Advance praise for COGNITIVE CAPITALISM, EDUCATION AND DIGITAL LABOR

"*Cognitive Capitalism, Education and Digital Labor* provides us with a series of very thoughtful and provocative analyses of the relationship among political economy, education and new forms of knowledge and labor. It is definitely worth reading and then discussing its implications at length."
— *Michael W. Apple, John Bascom Professor of Curriculum and Instruction*
and Educational Policy Studies, University of Wisconsin, Madison

"This volume is a *tour de force*. Through its chapters, a new space is opened for understanding education in the contemporary world. With an magisterial introduction by its indefatigable editor, Michael A. Peters, and his colleague Ergin Bulut, *Cognitive Capitalism, Education and Digital Labor* implicitly shows the limitations of postmodernism and offers a large conceptual framework that will surely be mined and critically examined for some years to come."
— *Ronald Barnett, Emeritus Professor of Higher Education, Institute of Education, London*

"*Cognitive Capitalism, Education and Digital Labor* is extraordinarily instructive in studying the living bestiary of capitalism, a provocative text that enervates capitalism through helping us cultivate our critical faculties creatively and exultantly in the service of its demise. An important advance in our understanding the production of subjectivity in capitalist societies."
— *Peter McLaren, School of Critical Studies in Education, Faculty of Education,*
University of Auckland

"This valuable, lithe volume explores the ever-evolving, mutating forms of capitalism. It is a work of craft, intelligence and provocation. It reflects on some of the most important subterranean trends in contemporary societies. These unite the material and the immaterial, biology and power, economics and education. The contributors parse the intersections of intellectual and physical labour, paid and unpaid work, labour and pedagogy, research and gaming, free information and multi-national corporations, autonomy and liberalism, accumulation and enclosure, class and creativity. They do so with verve, steel and tenacious insight."
— *Peter Murphy, Professor of Creative Arts and Social Aesthetics, James Cook University*

"If you read just a single book in the field of educational theory this year, make sure it's this one. Drawing on the rich tradition of Marxist autonomism, the contributors pinpoint what the transmutation of labor and opening of new domains of class struggle under cognitive capitalism mean for education. The editors have assembled an impressive team, all accomplished scholars adept at envisioning changes in the sites and forms of knowledge-making, acquisition and contestation. For anyone interested in the educational implications of technologically-driven shifts in capitalism's socio-economic structures, this is the volume to buy. Brimming with insight, balanced and lively—it will attract attention from scholars and students well beyond the confines of education faculties."
— *James Reveley, Associate Professor, Faculty of Commerce, University of Wollongong*

COGNITIVE CAPITALISM, EDUCATION AND DIGITAL LABOR

This book is part of the Peter Lang Education list.
Every volume is peer reviewed and meets
the highest quality standards for content and production.

PETER LANG
New York • Washington, D.C./Baltimore • Bern
Frankfurt • Berlin • Brussels • Vienna • Oxford

COGNITIVE CAPITALISM, EDUCATION AND DIGITAL LABOR

EDITED BY MICHAEL A. PETERS AND ERGIN BULUT

PETER LANG
New York • Washington, D.C./Baltimore • Bern
Frankfurt • Berlin • Brussels • Vienna • Oxford

Library of Congress Cataloging-in-Publication Data

Cognitive capitalism, education, and digital labor /
edited by Michael A. Peters, Ergin Bulut.
p. cm.
Includes bibliographical references and index.
1. Capitalism. 2. Knowledge management.
3. Education. I. Peters, Michael A. II. Bulut, Ergin.
HB501.C643   330.12'2—dc23   2011029138
ISBN 978-1-4331-0982-9 (hardcover)
ISBN 978-1-4331-0981-2 (paperback)
ISBN 978-1-4539-0148-9 (e-book)

Bibliographic information published by **Die Deutsche Nationalbibliothek**
Die Deutsche Nationalbibliothek lists this publication in the "Deutsche
Nationalbibliografie"; detailed bibliographic data is available
on the Internet at http://dnb.d-nb.de/.

The paper in this book meets the guidelines for permanence and durability
of the Committee on Production Guidelines for Book Longevity
of the Council of Library Resources.

© 2011 Peter Lang Publishing, Inc., New York
29 Broadway, 18th floor, New York, NY 10006
www.peterlang.com

Printed in the United States of America

Table of Contents

Part 2. Education and Labor in Cognitive Capitalism

Acknowledgements

The editors of this volume would like to thank some colleagues and friends for the realization of this project.

We would like to thank Peter Lang and its editors Bernadette Shade and Chris Myers for their meticulous work.

We thank Antonio Negri for letting us reprint his excellent material in this volume. In this respect, translators and editors of Negri (Mark Coté, Jennifer Pybus, Peter Graefe) should be acknowledged for their consent. Also, we want to thank the editorial board of *Mediations: Journal of the Marxist Literary Group* for their support.

Similarly, we thank Timothy Brennan for his reprint permission of his article 'Intellectual Labor', as well as *South Atlantic Quarterly* and Duke University Press.

We are grateful to Anil Kilic for sharing his creative cover work with us.

Our thanks also go to our friends we've fiercely debated and exchanged ideas with in Michael Peters's two graduate seminars: Contemporary Marxisms and Education and Creative Economy and Education. Among them especially Garett Gietzen, Lucinda Morgan, Dan Araya, James Thayer (The Canadian School), James Geary, John Jones, Huseyin Esen, Dave Ondercin, and George Liu deserve special thanks for igniting and balancing these debates. The intellectual support of our guest lecturers (Fazal Rizvi, Cris Mayo, James Anderson, Bill Cope, and Cameron McCarthy) is highly appreciated.

Ergin would also like to thank Evren Dincer, Bora Erdagi and Firat Kaplan for their constant support and critique regarding his work. He's also thankful to Michael for his inspiring (and never ending) questions to stir intellectual debates, which finally led Ergin to engage in his current research.

Michael extends his thanks to his partner Tina Besley and to Ergin Bulut who have been a delight to work with.

Foreword

The Labor of the Multitude and the Fabric of Biopolitics

ANTONIO NEGRI

Antonio Negri. "The Labor of the Multitude and the Fabric of Biopolitics." Trans. Sara Mayo, Peter Graefe and Mark Coté. Ed. Mark Coté. *Mediations* 23.2 (Spring 2008) 8–25. www.mediationsjournal.org/the-labor-of-the-multitude-and-the-fabric-of-biopolitics.

Editor's Note*

I had the pleasure of driving Toni Negri to the McMaster University campus for his brief stay as the Hooker Distinguished Visiting Professor. As contingency would have it, we approached the city from the east, since I had picked him up at Brock University. Anyone familiar with Hamilton knows that this necessitates driving past the heart of "Steeltown." Negri, in a driving practice true to his theoretical orientation, excitedly requested that we follow the route most proximal to the mills and smokestacks of Stelco and Dofasco. He asked many questions about the history of steelworkers' labor struggles, the composition of the labor force, its level and form of organization, and the role of heavy industry in the Canadian economy.

Negri's keen interest in the conditions of a quintessentially material form of industrial production provides a necessary counterpoint to the strong poststructuralist inflection of his lecture. After all, his stated focus was on the subjective, the cultural, and the creative as key modalities of labor under globalization. These contrapuntal elements bring us to the heart of Negri's project, wherein the conceptual deployments of Michel Foucault and Gilles Deleuze act as articulated elements of his longstanding and ongoing commitment to Marxist theory and praxis. It is, of course, an open Marxism, iterable as necessitated by our historical moment. But then innovation, as opposed to orthodoxy, has been a hallmark of Negri's distinguished and sometimes incendiary career.

Antonio Negri visited McMaster University as the Hooker Distinguished Visiting Professor in 2006. This lecture was delivered on 18 April 2006. [Ed.]

In the lecture that follows, Negri asks two basic questions. First, how can we understand the organization of labor under neoliberal globalization, where it has been anchored in the *bios*? Second, when and by which modalities does life itself enter into the field of power and become a central issue? In answering these questions, he offers an exciting reconceptualization of power (pace Foucault) that provides a unique and provocative lens through which to examine globalization in relation to the human condition. The purpose of this brief introduction will therefore be both to contextualize the work of Negri and to introduce key concepts used in the lecture, namely biopower-biopolitics and the crisis of measure.

Negri may be most familiar to some through his scholar-as-celebrity status achieved with the massive success of *Empire*.[1] In Italy, however, he has been producing important work since the 1960s. The autonomist Marxist tradition from which Negri emerged—historically called *operaismo* (workerism) in Italian—was distinguished by turning orthodox Marxism "on its head," as it were. Its fundamental conceptual innovation was to reverse the dynamic of labor-capital power relations. Rather than beginning with capital's domination over labor, the autonomists—via Mario Tronti in the early 1960s—began with the struggles of labor. In short, this new model understood capitalist power as having a reactive dynamic, only ever responding to the potential, the practices, and the struggles of labor. Thus capitalist development proceeds through the rearticulation of existing social and productive forms of labor. Under such a model, questions about the composition of labor are of preeminent importance, particularly as they can reveal the weakest points of capitalist control.

Negri attained another kind of prominence in the 1970s. At that time, the Left in Italy was certainly the largest and most febrile in Europe.[2] It was also polyvalent, active both within representative democracy and on an extraparliamentary level. Throughout the 1970s, the Eurocommunism of Enrico Berlinguer's Italian Communist Party was tantalizingly close to gaining power, falling only four percent short of plurality behind the ruling Christian Democrats in 1976. The Party's institutional successes created a wider swath for more critical and open Left politics. Negri was a preeminent part of this tradition, long active in the more radical extraparliamentary Left, both as a revolutionary militant and as professor and head of the Institute of Political Science Department of the University of Padova. Clashes grew more constant, not only between the variegated radical Left and the Italian state but with the Italian Communist Party as well. Indeed, Negri's work from that time cannot be properly understood without recognizing that the antagonism it expresses is directed as much against the Italian Communist Party as the state and capital. After the murder of Italian prime minister Aldo Moro in 1978 by the Red Brigades, the state went on the offensive with its net indiscriminately cast wide. Despite the lack of evidence, and the fact that Negri had been a vocal opponent of the Leninist-vanguardist Red Brigades, he was accused of being their theoretical wellspring.

He quickly fled to Paris, and while in exile there was invited by Louis Althusser to deliver a series of lectures at the prestigious École Normale Supérieure, eventually transcribed as *Marx Beyond Marx*.[3] Based on the *Grundrisse*, the lectures evinced not the despair of post-insurrectionary failure but a liberatory focus on making Marx more adequate to a historical moment in which post-Fordism was beginning to take flight through neoliberal globalization. As such, it signaled an expanded theoretical perspective that would lead Negri increasingly to Foucault, Deleuze, and the conceptual cornerstones of his Hooker lecture, which follows.

Negri identified a "crisis of measure" in the Marxist labor theory of value as *both* an emergent characteristic of global capital *and* a new path for radical political, social, and economic change. A key factor in the breakdown of a simple temporal measure of the productivity of labor is the radical transformation of the production process though information and communication technology. This facilitates the rise of "immaterial labor" and the "general intellect" as the dominant productive forces, as opposed to unmediated material labor.

What is innovative about the interpretation by Negri and other autonomists is that this is primarily a subjective process—hence the increasingly poststructuralist trajectory. Marx, in the *Grundrisse*, posited "general intellect" as accumulating in the fixed capital of machinery. However, the "subjective" reading of the autonomists situates this value in new laboring subjectivities, the technical, cultural, and linguistic knowledge that makes our high-tech economy possible. Such subjectivities become an immediate productive force. And, as autonomist Paolo Virno notes, "They are not units of measure, but rather are the measureless presupposition of heterogeneous operative possibilities."[4] The temporal disjunction provocatively situates immaterial labor beyond the commodity form, signaling a "scissor-like widening" of the gap between wage labor/exchange value and this new subjective productive force.

For Negri, such a force is diffused—albeit asymmetrically—in an individuated manner across society, and it expresses the "global potentiality which has within it that generalized social knowledge which is now an essential condition of production."[5] In short, this new "subjective" condition of labor is the liberatory potential of what Negri would later call the "multitude." Thus inscribed in this new power dynamic is the possibility of labor being not only antagonistic to capital but autonomous from—as opposed to within—capital.

Foucault's biopower offers a new conceptual foundation. Here Negri helps make visible the strong lines of affinity between Foucault (and Deleuze) and autonomist Marxism that have been largely overlooked. What is taken from Foucault is a thoroughly reconfigured understanding of power. What it enables us to see with greater precision is the intertwining of life and power in myriad productive formations. Foucault identified biopower as a form emergent since the end of the eighteenth century in the wake of the inadequacies of sovereign and disciplinary power. This is a productive form of power relations that "manages" populations (not individual bodies) in a "preventive fashion" to maximize their productivity as opposed to, say, punishing them after the fact as with sovereign power (Foucault offers sexual health and early epidemiology as initial examples). As Foucault notes, "biopower uses populations like a machine for production, for the production of wealth, goods, and other individuals."[6]

Thus far, biopower has been presented as a more sophisticated form of command, but such a unidimensional interpretation obscures the very aspects that make it so favored by autonomists. Maurizio Lazzarato emphasizes this in his important essay, "From Biopower to Biopolitics." Lazzarato reminds us that Foucault distinguished constituted biopower (a *dispositif* of command, management, and domination) from biopolitical becoming (creativity and resistance).[7] It is the latter biopolitical form that holds the capacity for freedom and transformation identified by Negri in his lecture. Power, be it in the labor-capital dyad or in biopolitical-biopower form, is always in an indissoluble linkage between resistance and control. The pursuit of its productive, creative, and liberatory potential is the real heart of Negri's lecture, and it contributes to bringing about more desirable forms of globalization. [Ed.]

The Labor of the Multitude and the Fabric of Biopolitics

I would like to discuss the problem of the anchoring of the organization of labor—and of the new postmodern political field which results—in the *bios*. We will see in a moment when and according to which modalities life enters into the field of power and becomes an essential issue.

Let's take as a starting point the Foucauldian definition of biopolitics. The term "biopolitics" indicates the manner in which power transforms itself in a certain period so it can govern not only individuals through a certain number of disciplinary procedures but also the set of living things constituted as "populations." Biopolitics (through local biopowers) takes control of the management of health, hygiene, diet, fertility, sexuality, etcetera, as each of these different fields of intervention have become political issues. Biopolitics thus comes to be involved, slowly but surely, in all aspects of life, which later become the sites for deploying the policies of the welfare state: its development is in effect entirely taken up with the aim of a better management of the labor force. As Foucault says, "the discovery of population is, at the same time as the discovery of the individual and the trainable [*dressable*] body, the other major technological nucleus around which the political procedures of the West were transformed."[8] Biopolitics is thus based on principles which develop the technologies of capitalism and sovereignty: these are largely modified by evolving from a first form—disciplinary—to a second, which adds to disciplines the *dispositifs* of control.[9] In effect, while discipline presented itself as an anatomo-policy of bodies and was applied essentially to individuals, biopolitics represents on the contrary a sort of grand "social medicine" that applies to the control of populations as a way to govern life. Life henceforth becomes part of the field of power.

The notion of biopolitics raises two problems. The first is tied to the contradiction that we find in Foucault himself: in the first texts where the term is used, it seems connected to what the Germans called in the nineteenth century the *Polizeiwissenschaft*, that is to say the maintenance of order and discipline through the growth of the State and its administrative organization. Later on, however, biopolitics seems on the contrary to signal the moment that the traditional nation/State dichotomy is overtaken by a political economy of life in general. And it is this second formulation that gives rise to the second problem: is it a question of thinking biopolitics as a set of biopowers? Or, to the extent that saying that power has invested life also signifies that life is a power, can we locate in life itself—that is to say, in labor and in language, but also in bodies, in desire, and in sexuality— the site of emergence of a counterpower, the site of a production of subjectivity that would present itself as a moment of desubjection (*désassujettisement*)? It is evident that this concept of biopolitics cannot be understood solely on the basis of the conception that Foucault had about power itself. And power, for Foucault, is never a coherent, stable, unitary entity but a set of "power relations" that imply complex historical conditions and multiple effects: power is a field of powers. Consequently, when Foucault writes of power, it is never about describing a first or fundamental principle but rather about a set of correlations where practices, knowledge, and institutions are interwoven.

The concept of power becomes totally different—almost totally post-modern—in relation to this Platonic tradition that has been permanent and hegemonic in a good part of modern thought. The juridical models of sovereignty are thus subject to a political critique of the State that reveals first the circulation of power in the social, and consequently the variability of phenomena of subjection to which these models give rise: paradoxically, it is precisely in the complexity of this circulation that the processes of subjectification, resistance, and insubordination can be given.

If we take these different elements, the genesis of the concept of biopower should then be modified as a function of the conditions in which these elements have been given. We will now seek to privilege the transformation of work in the organization of labor: we have here the possibility of working out a periodization of the organization of labor in the industrial era that permits us to understand the particular importance of the passage from the disciplinary regime to the control regime. It is this passage that we can see, for instance, in the crisis of Fordism, at the moment where the Taylorist organization of labor no longer sufficed to discipline the social movements, as well as the Keynesian macroeconomic techniques that were no longer able to evaluate the measure of labor. Starting in the 1970s, this transformation (which will provoke in turn a redefinition of biopowers) was most clearly seen in the "central" countries of capitalist development. It is thus in following the rhythm of this modification that we can understand the problematization of the theme of production of subjectivity in Foucault and Deleuze by underlining that these two schools of thought have common ground. In Deleuze, for instance, the displacement of what he takes to be the genuine matrix of the production of subjects—no longer a network of power relations extending throughout society but rather a dynamic center and a predisposition to subjectification—seems completely essential. From this point of view, when we speak of the themes of discipline and control and of the definition of power which follows, Deleuze does not limit himself to an interpretation of Foucault but integrates labor and develops his fundamental intuitions.

Once we have established that what we mean by biopolitics is a nonstatic, nonhypostatized process, a function of a moving history connected to a long process that brings the requirement of productivity to the center of the *dispositifs* of power, it is precisely that history that must be understood.

The danger to avoid is to read at the heart of biopolitics a sort of positivist vitalism (and/or materialist: in effect we could very well find ourselves before what Marx called "a sad materialism"). This is what we find, for instance, in certain recent interpretations of the political centrality of life. These interpretations develop a reading of biopolitics that creates a sort of confused, dangerous, even destructive magma:

a tendency which refers much more to a thanatopolitics, a politics of death, than to a genuine political affirmation of life. This slippage toward thanatopolitics is in reality permitted and fed by a great ambiguity that we lend to the word "life" itself: under the cover of a biopolitical reflection, we slide in reality to a biological and nat-uralistic understanding of life which takes away all its political power. We have thus reduced it to, at best, a set of flesh and bones. We would have to ask at what point a Heideggerian ontology doesn't find in this move from the *zo!* to *bios* an essential and tragic resource.[10]

Furthermore, the fundamental specificity of biopolitics in Foucault—the very form of the relationship between power and life—which immediately becomes, in Deleuze as in Foucault, the space for producing a free subjectivity was given an indis-criminately vitalistic interpretation. But as we well know, vitalism is a dirty beast! When it begins to emerge in the seventeenth century, after the crisis of Renaissance thought and from the interior of modern thought itself, it paralyzes the contradic-tions of the world and of society to the extent that it considers them as impossible to resolve. Or more exactly: it brings them to define the very essence of the world starting from the postulate of their invariability. In the confusion of vitalism, there is no capacity for discernment. Life and death are locked in a relation of great ambi-guity: the war between individuals becomes essential, the co-presence of an aggres-sive animal and a society exasperated by the market—what we call the dynamic of possessive individualism—is presented as a natural norm, that is to say, precisely as *life.*

Vitalism is thus always a reactionary philosophy, while the notion of *bios*, as it is presented in the biopolitical analysis of Foucault and Deleuze, is something entirely different: it was chosen in order to rupture this frame of mind. For us who follow their lead, biopolitics is not a return to origins, a manner of re-embedding thought in nature: it is on the contrary the attempt to construct thought starting from ways of life (whether individual or collective), to remove thought (and reflec-tion on the world) from artificiality—understood as the refusal of any natural foun-dation—and from the power of subjectification. Biopolitics is not an enigma, nor a set of such inextricable fuzzy relations that the only way out seems to be the immu-nization of life: it is on the contrary the recovered terrain of all political thought, to the extent that it is crossed by the power of processes of subjectification.

From this point of view, the idea of a biopolitics accompanies in an essential manner the passage to the postmodern—if we understand by this a historical moment where power relations are permanently interrupted by the resistance of the subjects to which they apply. If life has no "outside," if it must by consequence be totally lived "inside," its dynamic can only be one of power. Thanatopolitics is nei-ther an internal alternative nor an ambiguity of biopolitics but its exact opposite: an authoritarianism transcendent, a *dispositif* of corruption.

To finish this point, let me rapidly mention two last things regarding thanatopolitics. It is no accident that it was particularly affirmed in the experiences that are sometimes called "revolutionary conservatism" (let us think for example of a figure such as Ernest Jünger), that is to say, a type of thought where individualist and vitalistic anarchism functioned as a genuine foreshadowing of Nazi thought. We can think today of what is meant by the act of a kamikaze: if we make an abstraction of the suffering and desperation that leads to such choices—suffering and desperation that are absolutely political—we are then again face-to-face with the suicidal reduction of the *bios* to the *zo!* which suffices to remove all biopolitical power from the act that one commits (notwithstanding the judgment that we may have on this act).

It is important to note the type of methodological approach that biopolitics necessitates. It is only by confronting the problem from a constitutive (genealogical) point of view that we can construct an effective biopolitical discourse. This discourse must be founded on a series of *dispositifs* that have a subjective origin. We are perfectly aware that the concept of *dispositif*, as it appears in Foucault and in Deleuze, is used by the two philosophers as a group of homogeneous practices and strategies that characterize a state of power in a given era. We thus speak of *dispositifs* of control or of normative *dispositifs*. But to the extent to which the biopolitical problematization is ambiguous, because it is at the same time the exertion of power over life and the powerful and excessive reaction of life to power, it has seemed to us that the notion of *dispositif* should assume the same ambiguity: the *dispositif* could equally well be the name of a strategy of resistance.

When we speak of "*dispositif*," we want therefore to speak here of a type of genealogical thought whose development includes the movement of desires and reasonings: we thus subjectify the power relations that cross the world, society, institutional determinations, and individual practices.

However, this line of argument, which was that of Foucault and Deleuze, finds a profound anchoring in the non-teleological philosophies that have preceded *Historismus* or that have developed in parallel to this.[11] These schools of thought, from Georg Simmel to Walter Benjamin, have brought with them theoretical formulations that permitted, through the analysis of forms of life, the reconstruction of the ontological weave of culture and society. From this point of view, and beyond our legitimate insistence on the origins of the concept of biopolitics in French poststructuralist thought, it would be equally interesting to find in German thought at the end of the nineteenth and beginning of the twentieth centuries an epistemological development of the same type. The fundamental figure would clearly be Nietzsche: we would have in effect to analyze all the Nietzschian efforts to destroy positivist and vitalist teleology and the manner in which we find in this same effort the project of a genealogy of morals. The genealogy of morals is simultaneously an ensemble of subjectification processes and the space of a materialist teleology that both accepts the risk of projectuality and recognizes the finiteness of its own subjective source. This is what we have chosen to call, many years later, and following a postmodern reinvestment of Spinozist thought, a "dystopia."

It is therefore possible to push the analysis of biopolitics as it was in the liberal and mercantile era—and the resistance to it—toward the location of the functions it takes, once removed from modernity, in the context of the "real subsumption of society under capital" [to paraphrase Marx—Ed.]. When we speak of real subsumption of society under capital (that is to say, how capitalism is actually developing), we mean the mercantilization of life, the disappearance of use value and the colonization of forms of life by capital, but we also mean the construction of resistance inside this new horizon. Once again, one of the specificities of postmodernity is this character of reversibility that profoundly marks the phenomena which are present: all domination is also always resistance. On this point, one must underline the surprising convergence of certain theoretical experiences within Western or postcolonial Marxism (we can think here obviously of Italian *operaismo* or certain Indian culturalist schools) and the philosophical positions formulated by French poststructuralism. We will come back to this.

In addition, we have already insisted on the importance of "real subsumption," to the extent that one must consider it as the essential phenomenon around which the passage from the modern to the postmodern has occurred. But this transition's fundamental element seems also to be the generalization of resistance on each of the nodes that make up the great weave of real subsumption of society under capital. This discovery of resistance as a general phenomenon, as a paradoxical opening inside each of the links of power, as a multiform *dispositif* of subjective production, is precisely what comprises the postmodern affirmation.

Biopolitics is therefore a contradictory context of/within life. By its very definition, it represents the extension of the economic and political contradiction over the entire social fabric, but it also represents the emergence of the singularization of resistances that permanently cut across it.

What do we mean exactly by "production of subjectivity"? Here we'd like our analysis to go beyond the anthropological definition assumed in Foucault as in Deleuze. What seems important in this perspective is in effect the historical (also productive) concreteness of the constitution of the subject. The subject is productive: the production of subjectivity is thus a subjectivity that produces. Let us insist at present on the fact that the cause, the motor of this production of subjectivity, is found inside power relations, which is to say in the complex set of relationships that are nonetheless always traversed by a desire for life. However, to the extent that this desire for life signifies the emergence of a resistance to power, it is this resistance that becomes the genuine motor of production of subjectivity.

Some have judged this definition of the production of subjectivity to be unsatisfactory because it makes the mistake of reintroducing a sort of new dialectic: power includes resistance, resistance could even feed power. And, on another level, subjectivity would be productive; the productivity of resistances could even construct subjectivity. It is not difficult to stymie this argument: it only suffices to return to the concept of resistance we spoke of earlier, that is to say, the productive link that binds the concept of resistance to subjectivity and immediately determines the singularities in their antagonism to biopower. We do not understand very well why all allusion to antagonism must be necessarily reduced to a return to the dialectic. If this is truly a singularity that acts, the relationship that develops with power can in no case give rise to a moment of synthesis, of excess, of *Aufhebung*—in sum, the negation of negation in the Hegelian manner. On the contrary, what we're dealing with is absolutely a-teleological: singularity and resistance become exposed to risk, to the possibility of failure, but the production of subjectivity nonetheless always has the possibility—better still, the power—to give itself as an expression of surplus. The production of subjectivity can therefore not be reabsorbed into the heart of dialectical processes that seek to reconstitute the totality of the productive movement under transcendental forms. Certain effects of "reabsorption" are of course inevitable (as underlined by the particularly subtle schools of modern sociological thought such as Luc Boltanski and Richard Sennett), but it has to do in all cases with unpredictable phenomena, ones that go in all directions and never give rise to consequences that can be determined in advance. As we will insist again shortly, when it is obliged to pass from the exercise of government to the practice of governance, the machine of power reveals itself incapable of running its own mechanical dimension in a unilateral and necessary manner. Any attempt to reabsorb subjective productions can try to block new ways of life, but it will only immediately solicit other resistances, other surpluses. This becomes the only machine that we recognize in the function of postmodern societies and politics: a machine that is paradoxically not reducible to the mechanics of power.

We could object that politics and statism have always proceeded according to a logic which, in the heart of capitalism, would give to power relations the Leviathanian figure of a unilateral negotiator and resolver of problems: that is precisely what power consists of. In the eighteenth century, theories of the "raison d'État" included not only the arts of violence but also the arts of mediation. When we move the theme of power into the context of biopolitical relations, what appears—and what is new—is exactly opposed to this capacity of neutralization or immunization. It is in effect the emergence of rupture that forms alongside the production of subjectivity—the intensity of this surplus is its defining characteristic.

Two words on this concept of surplus—or, as we have sometimes called it, the notion of excessiveness. This idea was born inside a new analysis of the organization of labor, a moment at which value comes from the cognitive and immaterial product of a creative action, and when it escapes at the same time from the law of labor value (if we understand this in a strictly objective and economistic manner). The same idea is found at a different level in an ontological dissymmetry that exists between the functioning of biopower and the power of biopolitical resistance: where power is always measurable (and where the idea of the measure and the gap are in fact precise instruments of discipline and control) or power is on the contrary the non-measurable, the pure expression of non-reducible differences.

At a third level, one must be attentive to what is happening in State theories: the surplus is always described as a production of power—it takes, for example, the face of the "state of exception."[12] Yet this idea is inconsistent, even grotesque: the state of exception can only be defined on the inside of the relationship that links power and resistance in an indissoluble manner. State power is never absolute; it only represents itself as absolute, it offers a panorama of absoluteness. But it will always be made up of a complex set of relations that include resistance to what it is. It is not by chance if, in the theories of dictatorships that exist in Roman law—that is to say, in those of the state of exception—the dictatorship can only exist during brief periods. As Machiavelli noted, this temporal limitation cannot be referred to as a constitutional guarantee but to a reasoning in terms of efficiency. Consequently, the state of exception, even if it is in force for short periods, is unacceptable for free spirits and can thus only be valued as a desperate recourse in an equally desperate situation.

Finally, we find it grotesque that theories of totalitarianism (be they thought up by dictators themselves or, later on, by certain figures of contemporary political science, in particular during the cold war) make of it a version of power where all resistance is excluded. If totalitarianisms have existed—and if their sinister political practices continue to haunt our memories—the so-called absolute totality of their power is a mystifying idea that is long overdue for critical examination.

We must finally insist on one fundamental element: there is a sort of Marxist watermark that is found in all critiques of univocal conceptions of power—even if these, paradoxically, were produced in Marx's name. Capitalist power, according to what was put in evidence by the current critiques we have just mentioned, is always a relationship. Constant capital is confronted with variable capital, capitalist power is confronted with the resistance of labor power. It is this tension that produces the development of the economy and history. It is true that "official" Marxism locked labor power and variable capital inside relations that were objectively prefigured by the laws of the economy. But it is precisely this prefiguration having the value of necessity—more closely resembling the Heideggerian conception of technique than the liberation desire of proletarians—which certain Marxists, starting in 1968, began to break into pieces. This is the point of theoretical convergence between the *operaismo* of Laboratory Italy in the 1970s, schools of Indian postcolonial thought, and the analysis of power formulated by Foucault and Deleuze.

Let us return to the link between subjectivity and social labor. As we have said, labor possesses genuinely new dimensions. The first remarkable thing is without a doubt the transformation undergone by the temporal dimension in the postmodern modification of productive structures. In the Fordist era, temporality was measured according to the law of labor value: consequently it concerned an abstract, quantitative, analytic temporality, which, because it was opposed to living labor time, arrived at the composition of the productive value of capital. As it is described by Marx, capitalist production represents the synthesis of the living creativity of labor and of the exploitive structures organized by fixed capital and its temporal laws of productivity. In the era of post-Fordism, on the contrary, temporality is no longer—nor totally—enclosed within the structures of constant capital: as we have seen, intellectual, immaterial, and affective production (which characterizes post-Fordist labor) reveals a surplus. An abstract temporality—that is to say, the temporal *measure* of labor—is incapable of understanding the creative energy of labor itself.

On the inside of the new figure of the capitalist relation, the surplus permits the creation of spaces of self-valorization that cannot be entirely reabsorbed by capital: in the best case, it is only recuperated by a sort of permanent "pursuit-race" of this mass of autonomous labor—or, more exactly, of this multitude of productive singularities. The constitution of capitalist temporality (that is to say, capitalist power) can therefore no longer be acquired in a dialectical manner: the production of goods is always followed by the subjectivities that oppose it, under the form of a virtually antagonistic *dispositif* that comes to frustrate any capitalist synthesis of the process. The Foucauldian distinctions between regimes of power and regimes of subjectivity are therefore totally reinvested inside this new reality of capitalist organization; they are represented by the scission between capitalist time/value and the singular valorization of labor power.

We must thus return to an essential problem that we have already quickly mentioned: the problem of the simultaneous measure of capital's labor and time. If we start from the idea that living labor is the constituent cause and motor—material or immaterial—of all forms of development, if we think that the production of subjectivity is the fundamental element that permits us to escape the dialectic of biopower and to construct, on the contrary, a fabric of biopolitics to complete the passage from a simple disciplinary regime to a regime that equally integrates the control dimension and permits at the same time the emergence of powerful and common insurgencies, then the theme of measure (that is to say, of the quantified rationality of valorization) becomes central once again. Yet it only becomes central in a paradoxical manner because all the measures that capital wanted to discipline and control henceforth become evasive.

Without a doubt, it will be necessary to one day open a new field of research so we can understand if the thematic of measure can be proposed once again today on a terrain of social production, according to new forms and modalities that will have to be defined. In that case, the ontological rupture that we have located between living labor and constant capital will have to be considered as the presupposition of any analysis. The fact is that the surplus of living labor in relation to constant capital presents itself as production "beyond measure"—that is to say, as "outside" quantitative measurement—and it is in this that the difficulty forever reappears. Rather it is a production that goes *beyond* the idea of measure itself, that is to say, it ceases in reality to be defined as a negative passing of the limits of measurement to become simply—in an absolutely affirmative and positive manner—the power of living labor. This is how it becomes possible to foresee at least tendentially the end of exploitation. And it is without a doubt what Foucault and Deleuze allude to when they speak of the process of subjectification.

We have thus arrived at the edge of a new definition of capital as crisis—a capitalist relation which, from the point of view of constant capital, seems from now on totally parasitic; we have also arrived at the center of what is perhaps the possibility of a recomposition of antagonisms that engage with both the production of subjectivity and the expression of living labor.

We started by attempting to close in on the terms of biopower, biopolitics, discipline, and control. It seems now essential to address the question of multitude.

In effect, all our analyses constitute in reality this presupposition of the multitude. Let us therefore propose, as a point of provisionary support that we will have to reformulate and modify, the following definition. The concept of multitude is derived from the relationship between a constitutive form (that of singularity, of invention, of risk, to which all the transformation of labor and the new measure of time has brought us) and a practice of power (the destructive tendency of value/labor that capital is today obliged to put in effect). But while capital was in the past capable of reducing the multiplicity of singularities to something close to the organic and unitary—a class, a people, a mass, a set—this process has today failed intimately: it no longer works. The multitude should thus be necessarily thought of as a disorganized, differential, and powerful multiplicity. But this could be the subject of another lecture.

I thank you.

Notes

* For clarification, the editor of this piece is Mark Cote, not the editors of this volume.

1. Michael Hardt and Antonio Negri, *Empire* (Cambridge, MA: Harvard UP, 2000).[Ed.]

2. There are three excellent sources for an overview of the Italian autonomist Marxist move-
    ment. S. Lotringer and Christian Marazzi's *Italy: Autonomia—Post-Political Politics* (New
    York: Semiotext(e), 1980) has contributions from core members of the movement and was
    written in the wake of the state crackdown. Steve Wright's *Storming Heaven: Class
    Composition and Struggle in Italian Autonomist Marxism* (London: Pluto Press, 2002) offers
    a comprehensive historical overview. Finally, Michael Hardt and Paolo Virno's *Radical
    Thought in Italy: A Potential Politics* (Minneapolis: U of Minnesota P, 1996) is a collection
    of essays that both assess the tradition of autonomist thought and propose future directions.
    [Ed.]

3. Antonio Negri, *Marx beyond Marx: Lessons on the Grundrisse* (New York: Autonomedia,
    1989).[Ed.]

4. Paolo Virno, "Notes on the General Intellect," *Marxism beyond Marxism*, ed. Saree Makdisi,
    Cesare Casarino, and Rebecca E. Karl (New York: Routledge, 1996) 269. [Ed.]

5. Antonio Negri, "Archaeology and Project: The Mass Worker and the Social Worker,"
    *Revolution Retrieved: Writings on Marx, Keynes, Capitalist Crisis, and New Social Subjects
    (1967–1983)* (London: Red Notes, 1988) 224. [Ed.]

6. Michel Foucault, "Les mailles du pouvoir," *Dits et écrits, t. 2* (Paris: Gallimard, 1994) 1012.
    [Ed.]

7. Maurizio Lazzarato, "From Biopower to Biopolitics," *Pli: The Warwick Journal of Philosophy*
    13 (2002): 112–25. [Ed.]

8. Foucault, "Les mailles" 1012.

9. The *dispositif* is an important concept developed by Foucault that has been literally "lost in
    translation" and thus largely overlooked by English-language interlocutors. Most prominent-
    ly, it was used by Foucault in *Histoire de la sexualité, tome 1: La volonté de savoir* (Paris:
    Gallimard, 1976) as the "dispositif de sexualité." Inconsistently translated as "apparatus,"
    "arrangement," or "deployment," the *dispositif* is a methodological frame for understanding
    power. A *dispositif* is both discursive and non-discursive. Foucault describes it thusly: "[It is]
    firstly, a resolutely heterogeneous ensemble consisting of discourses, institutions, architec-
    tural forms, regulatory decisions, laws, administrative measures, scientific statements, philo-
    sophical, moral and philanthropic propositions—in short, the said as much as the unsaid"
    (299). Thus *dispositifs* are always in the middle of things, comprising a complex "system of
    relations" of discursive and non-discursive elements. We can see that the *dispositif* brings
    together heterogeneous elements that have distinct registers: from the *materiality* of insti-
    tutions, to the *regulation* of juridical processes, to the *expression* of what elsewhere might be
    called ideology, and finally to the *techniques* and *practices* of particular subjectivities. There
    is a complex composition to these distinct elements; yet this heterogeneity, in part, is
    designed to go beyond the reductive schema of an all-determining mode of production. This
    shift to more complex causal relations reflects Foucault's inexorable turn to seeing power as

diffused, decentralized, and arranged in microphysical relations. Methodologically, this means not just examining each element of this heterogeneous composition but focusing on the effects of a given dispositive—in terms of what we can say, see, or be. [Ed.]

10. Giorgio Agamben (*Homo Sacer: Sovereign Power and Bare Life*, trans. Daniel Heller-Roazen [Palo Alto, CA: Stanford UP, 1998]) revived the terms *zo!* and *bios* from Greek antiquity where they were key conceptual markers distinguishing "natural life" (*zo!*) and "political life" (*bios*)—the former refers to the home as the sphere of influence and the latter the polis. For Negri, *bios* expresses a dynamic of power—particularly in biopolitical form—which cannot be contained by older forms of sovereign power. In turn, this reveals the limits of such con-stituted power and necessitates the permanent turn to the "state of exception." Here Negri is expanding on key insights made by Maurizio Lazzarato ("From Biopower"), a contem-porary autonomist theorist who made important contributions to a more critical and polit-ical deployment of Foucauldian biopower. He notes, "The introduction of the *zo!* into the sphere of the polis is, for both Agamben and Foucault, the decisive event of modernity; it marks a radical transformation of the political and philosophical categories of classical thought. But is this impossibility of distinguishing between *zo!* and *bios*, between man as a living being and man as a political subject, the product of the action of sovereign power or the result of the action of new forces over which power has 'no control'? Agamben's response is very ambiguous and it oscillates continuously between these two alternatives. Foucault's response is entirely different: biopolitics is the form of government taken by a new dynam-ic of forces that, in conjunction, express power relations that the classical world could not have known. [Ed.]

11. *Historismus* is a German variant of Historicism initiated by Leopold von Ranke in the nine-teenth century. It is of relevance to Negri as it was an early methodological break with "uni-versal history" and instead emphasized the particularities of different historical periods and their unique conditions of possibility. This "relativism" was also a central characteristic of the Italian philosopher Benedetto Croce. [Ed.]

12. Carl Schmitt was a German political theorist who was active in the Nazi Party, attractive therein no doubt because he postulated that the actions of sovereign power are never lim-ited by the laws of the state. In other words, sovereign power has the permanent option of transgressing its own internal regulations, and at any time it can negate the rights of citi-zens through the "state of exception." What was a virtuous and functional insight for fas-cists takes on unintended consequences when critically deployed, most notably by Agamben. The "state of exception" is turned on its head, as it were, and presented as the manifest limit to safeguarding political rights and life under sovereign power. Agamben, who has long focused on the relationship between sovereign power and marginalized political subjectiv-ities, uses the "state of exception" as the permanent model for our historical moment, as seen in everything from Guantanamo Bay to the refugee camp. Negri has had a longstanding interest in Agamben's work and wrote an important review of *State of Exception* for the Italian paper *Il Manifesto*, which has been translated as "The Ripe Fruit of Redemption," trans. Arianna Bové, *Generation Online*, 2003, <http://www.generation-online.org/t/negriagamben.htm>. [Ed.]

Introduction
Cognitive Capitalism, Education and the Question of Immaterial Labor

MICHAEL A. PETERS & ERGIN BULUT

Introduction

'Cognitive capitalism' is a general term that has become significant in the discourse analyzing a new form of capitalism sometimes called the third phase of capitalism, after the earlier phases of mercantile and industrial capitalism, where the accumulation process is centered on immaterial assets utilizing immaterial or digital labor processes and production of symbolic goods and experiences. It is a term that focuses on the socio-economic changes ushered in with the Internet as platform and new Web 2.0 technologies that have impacted the mode of production and the nature of labor.

The core of cognitive capitalism is centered on digital labor processes that produce digital products cheaply utilizing new information and communications technologies that are protected through intellectual property rights regimes, which are increasingly subjected to interventions and negotiations of the nation states around the world. As Antonio Negri argues 'The originality of cognitive capitalism consists in capturing, within a generalized social activity, the innovative elements that produce value' where 'capitalist development and the capitalist creation of value and based more and more on the concept of social capture of value itself' (2008, p. 64). It is a term that has obvious significance for the analysis of the future of education and specific application in the field of educational policy analysis.

The theory of cognitive capitalism has its origins in French and Italian thinkers, particularly Gilles Deleuze and Felix Guattari's *Capitalism and Schizophrenia*, the work of Michel Foucault on biopolitics, Michael Hardt and Antonio Negri's trilogy *Empire, Multitude*, and *Commonwealth* as well as the Italian 'Autonomist' Marxist movement. The Autonomist tradition had its origins in the Italian 'Operaismo' ('workerism') in the 1960s, incorporating the work of Emilio Vesce, Luciano Ferrari Bravo, Mario Dalmaviva, Lauso Zagato, Oreste Scalzone, Pino Nicotri, Alisa del Re, Carmela di Rocco, Massimo Tramonte, Sandro Serafini, and Guido Bianchini, amongst others. There are a series of networks that have developed over many years that strengthened relationships among these thinkers.

Origins of Cognitive Capitalism

Frédéric Vandenberghe argues 'Contemporary capitalism is in effect, if not in intent, Deleuzian. As a network of networks, it is rhizomatic, flexible, chaosmotic, evolving, expanding' (2008, p. 877). Cognitive capitalism not only colonizes the life-world as Habermas (1984, 1987) holds, but life itself. Capitalism shifts to a more intensive mode of production that integrates 'the other spheres of life and, ultimately, the production of life itself, into its axiomatic'—the exploitation of *immaterial labor*—'that is, intellectual, communicative, symbolic or emotional labour that is produced outside of the sphere of production' (p. 884). Vandenberghe at one and the same time articulates the connecting thread among cybernetics, capitalism and self-regulating subjectivity:

> Deleuze and Guattari suggest that modern technology has successfully overcome the opposition between enslavement and subjection, domination and submission or alienation and subjectification. In the cybernetic 'human-machine systems' of advanced liberal capitalism, humans and machines have been coupled through a multiplicity of recursive processes and feedback loops and integrated in some kind of a living self-regulating mega-machine that operates globally on a single plane. When subjects are incorporated by the system as components of its own machinery, the subjects have become its living medium and mediation. (2008, p. 885)

The Deleuzian take on capitalism focused on the question of subjectivity and 'the society of control' (Peters, 1996, 2009) and provides an easy marriage with Foucault's notion of 'governing the self' and with his analysis of neoliberalism (Besley & Peters, 2007; Foucault, 2008; Peters et al., 2009). The understanding of biopower and biopolitics proves to be an important part of the analysis not only of the generalization of human capital theory and the notion of the entrepreneur but also an essential aspect of understanding the broader concept of biocapitalism (Lazzarato, n.d.).

Foucault (2008) provides an analysis of biopolitics of neoliberal capitalism. Foucault uses the term biopower to refer to the practice of modern states and their regulation of their subjects, integrating biology into the study of politics and understanding the ways in which the modern liberal state now utilizes techniques that operate on the body and the body politic as a societal organism. In his governmentality studies in the late 1970s, Foucault held a course at the Collège de France on the major forms of neoliberalism, examining the three theoretical schools of German ordoliberalism, the Austrian School characterized by Hayek, and American neoliberalism in the form of the Chicago School. Foucault's great insight was the critical link he observed in liberalism between the governance of the self and government of the state, understood as the exercise of political sovereignty over a territory and its population. For Foucault, liberal modes of governing are distinguished by the ways in which they utilize the capacities of free acting subjects and, consequently, modes of government differ according to the value and definition accorded the concept of freedom. Foucault's (2008) approach to governmentality details and analyzes German *ordoliberalism* as a source for the 'social market economy', and the EU's 'social model'. Foucault begins with an analysis of the self-limitation of governmental reason which is taken to be synonymous with liberalism which he suggests should be understood very broadly as:

1. Acceptance of the principle that somewhere there must be a limitation of government and that this is not just an external right.
2. Liberalism is also a practice: where exactly is the principle of the limitation of government to be found and how are the effects of this limitation to be calculated?
3. In a narrower sense, liberalism is the solution that consists in the maximum limitation of the forms and domains of government action.
4. Finally, liberalism is the organization of specific methods of transaction for defining the limitation of government practices:

—constitution, parliament

—opinion, the press

—commissions, inquiries (Foucault, 2008, pp. 20–21).

Liberalism, which in the second half of the twentieth century, 'is a word that comes to use from Germany' (Foucault, 2008, p. 22). In later chapters he jumps ahead to understand German neoliberalism beginning with Erhard in 1947, to examine contemporary German governmentality: economic freedom, the source of juridical legitimacy and political consensus. What preserves liberalism in its new formation is the way in which neoliberalism picks up on the classical liberal political practice of introducing a self-limitation on governmental reason while departing from it in terms of a theory of pure competition and the question of how to model the global exercise of political power on the principles of a market economy. Ordoliberalism thus issues in a critique of the protectionist economy according to Friedrich List (founder of the historical school of economics) including Bismarck's state socialism, the planned economy set up during the First World War, Keynesian interventionism, and the economic policy of National Socialism. The innovation of American neoliberalism for Foucault is the generalization of the model of *homo economicus* to all forms of behavior representing an extension of economic analysis to domains previously considered to be non-economic and the redefinition of *homo economicus* as entrepreneur of himself with an emphasis on acquired elements and the problem of the formation of human capital in education. Foucault goes on to discuss a resumption of the problem of social and economic innovation and the generalization of the "enterprise" form in the social field (see Peters et al., 2009).

Where Foucault can be seen as providing a post-Marxist radical political economy in the form of neoliberal governmentality, Deleuze and Guattari provide a libidinal economy that harnesses power and desire in a different register, utilizing the resources of Nietzsche. Deleuze (1995a: 171) remained a Marxist throughout his career even though he provided a Nietzschean analysis.[1] Deleuze indicates that any political philosophy must turn on the analysis of capitalism and its internal developments and recognizes Marx's notion of capitalism as an immanent system that constantly overcomes its own limitations. He observes that the analysis of capitalism in *A Thousand Plateaus* (Deleuze & Guattari, 1987) is characterized by three main directions: it defines society not by its contradictions[2] but through its *lines of flight*; it operates to define capitalism not through the analysis of class but through its *minorities*; it characterizes 'war machines' in a way that has nothing to do with war but rather 'to do with a particular way of occupying, taking up, space-time, or inventing new space-times' (p. 172). The concept that is central to the constant reconfiguration of capitalism is desire. As opposed to Freud, Deleuze and Guattari argue that unconscious is not passive and it is a factory which keeps producing. They "believe the unconscious has nothing in common with theatrical representation, but with something called a 'desiring-machine'" (Deleuze, 2004a, p. 232). Furthering their critique about Freud and his mommy-daddy method, Deleuze and Guattari maintain that "desire does not depend on lack, it is not a lack of something and it doesn't refer to any Law. Desire produces" (Deleuze, 2004a, p. 233). Their modification to Marx, on the other hand, is based on their notion of desire.[3] They modify Marx and state that capitalism "is demented and it works" (Deleuze, 2004b, p. 262). In other words, it is not doomed to collapse. And the reason why it works, according to them, is desire. They replace Marx's class struggle concept with desire and argue that "history is the history of desire" (Deleuze, 2004b, p. 263). Another critique they maintain is related to ideology. Marx argued that people do what they do and they don't know why they are doing it. "No," say Deleuze and Guattari and argue that "in capitalism, it is completely different: nothing is secret, at least in principle and according to the code (that's why capitalism is "democratic" and "publicizes" itself, even in the juridical sense of the term) (Deleuze, 2004b, p. 263). According to them, "the way in which desire is already in the economic, the way libido invests the economic, haunts the economic and fosters the political forms of oppression" (Deleuze, 2004b, p. 263). A very productive intervention they make is against the base/superstructure thesis. They rightly argue that ignoring superstructure as insignificant "is a perfect way to ignore how desire works on the infrastructure, invests it, belongs to it" (Deleuze, 2004b, p. 264). According to their assessment, "capitalism has always been, and still is a remarkable desiring-machine" and one has to "examine how inseparable from the phenomena of desire are its infrastructure and economy, and the extent to which it is a criss-crossing of desires" (Deleuze, 2004b, p. 267).

Deleuze (1995b) also uses the term 'societies of control' to denote a set of new forces and processes of free-floating control which Foucault foresaw as the basis of the immediate future society. Just as 'disciplinary societies' succeeded 'societies of sovereignty' in the eighteenth century to reach their apex in the early twentieth century, so too 'societies of control' have succeeded 'disciplinary societies', the development of which have accelerated in the post-war period. 'Disciplinary societies' can be distinguished, Deleuze argues in reference to Foucault, by the fact that they initiated the organization of vast spaces of enclosure and the individual moved from one enclosed space to another: the family, the school, the barracks, the factory, possibly the hospital and, paradigmatically, the prison. In this respect, it is safe to argue that we are in a period of universal crisis. Institutions built on the model of enclosed spaces, that is, the institutions of modernity—school, family, prison, factory, clinic—are in a struggle to redefine themselves. The modern institutions are struggling to survive within the crisis of flexible and informationalized capitalism whose survival is dependent on the very connections it promotes (Doran, 2011; Bulut, 2011).

What we are witnessing at this point of transition is the progressive and dispersed installation of a new system of domination based upon an open system where any element within it can be determined at any given instant. The key thing, Deleuze suggests, is to recognize that we are at the beginning of a new era. As he suggests, in the prison system, the attempt to find new forms of custody through electronic tagging; in the schools system, the introduction of new form of continuous assessment, perpetual retraining and the entry of business into education at every level; in the hospital system, deinstitutionalization of the mentally ill based upon new drug treatments, and the 'new medicine without doctors or patient' (p. 182); in the business system 'new ways of manipulating money, products, and men, no longer channeled through the old factory system' (Deleuze, 1995d: 182).

In an insightful interview, Eric Alliez (1997, p. 86) provides graphic description of Deleuze's 'societies of control,' linking it, above all, to the question of knowledge and the new spatialization of knowledge and education under a *capitalism of circulation* based upon the mode of information.

> The analysis that Deleuze gives us of the passage from 'disciplinary societies' to 'societies of control' aims to throw light on the forms taken by the accelerated substitution of a *capitalism of circulation and communication* for a capitalism of production centered on the exploitation of paid industrial labour alone (the factory being the paradigm for milieus of enclosure). The technological mutations of the age of planetary information-alization are thus related to a mutation of capitalism (a Hypercapitalism of services) which knows no discourse of legitimation other than the purely horizontal one of the market (from enlightened neo-liberalism to the hallucinated anarcho-capitalism of the Internet . . .), and no practice of domination other than that of a purely immanent social control by universal marketing in continuous variation and modulation (with the 3 M's ruling the New International order: Money, Media and Military).

The new spatialization of knowledge and education in the postmodern age is based on the 'soft architecture' of the *network*, which increasingly defines the nature of our institutions, our practices and our subjectivities.

Along the lines of Autonomous Marxist tradition,[4] Antonio Negri and Michael Hardt develop a single concept—'Empire'—to name and analyze the political constitution of global order. They work from a variety of sources in the Italian autonomist tradition and draw on the work of both Deleuze and Foucault to argue that we live in a "post-industrial, information-based" economy. In *Multitude* they argue:

> The current global recomposition of social classes, the hegemony of immaterial labor, and the forms of decision-making based on network structures all radically change the conditions of any revolutionary process.

They argue that with globalization we have witnessed the decline of the nation-state and the emergence of a new form of sovereignty that includes both national and supranational components that has led to a fundamental change in the labor process[5]:

> Since the production of services results in no material and durable good, we define the labor involved in this production as *immaterial labor*—that is, labor that produces an immaterial good, such as a service, a cultural product, knowledge, or communication. (2004, p. 290)

Services in the postmodern informational economy are characterized by the central role played by knowledge, information, affect and communication. They go on to distinguish three types of immaterial labor that drive the informational economy.

> The first is involved in an industrial production that has been informationalised and has incorporated communication technologies in a way that transforms the production process itself. Manufacturing is regarded as a service, and the material labor of the production of durable goods mixes with and tends toward immaterial labor. Second is the immaterial labor of analytical and symbolic tasks, which itself breaks down into creative and intelligent manipulation on the one hand and routine symbolic tasks on the other. Finally, a third type of immaterial labor involves the production and manipulation of affect and requires (virtual or actual) human contact, labor in the bodily mode. These are three types of labor that drive the postmodernisation of the global economy. (2004 , p. 293)

Negri himself has been strongly influenced by the Italian tradition of autonomist Marxism based on a journal launched in 1960 by Raniero Panzieri and Negri. The late 1960s were a time of student radicalization and industrial activism. The revolutionary left grew quicker and more than anywhere else in the world for many decades. Negri, himself, led *Potere Operaia,* a workerist grouping that developed a strong anarchism surviving through Negri's writings and reemerging in the 1990s leading to the 'autonomism' that characterizes the movement today. Harry Cleaver (2000) in his Preface to the 2nd edition of *Reading Capital Politically* writes:

> In short, in the history of the traditions that I call "autonomist Marxist" we find an evolution toward an extension of the political appreciation of the ability of workers to act autonomously, toward a reconceptualization of crisis theory that grasps it as a crisis of class power, toward a redefinition of 'working class' that both broadens it to include the unwaged, deepens the understanding of autonomy to intraclass relations and also recognizes the efforts of "workers" to escape their class status and to become something more (http://libcom.org/library/reading-capital-politically-cleaver-preface-two).

Cognitive Capitalism: A Characterization

The main theorists of cognitive capitalism suggest that a new accumulation regime based on immaterial assets constitutes a new phase of capitalism. Following mercantile and industrial capitalism, this new phase is based on new forms of labor—intellectual, immaterial and digital—developed by new technologies that spring from a concept of intellectual property and are enforced through intellectual property rights. Digital and web-based technologies have enhanced productive capacities that are now based on the human intellect rather than natural raw materials, which means that the production processes are more difficult to standardize, especially and in so far as they are based on forms of net*working* that often require the individual freedom and consent of the workers. In particular, in so far as the new labor processes depend ultimately on language and communication that can be digitized, the old industrial forms of labor organization (assembly lines, management hierarchies) are no longer appropriate or desirable. Under the new labor regimes processes of peer production become increasingly essential and by contrast old form of direct control become less important.

In the new regime of labor processes, knowledge and skills occupy the central place with an accent on education, training, and retraining and infrastructures that promote and facilitate new forms of learning and sharing ideas with greater worker individualization, discretion and judgment. Accordingly, worker subjectivities are intricately related to the creation of value through a new political economy of knowledge and learning that emphasizes consumption (e.g., reading, browsing, searching) as much as production, and personal investment in one's own cognitive labor.

Cognitive capitalism demonstrates characteristics as an emergent global economic system that depends upon the emergence of virtual (immaterial) economy ('third capitalism') based on the increasing informatization (digitization) of production where there is an increasing formalization, mathematicization and digitization of language, communication, and knowledge systems. Cognitive capitalism as a global system is also associated with the emergence of social media, social networking and social mode of production enhanced by Web 2.0 technologies. In this environment, public universities, community and schools become the public infrastructure for knowledge capitalism. Increasingly, distributed knowledge and learning systems, including online publication and archives leading to *open knowledge production* systems, become part of the open science economy from which the global info-utilities service multinationals recruit their talent. The public cyber infrastructure provides private benefits and decreasing costs of network access, knowledge-sharing and transmission, and greater 'borderless' interconnectedness of knowledge spaces is often theorized as emergence of a 'world brain'—a concept that while emphasizing interconnectedness does not indicate anything of worker autonomy. The new socio-technical 'cybernetic' paradigm of innovation is based on 'hothouse' social networking and social media where continuous endogenous innovation increasingly focused on science as a leading part of the accumulation regime.

Cognitive capitalism can be characterized in part by emphasizing the properties of emergent knowledge and learning systems where there has been a displacement of material production as a core of the system with a corresponding emphasis on interactive and dynamical relations between material and immaterial sectors (with the former the brain and the latter muscle power). Digitization and systematization of value (rather than chains) operate like natural ecologies based on collective intelligence. Increasingly co-production of symbolic goods reshape the production processes, but the private appropriation of global public knowledge goods can only be achieved through enforcement of arbitrary social conventions (patents, copyright, trademark) and are not reproduced spontaneously by market mechanisms. The growing capacity of computing, copying, file-sharing and storage of information are removing the technical fences to property rights that used to help enforcement of intellectual property rights. Scalable publishing and externalities within complex systems determine the general conditions of growth, investment and redistribution of revenue.

This characterization of cognitive capitalism rests also on an analysis of immaterial labor based on networked mass participation and collaboration rather than traditional Smithian division of labor. This represents a move to non-linear and dynamical systems of labor. Learning economies reinforce autonomy and collective intelligence as the main source of value in the market with emphasis on codification and contextualization of practical and implicit knowledge. Situated, personal and implicit knowledge not easily reduced to machine or to mere information (codified software or data) (Polanyi, 1958, 1966). Creative learning economies emphasize 'right brain' ascendancy with an accent on a psychology of openness, meta-cognition and 'learning by doing' where prosumption, co-creation and co-production of knowledge and information goods are the new norms. There is an infinite substitution of capital for labor for 'left brain' logical and sequential tasks releasing creative energies and the emergence of team or network as fundamental labor units. A new political economy of peer production ('interneting') based on cooperation and collaboration rather than competition replaces the old industrial labor process. In universities we see the internationalization of collaboration in global knowledge and research networks increasingly often in public-private, national and international partnerships that focus on science portals strongly wedded to major transnational corporations. In this respect there is an increasing importance of post-human network knowledge and learning practices based on mega-data bases and global portals where notions of individual performance have become global networks of labor governance where the traditional divisions between capital and labor are blurred.

Organization of this Book

The book is structured in two parts. While the first part mainly tackles broader questions as they relate to the very concept of immaterial labor and debates around it, the second part specifically attempts to link these debates the world of education, pedagogy and struggles around visuality, networks and university.

Part 1

This first part opens with Brennan's provocative and well-crafted essay where he questions the ambiguity around the notion of immaterial labor. He questions the affinities between anti-establishment thinkers and business circles and interrogates how they converge around the idea that knowledge has become a key factor in value creation. Emphasizing the geopolitical divide between the nature of intellectual labor and physical labor as it takes place within Global South, Brennan critiques the very activity of theorizing within anti-establishment circles.

In his piece, Fuchs provides a historical investigation of the notion of class and argues against the very notion of 'cognitive capitalism.' From a Marxist perspective, Fuchs finds both technologically objectivist and subjectivist understandings of capitalism insufficient. Instead, he offers his transnational theory of transnational informational capitalism as a more dialectical approach, arguing that "The search of capital for new strategies and forms of capital accumulation transforms labor in such a way that cognitive, communicative, and co-operative labor forms a significant amount of overall labor time (a development enforced by the rise of the ideology of self-discipline of 'participatory management'), but at the same time this labor is heavily mediated by information technologies and produces to a certain extent tangible informational goods (as well as intangible informational services" (Fuchs, this volume). Fuchs's chapter finally lays out the foundations for a transformative political project.

Providing a genealogy of the term 'cognitive capitalism', George Caffentzis points to the similarities between the theorists of cognitive capitalism and liberal definitions (WB, OECD) of the knowledge economy and criticizes both precisely because they do not provide a definition of knowledge or cognition. By evoking central concepts such as socially necessary labor time, Caffentiz welcomes the contributions from the theorists of cognitive capitalism but also objects to the claims that immaterial labor is immeasurable and easier to control, as well as underlining such burning issues as restructuring of social services to which knowledge work is central.

Silvia Federici's main concern in her chapter is to examine the concept of affective labor as it has been deployed by the Italian Autonomist Marxist school. Federici argues that while the concept of affective labor has its own utilities, taken to its extremes, it also underpins the gains of feminist movements during the 1970s and makes their struggle regarding the role of unpaid domestic labor invisible. Federici also interrogates the notion of immaterial labor and asks a useful question as to what is at stake when the differences between paid and unpaid labor are conflated, as well as pointing to the gendered and racialized nature of this metropolitan work.

Part 2

We have dedicated the second part of essays to those which not only focus on broader debates but also make the connection between education, pedagogy and labor.

In his treatment of the attention economy, Jonathan Beller argues that in the era of deeply interconnected capitalism, commodities themselves become productive power. For Beller, it is with the cinematicization of society that spectators are turned into workers on a visual assembly line and attention is transformed into a force of social production. In this fully mediatized society and commodification of senses, Beller rightly points to the uneven character of our current geopolitical condition and raises significant questions about what a transformative pedagogy in the 21st century should look like.

Ergin Bulut's chapter deals with the notion of creativity as it relates to the world of education and labor. Bulut argues that the discourse of creativity is an immensely elitist and First World-centric concept that disregards not only the stratified nature of the creative class but also the geopolitical nature of the totality of global commodity production where the fetish of 'creativity' and technology conceals the dependency of the creative class on the racialized and gendered laborers involved in the production of 'immaterial' goods and experiences.

Mark Coté and Jennifer Pybus take us to the world of social networks. Evoking the work of Paul Willis's *Learning to Labour* and contrasting it with contemporary reality, the authors make the case for a capitalism that has "taken a cultural and subjective turn" while they again acknowledge the fact that immaterial labor is not the dominant form of labor. Coté and Pybus also point to the pedagogical dimension of immaterial labor where youth learn how to effect "a kind of online personal brand management in a networked comprised by multiple lines of valorization".

From the world of networks, we move back to university and visit the very notion of critique and criticality with the help of Emma Dowling. Drawing on her own teaching experience and the ways in which her students view neoliberal governance in the UK, Dowling points to the ways in which critical learning skills are not at odds with the neoliberal restructuring of the university but are rather rearticulated within the very same process. Dowling makes a compelling case for understanding the university not only as an institution where critical thinking is taught but also as a web of social relations that cannot be thought of independently from its embeddedness within the broader nexus of capital and labor antagonism.

Alex Means connects the discourse of creativity with the research agenda of autonomist Marxism. Constructing education as a field of struggle over value and subjectivity and drawing on examples from the North American context, Means aptly makes the argument that policies around creativity are situated in an uneasy reality because of the very neoliberal policies that involve standardized testing, auditing and efficiency measures. According to Means, this leads to a 'double crisis' of education, which refers to the neoliberal restructuring of education, on the one hand, and the crisis of immaterial labor and its intersection with educational policy on the other. Means responds to the liberal literature on creativity from a critical perspective and raises a provocative and timely question as to whether the elite policy circles desire a creative and liberal education for all.

Toby Miller contributes to the volume by drawing a historical picture of the research university in the US and makes a case for the complicity of these educational institutions in the creation of militaristic video games as portrayed years ago by what he calls the Cold War futurists. Miller questions the complicity of the ideology of liberalism in the constitution of higher education institutions governed increasingly by profit and theories of human capital and free market. Within the intersection of university, video games and new media research, Miller reintroduces state and capital into the debate and calls for action to disrupt what scholars have called 'technological nationalism' (Charland, 1986).

Michael A. Peters harks back to the vents of May 6, 2010, when the U.S. equity market suffered one of the biggest instant declines in financial history to hypothesize the concept of 'algorithmic capitalism' that he sees as underlying most markets, as an aspect of informationalism linking markets and the rise of the new info-utility multinationals like Google and Amazon that now provide the service infrastructure for cognitive capitalism and for educational futures. Within this larger framework he explores the new logic and culture of social media as an aspect of what Siva Vaidhyanathan has called the "Googlization of education."

Alberto Toscano problematizes the concept of autonomy in his chapter. Discussing the narrative of cognitive capitalism as to what the crisis of the 1970s meant and led to, Toscano argues that the argument for autonomy is ironically unsubstantiated precisely because of the precarization of mental labor, loss of social rights such as health care and education. Toscano asks the crucial question to theorists of autonomy and cognitive capitalism: "*which* desire, freedom and autonomy are we talking about? One compatible with neoliberalism or at odds with it? And weren't many of the political struggle of the sixties and seventies ones around *needs* and around *security* which were precisely *not* being provided to the majority, rather than simply *against* the state as agent of reproduction?"

In his chapter, Nick Dyer-Witheford speaks to the recent financial crisis and its impact on the world of education, especially as it relates to what he calls "futuristic accumulation", implying the expropriation of scientific knowledge for capitalistic purposes. Making an analogy between futuristic accumulation and enclosure movements, Dyer-Witheford explores the links between these 'new enclosures' and processes of financialization and genetic research. Dyer-Witheford underlines the contested nature of the laboratories where futuristic accumulation takes place, and draws attention to similarities and differences of various struggles (radical reformism and terminal secession) but concludes by emphasizing the urgency of the need for a collective movement that aims not to discover some essentialist features of human beings but expand to life, cooperation and creativity on the basis of commons.

Tahir Wood's intervention has more to do with the utmost trust in innovation and growth and therefore deals with the uneven character and outcome of these processes. Based on data from South Africa, Wood demonstrates that innovation tied to capitalist motivation has a class character and does not always benefit the majority of the population. Wood's piece also deals with the problem of higher education not as an isolated case but rather in relation to the larger totality within which social relations are embedded.

Finally, Cameron McCarthy closes the volume by evoking the work of Walter Benjamin, among others, where he questions the relationship between progress, technology and education and highlights the need for forming communicative, reflexive and critical networks in our communities and educational institutions.

Notes

1. Indeed, he was reputedly writing a book on Marx when, suffering many years from a breathing affliction, he threw himself from his Paris apartment.
2. Here, we would like to go back to Marx and make the argument that while this introductory chapter mostly focuses on the poststructuralist take on capitalism, Marx's analysis of how capitalism in general works is still valid in many respects. We would like to argue that the depiction of capitalism in his magnum opus *Capital* stands in sharp contrast to what some critics argue to be a so-called causalistic and deterministic Marx. It should be taken into consideration that, as David Harvey (2010) aptly argues, under capitalism, everything is in motion and capital is not a thing but rather consists of a set of relations and processes.

3. Along with that, we should note that their account of capitalism is not totally against Marx's formulation. What was Marx saying? He was saying that capitalism is actually a rational system. However, Marx was politically criticizing capitalism and arguing for common ownership of the means of production. Likewise, Deleuze and Guattari do think that capitalism is both rational and irrational and say: "Reason is always a region carved out of the irrational—not sheltered from the irrational at all, but traversed by it and only defined by a particular kind of relationship among irrational factors" (Deleuze, 2004b, p. 262).

4. Nick Dyer-Witheford (1999) provides a very insightful analysis and description of this tradition. Very briefly, though, it can be stated that the Autonomous tradition focused on the resistant and creative potential of the labor power as opposed to the overwhelming dominance of capital. That is, the tradition constructs their analysis based on the primacy of labor rather than capital. It is not necessarily the capital that depends on labor but exactly the opposite. Hence the constant struggle over the control of labor power. Depending on how the labor power composes and recomposes itself, then capital attempts to reorganize the labor process within the workplace, nation and the globe. Then, we see the agency of the working classes as to why capital has to find new strategies to figure out new and more effective ways of extracting surplus value.

5. For an insightful critique of Hardt and Negri, see, among others, Dirlik (1997), especially the chapter, 'The Postmodernization and Its Organization: Flexible Production, Work and Culture.

References

Alliez, E. (1997). Questionnaire on Deleuze. *Theory, Culture and Society*, 14(2), 81–87.

Bogue, R. (1997). Art and Territory. *The South Atlantic Quarterly*, 96(3), 465–482.

Bulut, E. (2011). Labor and Totality in 'Participatory' Digital Capitalism. In C. McCarthy, H. Greenhalgh-Spencer, & R. Mejia (Eds.), *New Times: Making Sense of Critical/Cultural Theory in a Digital Age* (pp. 51–70). New York: Peter Lang.

Charland, Maurice. (1986). Technological Nationalism. *Canadian Journal of Political and Social Theory*, 10, no. 1: 196–220.

Cleaver, H. (2003). From *operaismo* to 'autonomist Marxism' A Response. Retrieved from http://www.eco.utexas.edu/facstaff/Cleaver/AufhebenResponse2.pdf

Cleaver, H. (2006). Deep Currents Rising: Some notes on the global challenge to capitalism. Retrieved from http://www.eco.utexas.edu/facstaff/Cleaver/DeepCurrentsRisingFinal2.htm

Deleuze, G. (1995). *A Thousand Plateaus*. In *Negotiations, 1972–1990*, trans. M. Joughin. New York: Columbia University Press: 25–34.

Deleuze, G. (1995a). Control and Becoming. In *Negotiations, 1972–1990*, trans. M. Joughin. New York: Columbia University Press: 169–176.

Deleuze, G. (1995b). On Philosophy. In *Negotiations, 1972–1990*, trans. M. Joughin. New York: Columbia University Press: 135–155.

Deleuze, G. (1995c). Letter to Serge Daney: Optimism, Pessimism, and Travel. In *Negotiations, 1972–1990*, trans. M. Joughin, New York, Columbia University Press: 68–80.

Deleuze, G. (1995d). Postscript on Control Societies, in *Negotiations, 1972–1990*, trans. M. Joughin. New York: Columbia University Press: 177–182.

Deleuze, G. (1998). *Essays Critical and Clinical*. trans. D. W. Smith and M. A. Greco. London and New York: Verso.

Deleuze, G. (1998). *Essays Critical and Clinical*, trans D. W. Smith and M. A. Greco, London and New York, Verso.

Deleuze, G. & Guattari, F. (1983). *Anti-Oedipus*. Preface by Michel Foucault. Trans. Robert Hurley, Mark Seem & Helen R. Lane. Minneapolis: University of Minnesota Press.

Deleuze, G. & Guattari, F. (1987). *A Thousand Plateaus*. Trans. & Foreword by Brian Massumi. Minneapolis: University of Minnesota Press.

Deleuze, G. & Guattari, F. (1994). *What Is Philosophy?* Trans. Graham Burchell and Hugh Tomlinson. London: Verso.

Deleuze, G. (2004a). Capitalism and Schizophrenia. In D. Lapoujade (Ed.), *Desert Islands and Other Texts* (pp. 232–242), Paris: Semiotext(e).

Deleuze, G. (2004b). On Capitalism and Desire. In D. Lapoujade (Ed.), *Desert Islands and Other Texts* (pp. 262–274). Paris: Semiotext(e).

Doran, S. (2011). Freedom Devices: Neoliberalism, Mobile Technologies and Governance. In C. McCarthy, H. Greenhalgh-Spencer, & R. Mejia (Eds.), *New Times: Making Sense of Critical/Cultural Theory in a Digital Age* (pp. 129–148). New York: Peter Lang.

Dyer-Witheford, N. (1999). *Cyber-Marx: Cycles and Circuits of Struggle in High-Technology Capitalism*. Urbana: University of Illinois Press.

Habermas, J. (1984). *Reason and the Rationalization of Society*, Volume 1 of *The Theory of Communicative Action*, trans. Thomas McCarthy. Boston: Beacon Press.

Habermas, J. (1987). *Lifeworld and System: A Critique of Functionalist Reason*, Volume 2 of *The Theory of Communicative Action*, trans. Thomas McCarthy. Boston: Beacon Press.

Holland, E. W. (1991). Deterritorializing Deterritorialization. From the *Anti-Oedipus* to *A Thousand Plateaus*, *SubStance* #66: 55–65.

Holland, E. W. (1993). A Schizoanalytic Reading of Baudelaire: The Modernist As Postmodernist. *Postmodern Culture*, v.4 n.1 (September).

Holland, E. W. (1998). From Schizophrenia to Social Control. In Eleanor Kaufman (Ed.) *Deleuze and Guattari: New Mappings in Politics, Philosophy, and Culture*. Minneapolis: University of Minnesota Press, 65–73.

Lazzarato, M. (1996). Immaterial Labour. In Paolo Virno and Michael Hardt (Eds.) *Radical Thought in Italy*. Minneapolis: University of Minnesota Press, pp. 132–146. Retrieved from http://www.generation-online.org/c/fcimmateriallabour3.htm.

Lazzarato, M. (n.d.). Biopolitics/Bioeconomics: A Politics of Multiplicity, trans. Arianna Bove & Erik Empson. Retrieved from http://www.generation-online.org/p/fplazzarato2.htm.

Lazzarato, M. (n.d.). From Biopower to Biopolitics. trans. Ivan A. Ramirez. Retrieved from http://www.generation-online.org/c/fcbiopolitics.htm.

Lefebvre, H. (1991). *The Production of Space*. Oxford: Blackwell.

Maurizio, L. & Negri, A. (1994). Travail Immaterial and Subjectivité. *Futur Antérieur* 6.

Maurizio, L. (1996). Immaterial Labour. In Paolo Virno & Michael Hardt (Eds.) *Radical Thought in Italy: A Potential Politics*. Minneapolis: University of Minnesota Press.

Negri, A. and Hardt, M. (2000). *Empire*. Cambridge, MA: Harvard University Press.

Negri, A. and Hardt, M. (2004). *Multitude: War and Democracy in the Age of Empire*. New York: Penguin.

Peters, M.A. (1996). Architecture of Resistance: Educational Theory, Postmodernism and the 'Politics of Space'. In *Poststructuralism, Politics and Education*, Westport, CT & London: Bergin & Garvey.

Peters, M.A. (2000a). Beyond Left and Right? Education, Equality and the 'Knowledge Economy'. Unpublished manuscript.

Peters, M.A. (2000b). 'Education, Work and the Global Knowledge Economy'. Unpublished manuscript.

Peters, M.A. (2001). *Poststructuralism, Marxism and Neoliberalism; Between Theory and Politics*. Lanham, MD; Boulder, CO;, New York; Oxford: Rowman & Littlefield.

Peters, M.A. (2003). *Knowledge Cultures: Education in the Age of Knowledge Capitalism*. Lanham, MD; Boulder, CO;, New York; Oxford: Rowman & Littlefield.

Peters, M.A. (2002). Education Policy in the Age of Knowledge Capitalism. World Comparative Education Forum Conference, Economic Globalisation and Education Reforms, Beijing Normal University, 14–16 October.

Polanyi, M. (1958). Personal Knowledge: Towards a Post-Critical Philosophy. Chicago: University of Chicago Press.

Polanyi, M. (1966). The Tacit Dimension. London: Routledge.

Vandenberghe, F. (2008). Deleuzian Capitalism. *Philosophy Social Criticism*, 34 (8) 877–903.

Wright, S. (2002). Storming Heaven: Class Composition and Struggle in Italian Autonomist Marxism. London: Pluto Press.

Part 1. Theoretical Foundations and Debates

CHAPTER ONE

Intellectual Labor

TIMOTHY BRENNAN

The intellect has become an increasingly privileged site in the production of value according to many theorists—both within processes of capitalist production and within perspectives for which the conceptual category of labor has once more become an object of hermeneutic interest. This shift derives at least some of its authority from influential sociological descriptions of the 1970s that pointed to structural changes in capitalism. The rise of a new caste of specialists created by the information economy and forecasts of a coming "postindustrial" society entailed the notion that industrial labor was, in any case, no longer a primary feature of productivity and had to be consigned to a second-order importance in a more heavily financialized and image-based system of global exchange.[1]

Out of this milieu, there arose a stronger version of the thesis: that theory itself (not simply the intellectual tasks of management and advertising) has become, for the first time, a material factor in the creation of economic value.[2] It is striking, though, that at the very moment that theory locates new ethereal sites that privilege the intellect in the production processes of capitalism, there is a general reluctance to explore the intellectual's role in the division of labor. A great deal is said in regard to its speaking about but very little about its manner of being within the system it diagnoses. Could it be that certain ideas rather than others have become prominent in theory as a result of obscuring that role? But also can it be that the ideas of moment and the styles of their delivery have a great deal to do with labor-saving operations—to a simplicity masked as complexity, which is a packaging that facilitates their circulation?

Before turning to these questions with examples, let me provide the setting. There has been, of course, an ongoing reliance by cultural theorists on terms and metaphors derived from economics: the "gift economy" (Marcel Mauss), the "libidinal economy" (Sigmund Freud), "expenditure" (Georges Bataille), "the spectacular commodity" (Guy Debord), "supplement as excess" (Jacques Derrida), and the term value itself as the register of an ambiguous middle realm between economics and aesthetics. But the converse is also true—a persistent borrowing from cultural theory by disciplinary discourses relating to economics seen in the use, for example, of the concept of "deterritorialization" in legal theories of sovereignty, of "multiculturalism" in corporate training programs, and postmodern tropes in chaos theory, which is now a large subfield in the usually less adventurous economics journals.[3]

This compulsion toward the economic is forced on all of us and is larger than any individual actor or position—part of a general inundation of society by economics as an everyday obsession, a new culture of economic forecasts, planning, and speculation, all following on the perceived new conditions at the "end of history," which has postulated that neoliberalism is the only possible system. Never before has investing, for instance, been such a populist activity; never before has charting the dips and rises of the market occupied the free time of ordinary people. New sections of daily newspapers on shopping, real estate speculation, home trading, and innovative pension fund packages show that finance and investment have become a form of entertainment and cultural curiosity that involve subjects at levels that exceed any interest in their own security.

The idea of living in a shareholder democracy, the idea that neoliberal ideology is not just popular in ruling circles but genuinely populist—this is the ambience within which present cultural theory has assumed its recent shape. Interestingly, and perhaps predictably, for a few years now there has been a recoil in theoretical discussions from an earlier investment in giving priority to the mediations of language and to vigorously emphasizing culture as a devised, artificial, constructed world of invented meaning—itself a revolt against the civic and governmental normativity of biopolitical orders and epistemic regimes seen as embodied in the tyranny of various "economisms."

What this represents is a turning away from an earlier rejection of discourses that stressed the economic determinations of culture, the economic roots of political ideologies, and any priority at all to the economic as such.[4] The setting that prompts this investigation, then, has to do in part with the recent return to the discourses of the economic within the very circles of theory that had before rejected them: the turn to "material culture" in anthropology and new historicist literary scholarship; to "real subsumption" and "immaterial labor" in the Deleuzian Marxism of the new Italians; to "thing theory" by high-end literary journals; and to the many sided attempts—Kojin Karatani's Transcritique is only one of many recent examples—to establish Kantian aesthetics as the foundation for all economic discourse and, indeed, to locate in original political economy itself a displaced and frustrated aesthetics.[5]

The stirrings of the apparent turn toward a new engagement with economics and aesthetics can be traced to ways that labor particularly has emerged as an ambiguous term in these debates. From its traditional usage in the nineteenth century as one of three primary categories within political economy—labor, capital, and rent—the term has experienced a scission between the exalted content with which it was endowed by the cultural theorist and the rather more degraded meaning it takes on as a sociological description of the theorist's social dilemma. Actually, the two halves of this fissure are intertwined. Summoned first as a grand economic category, it enters the conversation now in the form of a theory of the latest stage of capitalism in which "intellect" is considered the key productive force and in which, as a corollary, political activity is transformed into the art of living.

At the same time, this imputed productivity of the intellect inexorably refers (although now from the outside) to the hard work of thinking in a society that disparages critical theoretical effort as well as to the conditions of work under a regime of privatization involved in lowering the price of adversarial intellectual work. This process has been eagerly helped along by media intellectuals whose editorials mocking the humanities and applauding the defunding of the humanities have appeared in a variety of mainstream American and British publications. On the one hand, mental labor (performed by everyone from data entry technicians to brokers, script writers, management consultants, game show hosts, op-ed columnists, and Sunday morning political commentators on television) is considered more prevalent and vital in the levers of capitalist existence. On the other, intellectual (rather than merely "mental") labor assumes a new importance. The intellectual as entrepreneur—the breaker of icons, the imaginative creator of new modes of thought, new desires, new "potentialities"—has gripped dissident and conformist critics in equal measure and in identical terms. In place of domestic commodities and industrial objects of exchange, we are now directed to speed, creativity, information processing, and imagination, which are considered the nuts and bolts of the new economic regime.

Claims that primary labor is evanescent or immaterial in the new economy can be found, among other places, in the work of Thomas Friedman, David Brooks, and Jagdish Bhagwati. The work of ideas, concepts, and innovations takes on a new prominence, where the watchwords of yesterday—efficiency, productivity, and the workday—are replaced by terms such as intuition, adaptability, creativity, complexity, and play. Perhaps unexpectedly, this very assertion characterizes much of cultural theory as well, most clearly, perhaps, in Paolo Virno's recent contention that the world economy today is "post-Taylorist" and that in such an economy capitalism "puts to work . . . states of mind and inclinations," so that "modern forms of production" take on the shape of the "Intellect"—a public intellect existing "outside of work, and in opposition to it." [6] This appeal to the concept of a postindustrial society in the face of dramatic industrialization in China, India, Russia, and Brazil (dubbed by the business press the new "economic tigers") is oddly uncontroversial today, as is the idea that Taylorism is obsolete even as we witness the spread of the global maquiladora system in the textile, electronics, meat-processing, and service industries, which are so Taylorized as to include even proscriptions on the workers' use of free time. [7] But the assertion, however challenged it is by the facts, is a significant precondition of the turn we have been discussing. [8]

The theoretical warrant for these new departures in Left cultural theory (which are also and significantly a going back) is highly varied. It derives in part from the philosophies of difference forged by early-twentieth-century "economic psychologists" such as Gabriel Tarde and Gustave Le Bon, whose work on the "group mind" was taken up by the conservative Chicago school economists before being embraced by New Left Italian thinkers such as Maurizio Lazzarato (one of several such linkages between the new Italian school and its neoliberal counterparts). [9] Here, though, I would like to explore a different philosophical precursor—one that is more developed and more pervasive—which can be found in the current uses of Martin Heidegger. The Heideggerian orientation of contemporary theory can be seen as, among many other things, a skewed attempt to resolve this dilemma of triumphalization of intellect alongside the slipping status of the critical mind in the marketplace.

This is not to say that the influence of Heidegger is new or unusual or that it is the only problem to examine in the context of intellectual labor. After all, as both Theodor Adorno and Pierre Bourdieu have argued in brilliant, if neglected, studies, the exploration of existential being has been almost a habit in humanistic traditions of philosophy in the postwar period, even though it took many forms that did not exactly look forward to the current attractions of Heideggerianism.[10] Heidegger's themes and language seem perfectly suited to the present task. He rhetorically evokes the economic while abjuring it, pushing beyond the impasses of those language-based philosophies that began to be prominent during his early career and that took monopolistic hold in the last three decades. His writing's watchwords with little alteration significantly shadow economic discourses, with their focus on the "everyday," "experience," the utility and nonutility of objects, and the new "world picture" created by the fatal impact of technology supplanting techné. His is a return to a "materialism" based on thingliness, sensuousness, and the lonely intellect—a materialism, in other words, no longer associated with historical reckoning, dynamic intersubjectivity, or transformation (which are seen as political liabilities for critical humanists in an age of retreat and reassessment). This philosophical amalgam informs very disparate wings of contemporary thinking, including second-wave subaltern studies within postcolonial historiography; the philosophies of utterly diverse political figures such as Alain Badiou, Julia Kristeva, and Ian Hacking; the theology of David Bentley Hart; the new Italian political theory of Virno and Giorgio Agamben; and other, even more dissimilar, spheres of contemporary theory as well.

The contemporary shape of the Heideggerian gesture (and neither Adorno nor Bourdieu addressed this aspect of it) comes to us by way of the influence of two thinkers above all: Derrida within literary circles, and in the social sciences and political theory, the United States–inflected, demotic Heideggerianism of Hannah Arendt. Heidegger's famous shift in philosophy from epistemology to ontology has through various mediations come to resemble a move from knowing to a more consequential, purportedly more materialist, "being." What cannot be solved as thought is muscled forth as the realization of thought in action, but inactively: that is, in the crucial form of thought as action. For this purpose, labor has to be reconceptualized so that it can play the counterintuitive role of increasing the worth of primary intellectual work.

But here we confront still another paradox. To raise its value in the face of a disparaging or merely indifferent officialdom, labor has been made to seem, paradoxically, more expendable, more ethereal, and dispersed throughout the social strata without differentiation. The political consequences of this move are profound. If Antonio Gramsci had once famously pointed out in a widely cited passage that even workers are intellectuals, today's truism could be, paradoxically, that intellectuals are the only proletariat. Although this may seem overstated, it is the sense that underlies seriously debated positions today in the humanities: for example, that cosmopolitanism is a universal condition and equally shared globally and across all classes (the idea of the "vernacular" cosmopolitan), or that the category of the subaltern includes, for racial or civilizational reasons, everyone from a Gujarati peasant to United States–based history professors of Indian descent working in major universities or, indeed, foreign heads of state.

It would be all too easy, although perhaps still worthwhile, to interrogate this claim to dramatic centrality by intellectuals on the grounds of new German, French, or Italian ideology: that is, as the new "critical criticism" of the intellectual anxiously divorced from the world of affairs and, by way of overcompensation, all too eager to substitute the idea of transformation for the transformative powers of critique.[11] Much of that familiar line of attack is indeed still valid. But there are also other, and newer, ways of understanding the current hypostasis of intellectual—which is also to say, immaterial—labor as a symptom of the further commodification of knowledge rather than any resistance to it.

The Role of Arendt

Among the possibilities is that there are fully economic, and even vulgar, reasons for the trend toward thinking of the economic in terms of econopoiesis. I take this to be one of the more significant features of the Heideggerian turn, one based on Arendt's rehearsal of Heidegger's astounding practice of making claims about the present political world based on etymologies drawn from classical Greece. These etymologies were not philological in the sense that they did not establish buried connotations in key contemporary terminologies, thereby shedding light on present meanings. Rather, they were, as Arendt presented them, verities inscribed in a primary, uniquely emulatable civilization—the Greece out of which all later reality was (for her, and one might say also, for Heidegger and Nietzsche) a mere unfolding. In *The Human Condition* (1958)—Arendt's most profound and influential book— she uses the term poiesis to considerable effect.[12] In ancient Greek, it means an active making or crafting; by relying on the English homonym, Arendt summons poetry as productive labor: as the labor productive of truth. Her painstaking goal throughout the volume is to redefine politics by correcting our misconception of man as a "political animal."[13] The Greeks, she insists, preferred the vita contemplativa to the vita activa, the small revelations of the private sphere of the home to the repellent business of public affairs. The signal outrage of modernity for her is the rise of political economy, which dragged the former sphere into the latter, cheapening contemplation in the name of serving the grotesque bodily wants of a new god called by the name "society." Econo-poiesis, however, is much more than an argumentative gesture in Arendt's work. Her influence is such that it has become a general principle of contemporary theory and can be defined in the following way: the turning of economic categories into aesthetic artifacts with the authority of the Greek classics (as Agamben, another Arendtian, is doing with his appeals to the vocabulary of Roman law).

The project of *The Human Condition* is to dismantle the modern con- ception of labor as it was received from political economy and to contravene Hegel's epochal efforts in *The Philosophy of Right* to bring social labor squarely into the purview of philosophy, subjecting thought itself to a relationship of tension and debt to the physical labor that enables it. For Hegel this meant, ultimately, to realize the intellect socially—in part by witnessing the concrete form it had taken in governing institutions. Hegel's goal had, of course, already been revised, in its own way, by the Young Hegelians, including Marx, who instead set out to demonstrate that the intellect was the offspring, not the progenitor, of the world enveloping it. Alfred Sohn-Rethel in *Intellectual and Manual Labor*, aptly describes Marx's goal: "to dis- pel the fetishism of the intellect," a task Sohn-Rethel describes as requiring "infinitely deeper theoretical effort" than "to continue its worship."[14]

By drawing on distinctions she argued had prevailed in the Athens of antiquity, Arendt sets out first of all to extinguish the modern recognition of material labor as the foundation of value. She does this by making a distinction that she claims obtained in ancient Greece among the terms labor, work, and action. Labor referred to simple reproduction: that is, all the tasks associated with meeting the body's needs of clothing, food, and shelter. By contrast, work was artistic, referring to craftsmanship and the making of objects that, unlike basic necessities, were not immediately consumed and, therefore, were not useful only insofar as they were used up. Finally, action was perceived as the work of language, especially the rhetorical powers called forth in the political realm. In the significant setting of the U.S. 1950s,

Arendt launches a set of arguments that emerge again and again in contemporary cultural theory, most famously perhaps in the work of Michel Foucault, Agamben, Antonio Negri, and others, who share her idea that productivity is a degraded condition of a society whose bourgeois norms render sensibility, thinking, expressive love, and creative freedom impossible, reducing all to the servicing of physical needs and economic growth.

In this, Arendt conveys that profoundly Heideggerian sense of the revelatory properties of a new kind of action whose principal character is uselessness—a sublime disutility. In her tripartite division, labor is frightful and degraded because it is the toil associated with slaves whose plight is to expend effort on objects whose sole purpose is to be consumed, unlike work (as in "the work" of art), which is the sign of an effort whose exalted character lies precisely in its ability to live on, past consumption, bearing witness to the beauty of human effort. She deliberately divorces action from any sense of making. But it is not only the desired lack of practical activity that is her focus. The ideal state of Arendtian praxis is not necessarily to know anything as to experience everything and to be aware of one's everyday surroundings, surviving without guarantees in a world of objects whose mute solidity and quiet evidence of being are the only materialism worth seeking. Her effort, and here she is most faithful to her mentor, is to make of praxis not a doing but a state of availability.

The more utilitarian side of the oppositional intellectual's urge to resist a declining status by devising its economic centrality is here cast as the "discovery" (in the form of a rejection) of capitalism's obsession with utility, commodities, profits, and money. The effect of this confusion, although conceptual, is very real; activity and passivity are no longer distinct. Caught in a positional war, theory finds a way to increase its relative value. It presents itself as a labor-saving operation—a way of achieving "complexity" and "depth" with the artifice of style standing in for the shoddy empiricism of mere research and a repeatable (and, therefore, more easily transmissible) form.

The chief symptom in this operation is that, in place of argument, there emerges the virtual textual reading and the epigrammatic utterance. There need not be grounds for a declaration, since the declaration justifies itself by opening thought to new "potentialities." Authority is not based on reading, and reading need not correspond. In Arendt, who wrote at a time when reading still mattered, this takes the form of employing etymologies as splicing operations for complicated material processes, where the appeal to the Olympian serenity of antiquity emboldens the precepts without having to enter the messy world of plebeian documents such as international trade figures, real-wage charts, and so on, or even to contain any sense whatsoever of a world of conflicting interests.[15] We see this more generally today in the desires of publishers, given production costs, for minimalist, small-scale books—not unlike the compact discs in the recording industry on which only one song is original while the rest are recyclings of earlier work. Indeed, it is a common publishing practice today to parcel out an overall thesis across a number of short monographs in which isolated insights by major thinkers are blown up as programmatic statements that simultaneously maximize cover price. The semiroutine publications of Agamben, Slavoj Žižek, Jean-Luc Nancy, and Derrida are all examples of this trend.

This labor-saving move is part of an overall valorization of the aesthetics of complexity within contemporary criticism (which I will explore in the closing section of this essay), where complexity is seen as an absolute and unchallenged value: a physical sign, as it were, of immense critical labor embodied in a tangible, finely wrought, verbal artifact.[16] Such complexity is, of course, partly to be understood as a welcome riposte to a milieu of public discourse and propaganda in which ad copy proliferates and cynical campaign slogans abound. But this return to the fetish of intricacy also has an economic function unrelated to this element of protest. For complexity, among other things, offers the critic an opportunity to declare politically dissident ideas in the form of an ironic dissimulation—which is economic to the degree that it is a form of job protection in a regime of risk. Nonetheless, an idealization of complexity permits politically conformist ideas to take the form of dissident declarations in which the labor of thought is itself considered integral to oppositional modes of argument. Complexity thus becomes a use-value: the content as form of theoretically oppositional labor and, crucially, an instrument in making ambiguous the centrist movement of putatively oppositional thought.[17]

For Aristotle, to be alive was indistinguishable from being free—a condition made contingent by labor without rendering it impossible, depend- ing on how one defines the term labor, which is the initial justification for Arendt's toying with its meaning. The attempt of *The Human Condition* to translate observations regarding the slave-owning city-states of antiquity into projections of a modern bourgeois economy whose signature principle is "free labor" is a delicate move and requires some effort. In essence, what Arendt does is make the intellectual, rather than the citizen aristocrat, the new standard: he or she who does not labor (the new aristocracy, one might say), or, at least, he or she who should not simply labor, since it is clear from Arendt's analysis that intellectuals, too, have assumed the role of mere functionaries performing the scriptural tasks necessitated by bureaucracy like so many ancient craftspeople enlisted to do a useful job (the mental/ intellectual distinction referred to above). In making this gesture, Arendt attempts to undo Hegel's inauguration of modernity in *The Phenomenology of Spirit* when he brings slaves into the realm of freedom and labor into the heart of the processes of language, art, and reproduction.[18]

What has proven so disorienting for critics today is the strong antibourgeois strain of Arendt's thought, which seems to place her fully in the context of an undifferentiated radical critique. But we need to look at it more closely, because it is not what it seems. The rise of the commonwealth was tragic for Arendt in that it was a scheme of private owners to force the monarch to protect precisely their common wealth. It was less the case that they sought to employ their status as property holders to ensure a place in governance than to ask of government that it preserve and protect their property. Common wealth of this sort can never become a common inheritance throughout society; it must remain, strictly speaking, private. So what the rise of capitalism portends, for her, is the depressing insinuation of private concerns (considered disreputable by the Greeks) into an exalted public ideal. The response of subjects and citizens under this new arrangement was the development of a new arena or sphere of intimacy—a flight from the outer world into the inner subjectivity of the individual, which before had been sheltered (and left undiscussed) in the well-marked private realm of the household. Today, by contrast, the only way to hide the dark and secretive feelings, thoughts, and activities of the person is to have private property, which shields them from the prying eyes of publicity.

Modern property began to be perceived as pertaining not to movable goods in the world but to the human body itself—"labor power." Once again, there is a slippage for Arendt here (as elsewhere) between what we have in common and what we own privately. In different ways, and at different paces, capitalism and socialism alike represent a withering away of the private realm. For her, the equation of labor with "productivity" reduces all questions of importance to the reproduction "of the life processes." This is really her notion of biopolitics, which in this light can be seen (in a gesture made famous and generalized by Alexandre Kojève) of seeing capitalism and socialism alike as inventing the cruel logic of the disintegrating self. A completely socialized mankind makes no distinction between animal laborans and homo faber, so that the unuseful, beautiful, inquiring side of life is rendered unimportant. *The Human Condition* argues repeatedly that there is no distinction between labor and work in Marx. The animal laborans is unworldly because it is "imprisoned in the privacy of his own body, caught in the fulfillment of needs in which nobody can share."[19] Whatever is consumed is temporary and of short duration, and since the animal laborans produces only commodities for use, it can never attain to worldliness. In this way, the work of the hands and the labor of bodies are demarcated and distinguished by Arendt. The former, then, are those creations not used up in their use, those that are able to attain a persistence that bears witness to their having been made: the chair not reducible to its wood. This recognizable borrowing from Heidegger's "The Origin of the Work of Art" is, however, much more methodically adapted here by Arendt to the language and interests of Marx's *Capital*. And it is in the forging of this precise amalgam that Arendt has become so influential today and so widely copied by those theorists who consider themselves insurrectionary. The objectivity of the human-made world creates a feeling in common because more than one person over time can relate to the same object in the full knowledge that that object has been related to, in turn, before.

The subliminal disquiet that permeates *The Human Condition* ultimately lies in Arendt's antipathy toward equality (which she associates with conformity), toward the nation-state (which she consigns to bureaucracy), and to common needs. Given contemporary sensibilities, what seems most dated in her conceptions, among other things, is the complete absence in her outlook of the critiques by intellectuals from Africa, India, and Latin America that were already prominent, and growing, at the time of her writing. There is not a hint in any word she utters that Greece might have "come later."

The challenge of her perspective is not simply its cold war dimension or the not altogether ingenuous way in which she casts her arguments in an emotional tone of faux insouciance toward Marx and Left Hegelianism (even as she is involved throughout in a pitched battle with that philosophical lineage whose central themes she hopes to appropriate while pretending to include them in a long lineage in which they play a minor part). It is that there is a profound Helleno-centrism that fits somewhat awkwardly with the conventional wisdom of the U.S. 1950s, drawing on the same golden age rhetoric mobilized by writers and scholars such as Richmond Lattimore, Werner Jaeger, and, in the most egregious instance, Edith Hamilton. The latter two were, like Arendt, German American, and their works were used widely in the American school system for moral education.[20]

If Arendt follows Heidegger very closely in carrying on the proprietary relationship Germans feel toward Attic Greece (only they are its proper inheritors and interpreters), Arendt in effect creates a pop philosophical version of Hamilton for American audiences, translating the conventional American ideas of individualism (spelled out in her labor-work-action distinction) and the corruptness of all government as well as the purifying privacy of the home and of noncommercial property in a venerated, already established classical tradition. In short, she was making American political clichés classical and sanctifying them by association with the high philosophical tradition to which she belonged at one step removed.

Arendt's vision of a gentlewoman's circle of refined thinkers freed not from labor so much as from the obsessions of bourgeois politics and the degraded world of public affairs is shared by Derrida as well, who seeks to return the intellectual to that immersion in the purity of the concept characterized by an enticing bookishness in which text is venerated as an object of delight—a secularization of text in which the sacred is now beheld as an aesthetic aura (a move that conforms to the secularization of religion in Heidegger generally). He, like Arendt, is protesting against it. In Arendt and Derrida, the rejection of market efficiency, which they associate with the committed, participatory intellectual (who acts on and within civil society), is fashioned into a new model based on the heroic self-sufficiency of the poet and artistic amateur—aloof commentators on a society of which they feel themselves not a part but about which they concede to be thinking. The peasant philosopher becomes the poet philosopher, just as the radical critic becomes the aristocrat of the demimonde.

Complexity Is a Style

I begin this section with one last quotation in the spirit of our forgotten past and this return to economic thought as econo-poiesis. Take this passage from the Ludwig Feuerbach everyone knows from Marx's famous theses but which few actually take the time to read: "To have articulated what is such as it is, in other words, to have truthfully articulated what truly is, appears superficial. To have articulated what is such as it is not, in other words, to have falsely and distortedly articulated what truly is, appears profound. . . . Truthfulness, simplicity, and determinacy are the formal marks of the real philosophy."[21] Regardless of what one achieves in philosophy today, one is considered crude and reckless so long as one is unwilling to bow to a preapproved canon. The atmosphere is stifling, and the adversarial intellectual of the academic humanities is required by unwritten laws to work accord- ing to an imperious etiquette. Our valorized forms of theory operate only on the basis of a set of rules that are seldom acknowledged, some of which I have tried to describe above, while offering a story of how they came to be. I would like to counterpose to these another set of rules that negatively assess this particular version of theory as a mode of comportment (that is, what theory must look like in the current setting in order to be recognized as "theory" in the present division of labor). I hope it is clear that I am not taking a stand against theory as such, only "theory" where the designated scare quotes also intimate a self-arrogation. That is, I am making a case against the tyrannical identification of all theory with what is, in fact, only one currently hegemonic strand of it. I consider this itself a theoretical effort that a certain vulgar response wishes to discount without engagement, which would, again, require labor.

Rule 1: The work of "theory" is a mere prolegomenon to consequential theoretical work, although it does not see itself this way, of course. Its opposite—which is found in the symphonic sweep, the display of knowledge, the powers of synthesis, the carefully toned-down prose, and the emphasis on evidentiary argument of situated thinkers such as Giovanni Arrighi, Edward Said, Nancy Fraser, David Harvey, Arundhati Roy, and Alexander Kluge—does not register as "theory" because it has already internalized its lessons and expressed them in the investigation of an immanent set of unfolding social conflicts. The high theorists by contrast (and these can be very dissimilar politically and aesthetically—for example, Jean-Luc Nancy, Negri, Gilles Deleuze, Agamben, Badiou, and Gianni Vattimo) luxuriate in a preliminary intellectual space, whose value is enhanced by being, among other things, above productive work.

Rule 2: Theory (of the latter sort) is a sumptuous defanging of revolutionary ideas—only one reason why its underlying theatrics involve an activism rendered as immanent contemplation and illumination. The latest turn of the screw in theory's revolt against its own earlier generation has been to reject the mere word and substitute for it the thing. In this act, it mistakes itself for materialism. So, too, unlike the deconstructions of the 1980s and the fixations on identity of the 1990s, it now speaks of incompatibilities, remainders, antinomies, possibilities. With these slogans, it mistakes itself for dialectics. The move from the textual to the political in theory has thus been the move from a dynamic contradiction to a static paradox (what Georg Lukács had famously called "the antinomies of bourgeois thought" in "Reification and the Consciousness of the Proletariat").[22] Badiou, for instance, suggests as much in *Being and Event* in his decisive rejection of both earlier modes of theory in favor of the incontrovertible findings of the mathemes of Godelian and Cantorian logic and their scientific finalization of a being as fundamental as Heidegger's but now untied from its poetic enchantment.[23]

Rule 3: Precisely as the defanging of revolutionary ideas, theory—or better, the theoretical affect—relies on the promise of revolution, a sudden crystallization of formerly unkempt or rough-hewn ideas turned by the forces of genius after hard and heroic labor into a novum. What this ignores, and what the preapproved canon conspires to ignore, is the Vichian (and later, Saidian) lesson that all reading is a rereading and that every generation's task is to rediscover what others already knew; it also ignores Raymond Williams's lesson that the residual is embedded in the emergent and that history proceeds not in ruptures but in continuities that combine in haphazard and aesthetically unpleasing fashion the antiquated, the resili- ently contemporary, and the wholly unexpected and newly misrecognized. To put this another way, the safeguard of "theory," which sees itself as bold and entrepreneurially attuned to the immediate now (as opposed to nostalgic forms of older "economisms" and outdated Marxisms), is belated, drawing its resources from such cutting-edge figures as Heidegger, Schmitt, Nietzsche, Spinoza, and . . . Aristotle.

Rule 4: If theory cannot justify its grandeur on the basis of rupture, then a criterion must be established for the predominance of the prolegomenous theorist over the situated theorist. The former did not displace the latter on the basis of a collective judgment, on a conflict of arguments, or on the prima facie (and therefore unconscious) suitability of the former's ideas and formulations with a manifest present moment. It did so because of the lack of novelty lying at its core—its congruence, in other words, with the already existing prejudices of the now.

Rule 5: A permanent confusion supplies the fuel for theory as event. The theorist, especially the young theorist, impelled by the sacrificial desire to penetrate the malaise of powerlessness and desperate to solve the riddle of the social world without doing more harm, drinks in the plausible ideas emanating from a number of intellectual circles (which remain by him or her unanalyzed, uncategorized, and without origin).[24] These have to do with virtuality, information capitalism, an amorphous and decentered power that both characterizes corporate tyranny and is its most flagrant sales pitch.

Concepts of globalization, biotechnology, Internet hybridizations, post-political undergrounds, new diasporic enclaves, and so on all scream their complex approximations of a shifting and mutating present. These all form the background noise, as it were, for an inquiry that does not, for the most part, assess the actuality of these models as they are inherited (again, atmospherically) from sociology and media studies, discursive geography, punk anthropology, and pop journalism of the Tom Peters school. These ideas and inherited schemata are rather the point of departure for a much more demanding set of lucubrations in thought. They do not announce themselves as tarrying with the somewhat pedestrian practices of those who study labor statistics, quantify capital flows, keep track of ownership laws, or drag into their theses the time-tested and canonical opinions of social critics, economists, and sociologists. The response to the prospect of this kind of labor is never actually articulated, but what one is required to suppose, and quietly to affirm, for the purposes of avoiding contact with knowledge, or of feeling constrained actually to accumulate and assess it, is: "We already know this." All challenges to theory, then, must be viewed as ipso facto assaults on insight in the name of the superseded, attacks on the avant on behalf of the stubborn, sectarian, and inflexibly old.

The atmospheric convictions that inform theory all derive from an investment in the sensuality of thought—understood here in the sense of effeteness rather than thinking with or through the body.[25] The aestheticization of feeling as a sensuousness of thought (found in the new aristocratic sensibilities called forth by Arendt, for example) is considered by the situated theorist an embarrassing matter—a display not worthy of the objects of thought. What have to be made clear are the advantages to a mode of thought that instead confines itself to propositions that can achieve a bluntness precisely because of the precritical labor that has already been done prior to their articulation. While this opens itself up to misunderstanding among the sensualists, who decry such moves as "polemical," the sensualists must come to see that they are viewed in turn as involving themselves in wayward exhibitionism, as a "leading to" thought that is as yet naively expressed, often through allusion and citation rather than argument or debate.

This leads me to a final contrast I wish to draw in discussing intellectual labor: between the situated critic, who abjures an investment in the sensuality of thought, and the prolegomenous theorist, who dramatizes thought as dissidence but is, in fact, destructive of it.

Like the semantic indeterminacy of language or the epistemological impasse of ever "really" knowing the real, information capitalism in all its manifestations is already a banality to the situated theorist. The only interesting question for him or her lies in the details, emphases, or quality of the predictions of future trends within that established frame. In the situated theorist's eyes, then, the prolegomenous theorist fetishizes a banality—not because it is based on poorly understood ideas taken from linguists, economists, sociologists, or philosophers (which is frequently the case), but precisely because it is not philosophical but ethical. The prolegomenous theorist finds portents in an everyday that is perfectly meaningless without political agency or the bases of its historical becoming.

The prolegomenous theorist, drawing on Spinoza, Kant, Nietzsche, Machiavelli, and Schmitt, complains (oddly enough) of the datedness of his or her adversaries, implying that they have not kept pace. This dwelling in a highly selective past does not, even for a moment, give the theorist pause when assaulting the putatively antiquated categories of any oppositional position. The situated theorist, by contrast, abandons the modernist illusion of creation ex nihilo and finds in the prolegomenous theorist a bathing in thought as anodyne and the beatifying of the concept as event. The frightening possibility that theory has a social function that it cannot control or direct, and that works counter to its aims, is entertained only by the situated theorist; for the prolegomenous, it is a closed book.

For the prolegomenous theorist, social problems are solved by the very act of stipulating a poignant term. The reorientation of the real follows immediately on the utterance of a newly evoked reality. This is, and must be, a closed system, very much like a vacuum in which the laboratory specialist prevents a mote of dust or germ from infecting the carefully prepared sterility of the experiment—hence, the Saidian effort to trace the hidden fealty between the perennial modernism of beginnings and the disavowal of the places from which one's theory traveled.[26]

It would be inaccurate to say that these two discourses of situated and prolegomenous theory fail to understand one another. The situated understands the prolegomenous only too well, since the very act of situating itself requires studying what has outmaneuvered it and forced it into a defensive posture; whereas the prolegomenous ignores the situated with all the power and prejudice of its hegemony. In the end, each sees the other as simplistic.

In the struggle over interpretations, the situated theorist is at a structural disadvantage. He or she is constrained to wrestle with concepts, compare the shadings of views to eliminate inconsistencies, weigh not only his or her topics' conclusions but the environment of his or her composition. The prolegomenous, on the other hand, is driven by an immanent methodology in the service of a performative transcendence. He or she can move very rapidly from position to position, modeling his or her language on needs located in a fickle, flexible market. A quotation can stand for a corpus with little guilt or pause. By the time the situated theorist has uttered a syllable, the entire "debate" has shifted—although it never was a debate and is instinctively set up this way to avoid competition, since the anachronisms of historical thought, agency, will, and civic life are already "known" and no longer need to be attacked.

Focusing on the problem of intellectual labor is, among other things, to suggest that this bridging of fashions where antieconomisms effloresce as new economic theories within the cultural field has often taken place between radical political economic theory and some attempt to improve or update Marx by way of motifs drawn from his holy texts or in a return to anthropology, where the problematic essence of human character (usually captioned as its fundamental perversity) is once again probed as it had been in the earliest political economists with the goal of naturalizing the market. The distinctions on which philosophy had always been based are now collapsed into a single one: thinking is being, being is labor, labor is a poiesis or making, and therefore, economics is aesthetics under the regime of the general intellect.

It is better not to lose sight of the difference between reading laboriously in the hope of developing an approach that seeks an end (and that acknowledges its ends) and failing to do so out of the desire to run and dodge around points of contention for the purpose of pleasing the labored intellect. This pleasing is really a pacifying by means of the rhythms of a happily never-ending process and thereby reassures the intellect that its work will never be done, that there will always be employment. This is what is meant by Žižek's argument that the unsettled, unsatisfied lack is not the origin of desire but desire's end.[27] The alienation of the subject prompts its poetic reflection. For that particular natural resource to remain unexhausted, all of the objective world and its conditions of existence must remain exactly as they were. And this, and nothing else, is the meaning of the modern turn from knowing to being, which is the ground for the return to the economic and its dissimulation of intellectual labor.

Notes

1. Barbara Ehrenreich and John Ehrenreich, "The Professional-Managerial Class," in *Between Labor and Capital,* ed. Pat Walker (Boston: South End Press, 1979), 5–45; Daniel Bell, *The Coming of Post-Industrial Society: A Venture in Social Forecasting* (New York: Basic Books, 1973); and Alvin Toffler, The Third Wave (New York: Morrow, 1980).

2. Examples of this in mainstream business circles would be Robert B. Reich, *The Future of Success* (New York: Knopf, 2001); and Peter F. Drucker, *The Essential Drucker:*

Selections from the Management Works of Peter F. Drucker (New York: HarperCollins, 2001). For cultural theory, see André Gorz, *L'Immateriel—Connaissance, valeur et capital* (The Immaterial—Knowledge, Value, and Capital) (Paris: Galilée, 2003); and Félix Guattari and Toni Negri, *Communists Like Us: New Spaces of Liberty, New Lines of Alliance* (New York: Semiotext(e), 1990), 33–38.

3. On deterritorialization, see Martin Puchner, "Guantanamo Bay: A State of Exception," *London Review of Books,* December 16, 2004. On chaos theory in economics, see Tim Hay- ward and Judith Preston, "Chaos Theory, Economics, and Information: The Implications for Strategic Decision-Making," *Journal of Information Science* 25.3 (1999): 173–82; and James Gleick, *Chaos: Making a New Science* (New York: Penguin, 1987).

4. For brevity's sake, since the post-1970s reaction against economic explanations as represent- ing an older "base/superstructure" model was so pervasive, one might consult only the Routledge anthology on cultural studies from 1991, which captured the tone of the next decade. Stuart Hall's biting remarks on the "old mechanical economism" is paradigmatic of the mood I am describing, which was general. Stuart Hall, "Gramsci's Relevance for the Study of Race and Ethnicity," in *Stuart Hall: Critical Dialogues in Cultural Studies,* ed. David Morley and Kuan-Hsing Chen (London: Routledge, 1997), 411–40, 428. Apart from its influence, the cultural studies volume is a particularly apt example of the allergic response to economics in theory circles because of its identification with a tradition of thought (Marxism) that had always paid close attention to economics and, indeed, forced it into the discussion of early twentieth-century social theory.

5. A sampling of the turn to "material culture" in cultural anthropology and cultural studies can be found in Susanne Kuechler and Mike Rowlands, eds., *Journal of Material Culture,* which according to the editors "explores the relationship of artefacts to social relations." For "real subsumption," see Michael Hardt and Antonio Negri, *Empire* (Cambridge, MA: Harvard University Press, 2000); for thing theory, see the special issue of *Critical Inquiry* 28.1 (Fall 2001); and for Kantian aesthetics as a model for political economy, see Kojin Karatani, *Transcritique: On Kant and Marx* (Cambridge, MA: MIT Press, 2003).

6. Paolo Virno, "The Ambivalence of Disenchantment," in *Radical Thought in Italy: A Potential Politics,* ed. Paolo Virno and Michael Hardt (Minneapolis: University of Minnesota Press, 1996), 20, 26, 28. Virno is far from alone. Although not at all identical in his argu- ments, a mainstream version of the same thesis can be found in Thomas L. Friedman, *The World Is Flat: A Brief History of the Twenty-First Century* (New York: Farrar, Straus, and Giroux, 2005), as well as in left cultural theory: Maurizio Lazzarato, "Immaterial Labor," in *Radical Thought in Italy,* 133–50; and Michael Hardt and Antonio Negri, *Labor of Dionysus: A Critique of the State Form* (Minneapolis: University of Minnesota Press, 1994), 116–17, 277–79.

7. Andrew Downie, "Wanted: Skilled Workers for a Growing Economy in Brazil," *New York Times,* July 2, 2008.

8. Many of the premises of British cultural studies in its second-wave form set the stage for this analysis by drawing on André Gorz's *Farewell to the Working Class: An Essay on Post-*

Industrial Socialism (London: Pluto Press, 1982), for instance, or Scott Lash and John Urry's *The End of Organized Capitalism* (Madison: University of Wisconsin Press, 1987). Whether actually read and worked through by the humanists, these were nevertheless the points of departure for the theorization of "new times," from which the ideas of subversive consumption, niche marketing, and postindustrialization were ushered into cultural theory with a positive valence. The persistence of these ideas in academic humanities circles is demonstrable. See, for instance, Gary Hall and Claire Birchall, introduction to *New Cultural Studies: Adventures in Theory* (Athens: University of Georgia Press, 2007), 1–28.

9.   Maurizio Lazzarato, *Puissances de l'invention: La Psychologie économique de Gabriel Tarde contre l'économie politique* (The Powers of Invention: The Economic Psychology of Gabriel Tarde against Political Economy) (Paris: Les Empêcheurs de penser en rond, 2002).

10.   Theodor W. Adorno, *The Jargon of Authenticity* (Evanston, IL: Northwestern University Press, 1973); and Pierre Bourdieu, *The Political Ontology of Martin Heidegger* (Stanford, CA: Stanford University Press, 1991).

11.   The economic war over the price of ideas is explored outside the Marxist tradition in Georg Simmel, *The Philosophy of Money* (1900; London: Routledge and Kegan Paul, 1978). There Simmel describes how in a system of universal exchange (capitalism), where all relationships are mediated by money, "abstraction" reigns. The interchangeability and indifference of all objects was precisely suited to the tyranny of the intellect, now driven to "calculation" (that is, both in the sense of distinguishing among objects based on numerical quantities, and engaging in interpersonal relations based solely on a cost/benefit analysis. Simmel explicitly argues, in fact, that the one is the condition of the other). A year earlier in his *Theory of the Leisure Class,* Thorstein Veblen reminded his academic colleagues that their profession descended from the priestly classes trained "in the service of a supernatural agent." Intellectual work required "training for the domestic service of a temporal master" (the "Lord"), and was based on "acquiring facility in subservience." In such circles it was always highly valued to acquire knowledge with a (as Veblen put it) "spectacular effect, together with some sleight of hand"; "knowledge of the 'unknowable,' owed its serviceability for the sacerdotal purpose to its recondite character." Thorstein Veblen, *Theory of the Leisure Class: An Economic Study of Institutions* (1899; Norwalk, CT: Easton Press, 1994), 215–16.

12.   Hannah Arendt, *The Human Condition* (Chicago: University of Chicago Press, 1958).

13.   Ibid., 28–37, 68–73, 79–92, 167–81.

14.   Martin Sohn-Rethel, foreword to *Intellectual and Manual Labour: A Critique of Epistemology* (London: Macmillan, 1978), 3.

15.   There is a revealing passage along these lines in Friedrich A. Kittler, *Gramophone, Film, Typewriter* (Stanford, CA: Stanford University Press, 1999), 202–3, where he relates that when Nietzsche's eyesight began to fail him in later life, he enlisted a typewriter designer to fashion a type ball. It was at this moment that Nietzsche discovered the wisdom of aphorisms. Although Kittler presents this as a sign of Nietzsche's little-known effect on technology, there is another moral. Truth, always malleable for Nietzsche, here coincides apparently with whatever was less straining as activity for the philosopher.

16. I examine this problem of "complexity" (or, rather, one kind of claim to complexity) as a philosophical ruse in more detail in *At Home in the World: Cosmopolitanism Now* (Cambridge, MA: Harvard University Press, 1997), 66–78.

17. That this complexity has generally taken the form of a poetics of the intellect (the demonstration in language of its own plasticity and play) is not to say that there have not been wars on other fronts—for instance, Alain Badiou's effort to bridge continental and analytic traditions in philosophy by appealing to the very emblem of the unintelligibly complex, namely, math. This move may be seen as analogous to the decisive detour within political economy represented by the neoclassical revolution, which in the work of William Stanley Jevons and Alfred Marshall steered away from questions of value and human nature to the mathematical operations of "equilibrium" and "marginal utility."

18. For a full treatment of this remarkable moment in philosophy, see Susan Buck-Morss, *Hegel, Haiti, and Universal History* (Pittsburgh, PA: University of Pittsburgh Press, 2008).

19. Arendt, *The Human Condition,* 119.

20. Richmond Lattimore was (and in many places still is) considered one of the best translators of the Greek classics into English, known above all for his translation of "The Iliad," which dates from 1951. *Paideia* ("education," "instruction"), the three-volume magnum opus of the German American classicist Werner Jaeger, although published earlier, became a centerpiece of American college instruction in the 1950s. Edith Hamilton, another German American, published *The Greek Way* (1930) and *Mythology* (1942); they were both widely selling books that were (and are) used as introductory texts in U.S. colleges and high schools.

21. Ludwig Feuerbach, "Provisional Theses for the Reformation of Philosophy," in *The Young Hegelians: An Anthology,* ed. Lawrence S. Stepelevich (Atlantic Highlands, NJ: Humanities Press, 1983), 129–55.

22. Georg Lukács, "Reification and the Consciousness of the Proletariat," in *History and Class Consciousness: Studies in Marxist Dialectics,* trans. Rodney Livingstone (Cambridge, MA: MIT Press, 1968), 110.

23. Alain Badiou, *Being and Event,* trans. Oliver Feltham (London: Continuum, 2005), 14–15, 123–29.

24. To the degree that complexity is a style, we cannot exempt Badiou and Slavoj Žižek from these conclusions regarding thought's sumptuousness, despite their guerrilla encounter with and against the poetry of refuge and the linguistic attitude of "abstract objectivism" (in V. N. Vološinov's sense)—the structuralist normativity of language as pure langue. Within this mode of comportment they seek to enter and make a name in—on this particular terrain they have chosen for their political intervention (that is, that of "theory")—the prolegomenous reigns.

25. The relationship of thinking to the body, affect, and feeling in feminist theory has been well developed and has contributed to marking the hidden dimension of differential rationality based on sexual difference (Luce Irigaray, Jane Gallop, and others). This is, however, not the kind of problem I am addressing here. My focus is rather on the beholding of thought not as concept that approximates or clarifies but as a sumptuous object of consumption and dis-

play. This is, among other things, a by-product of a refinement and sophistication of thought serving as a social marker for those who live and work outside the need to reproduce themselves through physical labor.

26. Edward Said, *Beginnings: Intention and Method* (Baltimore, MD: Johns Hopkins University Press, 1975), 39–40, 354–57.
27. Slavoj Žižek, *The Parallax View* (Cambridge, MA: MIT Press, 2006), 25–28, 60, 107.

CHAPTER TWO

A Critique of "Cognitive Capitalism"

GEORGE CAFFENTZIS

But since money itself is an omnipresent means, the various elements of our existence are thus placed in an all-embracing teleological nexus in which no element is either the first or last. Furthermore, since it measures all objects with merciless objectivity, and since its standard of value so measured determines their relationship, a web of objective and personal aspects of life emerges which is similar to the natural cosmos with its continuous cohesion and strict causality (Simmel, 2004, p. 431).

Introduction

The last few years have witnessed both a major capitalist crisis (that is far from over) and a crisis of traditional Marxist explanations of capitalist crisis. That is why the development of the work of "post-operaist" or "Autonomous Marxists" like Hardt, Negri, Vercellone, Boutang, Virno, and Marrazi, has proven so attractive. They present a collection of new concepts or new approaches to old ones (e.g., cognitive capitalism, the General Intellect, immaterial labor, affective labor, biopower, common, Empire, multitude, rent, capture, singularity, formal and real subsumption, living knowledge) appropriate to conditions of post-post-Keynesian, post-post-Fordist capitalism, with a chance of providing a theory that might, finally, "grip the masses" or, in their terminology, "the multitude."

So much rides, then, upon the post-operaists' description of contemporary capitalism as "cognitive capitalism," or perhaps some of its cognates like "the informatization of production," "the knowledge economy," "informational capitalism." For it and these cognates are meant to describe a novel form of capitalism on the verge of collapse because the very forces of production and class struggle that brought it into existence far outpace the relations of production it offers. In other words, the time is ripe for (cognitive) revolution. However, in their laudable political effort to liberate the revolutionary energies of our time by portraying the hegemony of a new and inherently unstable capitalism, the theorists of cognitive capitalism dismiss the range and complexity of the forces in the field on both sides of the class line that make capitalism more unstable and, at the same time, potentially more enduring.

In this chapter I test the strength of the concept of "cognitive capitalism" (and its cognates) and find it (them) inadequate to the task of fully characterizing contemporary capitalism. I argue that there is no direct formula connecting capitalism, knowledge-production and political liberation, as the theorists of "cognitive capitalism" affirm. In the conclusion, I point to an alternative conception that escapes the strictures I brought against their "cognitivist" analyses.

The genealogy of cognitive capitalism

Capitalism=Rationality: Weber, Simmel, Hayek . . . sans Keynes with Marx in the middle

In order to test the concept of cognitive capitalism it is important to clarify which concept we are speaking about. Before the development of the concept of cognitive capitalism by Carlo Vercellone and other post-operaist or autonomous Marxist thinkers (see Edu-factory, 2009) there was an already highly developed notion of a knowledge economy and knowledge production in the academic, popular business, and OECD-World Bank literature. It is important to distinguish between these two traditions and discern their overlap and difference.

Indeed, there has been a long tradition connecting capitalism with cognition, rationality and the abstract quantitative spirit. Already in the period between the late 19th century and pre-WWI period a series of economists and sociologists in particular, German neo-Kantians like Georg Simmel and Max Weber, looked at capitalism as a "form of life" characterized by the spirit of rationality, calculation, and abstractness. Their work was part of a widespread lamentation on the sterility of existence in modern capitalism where formal structures take predominance over "life"—here also we have the seeds of the critique of bureaucracy that was so influential in the mid-20th century.

Simmel, for example, rooted capitalism in the inversion of means/ends polarity and the application of a quantitative value system based on the exchange of equal-for-equal to all forms of life. As we see in the epigraph, Simmel both praised and despaired of the soul-eviscerating, totalitarian form of life (or "second Nature") that such a rational capitalism promotes (Simmel, 2004). For Weber, capitalism was permeated with the "spirit" of rationality that leads to his famous "iron cage" image, i.e., capitalism drives humanity into a rational deployment of free labor, a rational form of accounting, and a rational form of industry responding to the market, but also to a soulless life world (Weber, 2002). True, this spirit operationalized only an instrumental rationality, but it was a rationality all the same that was superior to all previous economic forms as well as to its contemporary rivals (including socialism). It seemed inevitable.

Decades later, Hayek further developed these cognitive approaches to capitalism by his famous equation of the market with an epistemological tool providing information about the commodities up for sale (Hayek, 1949, pp. 77–91). In his view, any other effort to organize distribution would be continually dogged by a lack of measure leading to a system based on arbitrary, non-economic and inevitably corrupt choices. This approach led to his critique of socialism and his questioning of its long-term viability (Steele, 1992, pp. 119–122).

Not every bourgeois commentator on capitalism came to the same conclusion concerning the rational and cognitive character of capitalism. Keynes questioned the rationality of capitalism on a wide variety of contexts, e.g., from his remarks concerning "animal spirits," to the game-like character of most investment and gaming-like behavior of most investors, to the "bandwagon" effects of a stock market that comes down to betting on what the average bets of the bettors will be. His overall attitude is that capitalism was purely instrumental and he gave "one cheer" for it in the way that his fellow Bloomsburyian E.M. Forster gave "two cheers" for democracy. In fact, Keynes humorously expressed his attitude in his 1928 essay, "Economic Prospects of Our Grandchildren," in which he argued that once the accumulation process leads to the "solution" of the problem of scarcity (roughly in the early 21st century, i.e., now) humanity can finally assess the true value of the money-motive.

It is then that "The love of money as a possession—as distinguished from the love of money as a means to the enjoyments and realities of life—will be recognized for what it is, a somewhat disgusting morbidity, one of those semi-criminal, semi-pathological propensities which one hands over with a shudder to the specialists in mental disease" (Keynes, 1972: 329).

In a word, for Weber, Simmel and Hayek (but not for Keynes) the phrase *cognitive capitalism* was redundant. Though they undoubtedly had an important impact on cognitive capitalism theorists of the early 21ˢᵗ century, clearly the most important influence is Karl Marx. On the one side, Marx "recognized," with Weber, Simmel and Hayek, that all capitalist epochs had a cognitive aspect because the basic mechanisms of the system, even those he "emphasized"—like the exchange process, the labor time measure of value, the importance of reducing turnover time, the transformation of surplus-value into profit, rent and interest—create "concrete abstractions" that stimulate the development of an instrumental rationality. Indeed, Marx, for all his criticisms of the absurdity and barbarity of the system, was the original "immaterialist" and "cognitivist" as far as capitalism is concerned, since he argued that capitalists are not interested in things, but they definitely want to *know* their quantitative *value* and value is hardly a material stuff!

The Autonomist Marxist adherents of the theory of "cognitive capitalism" like Vercellone, however, are not particularly interested in Marx's general equation of capitalism with some form of quantitative (but fetishized) rationality, as was Alfred Sohn-Rethel (Sohn-Rethel, 1978). They place their emphasis on Marx as the student of the knowledge-capitalism relation and of the terrain where political economy and epistemology merge. In so doing they revalue Marx's collection of midnight notes, the *Grundrisse*, for it is there, they claim, that the basis for a political theory about the capitalist crisis generated by the application of knowledge to production and (potentially) leading to the liberation of workers from exploitation is laid out.

Marx's well-known argument in the *Fragment on Machines* in the *Grundrisse* is that with the advent of large-scale industry, a phase of capitalist development is inaugurated in which science becomes the main force of production, technology takes over the labor process and machines are substituted for human labor (with the consequent fall of the rate of profit). The worker is reduced to being an attendant to the machine but at the same time, the use of labor time to measure wealth is proving to be increasingly irrational (Marx, 1973, pp. 704–711).

The *Fragment on Machines* has been extremely influential on the Autonomist Marxists' conception of immaterial labor and cognitive capitalism, in their potential for fostering a transition to a different society, and exodus from capital. There is a general belief (prominent especially in the recent writings of Negri and Hardt), that we are in a stage in which capitalism is an obstacle to the further development of the productive forces, in which the historic contradiction between forces and relations of production is coming to a head, and that cognitive labor is the crucial element in the extremization of the contradiction.

Marxology, however, has not been the only force driving the development of a theory of cognitive capitalism. The epochal changes that followed the capitalist crisis of the mid-70s—a crisis clearly produced in great part by the cycle of struggles made by industrial workers worldwide—were crucial. It was the restructuring of the world economy in response to these—de-industrialization, globalization, and the computer/information revolution—that triggered the idea of cognitive capitalism. The geniality of the Autonomist Marxist theorists is to have turned the defeat of the industrial working class in the 1970s into a victory, by reading the deindustrialization of production, at least in the global North, as a response to and concretization of the refusal of the factory. Cognitive capitalism in this perspective is the step workers have forced capitalists to take, by refusing the assembly line, causing a productivity crisis and demonstrating that a whole industrial regime of life had to come to an end.

The OECD and World Bank

> The "promotion" of knowledge from the rank of an exogenous independent variable to that of an endogenous variable dependent on input, on the allocation of resources, is an important step.
>
> —FRITZ MACHLUP (1962, P. 5)

There is nothing new under the sun. This is true of an economic approach to knowledge and cognition and hence to "cognitive capitalism." Even though terms like "knowledge economy" began, by the mid-1990s, to be widely used by economists and sociologists as well as by the main capitalist planning institutions like the World Bank to define the new reality emerging from the economic restructuring responding to the crisis of the 1970s, economic theorists like Fritz Machlup had already developed the categories that would transform knowledge into a commodity and an industrial sector in the early 1960s (Machlup, 1962). Indeed, Machlup argued in 1962 that by 1958 more than 30% of the waged work force was constituted by "knowledge-producing persons" (Machlup, 1962, p. 393).

What adds complexity to this already complex genealogical picture is the fact that bourgeois economists and their antagonists, the post-operiasts or Autonomist Marxists, both use the term "cognitive" and its cognates ("knowledge" and "information") as adjectives to mark off a specific (indeed the latest) period in capitalism's history. "Cognitive" is used in the same way that "industrial" appears in phrases like "industrial capitalism" or "industry-based development," etc. The implication being that though knowledge and cognition were important in previous eras of capitalism, its latest phase should be properly baptized by terms like *cognitive* or *knowledge*.

What is it that has changed in capitalism that justifies the use of such terms? Is *knowledge qua* adjective functioning like *industry* in the past? Semantically, the notions of a knowledge-based economy, knowledge-related jobs, and knowledge-based industries began to be used with increasing frequency in the 1990s (although Robert Reich's term *symbolic analysis* he introduced in *The Work of Nations* would have been a more accurate phrase (Reich, 1992). Already by 1994, the World Bank was pointing to new trends like "the emerging role of knowledge as a major driver of economic development" (World Bank, 1994). This development seems to coincide with the "discovery" of the "new economy" in that first, post-Cold War decade.

Beginning in this period, slogans like "Knowledge has become the most important factor in economic development" or "Today, economic growth is as much a process of knowledge accumulation as of capital accumulation" became shibboleths (World Bank, 2002, p. 7). Certainly, the evidence that the World Bank, at least, used to justify these claims, and more generally to prepare us for a new, epistemic characterization of capitalism, begs more questions than it answers. For example, consider (a) the OECD has determined that the knowledge-based industry sector between 1985 and 1997 saw major increases in their share of total value added (51–59% in Germany, 45–51% in the UK, and from 34–42% in Finland), and (b) firms in the OECD devote at least one third of their investment to "knowledge-based intangibles" (OECD, 2001).

The problem with this "evidence" is the ambiguity of what is being measured: "the knowledge-based industry sector" and the "knowledge-based intangibles." What characterizes them as well as knowledge-jobs, knowledge-work and finally the knowledge economy? The OECD and the World Bank defined "the knowledge-based industry sector" as including "high and medium-high technology industries; communication services; finance, insurance, and other business services; and community, social, and personal services" (World Bank, 2002, p. 22) while "knowledge-based intangibles" include "training, R&D, patents, licensing, design, and market-ing" (World Bank, 2002, p. 9).

There is an extraordinary fuzziness in the terminology describing such serious matters. The knowledge-based industries and intangibles are no more connected with knowledge than non-knowledge-based industries and tangibles. They prompt an excess of questions over answers. What does reproducing labor power and constant capital, computing, communicating, or speculating make a firm, a job or an industrial sector "knowledge-based"? What makes an "intangible" non-knowledge-based? For example are "surveillance services" knowledge-based, but "guard-services" non-knowledge based? Are non-knowledge-based industries ignorance-based? What brings together banks, pornographic film companies, software design firms, communication corporations, airplane manufacturers under the knowledge-based industry sector rubric that excludes auto companies, real estate firms, restaurants, mines, and farms? Are the former more dependent on knowledge than the latter, do the former create significantly more knowledge than the latter, and/or do the workers in the former know more than those in the latter? Finally and most point-edly, why did the World Bank launch structural adjustment programs during the 1990s in African countries that defunded their educational systems when, presum-ably, it had recognized that knowledge and a knowledgeable work force was the most decisive "input" for any contemporary economy that hopes to survive in the glob-al market (Federici et al., 2000)?

II. Cognitive Capitalism from an anti-capitalist perspective

From Knowledge Economy to Cognitive Capitalism

The term "Cognitive Capitalism" seems to be of more recent origin than "knowl-edge economy," since the books and articles presenting it date from the dot.com crash in 2000–2001. The books that Vercellone and Boutang write with "Cognitive Capitalism" in the title are published in 2007 and the first references to a "cogni-tive capitalism" research program were from the year 2000 or so (Boutang, 2007, p. 11). In speaking of the Autonomist Marxist theory of cognitive capitalism, I refer to a theory that in many ways has been collectively elaborated by scholar-activists centered mostly in France and Italy, including Negri, Hardt, Boutang, and Virno. However, one author stands out: Carlo Vercellone, who in his work has stated the major outlines of the theory and has been responsible for many of its key insights. I will therefore concentrate on his work for my comments on the theory of cognitive capitalism with due qualifications and occasional references to the other theorists.

While recognizing the pitfalls of self-defined genealogies, it is useful to listen to Vercellone's efforts to place the notion of cognitive capitalism with respect to other theories of contemporary society and economy. He claims that "the hypothesis of cognitive capitalism develops from a critique of the political economy of the new theories of the knowledge-based economy" (Vercellone, 2007, p. 14) and then explains:

> The critical perspective on apologetic accounts of neoliberal inspiration is inscribed in two terms which compose the very concept of cognitive capitalism: i) the notion of 'capitalism' defines the enduring element in the change of the structural invariants of the capitalist mode of production: in particular, the driving role of profit and wage relation or, more precisely, the different forms of dependent labour on which the extraction of surplus labour is founded; ii) the term 'cognitive' emphasizes the new nature of the conflictual relation of capital and labour, and of the forms of property on which the accumulation of capital rests (Vercellone, 2007, p. 14).

One can appreciate the need for such a hypothesis at the turn of the millennium when the atmosphere was full of "new economy" rhetoric that pumped up the dot.com bubble, when pro-capitalist ideologists were proclaiming the arrival of an era of endless growth due to the fast approaching "singularity" (when presumably machines would outpace human intelligence), driven by exponentially increasing computing power (Kurzweil, 2000). This was the time when the day trader *qua* dot.com millionaire was being pointed to as the model of the worker in the 21st century. The "Capitalism" side of "Cognitive Capitalism" soberly reminded everyone that for all the changes in technology and psychology, capitalism was still capitalism and that workers' labor would have to be exploited in order for the system to exist and so, inevitably, the struggle between capital and labor would continue, and perhaps intensify.

Back to the Future

Man educated at the expense of much labor and time . . . may be compared to one of those expensive machines.
-ADAM SMITH, *THE WEALTH OF NATIONS* (MACHLUP, 1962, P. 5).

What makes this era's capitalism more "cognitive" than any other? The answer for Vercellone lies in a new periodization of the history of capitalism using the concepts found in Marx's unpublished "Results of the Immediate Process of Production"—real and formal subsumption of labor under capital—as well as terms from *Capital*, Vol. 1, absolute and relative surplus value. "Subsumption" itself is a technical term derived from formal logic and refers to the inclusion of one logically defined class by another, or even the minor premise of a syllogism which functions as mediating element in the larger argument. But Marx used this logical relation in his critique of political economy to distinguish two different ways that capital can subsume labor in the immediate process of production.

The formal subsumption of labor under capital is "viz., the takeover by capital of a mode of labor developed before the emergence of capitalist relations" (Marx, 1976, p. 1021). Marx claimed that with such modes "surplus-value can be created only by lengthening the working day, i.e., by increasing absolute surplus-value" (Marx, 1976, p. 1021). For Vercellone, the model of such formal subsumption of labor under capital is the "putting out system" (or "Verlagssystem") in the sixteenth to eighteenth centuries when mercantile and financial capital were dominant.

For Marx, the real subsumption of labor under capital happens when:

> The general features of the formal subsumption remain, viz., the direct subordination of the labour process to capital, irrespective of the state of its technological development. But on this foundation there now arises a technologically and otherwise specific mode of production which transforms the nature of the labour process and its actual conditions . . . The real subsumption of labour under capital is developed in all the forms evolved by relative as opposed to absolute surplus-value (Marx, 1976, pp. 1034–5).

This form of subsumption induces the direct application of science and technology to the production process. This period includes the Ford-Smith-Taylor-Mancunian (Manchester) model of production, i.e., from the 19th century to the crisis of the assembly-line worker of the 1960s and early 1970s. But he is also critical of those who find in the "Toyotist"/ "just-in-time" labor regime a new "post-Fordist" period, because it is still "bound to a factory-inspired vision of the new capitalism seen as a further development of the Fordist-industrial logic of the real subsumption of labor by capital" (Vercellone, 2007, p. 14). This model, however, does not show "the tendential crisis of some of the more structural invariants of the long-period dynamic that opened with the first industrial revolution" (Vercellone, 2007, p. 14). An example of such a "structural invariant" would be the capitalist's insistence on intervening in the labor process, whether by a Tayloristic time-motion study in the "Fordist" model, or by labor-management networking and the formation of "quality circles" in the "Post-Fordist" model. In other words, "Fordism" and "Post-Fordism" are not as different as the "Post-Fordists" avow. Vercellone claims that a better way of periodizing is to fold in many "post-Fordist" features to the previous stage of real subsumption and baptize the third stage of capitalism as "cognitive capitalism."

The supporters of cognitive capitalism are making a bold and attractive claim in the midst of what is clearly a historic crisis of capitalism and when the standard Marxism of our time has shown itself to be ineffective both politically and conceptually. They are asking us to take a new view of class struggle (that pits a parasitic capitalist against a collective, globally socialized knowledge worker) and to re-investigate the possibility of a direct transition from capitalism to communism without state socialism as mediator. So it is vital that we assess the claims and hypotheses that Vercellone and other supporters of cognitive capitalism provide.

The novelties of this "cognitive" stage of capitalism, Vercellone claims, are many. But a key feature is that capitalists have been driven out of the zone of the labor process and have returned to a formal subsumption of labor, although labor-time no longer is a measure of value. Vercellone argues that the ever intensifying capitalist drive for relative surplus-value accumulation that applied ever more scientific and technological knowledge to production and was typical of the second stage of capitalism is a thing of the past. Cognitive capitalism involves a return to a formal subsumption of labor under capital (in the sense that capital returns to a position external to the production process), but with two qualifications. Strictly speaking, formal subsumption ought to involve pre-capitalist forms of labor and absolute surplus-value accumulation but (a) instead of a return to pre-capitalist forms of labor we find new forms of labor that are not under capital's immediate control, and (b) instead of a return to absolute surplus-value accumulation, we have a form of labor that cannot be temporally measured (and hence the categories of relative and absolute surplus-value are inoperable in this era).

Consider the claim that capital is no longer an organizer of production, and that "the subsumption of labour is once again formal in the sense that it is based essentially on the relation of monetary dependence of the wage-laborer inside the process of circulation" (Vercellone, 2007, p. 31). Admittedly, Vercellone is rather abstract on this central point, but according to him capital apparently loses its control of the labor process due to "the new qualitative preponderance of living knowledge, incorporated and mobilized by labour over dead knowledge, incorporated in fixed capital (and the firm organization)" (Vercellone, 2005, pp. 6–7). The new knowledge-driven labor is no longer dependent upon machines and other forms of fixed capital (e.g., office buildings, fiber optic networks and management personnel). In fact, the tipping point for such a development was when "the share of intangible capital (R&D, education, health) incorporated essentially in people, exceeded that of material capital held in stock and became the principal factor of growth" (Vercellone, 2009, p. 120). This is reminiscent of the long period in U.S. history when the share of capital invested in slaves was larger than the value of the national stock of constant capital. He writes:

> In so far as the organization of labour becomes increasingly autonomous, white collar offices either disappear or become the avatar of times past. In this framework, control over labour no longer takes on the Taylorist role of direct allocation of tasks; it is mostly replaced by indirect mechanisms based on the imperative to deliver, the prescription of subjectivity and a pure and simple coercion linked to the precarization of the wage relation (Vercellone, 2008, p. 6).

This is a "back to the future" model of the autonomous and creative worker that tips its hat to Paolo Virno's characterization of contemporary work as a virtuoso communicative performance (Virno, 2004, pp. 61–63). As the category of immaterial labor—i.e., labor producing immaterial affects (affective labor) and knowledges (cognitive labor)—expands to tendentially dominate production, the nature of work inevitably changes. It can no longer be supervised or measured in the way that labor-producing material products can. Consequently, Vercellone suggests, it is in the nature of things that the capitalist employer treats such immaterial workers carefully and from the "outside," similar to the way that record and film industry bosses deal with their "artists." This is especially true of cognitive labor, the embodiment of "living knowledge." Instead of the factory, the production of contemporary cognitive capitalism has as its model the putting-out system, in which the merchant provides the wages, inputs and at times the machines, and receives the product in return.

In fact, there is a deep relationship between an increasing workers' autonomy in the production process and capital's tendency to "indirect forms of domination of production and of the mechanisms of surplus appropriation realized by means of the sphere of monetary and financial circulation" (Vercellone, 2007: 22).

The second qualification has to do with the intimate relation Marx drew between formal subsumption and absolute surplus-value. Since absolute surplus-value is based on a time measure of value it is entirely inappropriate when dealing with knowledge work. In that case, there is no relation between this cognitive capitalist subsumption and absolute surplus-value. In fact, this lack of relation constitutes a crisis of the law of value because a contradiction emerges between the knowledge-value of a production process's product and its time-value that capital insists on using even though it becomes, to paraphrase Marx, an increasingly "'wretched base' of the measure of wealth and norm of its distribution" (Vercellone, 2007, p. 30).

The return of rent

The next theoretical innovation with respect to Marx is Vercellone's reconfiguration of the relation between profit and rent. His thesis is that since "the law of value-labor time is in crisis and cooperation of labor appears to become increasingly autonomous from the managerial functions of capital, the very frontiers between rent and profit become in disintegrate" (Vercellone, 2008: 2). The key idea here is that since capital has retreated from organizing production (at least in the areas where the "cognitive" powers of labor are crucial) it, in effect, "leases" the means of production to the workers and receives a rent in return. I presume that, for example, a genetic laboratory owned by Merck is surreptitiously "leased out" to the scientific and technological workers who pay their "rent" to Merck management and stockholders by turning over to Merck Inc. the knowledge of the pharmacological powers of substances on certain genetic configurations that they research. Merck can then turn this knowledge into drug patents it can lease out to pharmacological firms throughout the world. "[W]e are witnessing the return of a mercantilist and financial logic that is reminiscent of pre-capitalism. . . ." (Vercellone, 2008).

This is a very different model from that of "productivist" capital that takes charge of each instant of the labor process to efficiently exude the greatest amount of production possible from a given worker. This concern for efficiency—from the smallest movement of a ditch digger to the color of the walls in a corporate headquarters office—is typical of the period of relative surplus-value (from the 19th century to the 1970s), when capital really subsumed labor. At that time, profit was the dominant form of revenue and it was sharply distinguished from rent. Indeed, from Ricardians to the neo-classical economists, the rentier and the rent-seeker were taken to task as a parasitic tumor on the body of capital. Rentiers were so cancerous to the system, that Keynes called for their euthanasia (Keynes, 1936).

However, Marx in his more prescient moments in *Capital*, Vol. 3, argues Vercellone, saw the "becoming rent of profit," a situation that he noted in the rise of the joint stock company that increasingly distinguished between owning capital and "performing capital", where the former extracts surplus-value "whilst no longer exercising any function in the organization of labor" while the latter "becomes increasingly embodied in the figure of the manager, where the functions of leadership and exploitation of labor take on the false appearance of a wage laborer practicing conceptual and organizational tasks in production" (Vercellone, 2008). But Marx went beyond Keynes' anathema on the rentiers (the owners of capital) in recognizing that even the performing capitalist's role as manager is bound for extinction once s/he is "confronted with a productive cooperation that is capable of organizing itself autonomously from capital" (Vercellone, 2008). But it is exactly this productive cooperation fostered by a diffused intellectuality generated by mass education and an increased level of training that displaces performing capitalists, increasingly making them superfluous to the production process.

With the estrangement of the performing capitalist from the production process, s/he finds a role as a "middle-(wo)man" between production and the market. By "capturing" the results of the production process autonomously run by workers, the new capitalist prepares it for the market both legally and through advertising. It is only due to the stranglehold the capitalist "middle-(wo)man" has on the production process (given the present relations of production, i.e., intellectual property law) that s/he has any claim to revenue from production. This is the reason why income from licensing the use of knowledge that is privatized by patents, copyrights, and trademarks has become so important to contemporary capitalism. For example, Gary Locke, the present Secretary of Commerce, in a recent speech claimed that "50 percent of our exports *depend* [emphasis added] on some form of intellectual property like software or complex technology" (Locke, 2010). This statement must be taken with a grain of salt, since only about 5% of U.S. exports are in the form of licenses and royalties (i.e., arising from *direct* intellectual property income)—not a small matter, but then again, not a major amount. Moreover, U.S. exports that depend on some form of intellectual property (however *this* is defined), like jet aircraft, are by no means costless to re-produce even after the design, testing and manufacturing work for the patented prototype is completed (i.e., the reproduction of intellectual property is not always costless in practice). Undoubtedly, however, revenue from renting intellectual property is an important source of corporate income.

This situation completely parallels the stranglehold aristocratic landowners had on agricultural production for centuries, that the Physiocrats decried when they called for taxing the land (cf. Marx's *Theories of Surplus Value*). The answer to their critique came with the French Revolution and the slide of the guillotine onto the aristocracy's neck. And in the case of knowledge, Vercellone, Hardt, Negri, and Boutang's call for breaking the fetters of archaic relations of production on the forces of production has been heard. Will its answer be long in coming?

Coda

Cognitive labor in the era of cognitive capitalism appears in Vercellone as a crucial element in the "transition"—a theme that has become more and more prominent in Autonomist Marxist writing. Not accidentally, autonomist Marxists refuse to take a gloomy view of precarity and precarization and all the concomitant changes in the work relation that are often condemned as generators of economic insecurity like flexibilization or casualization. Though recognizing the hardship consequent to the lack of an income, on the one hand, Autonomist Marxists see precarization in more positive terms, insofar as they read it both as the product of a struggle against the regimentation of work, a condition, they argue, to which no one wishes to return. On the other, they interpret it as expression of the fact that with the cognitivization of labor, areas of production become, in a way, zones liberated from immediate capitalist supervision and organization ("no management zones"), thereby becoming terrains of autonomy and self-organization.

It is easy to understand why such a theory has been so successful. It not only offers an optimistic view of contemporary society where the exodus from capitalism has already begun, and also offers a means of self-understanding to the vast population of "knowledge workers"—students, programmers, "creative" designers, architects, artists—who constitute a large segment of the work-force in the metropolitan areas of the world. To them Autonomist Marxists offer the self-definition of the "cognitariat" as the new subject of capitalist production, the one on whom the "transition" beyond capitalism depends. It is important to restate here that

Vercellone's views are now not unique. They have, so to speak, "gone viral" and now in different forms are a central component of most Autonomous Marxist theories.

A critique of cognitive capitalism

The rule and criterion of Truth is to have made it.

GIAMBATISTA VICO (1710)

Vercellone and his colleagues are to be praised for their efforts to both reintroduce Marxist analysis and anti-capitalist revolution into contemporary political discourse. However, there is much to criticize in their theory of cognitive capitalism from a political and conceptual perspective. In this section I will present a series of semantic, historical, and Marxist challenges to this theory, in the spirit of convivial dialogue leading to a stronger practice on both counts.

Who Knows What? (Semantics)

Garbage in, garbage out.

-ANONYMOUS

One of the most important, but confusing aspects of the writing of the adherents of cognitive capitalism is in their use of the terms "knowledge" and "cognitive." Vercellone frequently introduces these notions as arising from a radical critique of the "apologetic vision of the actual mutation entailed by the neoliberal theories of [a] knowledge-based economy" (Vercellone, 2005, p. 2). He argues that "the term 'cognitive' emphasizes the changed nature of the capital-labor relation and the forms of property upon which the accumulation of capital depends" (Vercellone, 2005, p. 2). This self-description of a concept by one of its creators is weighty evidence in any effort of semantic clarification. By Vercellone's own admission, the chief critique that he moves against the knowledge-based economy theorists is their *apologetic* conclusions. He does not question the notion of a knowledge-based economy, even though it waits on the answer to the vexed question: "what is knowledge?" Additionally, the term "cognitive" (instead of "industrial," I presume) is meant to *emphasize* the novel aspects of class struggle in a knowledge-based economy (that pits *living* against *dead* knowledge) as well as the newer forms of appropriation (e.g., licenses, royalties and rents based on copyright and patents instead of ownership of products).

On both counts, the issue is knowledge. The problem is that this problematic notion is not problematized. This lack of reflection on the meaning of "knowledge" is mirrored in the writing of their bourgeois opponents. What, indeed, is knowledge? Both the anti-capitalist theorists of cognitive capitalism and the neoliberal theorists of the knowledge-based economy depend upon *the lack of definition of knowledge* that circulates in the sphere of intellectual property law, for the simple reason that this sphere makes it possible to speak of intellectual commodities without referring to knowledge or cognition at all. We can copyright a cookbook entitled *Tasty Italian Sauces*, the recipes of which are perfectly wretched, and we can patent a mousetrap that actually traps no mice! For example, the form of property that is discussed by anti-capitalist and neoliberal theorists I have referred to has nothing *directly* to do with "knowledge" or "cognition." That is why theorists like Vercellone can use these terms so blithely. Otherwise, we would find their texts wrestling with some rather thorny philosophical issues, e.g., is truth a necessary condition of knowledge? What is a true proposition? Is induction a knowledge-producing process? Is any scientific theory ever completely falsified or confirmed? Are mathematical propositions necessarily true? Is scientific knowledge the paradigm of all knowledge; if not, what, if anything, is?

These questions can be sidestepped because what is crucial is the *commodification* of intellectual, computational, mental, digital (choose, for the moment, whatever adjective you wish) labor's products, *not* their status as knowledge or cognition. In fact, one can have a whole branch of industry of a "knowledge-based" economy or "cognitive" capitalism that produces propositions that are scientifically designed to be attractively deceptive, i.e., the advertising industry. Consequently, we have to be careful in interpreting theories of either sort, for they do not invoke a reprise of the older battles between ideology and science or between a false, fetishized, capitalist thought and the true proletarian perspective. Neither Vercellone et al. nor World Bank reps like Robert Solow are interested in such Cold War battles. The scene dramatically shifted in the 1990s, and the issue of globalized production built on a new communication infrastructure (completed by the Internet) has put both anti-capitalists and neoliberals on a path to an "end of ideology" in the old sense.

This simple observation, that much of this debate is operating under a misnomer, does not completely invalidate the insights of Vercellone et al. There is no doubt that however one measures it, the production of intellectual property commodities and—if one buys into the neologism—"intellectual property-intensive industries" (IPII) are important aspects of contemporary capitalist economy in the

United States. It is certainly true that immaterial labor, defined as labor producing immaterial products, seems to be an important way of characterizing the division of labor. IPIIs need to be studied and politically assessed (Caffentzis, 2005). But the idea puts under some stress Vercellone's vision of the struggle between workers and capital on the cognitive level, that he introduces into the irenic fairy tale of the knowledge economy told by Reich, Kurzweil or the World Bank. For Vercellone sees this new dimension of struggle as including: (a) "the time directly dedicated to the production of high-tech commodities becomes ever more insignificant, these commodities should be distributed for free" and (b) "the traditional opposition between dead labour and living labour, inherent to Industrial Capitalism, gives way to a new form of antagonism: that between the dead knowledge of capital and the living knowledge of labour" (Vercellone, 2005: 10).

The first site of struggle is a bit confused because though propositions in a text or images on a surface can be easily re-produced at insignificant cost, the production of the propositions or images might take decades and at not an insignificant cost. So there are two kinds of struggle here. (a) The one we are most familiar with is the battle between record corporations and free downloaders who are dramatically reducing the profits of the companies by appropriating songs, texts, still images and motion pictures off the net "for free." (b) The second one is that between the workers producing the texts or images who are making claims of their own as to how to produce and how much they will appropriate the value of the intellectual commodity produced and their corporate employer that claims the commodity to be its property and demands its "due" as profit.

These are very different struggles in dealing with intellectual property. A motion picture might take five years to make, involve hundreds of technicians, actors, artists, producers and directors and cost millions of dollars, but it takes only a couple of minutes to download a film from the net literally for free! Within that five years there will be struggles "on the set" over the work, how it is done, who gets the money, how much time it takes to do a particular animation, etc., while within that couple of minutes there will be the effort by the film company to electronically harass and threaten the determined "free" downloader. These are different struggles involving different agents—corporations like Sony, "artists," and audiences—allied and in conflict with each other.

For sure, however, it is not the case that "the time of labor directly dedicated to the production of high-tech commodities becomes ever more insignificant" (Vercellone, 2005, p. 10). After all, the duration and cost of shooting films, an archetypal high-tech commodity product of "immaterial labor," are not insignificant. It still takes between 60 and 96 hours to shoot a 45-minute television action-adventure show while the average "feature film" costs about $100 million (Wild, 2009). Moreover, it is not clear that there is any noticeable tendency for a reduction of either time or cost to insignificance. What is tending to zero is the time and cost of *re*-producing a film or television show. It is this contradiction between the cost of production and the cost of re-production that poses serious problems for capital, of course—see the declining profits of media corporations—but it also creates conflicts between actors and musicians and their audiences, i.e., between immaterial workers and other workers. What applies to film and song making also applies to science, for it is clear that in certain fields the cost of producing new knowledge is dramatically increasing (such as the need for near speed-of-light cyclotrons for subatomic physics) even though the cost of re-producing "old knowledge" (in the form of scientific journal articles) is dramatically decreasing.

The second place where Vercellone et al. face a problem, once we realize that the use of "knowledge" is an honorific misnomer in this discourse, is with the struggle between dead and living knowledge. This struggle parallels Marx's old distinction in *Capital* (and in the "Results of the Immediate Process of Production," an unpublished manuscript Marx wrote while drafting *Capital*) between, on the one side, dead, past, passive, barren, objectified labor and living, present, active, creative, subjective labor. These binaries are basic to the metaphorical life of Marxism. Vercellone and others have extended them to the realm of knowledge by contrasting living with dead knowledge. What does this contrast mean? It does not echo Wordsworth's romantic call to an original form of wisdom compared to the dull, lifeless knowledge of books in his poem, "The Tables Turned":

> Books! 'tis a dull and endless trifle:
> Come, hear the woodland linnet,
> How sweet his music! on my life,
> There's more of wisdom in it. . . .

But there is an echo of "the tables turned" theme in the account given by Vercellone and other theorists of living knowledge. For just as Marx pointed out in the mid-19th century that the huge agglomerations of capital in the form of machinery, factory buildings, titanic iron ships, and locomotives seem to dwarf the workers and make them appear insignificant, it is only the workers who create the value capitalists ultimately desire. So too a similar turning of the tables occurs on the plane of knowledge in the early 21ˢᵗ century.

The "intelligent" machines of the contemporary economy—the computer-communication-information net, the laboratories, the film production studios, the automated factories—that seem to be displacing human intelligence are, according to Vercellone and others, similarly dead capital. In order for them to be part of a process that can create value for capital they must be coupled with the living knowledge of cognitive workers; i.e., the net, the studios, the factories and the laboratories are all crystallizations of dead, objectified knowledge, and they await the vivifying, subjective action of a worker's living knowledge. The worker, as Marx himself put it, is the one "in whose brain exists the accumulated knowledge of society" (Vercellone, 2007, p. 31). Though it looks like the machines are eliminating the humans in this period of capitalism (as envisioned in many a science fiction novel and film), a new "humanism" arises from these anti-humanist Marxists claiming the renewed indispensable importance of knowledge embodied in humans.

My critique of this position is complex because there is an element in it that I agree with and have defended in many different venues, viz., that machines—whether simple machines, heat engines or Turing machines—cannot produce value (Caffentzis, 1997). I, like Vercellone and the other cognitive capitalist theorists, affirm the importance of living human labor in the creation of value. My points of criticism, however, are three fold:

(a) The living labor that is being exploited in IPIIs is not necessarily either knowledge or productive of knowledge. What is crucial is that it can create exchange value, irrespective of its epistemic value; so, for example, a commodity to have a value "must satisfy human needs of whatever kind. The nature of these needs, whether they arise, for example, from the stomach or the imagination, makes no difference" (Marx, 1976, p. 125). There is so much fraud, fallacy and fancy in this area of production (think of the work of derivative dealers!) that to call the labor power in action there "knowledge work" or "living knowledge" is to stretch the semantic tolerance of even a postmodern cultural theorist! But once I get past my verbal squeamishness I completely agree with Vercellone, Hardt and Negri, that capitalism still needs to transform labor power (including the powers to know, to imagine, to create) into labor in order to create value that it can later "capture."

(b) The claim that living knowledge creates value, but (unlike the living labor of the past) is measureless and uncontrollable, is problematic, because the process of creating propositions, objects, ideas and forms and other so-called "immaterial" products that could be transformed into intellectual property is a process in time that can be (*and is*) measured. Although the techniques used to control labor-time and to impose speed-ups differ from the assembly lines, workers in IPIIs are routinely given task-specific contracts with temporal deadlines. There is now a growing literature on the issue of the measurement and management of what Vercellone calls "living knowledge" in many different fields and the empirical results (e.g., see De Angelis and Harvie, 2008). We should remember two things concerning this immeasurability claim, one general (i) and the other specific to the measurement of work (ii):

(i) Claims of immeasurability are often simply a product of the limits of the tools and/or concepts of measurement. What can't be measured in time does not mean that it cannot be measured at time t+1. This should be clear in the main measuring discipline, mathematics:

> . . . one can look at the development of the notion of number as the continual confrontation with the "immeasurable" that is then integrated into an enlarged domain of number. The vocabulary of mathematics is littered with terms like "*imaginary* [emphasis added] number," "*complex* [emphasis added] number," "*transcendental* [emphasis added] number," "a cardinal number of an *uncountable* [emphasis added] set" that are semantic fossils of this transformation of the immeasurable into measurable (Caffentzis, 2005, p. 101).

The most dramatic conversion of the immeasurable into the measured was in trans-finite set theory in the late 19th century, where even infinity, the paradigm case of the immeasurable, was shown to have a measure and number (i.e., a cardinality).

(ii) Consequently, when the cognitive capitalism theorists claim that in a society where cooperation, interactivity, and autonomy are primary features of the work process, it is not possible for the value created by labor to be "measured on the basis of labor time directly dedicated to production" (Vercellone, 2007, p. 30), I can only reply that this has been a characteristic of all sorts of commodities—material or immaterial, high-tech and low-tech, from ones that

Dr. Johnson can kick to Berkeleyan ones that exist only when they are perceived—since the beginning of capitalism. As Marx pointed out, and has been repeated in a thousand Marxism 101 courses, clock-time and labor-time are by no means the same. For the value of a commodity is dependent on "the socially necessary labor-time [that] is the labor-time required to produce any use-value under the conditions of production normal for a given society and with the average degree of skill and intensity of labor prevalent in that society" (Marx, 1976, p. 129). Socially necessary labor-time (SNLT) is not determined by the clock-time of labor directly employed in production. It is affected in a thousand different ways that cannot be measured "locally." For example, the value of the fabric produced by the English hand-loom weaver, once power looms were introduced, was cut by one half. So why should it be surprising that the clock-time of production has a tangential relation to the labor-time value of a commodity (which includes, e.g., the fact that the distinction between the work-day and the rest seems to be unwavering). The mechanisms for determining value through SNLT might appear useless by Hardt and Negri, but they are still operative in the actual functioning of capitalist production, from Google to the sweatshops.

(c)   The amount of reproductive labor (here I am *not* referring to "affective labor," see Silvia Federici's article in this volume) that goes into the production of labor power (from a mother's nursing to graduate seminars in postcolonial theory) can account for the value of the labor power in the industries that have a high capital-to-labor ratio. Indeed, there is a struggle as to who will bear the costs of that reproductive labor and suffer the consequences of the autonomy and insubordination it implies. As Ure said of the skilled workmen of the manufacturing period: "By the infirmity of human nature it happens the more skilful the workman, the more self-willed and intractable he is apt to become, and of course the less fit a component of a mechanical system in which . . . he may do great damage to the whole" (Marx, 1976, p. 490). This increased training of the contemporary worker (the "diffuse intellectuality" of those in the IPII, as Vercellone would phrase it) adds additional value to the average labor-time, similar to the constant capital transferred to the product. Just as the skilled workmen in the period of manufacture here too one finds the autonomy ("self-willed and intractable") of the contemporary worker in IPIIs . . . as well as his/her vulnerability.

"If we're so smart, why aren't we free?" (History)

A surprising feature of Vercellone's and other cognitive capitalism theorists' perspective has been its "back to the future" character. It presents a vision antithetical to the Matrix image of a world controlled by machines with the human worker "step[ping] to the side of the production process instead of being its chief actor" and playing the role of "watchman and regulator to the production process" (Marx, 1973, p. 705). In the theory of cognitive capitalism, cognitive workers' living knowledge is still essential to the production of wealth while the capitalists, since the 1970s, mass worker revolts, have been literally chased out of their role as supervisors of production in the knowledge-based industrial sectors. We have reached the stage that Marx discussed in *Capital 3* where:

> The capitalist mode of production has brought matters to a point where the work of supervision, entirely divorced from the ownership of capital, is always readily obtainable. It has, therefore, come to be useless for the capitalist to perform it . . . Co-operative factories furnish proof that the capitalist has become no less redundant as a functionary in production as he himself, looking down from his high perch, finds the big landowner redundant (Marx 1966: 386–87).

Vercellone then notes an ingenious historical parallel between the contemporary forms of production and the putting-out system (or domestic industry, or cottage industry, or the *Verlagssystem*) of the 16th through 18th centuries. The key similarity is the autonomy of the workers from their bosses in both periods. Moreover, one can find further parallels in the erasure of the divisions of work/nonwork and production/ reproduction, since in the putting-out system the work is done at home (hence terms like "cottage" and "domestic" are used to describe it as well).

But if there is indeed a parallelism between these two forms of production, a careful examination of the catastrophe of the domestic-industry workers will be especially important for their contemporary equivalents. Let us examine, then, this parallel in some more detail to note a fatal problem for workers inscribed in the history of the putting-out system and, perhaps, for the contemporary cognitariat.

The putting-out system is so called because the merchant "puts out" to the worker (or, more correctly, to his family) the raw materials to be worked, often leasing out to the worker the machines to be used in the production process as well. He would then come to pick up the finished goods and pay the cottager for the "pieces" he, actually his family, produced (after docking him for the wasted raw materials or damage to the leased machines and tools). Though his ownership of the raw materials and tools/machines projected the merchant capitalist into the process of production, he did not supervise it. As Peter Kreidte put it:

> ... when [the merchant] advanced credit for the acquisition of raw materials and/or provided raw materials, in some cases even the tools ... the merchant thus intruded into the production sphere without, however, taking full control of it. The *Verleger* assumed control of the product; the small producer, on the other hand, kept control of the work process (1983, p. 138).

The delicate balance between control of the product and control of the work process completely unraveled when:

> ... the instruments of production became the property of the putter-out as well. In this case, capital dominated the sphere of production almost completely. The direct producers no longer manufactured commodities which they sold as their property; they merely sold their labour power for piece-wages (which included the upkeep of the workshops which were also their homes) (Schlumbohm, 1981, p. 102).

Thus the image that Vercellone paints of the parallelism between contemporary cognitive workers and the proto-industrial cottage-industry workers of the 16th to 18th centuries should be taken either as a grain of salt or as a seed of truth. For Vercellone sees in the old putting-out system a place where the direct producers were autonomous from the capitalist and need only meet him at the end of the labor process, i.e., at the point of "capture." However, the historical accounts of the putting-out system show the merchant capitalist deeply involved in the planning and organizing of the work process. At times he was so involved that the so-called legally autonomous worker virtually became a pieceworker with, at best, "the semblance of power over the instruments of production" (Schlumbohm, 1981, p. 103). The connection was so close that Marx, in fact, identified piece wages as the "basis for modern 'domestic labor'" (Marx, 1976, p. 695).

This tendency of piecewages to organize payment in the putting-out system is very important, especially if we run Vercellone's parallel the other way and see the contemporary cognitariat as the domestic industry laborers of our time. For piece wages are, of course, an obscured and fetishized form of time-wages, but they also have a number of very important characteristics that Marx noted long ago, as if seeing in a vision the 21st century's cognitariat's plight.

First, "since the quality and intensity of the work are here controlled by the very form of the wage, superintendence of labor becomes to a great extent superfluous" (Marx, 1976: 695). This describes the famous "autonomy" of the knowledge worker, who because s/he is not working by the clock can work "at his/her pace." But, of course, this pace ultimately is constrained by the demands of the piecework schedule (whether it be the fifty phone calls to make from home in the evening or the six "ideas" to create while "vacationing"). Consequently, the capitalists save superintendence costs via the action at a distance that the piecework wage system provides . . . a bitter autonomy indeed.

Second, piecewages "form the basis . . . for a hierarchically organized system of exploitation and oppression" (Marx, 1976, p. 695). In this passage Marx describes the cooperative work that is so touted by the theorists of cognitive capitalism in a somewhat different light. For Marx argues that the piece-wage system gives rise to what we call sub-contracting and what in his time was called "subletting of labor." This is a form of labor that is standard in the world of the computer programmers, artists and designers, "social entrepreneurs," etc. In a way, domestic industry involves a capitalist subletting of labor, with the artisan's and his family's hands as the items to be sublet. But in the 19th century, sometimes these "middlemen" subletters were capitalists who organized the subcontracting and got their profits from "the difference between the price of labor which the capitalist pays, and the part of that price they actually allow the worker to receive;" this was appropriately enough called the "sweating system" (Marx, 1976, p. 695). Sometimes capitalists hire "important workers . . . at a price for which this man himself undertakes the enlisting and payment of his assistants." (Marx, 1976, p. 695). The result here, however, is that "the exploitation of the worker by capital takes place through the medium of the exploitation of one worker by another" (Marx, 1976, p. 695). In both cases, of course, the middleman and the "important worker" mediator must generate a level of cooperation that could guarantee a profit for them and their ultimate boss.

Third, the 21st century cognitariat's ideology or "subjectivity" that is generated by piecework is similar to the one that was found among the piece workers of the past (including those in domestic industry). Marx connected the latter's subjectivity with the form of the wage: "But the wider scope that piece-wages give to individuality, and with it the worker's sense of liberty, independence and self-control, and also the competition of workers with each other" (Marx, 1976, p. 697). This sense of "autonomy" that is touted as being basic to the cognitariat can also be expressed as a divisive individualism and competitiveness that is a well-known aspect of the "subjectivities" created in the IPIIs.

These parallels between the putting-out system workers and the so-called cognitariat bring us to ask: how did the struggle between worker and capital in the putting-out system proceed and how were the workers defeated and transformed into wage workers in the factories of the 19th and 20th centuries? Historians of the *Verlagssystem* analyze the struggle between merchant capitalists and the direct producers on at least two levels: (1) over the materials (and sometimes the tools) that are worked on, (2) the withdrawal of labor in the boom periods, i.e., the infamous "backward bending labor supply curve."

Level (1) was a perennial issue in the putting-out system, for the *Verleger*, as the putter-out was called in German, had to "protect himself against the fraudulent use of the raw materials he was distributing to the families which were part of his network" (Kreidte, 1983, p. 142). Whenever in the class relationship wages are paid before work is completed or constant capital is entrusted into the hands of the unpoliced workers a chronic guerilla war frequently follows over the work paid for or the fate of the constant capital. The *Verleger's* need to keep a constant surveillance over the materials put out put an inevitable limit as to the number of "cottages" he could employ. This limit was especially problematic, of course, during the boom part of the cycle. The different strategies employed by the *Verleger* and the often rural domestic industry workers are part of the wider struggle in the European countryside that took place in the period of the 16th through 18th centuries under the rubric of "protoindustrialization," including the struggle against enclosure (Kisch, 1989).

Level (2) was an even greater arena of struggle, since it expressed a basic clash of values and put a stranglehold on the expansion of capitalism in Europe. The *Verleger* was driven by the capitalist ethos (or even religion) to "accumulate, accumulate," while the families involved in the domestic industries throughout Europe were still committed to a subsistence form of life, where the artisan work was a supplement to other forms of rural labor (Braudel, 1982, pp. 304–306). This clash of values was most clearly seen during the "boom" portion of the proto-industrial business cycle. As Kreidte writes: "the proto-industrial family had a propensity to reduce its output precisely in periods of boom; this was because as the return per unit rose, its subsistence needs could be satisfied with a smaller labor effort" (Kreidte, 1983: p. 142). This sort of behavior has often been described in the economics literature by "the backward-bending supply of labor" curve [BBSLC], i.e., this curve describes a situation where there comes a point when an increase in wages leads to a reduction in the hours worked. This "paradoxical" behavior was conditional, of course, on the extent of capital's penetration in the sphere of production and whether it had "subjected the laborers to its interests by way of suppression or consumer incentives" (Schlumbohm, 1981, p. 100). So, for example, if domestic workers had less and less access to land (common or freehold) for subsistence purposes, they were more dependent on the vagaries of the economic cycle and hence less able to cut back on the labor offered by the *Verleger*.

Indeed, the BBSLC was a fundamental constraint on capitalist development in Europe that was broken by both the "blood and fire" of primitive accumulation (which reduced the land available for subsistence agriculture) and the rise of the factory system that both increased the centralization of the workers and allowed for the technological transformation of production. The leader in responding to the resistance to the putting-out system (and to the power for the artisans in the manufacturing centers) was the textile industry in Britain beginning in the last half of the 18th century (Kreidte, 1983, pp. 142–145). What in effect happened was the substitution of new and expensive machinery for the traditional equipment, the centralization of workers in the urban factories and the use of slave labor in Brazil, the Caribbean and the American South for the cotton inputs to production. Eric Hobsbawm wrote of this development, "The most modern centre of production thus preserved and extended the most primitive form of exploitation" (Kreidte, 1983, p. 145). Although it was barbaric, the form of capitalist slavery that marked the Atlantic slave trade was no more "primitive" than the technologically refined Nazi death camps.

In conclusion, we should apply our excursus on the putting-out system to our meditation on the fate of the cognitariat of the beginning 21st century. For if Vercellone's parallel between the cognitariat and the workers of the putting-out system is more a seed of truth than a grain of salt, then we should prepare for a similar outcome for a set of workers who claim that they cannot be replaced and that the value of their work is immeasurable. If the experience of the domestic industry workers of the past is any guide, one should then expect (in the words of cognitive capitalism theorists) a counter-attack on a number of sides: (a) an internationalization of the sources of "living knowledge," (b) the substitution of machinery (dead knowledge) for the workers' "living knowledge," (c) the creation of new techniques of centralization of cognitive workers, (d) the development of new systems of measurement of cognitive labor, (e) the development of new methods of payment.

It does not take too much imagination to see this scenario being played in the present crisis. For example, the "knowledge workers" in education (actual or perspective) in Europe and North America are facing unprecedented cut-backs and deficits, layoffs of faculty and staff, etc. from kindergartens to graduate schools and are being told that they and their children must face competition from workers internationally who now are operating on the same cognitive level as they are. That is, "knowledge work," cognitive labor, etc. is becoming normalized, measurable (since only then can there be competition!) and put under direct capitalist control. Is that impossible? That is the cry of all skilled workers throughout the history of capitalism: "They can't take my job from me; my contribution is immeasurable; I know too much!" However, skilled worker self-confidence has failed time and again as a defense against restructuring, replacement and displacement. I fear that the optimism of the theory of cognitive capitalism, however, does not prepare us for such a challenge.

The becoming profit, rent and interest of surplus-value or the becoming rent of profit? (Marxology)

> Here, then, we have a mathematically precise proof why capitalists form a veritable freemason society vis-à-vis the whole working class, while there is little love lost between them in competition among themselves.
>
> –KARL MARX (MARX, 1966, P. 198)

An important claim of the cognitive capitalism theorists is that with the rise of cognitive capitalism there has been a major categorical change in the revenues that Marx analyzed—profit, interest, rent and wages. The category of profit, especially, is merging into that of rent. Indeed, these theorists claim that Marx had some premonition of such changes, especially in two texts he never finished, *Capital 3* and the *Grundrisse*. The key evidence they use is the presumably changing role that the capitalists play vis-à-vis the production process. One of their central tenets is that capitalists no longer plan, organize and directly supervise production in the way that they did in the period of real subsumption. Consequently, if profit is the revenue earned by bosses when they do what bosses should be doing (i.e., finding new ways to exploit workers, intensify work, by-pass workers' refusal of work and, in general, increasing the length, intensity and/or productivity of work), then the importance and integrity of the category of profit is bound to be diminishing.

But even if this were the case—and there is much evidence to question this claim for most branches of industry, including the knowledge-producing sector—this thesis would not fare well in the light of Marx's theory. Marx himself made a sharp differentiation between "the profit of enterprise," and the "wages of supervision," and the former was not dependent on the latter (Marx, 1966, p. 387). The profit of enterprise is not "locally produced," it is a "field" variable that is the result of a transformation process taking the collectively generated surplus value throughout the system (something of a capitalist common) and redistributing it according to a specific rule of return: if c is the constant capital, v is the variable in a branch of industry and R is the average rate of profit across all industries, then the profit would (c+v)R, with the proviso that there was free movement of capital and labor. Or, in Marx's words, "In a capitalist society, this surplus-value . . . is divided among capitalists as dividends proportionate to the share of social capital each holds" (Marx, 1966, p. 820).

Consequently, there is no correlation between the cleverness, self-discipline, charisma or brutality of the individual boss and the rate of profit of his/her firm or industry. Some capitalists might be exploiting the hell out of their workers, say in a branch of industry in which the exploitation rate is 100%, but if their firms are in a low organic composition industry (roughly, the ratio between machines and labor power employed in the production process), they must "share" the surplus value created in their industry with the capitalists in industries at the high organic composition end of the system of production whose actual exploitation rate is 10%! The key is the amount of capital (constant and variable) employed in the production process. This is capitalist justice: capital itself must get its due, even if individual capitalists, especially the "hard working" ones operating at the lower end of the system and squeezing the most surplus value out of their workers in the face of the greatest resistance, are rewarded by being allowed to keep only a miniscule amount of surplus labor they extracted.

This surplus-value transformation process is the material basis of the existence of a single capitalist class. That is what Marx meant in his reference to capitalists' "freemason society" in the epigraph to this section, i.e., a secret society that creates solidarity among members behind the backs of those who see them as competitors in "the religion of everyday life" (Marx, 1966, p. 830). Marx expressed this solidarity as: " . . . a capitalist who would not in his line of production employ any variable capital, and therefore any laborer (in reality an exaggerated assumption), would nevertheless be as much interested in the exploitation of the working-class by capital, and would derive his profit quite as much from unpaid surplus-labor as , say, a capitalist who would employ only variable capital (another exaggeration), and who would thus invest his entire capital in wages" (Marx, 1966, p. 197). Thus a crucial aspect of the category of profit has nothing directly to do with the behavior of the capitalist with respect to the production process; whether capitalists resembled either absconding gods who pay managers to do the dirty work or crucified ones suffering in the bowels of the firm for their salvation is ultimately irrelevant to the functioning of the flow of surplus-value into the form of profit. Consequently, cognitive capitalism theorists' argument concerning the withdrawal of capitalists from the production process does not quite reach its conclusion unless the very transformation process by which capitalism becomes itself is jettisoned.

The fact that profit of a firm is not determined simply by what goes on in the firm applies in different ways to the other forms of revenue Marx reviewed in the "Trinity Formula" (Marx, 1966, pp. 814–831). Marx was anxious to escape from the pathos of a "factors of production" approach to revenues, positing a one-to-one relationship between a revenue category (profit, interest, rent, wage) and its separate sources. He refused to allow that each category of revenue is "justified" to receive "its share" of the value of commodities and is scathing in his contempt for this piece of "vulgar economy [that] actually does no more than interpret, systematize and defend in doctrinaire fashion the conceptions of the agents of bourgeois production, who are entrapped in bourgeois production relations" (Marx, 1966, p. 817). For in reality, no one was justified the receive their revenues according to the tale they tell about their "contribution" to the value creation.

Marx's perspective on the categories of revenue combines objective metabolic transformation of surplus-value and subjective confusion and illusion, i.e., everything happens behind everyone's back; what is private becoming common and vice versa. Thus the "trinity formula," capital—profit/interest, land—rent, labor—wages, systematically fetishizes capital, land and labor as the sources of the revenues interest, rent, and wages, respectively. But how can capital (in the form of money, machines or raw material) expand itself to earn a profit or pay interest thus making, as Marx derides, 4 equal 5? How can land, which has use-value but no exchange value produce *ex nihilo* an exchange value, rent? How can "a social relation conceived as a thing [be] made proportional to Nature" (Marx 1966, p. 817)? Finally, how can labor, which creates value, have a price? Isn't the term "the price of labor" "as irrational as a yellow logarithm" (Marx 1966, p. 818)? In the face of these absurdities,

Marx proposes another "source" for these revenues: value creating living labor in a vast common pool that appears in another mode as an equally vast mountain of commodities, bodies, money, and machines.

The problem with the cognitive capitalist theorists is that they attribute the sources of revenues like profit and rent to the behavior of profit-making capitalists and to rentiers. Their argument seems to be: if capitalists begin to behave as rentiers, their revenue will stop being profit and begin to become rent. But this behavior *qua* profit-making capitalist or qua rentier was not the source of the value appearing as profit and rent, consequently these changes (whatever their empirical status) are logically disconnected with the behavior of the revenues. Cognitive capitalism theorists like Vercellone and Boutang do not take into account the relationship between the lowest and highest organic composition poles of the system and the transfer of surplus-value from lower to higher branches for the latter to be able to achieve at least an average rate of profit.

This appears to be a "mathematical" constraint, but, on the contrary, it is based on the vagaries of class relations. For the only way to resist the falling rate of profit throughout the system is to continue to introduce industries with low organic composition to off-set the growing organic composition of the industries that are usually associated with the knowledge sector. But where are these industries to come from? They arise in areas where there is relative over-population that makes labor power cheap, since there is an "abundance of disposable o unemployed wage-laborers" (Marx, 1966, p. 237). It is exactly in these regions that low organic composition industries can start up and make it possible to transfer surplus-value created there to the high organic composition industries and also produce a countertendency to the falling rate of profit. This is exactly the story of the industrialization of China in the context of the increasing organic composition of production associated with IPIIs in the U.S. and Western Europe. The increasing power of Chinese factory workers will have epochal consequences for the profits of capitalists around the planet, independent of whether they have invested in Chinese firms or not.

Conclusion: Searching for a synoptic view of global struggles

Let us imagine, with your permission, a little worm, living in the blood, able to distinguish by sight the particles of blood, lymph, &c., and to reflect on the manner in which each particle, on meeting with another particle, either is repulsed, or communicates a portion of its own motion . . . He would be unable to determine, how all the parts are modified by the general nature of blood, and are compelled by it to adapt themselves, so as to stand in a fixed relation to one another.

SPINOZA TO OLDENBURG (1665–6) (SPINOZA 1955: 291)

The cognitive capitalism theorists' work has brought a welcome excitement to the study of contemporary capitalism. Their approach is certainly unconventional and filled with categorical topsy-turvies where apparent victory becomes real defeat and apparent weakness becomes real strength. For example, what conventional Marxist wisdom racks up as a defeat—deindustrialization and globalization—has, in cognitive capitalism theorists' eyes, been a victory for the proletariat in Europe and the United States (since their struggles have, in effect, driven capitalists out of the production process). Moreover, capitalism in its cognitive stage is extremely vulnerable, since workers now are using their powers of cooperation and self-determination in the very process of applying their living knowledge on the job, while, shades of Hegel's master/slave dialectic, capitalists are reduced to the role of middle-(wo)men, no longer in touch with the production process. By arguing that capital suffers from a deep weakness, and that the cognitariat possesses an even deeper strength, the cognitive capitalist theorists aim to revive the revolutionary élan of the age.

Far be it from me to hinder a path to revolutionary enthusiasm and joy, for no great transformation can take place without them. But I agree with Spinoza in the importance of adequate ideas whose presence or absence differentiates between joy from pride. The characteristic measure of such a conceptual adequacy is the synoptic breadth of the analysis, so that we are not stuck with the "worm in the blood's" limited vision of the human (or social) body (as in this section's epigraph). It is in its lack of a synoptic comprehension that I find the theory of cognitive capitalism most deficient.

The cognitive capitalism theorists' focused scrutiny of the struggles in the knowledge-based sector inevitably makes it possible for them to neglect the class struggle taking place in the huge area of agriculture (especially in the struggles against land displacement) and in factory production worldwide. Just because factory and agricultural production now account for only a quarter of employment in the United States does not discount the fact that factory and agricultural production constitute nearly two thirds of global employment, and that is based on ILO statistics that emphasize waged employment. Therefore, the most vital questions concerning the contradictory political impulses arising from the complex composition of the contemporary proletariat of our time are not addressed. This is especially problematic because there seems to be an assumption that workers that are at the highest spheres of capitalist productivity are the most revolutionary.

Silvia Federici and I recently noted that this assumption is false. Thus in the period of industrial work, it was not the industrial workers who made the revolutions:

> Ironically, under the regime of industrial capitalism and factory work, it was the peasant movements of Mexico, China, Vietnam, and to a great extent Russia who made the revolutions of the 20th century. In the 1960s as well, the impetus for change at the global level came from the anti-colonial struggle, including the struggle against apartheid and for Black Power in the US (Caffentzis and Federici, 2009, pp. 128–129).

Similar ironies seem to be playing out in this period of cognitive capitalism when "it is the indigenous people, the campesinos, the unemployed of Mexico (Chiapas, Oaxaca), Bolivia, Ecuador, Brazil, Venezuela, the farmers of India, the maquila workers of the U.S. border, the immigrant workers of the United States, etc. who are conducting the most "advanced" struggles against the global extension of capitalist relation" (Caffentzis and Federici, 2009, p. 129). Indeed, it appears that we are facing a 21st-century version of the question, will "the hammer" (in the form of the silicon chip and fiber optic cable) once again dominate "the sickle"? (Midnight Notes, 2001).

A synoptic theory that can bring together the poles of organic composition and class composition and escape the worm in the blood's dilemma will become the source of the adequate ideas for revolutionary transition from capitalism in the 21st century. The theorists of cognitive capitalism have only accomplished part of the job of constructing this theory, and for that we must thank them. The whole, however, remains undone.

Bibliography

Boutang, Y.M. (2007). *Cognitive Capitalism and entrepreneurship. Decline in industrial entrepreneurship and the rising of collective intelligence.* Paper presented at the Conference on Capitalism and Entrepreneurship at Cornell University, Sept. 28–29.

Braudel, F. (1982.) *The Wheels of Commerce.* New York: Harper & Row.

Caffentzis, G. (1997). "Why Machines Cannot Create Value: Marx's Theory of Machines," in Jim Davis, Thomas Hirschl and Michael Stack (eds.), *Cutting Edge: Technology, Information Capitalism and Social Revolution.* (London: Verso, 1997), pp. 29–56.

Caffentzis, G. (2005). Immeasurable Value? An Essay on Marx's Legacy. *The Commoner*, N. 10. http://www.commoner.org.uk/10caffentzis.pdf last accessed May 31, 2010.

De Angelis, M. and David, H. (2009). Cognitive capitalism and the rat race: How capital measures immaterial labour in British universities. *Historical Materialism*, 17(3): 3–30.

Edu-factory Collective (2009). *Towards a Global Autonomous University: Cognitive Labor, the Production of Knowledge and Exodus from the Education Factory.* New York: Autonomedia.

Federici, S., Caffentzis, G. & Alidou, O. (eds.) (2000). *A Thousand Flowers: Social Struggles against Structural Adjustment in African Universities.* Trenton, NJ: Africa World Press.

Hardt, M. & Negri, A. (2009). *Commonwealth.* Cambridge, MA: Harvard University Press.

Hayek, F. A. (1949). *Individualism and the Economic Order.* London: Routledge and Kegan Paul.

Keynes, J.M. (1972). *Essays in Persuasion. The Collected Writings of John Maynard Keynes, Vol. X.* London: The Macmillan Press.

Kisch, H. (1989). *From Domestic Manufacture to Industrial Revolution: The Case of the Rhineland Textile Districts.* New York: Oxford University Press.

Kriedte, P. (1983). *Peasants, Landlords and Merchant Capitalists: Europe and the World Economy 1500–1800.* Cambridge: Cambridge University Press.

Kurzweil, R. (2000). *The Age of Spiritual Machines: When Computers Exceed Human Intelligence.* New York: Penguin.

Machlup, F. (1962). *The Production and Distribution of Knowledge in the United States.* Princeton, NJ: Princeton University Press.

Marx, K. (1976). *Capital, Vol. 1.* Harmondsworth, United Kingdom: Penguin Books.

Marx, K. (1966). *Capital, Vol. 3.* Moscow: Progress Publishers.

Midnight Notes Collective (eds.) (2001). Introduction. *Auroras of the Zapatistas: Local and Global Struggles in the Fourth World War.* Brooklyn, NY: Auronomedia.

Reich, R. (1992). *The Work of Nations.* New York: Random House.

Schlumbohm, J. (1981). "Relations of Production—Productive Forces—Crises. In *Industrialization before Industrialization: Rural Industry in the Genesis of Capitalism.* Edited by Peter Kriedte, Hans Medick, Jurgen Schlumbohm. Cambridge: Cambridge University Press.

Simmel, G. (2004). *The Philosophy of Money.* Third Edition. London: Routledge.

Sohn-Rethel, A. (1978). *Intellectual and Manual Labour: A Critique of Epistemology.* London: Macmillan.

de Spinoza, B. (1955). *On the Improvement of the Understanding, The Ethics, Correspondence*. New York: Dover.

Steele, D.R. (1992). *From Marx to Mises: Post-Capitalist Society and the Challenge of Economic Calculation*. La Salle, IL: Open Court.

Vercellone, C. (2005). The Hypothesis of Cognitive Capitalism. Paper read at Historical Materialism Annual Conference, London.

Vercellone, C. (2007). "From Formal Subsumption to General Intellect: Elements for a Marxist Reading to the Thesis of Cognitive Capitalism." *Historical Materialism* 15: 13–36.

Vercellone, C. (2008). The New Articulation of Wages, Rent and Profit in Cognitive Capitalism. Paper read at the conference, "The Art of Rent," Queen Mary University School of Business and Management, London.

Vercellone, C. (2009). "Cognitive Capitalism and Models for the Regulation of Wages." In *Towards a Global Autonomous University: Cognitive Labor, The Production of Knowledge and Exodus from the Education Factory*, edited by The Edu-factory Collective. Brooklyn, NY: Autonomedia.

Virno, P. (2004). *A Grammar of the Multitude*. New York: Semiotext(e).

Weber, M. (2002). The Protestant Ethic and "the Spirit of Capitalism." trans. Peter Baehr and Gordon C. Wells. London: Penguin Books.

Wild, L. (2009). Film Production. Retrieved from http://www3.northern.edu/wild/th100/flm-prod.htm

World Bank (1994). *Higher Education: The Lessons of Experience. Development in Practice Series*. Washington, D.C.: World Bank.

World Bank (2002). *Constructing Knowledge Societies: New Challenges for Tertiary Education*. Washington, D.C.: World Bank.

CHAPTER THREE

On Affective Labor

SILVIA FEDERICI

Coined in the mid-1990s by Marxist Autonomists reflecting on the new forms of work that the restructuring of the world economy has produced, 'affective labor' has become a common notion in radical circles, proving to be a protean concept. Through its brief lifespan, its latitude has expanded, making attempts to provide a precise definition a difficult task. 'Affective Labor' (AL) is presently used to describe new work-activities in the service sector or conceptualize the nature of work in the 'post-Fordist' era; for some it is a synonym of reproductive work or a springboard for rethinking the fundamentals of feminist discourse.

Clearly, it is a concept that has captured the radical imagination. In what follows I discuss the reasons for this attraction, asking how it reframes our vision of the changes that have taken place in the social organization of production and what political projects it sustains.

In particular I consider how AL compares with the categorical framework by which Marxist Feminists have understood the work of reproduction in capitalism and the women-capital relation. My argument is that AL highlights significant aspects of the commercialization of reproduction but becomes problematic if taken as the main signifier for the activities and relations underpinning the reproduction of labor-power in our time. In this case it marks a retreat with respect to the understanding of social relations that the feminist movement of the 1970s provided. For it hides the continuing exploitation of women's unpaid domestic labor and makes the struggles that women are waging on the terrain of reproduction invisible again.

In support of these claims I examine the theory of AL in the works of Negri and Hardt, its main proponents, but also consider its use in contemporary social theory and reception by feminist writers. My interest is predominantly a political one. It is to see what resources and tools the concept of AL and the theory on which it rests provide to an understanding of contemporary anti-capitalist struggle, what possibilities it enables us to think and how it expands our collective imagination.

My approach in this context is a partisan one, for some of the answers given to these questions by Autonomous Marxists challenge the analysis of social reproduction that has been at the center of my work over the course of at least three decades. This analysis is founded on the assumption of qualitative differences in capitalism between the production of commodities and the production of labor power, and between waged and unwaged work, a thesis that is rejected by the theory of Affective Labor, at least as argued by Autonomous Marxists.

Affective Labor and Immaterial Labor from *Empire* to *Multitude* and *Commonwealth*

An analysis of AL must begin with the work of Negri and Hardt because it is here that the concept of AL was first developed, and their treatment of it has set a frame that has shaped later discussions. AL, however, in Negri and Hardt's writing is not a self-subsistent concept. Rather, it is an aspect of the theory of Immaterial Labor that is the core of their work. Thus, I focus first on this broader frame in which AL is inserted and the political/theoretical project to which Negri and Hardt have been committed in the trilogy from *Empire* (2000) to *Multitude* (2004) and *Commonwealth* (2009).

This can be described as an attempt to re-launch Marxist theory for a generation of activists and intellectuals for whom communism, in Maurizio Lazzarato's words (Lazzarato, 2008) has become a "dead hypothesis," and dispel the pessimism generated by the postmodern conception of history. In pursuance of these tasks, Negri and Hardt have elaborated a theory that argues that the struggles of the '60s have forced capitalism to institute a new economic order that already represents a transition to a post-capitalist society, in that it makes labor more autonomous from capital, more productive of social cooperation and dissolves the material grounds on which unequal power relations have flourished, fostering a political re-composition of the global workforce.

In its broad outlines (for its main arguments have been the subject of a wide debate) this theory maintains that the restructuring of the world economy, and in particular the computer and information revolutions, have ushered in a phase of cap-italist development, partially anticipated by Marx in the *Grundrisse,* in which sci-ence becomes the main productive force and the cognitive/cultural component of commodities is the fuel of the valorization process, so that Immaterial Labor (IL) becomes the dominant form of work.

Defined as labor that produces non-physical objects—codes, data, symbols, images, ideas, knowledges, subjectivities, social relations (Hardt and Negri, 2004, pp. 65–66; Hardt and Negri, 2009, pp. 132, 287), IL would seem to define a spe-cific sphere of activities and workers (e.g., computer operators, artists, designers) and perhaps signify a widening of the hierarchies imposed by the social division of work. We are assured, however, that this is not the case. IL does not select, nor does it cre-ate hierarchies or other significant distinctions, for in time, it is argued, all forms of work will become immaterial (Hardt and Negri, 2004, pp. 107, 338, 349), in accordance with the principle articulated by Marx in the chapter on "Machinery and Large-scale Industry" (*Capital* Vol.1) stipulating that in each phase of capitalist development the dominant form of work hegemonically assimilates to itself all the others, imposing its qualities on them, thereby transforming them in its own image. (Hardt and Negri, 2004, p. 107; Hardt and Negri, 2000, p. 292) IL, therefore, in the current global economy, no longer institutes a dividing line between intellectu-al and manual labor, the head and the hand, nor is a product of the separation of the worker from the intellectual faculties of production as intellectual labor was in earlier phases of capitalism discussed, for instance, by Alfred Sohn-Rethel (Sohn-Rethel, 1978).

On the contrary, IL institutes a qualitatively new, positive relation between labor and capital whereby work becomes autonomous, self-organized and productive of social cooperation, a reality to which Negri and Hardt refer to as "the common." Two reasons are offered for this transformation. On one side, workers' struggles have forced capital to flee from the terrain of production to the safer terrain of financial-ization, leaving workers masters of the field (Hardt and Negri, 2009, p. 289). Second, unlike physical labor, knowledge/information-based work cannot be controlled or supervised, for it cannot be confined to any specific locality and time. (Hardt and Negri, 2009, p. 266) Thus, we presumably have a qualitatively new phenomenon: the emergence of liberated zones in the heart of high-tech capitalism, co-existing with the continuation of exploitation now occurring, however, not through the direct organization of production but through an act of dispossession, which the capitalists perform at the end of the work process, "capturing" its product, for example, through the imposition of Intellectual Property Laws. (Hardt and Negri, 2004, pp. 184–188; Hardt and Negri, 2009, p. 141).

Third, and most important, Negri and Hardt maintain that with the immaterialization of production, all the contrasts that characterized labor in the industrial era—productive/unproductive, production/reproduction, labor/leisure, life-time/labor-time, waged/unwaged work—vanish, so that labor ceases to be a source of differentiation and unequal power relations (Hardt and Negri, 2004, pp. 134–135). In place of the former divisions, Negri and Hardt envision a Gargantuan process of social reproduction such that every articulation of social life becomes a point of production and society itself becomes an immense work-machine producing value for capital but also knowledges, cultures, subjectivities. Echoing Foucault, Negri and Hardt name this new regime *bio-political production* (Hardt and Negri, 2009, pp. 132–137), arguing that within it work becomes a political act as it acquires the traits typical of political intercourse—it becomes communicative, interactive, affective—and a training ground in self-government for workers. Most important, within it no material grounds subsist for hierarchy producing differentiations, as all social subjects are equally creative of the wealth produced. Hence the image of the 'Multitude' as the political subject of Immaterial Labor, presumably incorporating differences but without establishing any ranking or divisions. As Hardt and Negri write:

> There is no qualitative difference that divides the poor from the classes of employed workers. Instead, there is an increasingly common condition of existence and creative activity that defines the entire Multitude . . . The old Marxist distinctions between productive and unproductive labor, as well that between productive and reproductive labor, which were always dubious, should now be completely thrown out. (2004, pp. 134–135)

In sum, according to Negri and Hardt, the possibility of a major social transformation is now on the agenda, the advent of IL and bio-politics signifying that we can construct the alternative starting from our everyday life, and what remains to be done is expanding our capacity for collective production and knowledge exchange and educating ourselves for self-government (Hardt and Negri, 2009, pp. 314–321).

This is a prospect that is highly empowering and it is easy to see why this theory has been so successful. Its affirmative message and focus on work and class antagonism have made it a welcome turn after years of post-modernist 'deconstruction.' Most attractive, perhaps, is that it re-launches the idea that revolution is *now*, rather than something confined to an indefinite, constantly postponed future, and it places at the center of political analysis the problematic of the 'transition.' At the same time, its main tenets have shaky empirical foundations, being over-dependent on the assumption of 'tendencies' and 'trends' for their validation, and its political message is often ridden with contradictions.

The evidence that capitalism today feeds primarily on immaterial forms of production is questionable, factually and politically, even if we accept that what Negri and Hardt are describing is presently only a trend. (Federici and Caffentzis, 2009) With more weight, it can be demonstrated that the force driving the world economy has been international capital's ability to throw on the global labor-market masses of expropriated peasants and housewives, that is, immense quantities of non-contractual labor, exponentially increasing the rate of surplus extraction. Also disputable is the postulated autonomy of "immaterial workers." Two decades after the 'dot.com revolution' the illusion that digital work may provide an oasis of creativity and freedom has largely dissolved, as the term 'net-slaves' indicates (Terranova 2000). Even for the most creative workers, autonomy has turned out to be a transitory, unsustainable experience or the effect of a complete identification with the interests of the employers. We should also be skeptical of celebrations of social cooperation in the organization of work that do not specify to what purposes it is finalized. What, for instance, is the political potential of the cooperation IL requires and creates if in the realm of the bio-political producing the tools of war is as much of a 'commoning' activity as child-raising, and if all differences are conflated between paid and unpaid labor?

There are also troubles with the concept of the 'Multitude,' the mythical figure described as the one and the many, singularity and multiplicity, undefined as far as gender, race, ethnic origin, occupation, which Negri and Hardt have appointed as the signifier for the global workforce. Its disembodied character makes it suspicious, especially as we imagine it composed of computer literate Immaterial Laborers, immersed in a worldwide flow of online communications. Could it be (paraphrasing Antonella Corsani) that this amorphous creature is the last haven of a male metropolitan workforce that has no need of identity because its dominance is not disputed (Corsani, 2007)?

There is other evidence indicating that the Multitude is mostly composed of male metropolitan workers. Negri and Hardt, for instance, describe the 'post-Fordist' restructuring of production as work spilling from the factory into the territory. But in reality, the bulk of industrial labor has actually "spilled" into the "third world," while the growth of the service sector has mostly been a product of the commercialization of reproductive work and, therefore, a "spill" into the "territory" not from the factory but from the home.

Last, the hypothesis of an inevitable homogenization of labor under the hegemony of IL cannot be validated. Marx was mistaken on this account. For capitalism has historically required and profited from drastically different forms of work. This is evident if we look at capitalist development from the viewpoint of domestic labor and reproduction (as well as the viewpoint of those whom capitalist development has systematically 'underdeveloped'). As feminist historians have shown, capitalism never industrialized domestic work, although the nuclear family cannot be considered a legacy of pre-capitalist relations. Domestic work was a creation of late 19th century capitalism constructed at the peak of industrialization, both to pacify male workers and to support the shift from textile to heavy industry (in Marxian terms, from absolute to relative surplus) that required a more intensive exploitation of labor and thus a leap in the investment made in its reproduction. Its creation was part of the same capitalist strategy that led to the institution of the family-wage and culminated in Fordism. A full industrialization of housework of the kind attempted in the early years of the Bolshevik Revolution was undoubtedly an option and one that some socialists and even some feminists recommended. Yet, neither in the 19th century nor in the subsequent decades of the 20th was it actually attempted. Despite the epochal changes capitalism underwent, housework was never industrialized.

What this demonstrates is that the Marxian rule that the dominant form of work makes all others equal to itself must be revised when tested against the experience of unwaged domestic labor/ers. It must also be bent to accommodate for non-directly economic factors, such as the need to disaggregate/ deconcentrate workers once they are outside of the factory and/or the inability to break their resistance to a full regimentation of their lives. This means that a "real subsumption" regime can obtain without a full process of homogenization in the forms and condition of work and that discontinuities are fundamental to the reproduction of capitalist relations.

What remains to be seen is the role that AL plays in IL theory. IL, in fact, has both a cognitive and affective component, a partition suggestive of two main aspects of the restructuring of the global economy in the metropolitan areas: the growth of the service sector and the computerization of work. In this sense, IL can be disaggregated, and indeed AL is often used to describe marketized reproductive work. But it would be a mistake to conclude that AL is an expression of a gendered division of work. This is an equivocation that Negri and Hardt are willing to encourage, by referring to the cognitive component of IL as "the becoming intelligent of labor" (Hardt and Negri 2004, p. 109) and to the affective one (quoting Dorothy Smith) as "labor in the bodily mode" (Hardt and Negri, 2000, p. 293). By this gendered, hierarchical mapping of activities, Negri and Hardt nod to the feminist movement, signaling that the feminine side of the social equation has not been forgotten and their vision of the new productive forces embraces the totality of social life (Schultz, 2006). I argue, however, that rather than highlighting a gendered division of work, AL takes us beyond it. Affective Labor does not refer to gender-specific forms of work, although at times defined as "women's work." AL refers to the interactive character of work, to its capacity to promote flows of communication, thus it is polyvalent with regard to the activities associated with it. This becomes evident when we consider how the concept of AL is constructed and how it is deployed on the current labor map.

The Origin of Affective Labor and Affect

The concept of AL originates in the philosophy of Spinoza, the 17th century Dutch philosopher who in the 1970s and 1980s became the flag of the anti-Hegelian revolt in French and Italian radical thought and a reference point in the investigation of the nature of power inspired by Foucault's work. Spinoza is an author that both Negri and Hardt have studied, written about and found profoundly inspiring as indicated by the increasing presence of his ontological framework in their works, especially *Commonwealth* . Spinoza provides the spirit, the philosophy, and the wisdom to the reconstructed Marxist theory that Negri and Hardt propose. As already in Deleuze and Guattari, in Negri and Hardt as well, Spinoza's Renaissance naturalism and immanentist materialist ontology is the answer to the Hegelian view of history as the unfolding of transcendent forces, which relegates would-be revolutionaries to the role of hands of historical becoming. Spinoza also provides a crucial connection between "human nature" and political economy precisely through the notion of "Affect," the ontological seed from which AL has grown.

The crucial text for a genealogy of Affect and Affective Labor is Part 3 of the *Ethics* (1677), where Spinoza develops a non-Cartesian, materialist view of the mind-body relation rooted on the idea of 'being' as affectivity, i.e., a constant process of interaction and self-production (Spinoza, 1955).

"Affects" in Spinoza are modifications of the body that increase or diminish its capacity to act (Spinoza, 1955, p. 130). Spinoza specifies that these can be active, positive forces if they come from within us, or passive, negative ones ('passions') if what provokes them is outside of us. Thus, his ethics is an exhortation to cultivate active, empowering affects, like joy, and free ourselves from passive, negative ones that may prevent us from acting and put us in the bondage of passions. It is this notion of 'affectivity' as capacity to act and be acted upon that is incorporated in Negri and Hardt's political vision. "Affect" does not signify a feeling of fondness or love. Rather it signifies our capacity for interactivity, our capacity to move and to be moved in an endless flow of exchanges and encounters presumably expanding our powers and demonstrating not only the infinite productivity of our being but the transformative and thus already political character of everyday life (Hardt and Negri, 2009, p. 379).

It is one of the functions of the theory of Affective Labor to transpose the philosophical concept of "Affect" onto an economic and political plane, and in this process demonstrate that in today's capitalist society labor realizes and amplifies *this ontological disposition of our being* fostering that capacity for self-organization and self-transformation that the concept of "Affect" evokes. This is how I read the thesis that *in contemporary capitalism Affectivity has become a component of every form of work*, for IL is highly interactive and mobilizes not only the physical energies but also the entire subjectivity of the workers (Hardt and Negri, 2004, p. 108). By this claim Negri and Hardt suggest a unique alignment between the ontological possibilities of our being and the activities comprising our economic life, signaling the advent of a new historic phase, the 'beginning of history,' as it were (Hardt and Negri, 2009, p. 377). AL also serves to extend the reach of IL to include within it a broad range of activities characteristic of commodified reproductive work and, more ambiguously, reproduction outside of the market. But, as we will see, later, the main function AL performs is the *ungendering of labor*, suggesting that the traits once associated with "women's reproductive" work are now being generalized, so that work-wise men are increasingly becoming like women. This is why, as stated earlier, rather than evoking a sexual division of labor, AL *spells the end of this division*, at least as a significant factor of social life and a foundation for a feminist standpoint.

Affective Labor and the Ungendering of Labor

How the 'ungendering' of labor is accomplished can be seen by following the mutations of affective work in its transition from the ontological to the economic plane. As already suggested, AL has a sociological as well as ontological dimension. In the same way as the cognitive part of IL is concretized in the activities spawned by the computerization of work and the Internet, so AL is often said to describe activities in the service sector especially referring to the commercialization of reproduction. In this respect, a clear influence on the theory of AL has been the work of the feminist sociologist Arlie Hochschild on the 'commodification of emotions' and 'emotional labor' (Hardt and Negri, 2004, p. 375; Hardt and Negri, 2009, p. 407).

Hochschild's analysis, in *The Managed Heart* (1983), of the changes that by 1980 had taken place in the American workplace, is a precursor to their efforts. Already in this book, quoting Daniel Bell's *The Coming Post-Industrial Society* (1973), Hochschild had argued that with the decline of industrial production (reduced by 1983 to 6% of all employment) and the rise of the service sector "nowadays most jobs call for a capacity to deal with people rather than with things, [and call] for more interpersonal skills rather than mechanical skills" (Hochschild, 1983, p. 9). She had then put under the spotlight the "emotional labor" that flight attendants in the airline industry must perform to dispel the passengers' anxiety, project a sense of confidence and ease, repress anger or irritation in front of abuse and make those they served feel valorized. In subsequent works as well, Hochschild returned to the subject to investigate the psychological and social consequences of the commercialization of services that the family once provided, but have now been taken out of the home in the wake of women's massive entrance into the waged workforce.

From the viewpoint of how AL is described by Negri and Hardt, the industries they occasionally associate it with and the types of workers it refers to, everything would indicate that this is a close kin to Hochschild's "emotional labor". AL is "labor that produces or manipulates affects, such as a feeling of ease, well-being, satisfaction, excitement, or passion" (Hardt and Negri, 2004, p. 108). We are told that it is the sort of work that we find in the entertainment or advertising industries; that we can deduce its growing importance from the employers' demand that workers have good attitudes, good social skills, and education; affective workers are said to include "legal assistants, flight attendants," and fast-food workers who must "service with a smile" (Hardt and Negri, 2004, p. 108).

There are, however, significant differences between Hochschild's theory and Negri and Hardt's. Hochschild's analysis leaves no doubt that *women are the central subjects of emotional labor* and, though this is waged work performed on a public basis, she maintains that in essence it is work that women have always done. As she points out, lacking other resources and depending on men for money, women have always made an asset of their feelings, giving them to men in return for the material resources they lacked. The rise of the service sector has [in her words] made emotional work more systematized, standardized, and mass produced, but its existence still capitalizes on the fact that from childhood, women have been trained to have an instrumental relation to their emotions (Hochschild, 1983, p. 171).

Hochschild further establishes a direct connection between the commercialization of emotions and women's refusal of unpaid domestic work. Indeed, her analysis of emotional labor is part of a broader investigation into the effects of the 'feminist revolution' on women's social position and family relations. One of her main concerns is the crisis of care that women's waged employment has sparked off (Hochschild, 2003, pp. 1–3, 37–8) in the absence of changes in the (waged) workplace or increased institutional support for reproductive work or increased men's readiness to share the housework (Hochschild, 2003, pp. 1–3, 37–8). The picture that she paints is a troubling one: children entrusted to 'self-care,' frequently so resentful of their parents' daily absence that the latter at times extend their workday to avoid confrontations with them; elderly destined to nursing homes and a life of isolation, and a generally harsher world where relationships not leading to monetary reward are more and more devalued (Hochschild, 2003, pp. 131,145; Hochschild, 1997, pp. 212–225).

On all these counts, Negri and Hardt's theory of AL is a departure from Hochschild's. Although examples for AL are drawn from service sector-jobs usually performed by women and though is often labeled "women's work" (Hardt and Negri, 2000 , p. 293), AL does not describe a gendered form of work. On the contrary, as we have seen, it is said to be a component of most forms of IL, all forms of work presumably becoming more communicative, interactive, and productive of social relations (Hardt and Negri, 2004, p. 108). It is in this sense Negri and Hardt speak of the "feminization of work". Their reference here is not primarily to the massive entrance of women into (waged) labor-force, but to the becoming 'feminine' of the work done by men, which explains why there are nothing more than passing references to gender-specific forms of work, like procreation and child care, in any of their texts (Hardt and Negri, 2009, p. 133). Negri and Hardt are not interested in "female labor" as such, whether paid or unpaid, inside or outside the home, though we may describe it as the largest pool of "affective work" on the planet. Similarly, they seem unaware of the massive struggles, visible and invisible, that women have made against the blackmail of "affectivity," culminating in the struggle of welfare mothers and the women's liberation movement. When describing the workers' revolts of the 1960s and 1970s, which in their view have driven the restructuring of the global economy, Negri and Hardt focus exclusively on the industrial proletariat. It is the mass-worker of Fiat and River Rouge that they recognize as the force driving capital's shift to a different form of production (Hardt and Negri 2000, pp. 261–279). By contrast, nothing transpires in their texts of women's 'refusal of housework,' though it is generally recognized that this has been the most important, most transformative social/cultural revolution in our time. A consequence of this omission is that the theory of AL cannot explain *the dynamics driving the socialization of reproduction* and the new international division of reproductive work. As we have seen, Negri and Hardt speak of work spilling over from the factory into society, oblivious to the revolution that in the '60s and '70s has occurred on the home, which has propelled many formerly home-based activities into the labor market. They also miss the fact that rather than merging with production, reproductive work, as reconfigured in the post-Fordist era, has largely been unloaded on the shoulders of immigrant women (Federici, 1999; Ongero, 2003; Parrenas, 2001).

Indeed, AL and Bio-political Production cannot speak to the key questions in women's lives today: the crisis that women are facing trying to reconcile paid labor with reproduction, the fact that social reproduction still relies on women's unwaged work, that as much reproductive work has returned to the home as has gone out of it, due to cuts in healthcare, hospital care, retail work, due also to the (worldwide) expansion of home-work but above all the continuing function of the home as a magnet for unpaid/low paid labor (Glazer, 1993, Staples 2006).

In view of the above, we can then draw some preliminary conclusions. The generalization of affective labor, i.e., its dispersal over every form of work, takes us back to a pre-feminist situation, where not only the specificity but the very existence of women's reproductive work and the struggle women are making on this terrain become invisible again.

Affective Labor in Feminist Writing

While in Negri and Hardt's thought AL stands for a general characteristic of work in the post-Fordist era, among feminist scholars the concept has provided an analytic tool for exploring new forms of (mostly female) labor exploitation, as well as new modes of subjectivity and projectuality, stimulating empirical research on the changes that reproductive work and its subjects have undergone in entering the public/commercial sphere. These analyses, in the form of case studies of reproductive activities in the service sector, have not supported Negri and Hardt's 'autonomy hypothesis,' however. Compared with assembly-line work, 'affective labor' may appear more creative, as workers must engage in a constant re-articulation/ reinvention of their subjectivity, choose how much of their 'selves' to give to the job, mediate conflicting interests. But they must do so under the pressure of precarious labor conditions, an intense pace of work, and a neo-Taylorist rationalization and regimentation of work that one would have imagined foregone with the decline of the Fordist regime.

The contradictions affective workers face when work relations become 'affective' and subjectivized are well documented in the research conducted by Emma Dowling, Kristin Carls, Elizabeth Wissinger and Alison Hearn (among others) on AL in [respectively] waitressing, large scale retail work, modeling and 'self-branding' in TV reality shows. Each provides a fascinating description of what putting one's subjectivity, one's personality and affects to work implies in the sphere of waged labor, under conditions of increasing competition and enhanced employers' capacity for technological supervision. Dowling points out, for instance, that she was not only instructed (as a waitress in a high-class restaurant in London) to place 'affective' elements (conversation, entertainment, valorization of the client) at the center of her serving, to produce a 'dining experience,' but had to do so according to highly structured and codified guidelines "meticulously set out in a 25-point 'sequence of service'" specifying at what distances to make eye contact, shake hands and so forth (Dowling, 2007, pp. 120–121).

Carls, as well, argues, this time with reference to the retail industry, that rather than opening new possibilities for workers' cooperation and 'collective appropriation of working conditions,' the growing focus on affect is a central mechanism and strategy for labor control (Carls, 2007, p. 46). In a work context characterized by cost-cutting, competition, and a strict regimentation of work, such that everything, from dress codes to toilet breaks, is regulated and enforced through multiple forms of surveillance, focus on affect and interactivity in worker-management and worker-customer relations is more conducive to the internalization of codes of conduct, the internalization of responsibility for the success of the company's objectives, and the individualization of labor practices rather than solidarity with other workers—all dynamics that the precarization of labor and permanent insecurity as to future employment intensify (Carls, 2007, pp. 49–51).

Precarity, as an essential component of work-discipline, emerges as a theme also in Elizabeth Wissinger's analysis of affective labor in the fashion industry, modeling in particular. This is an activity where life truly blurs with work as continuous working on one's body, one's sense of self, and projected image, is central to the life of a model. But the seeming self-valorization hides high levels of unpaid labor and makes workers acceptant of constantly deferred rewards and a regime of total expendability whereby they can be immediately dismissed if they cease to be 'fun,' "sometimes even before a job is finished" (Wissinger, 2007, pp. 252–53, 255–57).

Last, Hearn's discussion of "self-branding" in reality TV directly challenges the assumption that affective labor is a creative activity or a vehicle for self-expression. It shows that while drawing from the emotions and personality of the workers, the selfhood performed is shaped by specific dictates and disciplinary structures, and the selling of "subjectivity" and life experiences is a managerial ruse to cut production cost, pretending no labor is truly involved (Hearn, 2010).

Examples could be multiplied, but with similar results. In sum, rather than being an autonomous, self-organized form of work, spontaneously producing forms of "elementary communism," AL for workers is a mechanical, alienating experience performed under command, spied upon and certainly measured and quantified in its value producing capacity as much as any form of physical labor (Dowling, pp. 121, 128). It is also a form of work that generates a more intense sense of responsibility and occasionally pride in the workers, thus undermining any potential rebellion against the sense of suffered injustice.

The above descriptions of AL can be generalized. Few work-activities qualifying as AL create the common 'internal to labor' and 'external to capital' that Negri and Hardt imagine produced by this work. As Carls points out, "the development of cooperation and collective agency is not a spontaneous process, inherent in the logic of the post-Fordist reorganization of work . . ." (Carls, 2007, p. 58). Relations between waitresses or retail workers and clients, baby sitters and the children they care for, nurses or aides and hospital patients, are not spontaneously productive of "the common". In the neoliberal workplace, where understaffing makes speed-ups the order of the day and precarity generates a high level of insecurity and anxiety, AL is more conducive to tensions and conflicts than the discovery of commonalities (Carls, 2007, p. 46). Indeed, it is an illusion to believe that in a labor regime in which work relations are structured for the sake of accumulation, work can have an autonomous character, be self-organizing, and escape measurements and quantification.

That capitalism cannot "capture" all the energy/productivity of living labor does not detract from the fact that work subsumed under a capitalist logic reaches into the workers' psyche, manipulating, distorting and structuring their very souls. This is recognized by Maurizio Lazzarato (1996) when he states that under the hegemony of IL "the worker's personality and subjectivity have to be made susceptible to organization and command" (Dowling, 2007, p. 121). Hochschild would agree. She finds that there are different strategies that 'emotional workers' resort to in order to respond to the techniques management employs to appropriate their emotional energy. Some give their soul, their whole self to the job, making the customers' concerns their own, others completely dissociate themselves from the job, mechanically "acting out" the affective content of the labor expected of them, others for their part try to navigate between these two extremes (Hochschild, 1983). But in no case is "commoning" a given, an automatic development immanent in the work itself. Put in different terms, "commoning" cannot be produced when we must offer the customers drinks, regardless of possible kidney problems, or must convince them to buy the dress, the car, the furniture they might not be able to afford, or lavish on them ego-boosting, flattering comments according to prescription. Indeed, as already mentioned, what appears as "autonomy" is most often interiorization of the employers' needs.

Nevertheless, as dramatized by flight attendant Steven Slater's decision to stop 'yessing' his customers and 'Go Down the Chute,' struggles against AL do occur and it is perhaps one of the main limits of Negri and Hardt's work to have ignored this reality (King, 2010).

This is not accidental. Negri and Hardt's insistence on defining affectivity as primarily interactivity, self-organization and cooperation precludes the recognition of the antagonistic relations that are constitutive of this work. It also precludes the elaboration of strategies enabling affective laborers to overcome the sense of guilt that comes with refusing a work on which the reproduction of other people's depends. It is only when we think of affective work as reproductive work in its double, contradictory function, as reproduction of human beings and reproduction of labor-power, that we can imagine forms of struggles and refusal that empower rather than destroying those we care for. The lesson of the feminist movement has been crucial in this respect, as it has recognized that women's refusal of the exploitation and emotional blackmail, which is at the core of unpaid domestic labor as well as paid care-work, also liberated those dependent on this work.

This recognition and strategic approach to AL is not possible, however, if this activity is presented not as work organized by and for capital, but as an activity already exemplifying work in post-capitalist society.

Conclusions

It is significant that analyses conducted under the label of affective labor have concentrated on new forms of market work and especially on (mostly female) commercialized reproductive work. This, on one side, is not surprising, for the marketization of many reproductive tasks has been one of the main novelties in the new world economy that has emerged also in response to womens struggles against unpaid labor in the 1980s and 1990s. On the other side, this turn is problematic. For the focus on marketized reproductive work risks hiding again the archipelagos of unpaid activities that are still carried out in the home and their effect on the position of women also as waged workers. More important, the dominant stress on market work and (in Negri and Hardt's view) the collapsing of distinctions between production/reproduction, waged/unwaged risk obscures a fundamental fact about the nature of capitalism, which the struggle of the wageless in the 1960s brought forcefully to the foreground. That is, capital accumulation feeds upon an immense amount of unpaid labor; above all it feeds upon the systematic devaluation of reproductive work that is translated into the devaluation of large sectors of the world proletariat. It is this recognition that risks being lost when 'affective labor' becomes the exclusive prism through which we read the restructuring of reproduction or it becomes the signpost for a worldview where distinctions between production/reproduction, waged/unwaged labor are completely obliterated.

Bibliography

Boris, E. & Klein, J. (2007). "We Are the Invisible Workforce. Unionizing Home Care." In D. S. Cobble ed, *The Sex of Class, Women Transform American Labor*. Ithaca, NY: Cornell University Press.

Carls, K. (2007). Affective Labor in Milanese Large Scale Retailing: Labor Control and Employees' Coping Strategies. *Ephemera*, Vol. 7(1): 46–59.

Casarino, C. & Negri A. (2008). *A Conversation on Philosophy in Praise of the Commons and Politics*. Minneapolis: University of Minnesota Press.

Corsani, A. (2007). Beyond the Myth of Woman: The Becoming-Transfeminist of (Post-) Marxism. *SubStance* # 112, Vol. 36, no.1, 2007, 107–138.

Dowling, E. (2007). Producing the Dining Experience: Measure Subjectivity and the Affective Worker. *Ephemera*, Vol. 7(1): 117–132.

Federici, S. (1980). Wages against Housework. In E. Malos (ed.), *The Politics of Housework*. Cheltenham: New Clarion Press.

Federici, S. (1999). Reproduction and Feminist Struggle in the New International Division of Labor. In M. Dalla Costa and F. Dalla Costa eds. (1999) *Women, Development and Labor Reproduction*. Trenton, NJ: Africa World Press.

Federici, S. (2008). Precarious Labour: A Feminist Viewpoint, *In the Middle of a Whirlwind. 2008 Convention Protests, Movement and Movements*. Retrieved from www.inthemiddleofawhirl-wind.info

Federici, S. (n.d.). The Development of Domestic Work in the Transition from Absolute to Relative Surplus Value. Unpublished manuscript. For copies contact S. Federici at silvia.federici@hofstra.edu.

Federici, S. & Caffentzis, G. (2009). Notes on the Edu–factory and Cognitive Capitalism (with Caffentzis, G. In Edu-factory Collective Eds., *Towards a Global University. Cognitive Labor, the Production of Knowledge and Exodus from the Education Factory*. Brooklyn, NY: Autonomedia.

Gilman, C.P. (1903). *The Home, Its Work and Influence*. New York: McClure, Phillips, & Co.

Hardt, M. (1993). *Gilles Deleuze: An Apprenticeship in Philosophy*. Minneapolis: University of Minnesota Press.

Hardt, M. (1999). Affective Labor, *Boundary* 2 26.2 (1999): 89–100.

Hardt, M. & Negri, A. (2000). *Empire*. Cambridge, MA: Harvard University Press.

Hardt, M. & Negri, A. (2004). *Multitude—War and Democracy in an Age of Empire*. London: Penguin Press.

Hardt, M. & Negri, A. (2009). *Commonwealth*. Cambridge, MA: Harvard University Press.

Hayden, D. (1985). *The Grand Domestic Revolution: A History of Feminist Designs for American Homes, Neighborhoods, and Cities*. Cambridge, MA: The MIT Press.

Hearn, A. (2010). Reality Television, *The Hills*, and the Limits of the Immaterial Labor Thesis. *tripleC-Cognition, Communication, Co-operation*, Vol. 8, No. 1

Hochschild, A.R. (1983). *The Managed Heart. Commercialization of Human Feeling*. Berkeley: University of California Press.

Hochschild, A.R. (1997). *Time Bind. When Work Becomes Home and Home Becomes Work*. New York: Metropolitan Book.

Hochschild, A.R. (2003). *The Commercialization of Intimate Life*. Berkeley: University of California Press.

King, L. (2010). Interview with Steven Slater. Retrieved from transcripts.cnn.com/TRAN-SCRIPTS/1010/26/lkl.01.html.

Kopp, A. (1967). *Ville et Revolution: Architecture et Urbanisme Sovietiques des Annees Vingt*. Paris: Editions Anthropos.

Lazzarato, M. (2008). From Knowledge to Belief, from Critique to the Production of Subjectivity. European Institute for Progressive Cultural Policies (eipcp). Retrieved from Eipcp.net/transversal/0808/lazzarato/en.

Negri, A. (1991). *The Savage Anomaly. The Power of Spinoza's Metaphysics and Politics*, trans. Michael Hardt. Minneapolis: University of Minnesota Press.

Ongaro, S. (2003). De la reproduction productive a la production reproductive. Association Multitudes, *Multitudes*, 2003/2–n. 12, pp. 145–153.

Parreñas, R.S. (2001). *Servants of Globalization: Women, Migration and Domestic Work*. Stanford, CA: Stanford University Press.

De Spinoza, B. (1955). *On the Improvement of the Understanding, The Ethics, The Correspondence*. New York: Dover Publication.

Schultz, S. (2006). Dissolved Boundaries and "Affective Labor": On the Disappearance of Reproductive Labor and Feminist Critique in Empire. *Capitalism, Nature and Socialism*, Vol. 17, no. 1, March (2006): pp. 77–82(6).

Sohn-Rethel, A. (1978). *Intellectual and Manual Labor: A Critique of Epistemology*. London: Macmillan.

Terranova, T. (2000). Free Labor: Producing Culture for the Digital Economy. *Social Text*, no. 63: 33–58.

Weeks, K. (2007). Life Within and Against Work: Affective Labor, Feminist Critique, and Post-Fordist Politics. *Ephemera*, Vol. 7(1): 233–249

Wissinger, E. (2007)\. Modelling a Way of Life: Immaterial and Affective Labour in the Fashion Modelling Industry. *Ephemera*, Vol. 7(1): 250–269.

CHAPTER FOUR

Cognitive Capitalism or Informational Capitalism?
The Role of Class in the Informational Economy

CHRISTIAN FUCHS

Introduction

This chapter poses the question of class in the information age. It wants to contribute to the renewal of class analysis in the 21st century and wants to show that class is a central concept for analyzing contemporary society and the role of information in contemporary society.

The two main approaches on class in the social sciences are the Marxian and the Weberian concepts of class (Wright, 2005). Whereas the Marxian class concept stresses exploitation, the Weberian concept takes class as a group of people who have certain life chances in the market in common. These chances would have to do with the possession of goods and opportunities for earning income and would be represented under the conditions of the commodity or labour market (Weber, 1978, p. 926). The Marxian concept of class "figures centrally in a political project of emancipatory social change" (Wright, 2005, 718). The Marxian notion is dynamic, historical, and relational—class is a historical social relationship between antagonistic, opposing classes that have conflicting interests (Thompson, 1960b, p. 24; Thompson, 1968, pp. 8–10).

If one assumes that we can speak of informational capitalism today, it is important to pose the question of class in the digital age and to discuss its continuities and discontinuities. For Manuel Castells, the economy consists of an interrelation between a mode of production (capitalism) and a mode of development (informationalism) (Castells, 2000, p. 14). He argues that informationalism is a new mode of development that has been accelerated, channelled, and shaped by "the process of capitalist restructuring undertaken since the 1980s, so that the new techno-economic system can be adequately characterized as informational capitalism" (Castells, 2000, p. 18). The informational productive forces are dialectically connected to class relationships. This dialectic produces the dynamic and antagonisms of the contemporary capitalist economy (Fuchs, 2008b). The informational productive forces are medium and outcome of capitalist interests, strategies, and restructuring—technology is shaped by and shapes society in complex ways. A historical novelty of contemporary society is not that there are networks in society, but that processes of production, power, exploitation, hegemony, and struggles take on the form of transnational networks that are mediated by networked information and communication technologies and knowledge processes (Fuchs, 2008b). Informational capitalism is based on a transnational organizational model, organizations cross national boundaries, the novel aspect is that organizations and social networks are increasingly globally distributed, that actors and substructures are located globally and change dynamically (new nodes can be continuously added and removed), and that the flows of capital, power, money, commodities, people, and information are processed globally at high speed. Global informational network capitalism is a nomadic dynamic system in the sense that it and its parts permanently reorganize by changing their boundaries and including or excluding various systems by establishing links, unions, and alliances or getting rid of or ignoring those actors that do not serve or contribute to the aim of capital accumulation. Informational capitalism is a category that is used for describing those parts of contemporary societies that are basing their operations predominantly on information, which is understood as processes of cognition, communication, and cooperation, and on information technologies (Fuchs, 2007, 2008b, 2009).

The central concept of this book is the one of cognitive capitalism. I will therefore argue in section 2 of this chapter why I prefer the notion of informational capitalism to the one of cognitive capitalism, and that in any case care must be taken in making claims about informatization. In section 3, foundations of Marxian class analysis are introduced. In section 4, I discuss the connection of class, information labour, and digital media. Finally, some conclusions are drawn in section 5.

Information society theory and informational capitalism

Discussions about the concept of cognitive capitalism are situated in the information society debate. This discourse can be theoretically categorized by distinguishing two axes that characterize information society theories: the first axis distinguishes aspects of societal change, the second one the informational qualities of these changes. There are theories that conceive the transformations of the past decades as constituting radical societal change. These are discontinuous theories. Other theories stress the continuities of modern society. More Subjective social theories stress the importance of human individuals and their thinking and actions in society, whereas objective social theories stress structures that transcend single individuals (Giddens, 1984, p. xx). Subjective information society theories stress the importance of human knowledge (thought, mental activities) in contemporary society, whereas objective information society theories emphasize the role of information technologies such as the mass media, the computer, the Internet, or the mobile phone. Figure 1 shows a typology of information society theories.

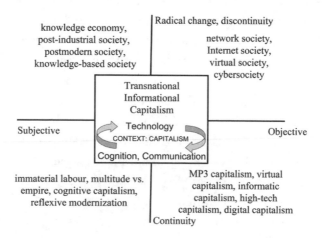

Figure 1: A typology of information society theories

Discontinuous subjective concepts are, for example, the knowledge economy (Machlup, 1962; Drucker, 1969; Porat, 1977), the post-industrial society (Bell, 1976; Touraine, 1971), the postmodern society (Lyotard, 1984), or the knowledge-based society (Stehr, 2002). Objective discontinuous notions that stress the importance of information technologies are, for example, the network society (Castells, 2000; van Dijk, 2006), the virtual society (Bühl, 2000; Woolgar, 2002), cybersociety (Jones, 1998), or the Internet society (Bakardjieva 2005).

Discontinuous information society theories prefix certain terms to macro-sociological categories such as society or economy, which implies that they assume that society or the economy has undergone a radical transformation in the past decades and that we now live in a new society or economy. These approaches stress discontinuity, as if contemporary society had nothing in common with society as it was 100 or 150 years ago. "If there is just more information then it is hard to understand why anyone should suggest that we have before us something radically new" (Webster, 2002a, p. 259). Nicholas Garnham (2004) therefore characterizes information society theory as ideology. Such assumptions have ideological character because they fit with the view that we can do nothing about change and have to adapt to existing political realities (Webster, 2002b, p. 267). Peter Golding argues that information society discourse is an ideology that "anticipates and celebrates the privatization of information, and the incorporation of ICT developments into the expansion of the free market" (2000, p. 170). The danger in sociology's fascination of the new would be that it would be distracted from the focus on radical potentials and the critique of how these potentials are suppressed (Golding, 2000, p. 171).

I agree with these critiques, that discontinuous information society theories occlude viewing the continuity of capitalist structures. But such critiques tend to assume that the capitalist character of contemporary society is self-evident and therefore do not or hardly ground their criticism of discontinuous information society theories in empirical data. Qualities of society can only be presented in a convincing manner if theoretical assumptions are supported by data. It therefore needs to be shown that we have been living in a capitalist society in the past decades and that therefore there is a continuity of capitalist structures. Karl Marx characterized capitalism with the following words: "The driving notion and determining purpose of capitalist production is the self-valorization of capital to the greatest possible extent, i.e. the greatest possible production of surplus-value, hence the greatest possible exploitation of labour-power by the capitalist" (Marx, 1867, p. 449). Capitalism is a dynamic economic system that is based on the need for permanent capital accumulation in order to continue to exist. Capital can only be increased by the extraction of unpaid labour from workers that is transformed into money profit. "The employment of surplus-value as capital, or its reconversion into capital, is called accumulation of capital" (Marx, 1867, p. 725). A central characteristic of capitalism, therefore, is the class relationship between capitalists and workers, in which surplus value is produced that is objectified in commodities that are sold on markets, so that surplus value is transformed into profit and the initial capital is increased and reinvested. This is a dynamic process. In order to show the continuity of capitalism, we therefore need to analyze the development of capital and labour in time.

Figure 2 shows the development of the worldwide gross domestic product (GDP) in the years 1961–2008. GDP growth seems to develop in cycles that include upswings and downswings. The combination of these cycles can result in longer waves of GDP growth or sudden phases of stagnation/crisis. Except for the year 2008, there was an overall growth of the world GDP, which is an indication for continuous capital accumulation in the outlined period. But GDP is an indicator that contains both wages and profits and therefore obscures the class relations that are at the heart of capitalism. In order to analyze the development of class relations, we therefore need to refer to other data.

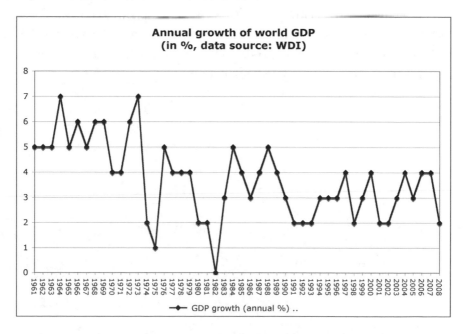

Figure 2

Figure 3 shows the development of the wage shares for the EU15 countries, the United States, and Japan in the years 1960–2009. The wage share measures the share of total wages in the gross domestic product. The wage share decreased from 65–75% in the mid-1970s to 55–60% at the end of the first decade of the new millennium. This means that wages have relatively decreased in relationship to profits: lowering wages has radically increased profits. Capitalism in the past 35 years has been characterized by an intensification of class struggle from above: corporations have combated labour by relatively lowering wages. They have been supported in this endeavour by state policies that deregulated markets, labour laws, and decreased corporate taxes. Capital accumulation has therefore remained continuously at high levels for most of the time in the years 1960–2008. An indication for this circumstance is that world cross capital formation, which measures the total value of additions to fixed assets, has remained at more than 20% in all of these years (Figure 4). The combined value of all stocks has remained continuously at rates above 40% of world GDP in the years 1960–2008 (Figure 5). Figure 6 shows the growth of total capital assets in the EU15 countries and the United States for the years 1960–2008. The continuous growth of capital assets shows that capital accumulation has continuously yielded profits in the past decades. The continuous growth of world GDP, capital assets, cross capital formation, and stock market values in the past decades is an indication that we live in a capitalist economy. The tendency for the growth of profits by decreasing the wage share is an indication for an intensification of class struggle by capital in the past decades, which shows the continuous class character of the contemporary economy.

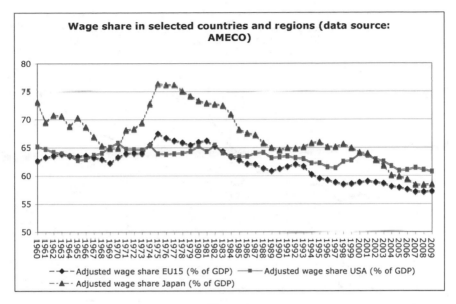

Figure 3

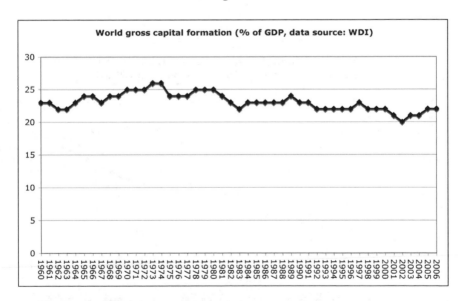

Figure 4

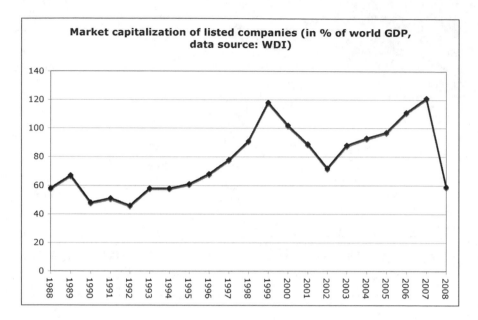

Figure 5

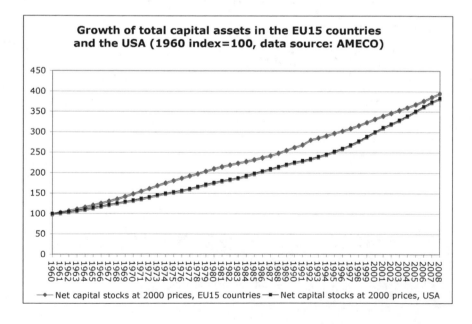

Figure 6

Continuous information society theories stress that we still live in a modern capitalist society but that certain changes of the forms that express basic capitalist structures have taken place. Subjective continuous information society concepts are, for example, reflexive modernization (Beck, Giddens and Lash, 1994), cognitive capitalism (Vercellone, 2007), semio-capitalism (Berardi, 2009a, 2009b), and general intellect and immaterial labour (Hardt and Negri, 2000, 2004; Virno, 2004). They stress the importance of mental labour for capital accumulation in contemporary capitalism. Objective continuous information society concepts include, for example, digital capitalism (Glotz, 1999; Schiller, 2000), virtual capitalism (Dawson and Foster, 1998), high-tech capitalism (Haug, 2003), MP3 capitalism (Sennett, 2006), and informatic capitalism (Fitzpatrick, 2002).

Based on Negri and Hardt's (2000, 2004) focus on immaterial labor, there are some Marxist approaches that frame the current transformation not as objective approaches as a technological transformation but as a subjective turn. Maurizio Lazzarato introduced the term *immaterial labour*, by which he means "labor that produces the informational and cultural content of the commodity" (Lazzarato, 1996, p. 133). Michael Hardt and Antonio Negri have popularized the term, and define immaterial labour as labour "that creates immaterial products, such as knowledge, information, communication, a relationship, or an emotional response" (Hardt and Negri, 2004, p. 108).

Franco Berardi stresses the subjective character of what he terms semio-capitalism: "Semio-capital, in fact, is not about the production of material goods, but about the production of psychic stimulation" (Berardi, 2009a, p. 45). The "intellectual becomes a mass social subject that tends to become an integral part of the general productive process" (Berardi, 2009a, p. 63). Semio-capitalism means for Berardi the "integration of language in the valorization process" (2009a, p. 149). Semiocapitalism "takes the mind, language and creativity as its primary tools for the production of value" (Berardi, 2009b, p. 21), Berardi says that semiocapitalism puts the soul at work: "Not the body but the soul becomes the subject of techno-social domination" (2009b, p. 200).

Christian Marazzi and Paolo Virno say that contemporary capitalism is shaped by the general intellect, which they conceive (other than Marx) as a purely subjective concept. Christian Marazzi writes that in "post-Fordism the general intellect is not fixed in machines, but in the bodies of workers" (2008, p. 44). The "primary productive resource of contemporary capitalism lies in the linguistic-relational abilities of humankind, in the complex of communicative and cognitive faculties (dynameis, powers) which distinguish humans" (Virno, 2004, p. 98). The notion of general intellect refers for Virno to the mind and linguistic-cognitive faculties of the human (2004, p. 42). Virno says that today general intellect "instead of being incarnated" into "the system of machines, exists as attribute of living labor" (2004, p. 65). He uses the notion of the intellectuality of the masses for "the whole of post-Ford era living labor . . . in that it is a depository of cognitive and communicative skills which cannot be objectified within the system of machines" (2004, p. 107). Negri uses the term cognitive capitalism for stressing that "the production of value depends increasingly on creative intellectual activity which, apart from placing itself beyond any valorization related to scarcity, also places itself beyond mass accumulation, factory accumulation and the like" (Negri, 2008, p. 64). Nick Dyer-Witheford (2005) sees cognitive capitalism as "the commercial appropriation of general intellect", but also stresses that one "of the defining features of cognitive capitalism is its elaboration of high technology communications systems, of which the most famous is the Internet". Carlo Vercellone (2007) sees the transformation of capitalism as a subjective turn and hence speaks of "cognitive capitalism" as a formation that is characterized by "the hegemony of knowledges, by a diffuse intellectuality, and by the driving role of the production of knowledges by means of knowledges connected to the increasingly immaterial and cognitive character of labor" (Vercellone, 2007, p. 16). There would be a "preponderance of the knowledges of living labor over knowledges incorporated in fixed capital and in corporate organization" (Vercellone, 2007, p. 32). The emerging antagonism between the living knowledge of labour and the dead knowledge of fixed constant capital would cause a crisis of the law of value, and an antagonism between capital's attempt to enforce the law of value artificially (e.g., by intellectual property rights) and the socialization of knowledge by its incorporation in the brains of the collective workers of the general intellect. Paolo Virno (2004) formulates this assumption as his thesis no. 7: that in post-Fordism, the general intellect does not coincide with fixed capital, but manifests itself principally as a linguistic reiteration of living labour.

That the role of technology does not vanish as claimed by Negri, Vercellone, Virno and others can, for example, be seen by the fact that among the worldwide largest corporations (measured by a composite index of sales, market value, assets and profits, for example the Forbes Global 2000 list from 2009) there are not only financial, banking, insurance institutions and oil corporations but increasingly also information technology-producers like AT&T, Verizon Communications, IBM,

Telefónica, Hewlett-Packard, Deutsche Telekom, Nippon, or Microsoft. The notion of cognitive capitalism ignores that human knowledge not only is a productive force, but that knowledge is also stored, shared, communicated, and networked with the help of information technologies such as the computer, the Internet, and the mobile phone. Informational productive forces involve both human knowledge and information technologies. Humans make use of technologies for diffusing, using, sharing, and storing data. Knowledge becomes networked with the help of technologies. Notions such as immaterial labour and cognitive capitalism are subjectivistic and idealistic, they ignore the technical features of contemporary society that mediate human cognition, communication, and cooperation.

If one applies a dialectical methodology, the rise of transnational informational capitalism is neither only a subjective nor only an objective transformation but based on a subject-object-dialectic. Objective approaches are techno-deterministic and neglect how forms of labour and agency have changed, subjective approaches neglect that technology is a force that shapes and is shaped by agency. Hence both the technology-oriented objective and the subjective knowledge-oriented Marxist approaches are insufficient. But at the same time they are right in stressing one pole of a dialectic of a larger framework: The notion of transnational informational capitalism sublates both lines of thinking dialectically because information and networks have both an objective and a subjective aspect; they transform the means of production and the relations of production. The search of capital for new strategies and forms of capital accumulation transforms labour in such a way that cognitive, communicative, and cooperative labour forms a significant amount of overall labour time (a development enforced by the rise of the ideology of self-discipline of 'participatory management'), but at the same time this labour is heavily mediated by information technologies and produces to a certain extent tangible informational goods (as well as intangible informational services) (Fuchs, 2008b). The notion of transnational informational capitalism grasps this subject-object-dialectic, it conceptualizes contemporary capitalism based on the rise of cognitive, communicative, and cooperative labour that is interconnected with the rise of technologies of and goods that objectify human cognition, communication, and cooperation. Informational capitalism is based on the dialectical interconnection of subjective knowledge and knowledge objectified in information. The reason why I think that this approach is better grounded is that dialectics allow for the conception of reality as complex and dynamic, which questions one-dimensional and static-ideological accounts of reality.

Transnational informational capitalism is the result of the dialectic of continuity and discontinuity that shapes capitalist development. Surplus value, exchange value, capital, commodities and competition are basic aspects of capitalism, how such forms are exactly produced, objectified, accumulated, and circulated is contingent and historical. They manifest themselves differently in different capitalist modes of development. In the informational mode of development surplus value production and capital accumunication manifest themselves increasingly in symbolic, "immaterial", informational commodities and cognitive, communicative, and cooperative labour. The accumulation of capital, power, and definition-capacities on a transnational scale is strongly mediated by new media. Roy Bhaskar (1993, p. 12) has distinguished between real negation ≥ transformative negation ≥ radical negation in order to stress the non-deterministic and complex character of sublation. Not all negations of negations are at the fundamental level, there are also partial sublations that are transformative but not radical. The emergence of transnational informational capitalism is a transformational sublation but not a radical one.

After the second world economic crisis in the mid-1970s there was a transition from the Fordist mode of development to the post-Fordist mode of capitalist development. In order to increase profits new strategies and a flexible regime of accumulation and domination (Harvey, 1989) emerged, the main idea is to increase profits by putting pressure on nation states to lower wages and by decentralizing and globalizing the production process in order to reduce wage costs and investment and reproduction costs of capital so that variable and constant capital decrease, which results in an increased production of surplus value and hence in rising profits.

The increasing importance of computer networks and global network organizations is an instrumental result of capitalist development. Computer technology and the Internet were not invented and introduced in an economic but in a military context. But the societal diffusion of these technologies is due to the role they have played primarily for the economic restructuration of capitalism. Computer networks are the technological foundation that has allowed the emergence of global network capitalism, i.e., regimes of accumulation, regulation, and discipline that are helping to increasingly base the accumulation of economic, political, and cultural capital on transnational network organizations that make use of cyberspace and other new technologies for global coordination and communication.

Globalization can generally be defined as the stretching of social relationships, i.e., communication networks, in space-time, a globalizing social system enlarges its border in space-time, as a result social relationships can be maintained across larger temporal and spatial distances. In modern society, processes of globalization are based on the logic of accumulation of natural resources, tools, money capital, power, and hegemony. The main problem that modern society tries to solve is how to accumulate ever more capital. Whenever an existing regime/mode of accumulation reaches its inherent limits and enters a crisis, new strategies and areas of accumulation are needed in order to revert to ordered processes of accumulation. Hence globalization is in modern society inherently driven by the logic of capital accumulation that results in the appropriation and production of new spaces and systems of accumulation. The antagonism between structures and actors characteristic for modern society (social structures are alienated from their producers, i.e., they are controlled by certain groups that exclude others from control) results in a clash of estrangement and self-determination that is characteristic for all subsystems of modern society. The basic conflict is that many people cannot cope with the increased complexity of the world because their lives are increasingly shaped by global alienated structures that are out of their reach and that they cannot participate in.

Contemporary capitalism is based on a transnational organizational model: Organizations cross national boundaries; the novel aspect is that organizations and social networks are increasingly globally distributed, that actors and substructures are located globally and change dynamically (new nodes can be continuously added and removed), and that the flows of capital, power, money, commodities, people, and information are processed globally at highspeed. Global network capitalism is a nomadic dynamic system in the sense that it and its parts permanently reorganize by changing their boundaries and including or excluding various systems by establishing links, unions, and alliances or getting rid of or ignoring those actors that don't serve or contribute to the overall aim of capital accumulation.

Network technologies like the Internet—due to their global reach, decentralized structure, and high speed—support communication and social relations across spatial and temporal distances. Phil Graham (2006, pp. 1, 72) sees the high speed and extent of communication as the central characteristic of what he terms hypercapitalism. High speed is just one quantitative feature of a new quality of capitalism, a networked transnationalism regime of rule. It might be better to focus on qualities and not on quantities in choosing a key concept because in dialectical thinking the transformations that emerge from the overturn on quantitative features are decisive. A global space is constituted by the interaction of global technological systems and [SH1]transnational (economic, political, cultural) organizations and institutions. This space is a space of global flows of capital, power, and ideology that create and permanently recreate a new transnational regime of domination.

The accumulation of money capital, power, and cultural definition-capacities, i.e., exploitation, domination, and ideological legitimization, have become more transnational and are influenced by knowledge production (subjective aspect) and networked digital information and communication technologies (objective aspect). Transnational network capitalism has an antagonistic character, knowledge and new technologies don't have one-sided effects but should be analyzed dialectically: They are embedded into a fundamental antagonism of capitalism the one between cooperation and competition, that has specific manifestations in the various subsystems of society. The computer is a universal machine that is simultaneously a means of production, circulation, and consumption. This feature combined with networking has resulted in the emergence of the figure of the prosumer that on the one hand promises a new model of cooperative production and socialization of the means of production, but on the other hand is antagonistically subsumed under the rule of capital.

FDI flows have increased from approximately 0.5% of world GDP at the beginning of the 1970s to a share between 2% and 4.5% since the end of the millennium (data source: UNCTAD). FDI stocks have increased from a level of about 5% of world GDP at the beginning of the 1980s to 25% of world GDP in 2006. In 2006, the top 100 transnational corporations (TNCs) listed in the World Investment Report had an average transnationality index (a composite index that measures the degree to which asset, sales, employees are operating outside the home base of a TNC) of 61.6% (World Investment Report, 2008, p. 28), which shows that large multi- and transnationals indeed do have transnational value-sources. World exports and World imports have increased from approximately 10% of the world GDP in 1965 to more than 25% in 2007. These are empirical indicators that contemporary capitalism is more global in character than Fordist capitalism. Global capitalism is therefore a term that denotes an extension and intensification of the globalization of contemporary capitalism in comparison to Fordist capitalism (1945–1975).

But can we indeed maintain that transnational capitalism is informational in character?

If one defines information as cognitive and communicative process (Fuchs, 2008b), then one can see the information sector of the economy as being comprised of the generation, distribution, and consumption of informational goods and services (affective labour, production of information technologies, communication equipment, media infrastructure, media content, research, education, recreation, culture, entertainment). The United Nations (UN) International Standard Industrial Classification of All Economic Activities (ISIC Rev 3.1) distinguishes various economic activities that can be mapped to four economic sectors: the primary (agriculture and mining), the secondary (traditional manufacturing), the tertiary (non-informational services), and the quaternary (informational goods and services) sector (see Fuchs, 2008b, 194ff).

The information economy constitutes the quaternary sector. Statistical analysis (based on data from the Organisation for Economic Co-operation and Development (OECD) Database for Structural Analysis (STAN)) allows analysis of how value added and employees are distributed within various countries across these four sectors. Tables 1 and 2 show the results for a number of countries. The selected advanced countries display uniform structural patterns: the informational economy is the dominant employment sector in all selected countries (Italy excepted). The secondary sector is the dominant locus of value production in all selected countries. In all of the selected countries, the informational sector is the second largest locus of value production. These statistics allow analyzing the role of information in national economies. Structural analysis shows that information is important in the economies of some of the dominant countries, although it is only dominant in the employment structure and not in value production. What is the role of information in transnational economic relationships? Does it play an important or a rather minor role in foreign investments, transnational business operations, and world trade? It is one of the tasks of this chapter to answer these questions by treating the topic of the information economy within the context of the debate on the new imperialism and global capitalism.

Economic Sector	U.S.	Germany	Norway	France	Austria	Finland	Italy
1st	2.0%	2.3%	4.8%	3.5%	12.0%	5.3%	4.3%
2nd	15.9%	23.7%	17.5%	19.2%	20.7%	22.8%	27.1%
3rd	34.2%	32.2%	29.2%	28.7%	31.8%	26.0%	34.4%
4th	47.9%	41.7%	48.5%	48.7%	35.4%	46.0%	34.1%

Table1

Distribution of employees in four economic sectors (2006 data for total employment, data source: author's calculations based on data from OECD Database for Structural Analysis)

Economic Sector	U.S.	Germany	Norway	France	Austria	Finland	Italy
1st	3.0%	1.1%	29.3%	2.1%	2.2%	2.9%	2.5%
2nd	40.5%	42.9%	32.8%	38.2%	51.3%	44.6%	46.8%
3rd	25.2%	27.8%	14.7%	28.7%	20.4%	19.6%	24.0%
4th	31.2%	28.3%	23.2%	31.0%	26.1%	33.0%	26.8%

Table2

Distribution of value added in four economic sectors (2006 data: value added at current prices, data source: author's calculations based on data from OECD Database for Structural Analysis)

Figure 7 shows an analysis of the distribution of the capital assets of the world's largest 2,000 corporations between various economic sectors. Finance capital is the dominant fraction of capital today, which shows that an important characteristic of imperialistic capitalism is present today. Fossil fuels are also still very important in the contemporary economy. This is an indication that industrial society is not over, and that we have entered a hyper-industrial era in which information production, selling, and consumption becomes an important factor of the overall economy, but does not substitute for the economic importance of finance capital and fossil fuels. Financialization, hyper-industrialism, and informatization characterize contemporary imperialist capitalism. Information companies are important in the global capitalist economy, which reflects a trend towards informatization, that is, the rise of the importance of information in the economy, but they are far less important than finance and the oil and gas industry.

Share of Selected Industries in Total Capital Assets of the World's Largest 2000 Corporations (Source: Forbes 2000, 2008 List)

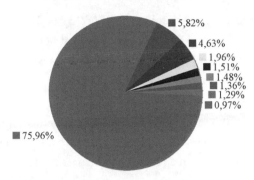

■ 5,82%
■ 4,63%
■ 1,96%
■ 1,51%
■ 1,48%
■ 1,36%
■ 1,29%
■ 0,97%

■ 75,96%

■ Finance (Banking, Financials, Insurance)
■ Oil & Gas Operations, Utilities
■ Information (Telecommunications, Technology Hardware & Equipment, Media, Software & Services, Semiconductors)
  Consumer Durables
■ Food (Food, Drinks & Tobacco; Food Markets; Hotel, Restaurants & Leisure)
■ Conglomerates
■ Materials
■ Transportation
■ Construction

Figure 7: Share of selected industries in total capital assets of the world's largest 2000 corporations in 2008 (data source: Forbes, 2000, 2009, list)

Data for the employment structure, value added, and capital assets show that depending on which indicator we use, we will achieve different results to the question to which extent contemporary capitalism is informational. Furthermore these data show that contemporary capitalism is not only informational, but also imperialistic and hyper-industrial (Fuchs, 2010a, 2010b, 2011). I therefore use the notion of informational capitalism not for designating that information, knowledge, or information technologies are the central aspects of contemporary society or economy but argue in a more pragmatic way that informational capitalism should be used as a term that characterizes all those parts of the economy that create informational goods or services. To which extent the capitalist economy is information-based can only be determined by empirical research.

I have already mentioned that class is a central characteristic of capitalism. For constructing a theory of informational capitalism, it is therefore necessary to discuss the notion of informational labour in relation to class analysis. In section 3, foundations of Marxian class analysis are introduced. In section 4, Marxian class analysis is related to informational labour.

Class analysis

Marx and Engels defined class in the following way: "By bourgeoisie is meant the class of modern capitalists, owners of the means of social production and employers of wage labour. By proletariat, the class of modern wage labourers, who, having no means of production of their own, are reduced to selling their labour power in order to live" (Marx and Engels, 1848, p. 35).

In contemporary society, also large groups that are outside of traditional wage-labour work live under precarious conditions. In the EU25 countries, the combined unemployment rate has always been above 7% in the past ten years, reaching 9% in 2002 and 2003 (Eurostat, online). In many of these countries (like Bulgaria, France, Greece, Italy, Latvia, Lithuania, Poland, Slovakia, Spain) an unemployment rate well above 10 or even 15% has not been an exception from the rule (Eurostat, online). The peak between the years 1996–2007 was a rate of 20.0% in 2002 in Poland (Eurostat, online). In the course of the new global economic crisis, the unemployment rate rose from 7.0% in June 2008 to 9.0% in May 2009 in the EU25 countries. The national rates reached peak levels in countries like Spain (18.7%), Latvia (16.3%), Estonia (15.6%), Lithuania (14.3%), Ireland (11.7%), Slovakia (11.1%), and Hungary (10.2%). These data are an indication that unemployment (and its consequences like increased poverty) is a pressing structural problem of contemporary society. Self-employed persons in Europe have an in-work poverty risk that is 2.5 times greater than the one of regular employees. 16% of the self-employed in the EU15 countries have an in-work poverty risk, compared to 6% of dependent employees (European Foundation for the Improvement of Living and Working Conditions, 2007). These data are an indication that many people outside of regular employment relations are facing precarious living and working conditions. Nonetheless, their material situation is comparable to many people who are wage labourers. Therefore it would be an analytical and political error to not include these people into the category of the proletariat. The data are an indication that today the category of the proletariat should not be limited to industrial wage labour. These days the definition of the proletariat as "the class of modern wage labourers" is not suitable anymore.

But there is a second line of thought in Marx's class theory that is more appropriate under contemporary conditions. Marx highlights exploitation as the fundamental aspect of class in another passage where he says that "the driving motive and determining purpose of capitalist production" is "the greatest possible exploitation of labour-power by the capitalist" (Marx, 1867, p. 449). Antagonistic class relations arise due to exploitation: "The control exercised by the capitalist is not only a special function arising from the nature of the social labour process, and peculiar to that process, but it is at the same time a function of the exploitation of a social labour process, and is consequently conditioned by the unavoidable antagonism between the exploiter and the raw material of his exploitation" (Marx, 1867, p. 449).

The exploited class is "free from, unencumbered by, any means of production of their own", which would mean the "complete separation between the workers and the ownership of the conditions or the realization of their labour" (Marx, 1867, p. 874). The proletariat is "a machine for the production of surplus-value", capitalists are "a machine for the transformation of this surplus-value into surplus capital" (Marx, 1867, p. 742). In his analysis, Marx had to limit the class concept to wage labour under the conditions of 19th century industrialism.

In the three volumes of *Capital*, Marx analyzes the accumulation process of capital. This process, as described by Marx, is visualized in figure 8. The introduction of some important categories that Marx employs can summarize this account.

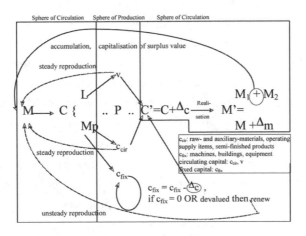

Figure 8: The accumulation/expanded reproduction of capital

Marx's theory is a labour theory of value, which is a theory that draws conclusion from the analysis of the total labour time that is needed for the production of goods. It is also a critique of value, which means that the forms that value takes in capitalism and the practices and ideologies that are based on this form are questioned. The value of a good is the total time that is needed for its production. The more value a good has, the longer its production takes. At the level of prices, this can be observed by the fact that labour-intensive goods are frequently more expensive than goods with low labour intensity. Marx argues that the cell form of capitalism is the commodity, goods that are exchanged in a certain quantitative relationship with money (x amount of commodity A = y units of money). He says that in societies that are based on the economic principle of exchange, goods have a use value and an exchange value. The use value is the qualitative aspect of a good; it is a utility that satisfies certain human needs. In exchange-based societies, humans can only get hold of such goods by exchanging other goods (such as money or their labour power) with the needed goods in certain quantitative relationships (x commodity A = y commodity B). Concrete labour is a category that is used for describing the creation of the use value of a good by humans. Abstract labour is a category employed for signifying the creation of the value of a good, i.e., the objectified labour time needed for its production. Marx sees money as the general equivalent of exchange; it simplifies the exchange of commodities and is therefore a general commodity.

In the accumulation of capital, capitalists buy labour power and means of production (raw materials, technologies, etc.) in order to produce new commodities that are sold with the expectation to make money profit that is partly reinvested. Marx distinguishes two spheres of capital accumulation: the circulation sphere and the sphere of production. In the circulation sphere, capital transforms its value form: First money M is transformed into commodities (from the standpoint of the capitalist as buyer), the capitalist purchases the commodities labour power L and means of production Mp. M-C is based on the two purchases M-L and M-Mp. In capitalism, labour power is separated from the means of production, "the mass of the people, the workers, [. . .] come face to face with the non-workers, the former as non-owners, the latter as the owners, of these means of production" (Marx, 1885, p. 116). This means that due to private property structures, workers do not own the means of production, the products they produce, and the profit they generate. Capitalists own these resources.

In the sphere of production, a new good is produced: the value of labour power and the value of the means of production are added to the product. Value takes on the form of productive capital P. The value form of labour is variable capital v (which can be observed as wages), the value form of the means of production constant capital c (which can be observed as the total price of the means of production/producer goods).

That part of capital, therefore, which is turned into means of production, i.e. the raw material, the auxiliary material and the instruments of labour, does not undergo any quantitative alteration of value in the process of production. For this reason, I call it the constant part of capital, or more briefly, constant capital. On the other hand, that part of capital which is turned into labour-power does undergo an alteration of value in the process of production. It both reproduces the equivalent of its own value and produces an excess, a surplus-value, which may itself vary, and be more or less according to circumstances. This part of capital is continually being transformed from a constant into a variable magnitude. I therefore call it the variable part of capital, or more briefly, variable capital. (Marx, 1867, p. 317)

Constant capital consists of two parts: circulating constant capital c_{cir} (the value of the utilized raw materials, auxiliary materials, operating supply items and semi-finished products) and fixed constant capital c_{fix} (the value of the utilized machines, buildings and equipment) (Marx 1885, chapter 8). c_{cir} and v together form circulating capital: They transfuse their value totally to the product and must be constantly renewed. c_{fix} remains fixed in the production process for many turnovers of capital. The turnover time of capital is the sum of its circulation time and its production time (Marx, 1885, p. 236). Circulation time is the time that capital takes to be transformed from its commodity form into the money form and later from its money form to its commodity form. Production time is the time that capital takes in the sphere of production.

Fixed constant capital decreases its value in each turnover of capital. Its value is decreased by the amount of (c, which is a flexible value. Fixed constant capital like machinery does not create value and its value is never entirely transfused to capital at once. It is depreciated by wear and tear, non-usage, and moral depreciation (i.e., the emergence of new machinery with increased productivity).

A part of the capital value advanced is fixed in this form, which is determined by the function of the means of labour in the process. As a means of labour functions and is used up, one part of its value passes over to the product, while another part remains fixed in the means of labour and hence in the production process. The value fixed in this way steadily declines, until the means of labour is worn out and has therefore distributed its value, in a longer or shorter period, over the volume of products that has emerged from a series of continually repeated labour processes. (Marx, 1885, p. 237).

In the sphere of production, capital stops its metamorphosis so that capital circulation comes to a halt. New value V' of the commodity is produced, V' contains the value of the necessary constant and variable capital and surplus value (s of the surplus product. Surplus value is generated by unpaid labour. Capitalists do not pay for the production of surplus, therefore the production of surplus value can be considered as a process of exploitation. The value V' of the new commodity after production is V' = c + v + s. The commodity then leaves the sphere of production and again enters the circulation sphere, in which capital conducts its next metamorphosis: By being sold on the market it is transformed from the commodity form back into the money form. Surplus value is realized in the form of money value. The initial money capital M now takes on the form M' = M + (m, it has been increased by an increment (m. Accumulation of capital means that the produced surplus value is (partly) reinvested/capitalized. The end point of one process M' becomes the starting point of a new accumulation process. One part of M', M_1, is reinvested. Accumulation means the aggregation of capital by investment and exploitation in the capital circuit M-C. .P. .C'-M', in which the end product M' becomes a new starting point M. The total process makes up the dynamic character of capital. Capital is money that is permanently increasing due to the exploitation of surplus value.

Commodities are sold at prices that are higher than the investment costs so that money profit is generated. For Marx, one decisive quality of capital accumulation is that profit is an emergent property of production that is produced by labour, but owned by the capitalists. Without labour no profit could be made. Workers are forced to enter class relations and to produce profit in order to survive, which enables capital to appropriate surplus. The notion of exploited surplus value is the main concept of Marx's theory, by which he intends to show that capitalism is a class society. "The theory of surplus value is in consequence immediately the theory of exploitation" (Negri, 1991, p. 74) and, one can add, the theory of class and as a consequence the political demand for a classless society.

Enrique Dussel argues that in his work on the *Grundrisse*, Marx had "for the first time in his work . . . discovered the category of surplus value" (Dussel, 2008, p. 77) in December, 1857. "If the worker needs only half a working day in order to live a whole day, then, in order to keep alive as a worker, he needs to work only half a day. The second half of the day is forced labour; surplus labour" (Marx, 1857/58, p. 324). Surplus value also means that workers are compelled to work more than necessary for satisfying their immediate needs, they produce an excess for free that is appropriated by capitalists: "What appears as surplus value on capital's side appears identically on the worker's side as surplus labour in excess of his requirements as worker, hence in excess of his immediate requirements for keeping himself alive" (Marx, 1857/58, p. 324f).

> The surplus value which capital obtains through the production process consists only of the excess of surplus labour over necessary labour. The increase in productive force can increase surplus labour—i.e. the excess of labour objectified in capital as product over the labour objectified in the exchange value of the working day—only to the extent that it diminishes the relation of necessary labour to surplus labour, and only in the pro- portion in which it diminishes this relation. Surplus value is exactly equal to surplus labour; the increase of one [is] exactly measured by the diminution of necessary labour. (Marx 1857/58, 339)

The capitalist "wants to produce a commodity greater in value than the sum of the values of the commodities used to produce it, namely the means of production and the labour-power he purchased with his good money on the open market. His aim is to produce not only a use-value, but a commodity; not only use-value, but value; and not just value, but also surplus value [. . .] The cotton originally bought for £100 is for example re-sold at £100 + £10, i.e. £110. The complete form of this process is therefore M-C-M', where M' = M + ΔM, i.e. the original sum advanced plus an increment. This increment or excess over the original value I call 'surplus-value'" (Marx, 1867, pp. 293, 251).

Capital is not money, but money that is increased through accumulation, "money which begets money" (Marx, 1867, p. 256). Marx argues that the value of labour power is the average amount of time that is needed for the production of goods that are necessary for survival (necessary labour time), which in capitalism is paid for by workers with their wages. Surplus labour time is all labour time that exceeds necessary labour time, remains unpaid, is appropriated for free by capital- ists, and transformed into money profit.

Surplus value "is in substance the materialization of unpaid labour-time. The secret of the self-valorization of capital resolves itself into the fact that it has at its disposal a definite quantity of the unpaid labour of other people" (Marx, 1867, p. 672). Surplus value "costs the worker labour but the capitalist nothing", but "none the less becomes the legitimate property of the capitalist" (Marx, 1867, p. 672). "Capital also developed into a coercive relation, and this compels the working class to do more work than would be required by the narrow circle of its own needs. As an agent in producing the activity of others, as an extractor of surplus labour and an exploiter of labour-power, it surpasses all earlier systems of production, which were based on directly compulsory labour, in its energy and its quality of unbounded and ruthless activity" (Marx, 1867, p. 425). Surplus value also means that workers are compelled to work more than necessary for satisfying their immediate needs, they produce an excess for free that is appropriated by capitalists: "What appears as surplus value on capital's side appears identically on the worker's side as surplus labour in excess of his requirements as worker, hence in excess of his immediate requirements for keeping himself alive" (Marx, 1857/58, p. 324f).

Marx argues that capitalists are unproductive, they do not produce value, and that profit stems from the production of value by workers that is exploited and appropriated by capitalists. He uses the term productive labour in this context: Productive labour "produces surplus-value for the capitalist, or in other words contributes towards the self-valorization of capital" (Marx, 1867, p. 644). For Marx, capitalism is based on the permanent theft of unpaid labour from workers by capitalists. This is the reason why he characterizes capital as vampire and werewolf. "Capital is dead labour which, vampire-like, lives only by sucking living labour, and lives the more, the more labour it sucks" (Marx, 1867, p. 342). The production of surplus value "forms the specific content and purpose of capitalist production" (Marx, 1867, p. 411), it is "the *differentia specifica* of capitalist production", "the absolute law of this mode of production" (Marx, 1867, p. 769), the "driving force and the final result of the capitalist process of production" (Marx, 1867, p. 976).

The production and exploitation of surplus value is according to Marx the heart of class structuration and capitalism. Therefore we today have to deal with the question who the producers of surplus value are in an information age.

Informational Labour and Class

If one defines economic exploitation as the existence of an exploiting class that deprives at least one exploited class of its resources, excludes it from ownership, and appropriates resources produced by the exploited, one stays within a Marxist framework of class, but must not necessarily exclude the "underclasses" from this concept if one considers knowledge labour as central to contemporary society. Knowledge labour is labour that produces and distributes information, communication, social relationships, affects, and information and communication technologies. It is a direct and indirect aspect of the accumulation of capital in informational capitalism: there are direct knowledge workers (either employed as wage labour in firms or outsourced, self-employed labour) that produce knowledge goods and services that are sold as commodities on the market (for example software, data, statistics, expertise, consultancy, advertisements, media content, films, music, etc.) and indirect knowledge workers that produce and reproduce the social conditions of the existence of capital and wage labour such as education, social relationships, affects, communication, sex, housework, common knowledge in everyday life, natural resources, nurture, care, etc. These are forms of unpaid labour that are necessary for the existence of society, they are performed not exclusively, but to a certain extent by those who do not have regular wage labour–houseworkers, the unemployed, retirees, students, precarious and informal workers, underpaid workers in temporal or part-time jobs, and migrants. This unpaid labour is reproductive in the sense that it reproduces and enables the existence of capital and wage labour that consume the goods and services of unpaid reproductive workers for free. Therefore both capital and wage labour exploit reproductive workers—which is just another term for indirect knowledge workers. Capital could not be accumulated without activities in a common societal infrastructure in the areas of education, spare time, health and social care, natural resources, culture, art, sexuality, friendship, science, media, morals, sports, housework, etc. that are taken for granted and do not have to be paid for by capital (in the form of shares of its profits). Marx remarks in this context that the rise in the rate of profit in one line of industry depends on the development of the productive power of labour in another sector of the economy (1894, p. 175). This can also mean that accumulation in the wage labour economy is not only based on its own advances but also on the non-wage labour economy. "What the capitalist makes use of here are the benefits of the entire system of the social division of labour" (Marx, 1894, p. 175). This system of the division of labour also includes a non-wage economy that is dialectically separated from and connected to the wage economy and is exploited by capital.

By consuming reproductive labour and public goods and services, wage labour is reproducing itself. Wage labourers exploit reproductive workers in order to be able to be exploited by capital. Therefore we can define the multitude, the contemporary proletariat, as the class of those who produce material or knowledge goods and services directly or indirectly for capital and are deprived and expropriated of resources by capital. Such exploited resources are consumed by capital for free. In informational capitalism, knowledge has become a productive force, but knowledge is not only produced in corporations in the form of knowledge goods but also in everyday life, for example by parents who educate their children, citizens who engage in everyday politics, consumers of media who produce social meaning and hence are prosumers, users of MySpace, YouTube, Facebook, etc. who produce informational content that is appropriated by capital, radio listeners and television viewers who call in live on air in order to discuss with studio guests and convey their ideas that are instantly commodified in the real-time economy, etc. The production process of knowledge is a social, common process, but knowledge is appropriated by capital. By this appropriation, the producers of knowledge become just like traditional industrial labour an exploited class that can with reference to Hardt and Negri (2000, 2004) be termed the multitude. The multitude is an expanded notion of class that goes beyond manual wage labour and takes into account that labour has become more common.

Hardt and Negri (2000, 2004, 2009) never outlined the subclasses of the multitude. The multitude, as the class of all those who are in some sense exploited, in my opinion consists of the following class fractions:

1. Traditional industrial workers, who are wage labourers and produce physical goods. Capital appropriates the physical goods of these workers and the surplus value contained in them.

2. Knowledge workers, who are wage labourers and produce knowledge goods and services in wage-relationships or self-employed labour relations. Capital appropriates the knowledge goods and services of these workers and the surplus value contained in them. One must note that public servants in areas such as health, education, transport, social care, housing, energy, and so on, are not under the direct command of capital. Most of them are waged knowledge workers who produce parts of the commons that are a necessary condition for the existence of society and capital. The latter exploits these public goods in an indirect way.

3. Houseworkers: These workers—who are still predominantly female—produce knowledge in the broad sense of communication, affects, sexuality, domestic goods and services that are not sold as commodities but consumed by capitalists and wage labourers for free in order to reproduce manpower.

4. The unemployed: This class is deprived of job assets by capital and wage labour. It is the result of the tendency of the organic composition of capital to rise (the relationship of constant and variable capital), which is due to technological progress. The unemployed are, just like houseworkers, involved in unpaid reproductive knowledge labour that is a necessary con-

dition for the existence of capital. Furthermore, the unemployed are frequently forced to take on very low-paid and often precarious or illegal jobs and hence are also subjected to extreme economic appropriation. Unemployed persons are in numerous instances forced by the state to perform extremely low-paid, compulsory, over-exploited work.

5. Migrants and workers in developing countries: Migrants are frequently subjected to extreme economic exploitation in racist relations of production as illegal, over-exploited workers. They are exploited by capital. A certain share of wage labourers who hope to increase their wages and to reach better positions if migrants can be forced to do unpaid or extremely low-paid unskilled work, ideologically supports this exploitation. Developing countries are either completely excluded from exploitation or they are considered as a sphere of cheap, unskilled wage labour that is over-exploited by capital by paying extremely low wages and ignoring labour rights and standards.

6. Retirees: Retirees are exploited to the extent that they act as unpaid reproductive workers in spheres such as the family, social care, home care, and education.

7. Students: Students are exploited in the sense that they produce and reproduce intellectual knowledge and skills that are appropriated by capital for free as part of the commons. Students are furthermore frequently over-exploited as precarious workers, a phenomenon for which terms such as "precariat", "generation internship", or "praktikariat" (from the German term "Praktikum", which means internship, combined with the term "precariat") can be employed.

8. Precarious and informal workers: Part-time workers, temporary workers, the fractionally employed, contract labour, bogus self-employment, etc., are work relations that are temporary, insecure, and low paid. Hence these workers are over-exploited by capital in the sense that such jobs would cost much more for capital if they were performed by regularly employed workers. The same situation can be found in the case of racist labour relations and compulsory work performed by unemployed persons. Self-employed persons who do not employ others themselves are forced to sell their own labour power by contracts. They control their means of production, but produce surplus for others who control capital and use the appropriated labour for achieving profit.

I have used the term over-exploitation here several times. Capital can gain extra surplus value by over-exploitation. Extra surplus value is a term coined by Marx for describing relations of production, in which goods are produced in a way that the "individual value of these articles is now below their social value" (Marx, 1867, p. 434). By employing illegal migrants, unemployed compulsory or illegal workers, students, precarious and informal workers, capital can produce goods at a value that is lower than the average social value because its wage costs are lower than in a regular employment relationship. As a result the commodities produced contain less variable capital but are nonetheless sold at regular prices so that an extra profit can be obtained. By employing or outsourcing labour to over-exploited workers, the wage costs for capital are lower then in the case that the same work is conducted by regularly paid wage labour. As a result, more profit can be achieved. The total value of a commodity is $V = c + v + s$ (constant capital + variable capital + surplus value). By over-exploitation, variable capital and the total value of the commodity are lowered, the commodity can be sold at regular market prices and thus extra profit can be achieved. Those who are outside of regular employment, such as students, pensioners, the unemployed, and illegal immigrants, are particularly active in reproductive labour that produces the social, educational, and knowledge commons of society. All of these activities indirectly benefit capital accumulation. If capital had to pay for this labour, its profits would probably decrease drastically. Therefore it can be argued that capital accumulation is advanced by outsourcing reproductive labour from corporations to the private and public realm, where especially groups like young people, parents, teachers, the unemployed, pensioners, and illegal immigrants engage in producing the commons of society that are a necessary condition for the existence of the capitalist economy. This process of outsourcing is free for capital, the informal workers are over-exploited to an extreme extent (if they receive no money at all, the rate of exploitation is infinite). Capital makes use of gratis labour, which is just another formulation for saying that capital exploits all members of society except for itself.

Rosa Luxemburg (1913/2003) argued that capital accumulation feeds on the exploitation of milieus that are drawn into the capitalist system: "Capital feeds on the ruins of such organisations, and, although this non-capitalist milieu is indispensable for accumulation, the latter proceeds, at the cost of this medium nevertheless, by eating it up" (1913/2003, p. 363). This idea was used for explaining the existence of colonies of imperialism by Luxemburg and was applied by Marxist Feminism in order to argue that unpaid reproductive labour can be considered as an inner colony and milieu of primitive accumulation of capitalism (Mies, Bennholdt-Thomsen and Werlhof, 1988; Mies, 1986; Werlhof, 1991). Non-wage labour "ensures the reproduction of labour power and living conditions" (Mies et al., 1988, p. 18). It is labour spent "in the production of life, or subsistence production" (Mies et al., 1988, p. 70). Primitive accumulation "is overt violence, with the aim of robbery [VSA2]wherever, whenever, and against whomever this is 'economically' necessary, politically possible and technically feasible" (Mies et al., 1988, p. 102). In post-Fordist capitalism, the inner colonies of capitalism are expanded so that profits rise by generating milieus of low-paid and unpaid labour. The formation of these colonies is a form of ongoing primitive accumulation that uses violence for expropriating labour. "Women, colonies and nature" are "the main targets of this process of ongoing primitive accumulation" (Mies et al., 1988, p. 6). This phenomenon has been termed "housewifization" (Mies et al., 1988; Mies, 1986): more and more people live and work under precarious conditions that have traditionally been characteristic for patriarchal relations. People working under such conditions are, like housewives, a source of uncontrolled and unlimited exploitation. Housewifization transforms labour so that it "bears the characteristics of housework, namely, labour not protected by trade unions or labour laws, that is available at any time, for any price, that is not recognized as 'labour' but as an 'activity', as in the 'income generating activities', meaning isolated and unorganized and so on" (Mies, Benholdt-Thomsen and Werlhof, 1988, p. 10). Housewifized labour is characterized by "no job permanency, the lowest wages, longest working hours, most monotonous work, no trade unions, no opportunity to obtain higher qualifications, no promotion, no rights and no social security" (Mies et al., 1988, p. 169). Such informal work is "a source of unchecked, unlimited exploitation" (Mies, 1986, p. 16). Housewifized labour is "superexploitation of non-wage labourers . . . upon which wage labour exploitation then is possible" (Mies, 1986, p. 48) because it involves the "externalization, or ex-territorialization of costs which otherwise would have to be covered by the capitalists" (Mies, 1986, p. 110).

Toni Negri uses the term "social worker" for arguing that there is a broadening of the proletariat that is "now extended throughout the entire span of production and reproduction" (Negri, 1982, p. 209). The concept of the social worker has been combined with the one of immaterial labour in the category of the multitude. According to Hardt and Negri, relationships, communication, and knowledge are goods that are produced in common but appropriated by capital for economic ends. Hence, exploitation today is "the expropriation of the common" (Hardt and

Negri, 2004, p. 150). Exploitation today is also the exploitation of human creative capacities. The multitude or proletariat is formed by "all those who labour and produce under the rule of capital" (Hardt and Negri, 2004, p. 106), "all those whose labour is directly or indirectly exploited by and subjected to capitalist norms of production and reproduction" (Hardt and Negri, 2000, p. 52), the "entire cooperating multitude" (Hardt and Negri, 2000, p. 402). The formation of the multitude can be seen as the colonization and housewifization of all of society. Marxist feminism and autonomist Marxism share the view that the exploitation of non-wage labour is a crucial feature of class in capitalism.

Rosa Luxemburg's work showed that capital generates new spheres of exploitation. Marxist feminist analyses applied these accounts to housework. We can base our analyses on these insights, but need to go beyond them because these accounts did not discuss the role of knowledge and new media in capitalism. Hardt and Negri can be read as expanded concretization of Luxemburg and the notion of reproductive labour. Their category of immaterial labour broaches the issue of knowledge labour in capitalism but still remains at a level of high abstraction so that their account does not identify which groups exactly belong to the multitude and lacks a theoretical class model. It is therefore necessary to build on and go beyond these approaches.

Class relationships have become generalized. The production of surplus value and hence exploitation are not limited to wage-labour but reach society as a whole. Houseworkers, the unemployed, migrants, developing countries, retirees working in reproduction, students, precarious and informal workers should, besides wage labour, be considered as exploited classes that form part of the multitude. The latter is antagonistic in character and traversed by inner lines of exploitation, oppression, and domination that segment the multitude and create inner classes and class fractions. Nonetheless, the multitude is objectively united by the fact that it consists of all those individuals and groups that are exploited by the capital, live and produce directly and indirectly for the capital that expropriates and appropriates resources (commodities, labour power, the commons, knowledge, nature, public infrastructures and services) that are produced and reproduced by the multitude in common.

The growing number of those who produce the commons and are exploited outside of regular wage relationships can be included in a class model as exploited classes (see Figure 7.1). In this model, wage labour is subdivided by the amount of skills and authority that it possesses in the production process (Wright, 1997). Note that an individual can be positioned in more than one class at a time. Class positions are not fixed, but dynamic, meaning that in informational capitalism people have a fluid and transit class status. So, for example, female wage workers are frequently at the same time houseworkers; many students are also precarious workers; many precarious workers form a type of self-employed labour, and so on. That class positions are antagonistic also means that there is no clear-cut separation between the multitude and the capitalist class, so, for example managers can be considered to have a contradictory class position: they work for a wage, but at the same time execute the command over workers in the name of capital.

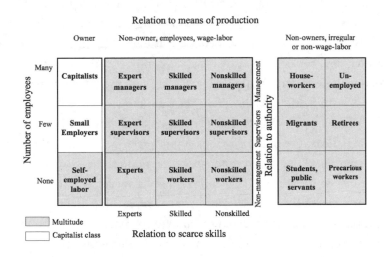

Figure 9: An expanded class model

Knowledge is a social and historical product; new knowledge emerges from the historical heritage of knowledge in society and is in many cases produced co-operatively. Hence, Marx argued that knowledge is "universal labour" that is "brought about partly by the cooperation of men now living, but partly also by building on earlier work" (Marx, 1894, p. 199). Nature, knowledge, and societal infra-structures due to their collective or natural form of production are common aspects of society. They are not produced by single individuals. "Communal labour, however, simply involves the direct cooperation of individuals" (Marx, 1894, p. 199): Marx stressed the co-operative character of knowledge production. Knowledge and infrastructures can only exist due to the collective activities of many. Nature produces itself and is transformed into resources by metabolic processes organized by many. Knowledge, nature, and infrastructures are collective goods that cost nothing for capital, but they are a necessary condition for capital accumulation. They enter production processes and capital profits from them. Capital consumes the commons for free; it exploits the results of societal and natural production processes such as education, science, health, reproductive labour, and so on. The essence of the commons is its social character, but in capitalism the commons are individually appropriated by capital. In categories of the Hegelian logic, one can argue that essence and existence of knowledge and the commons are non-identical. Exploitation alienates the existence of the commons from their essence and their truth, reason, and reality.

All humans benefit from knowledge in society that was produced in the past (inherited, historical knowledge) in the form of organizations that allow the development of skills (educational knowledge), cultural goods (music, theatre performances, literature, books, films, artworks, philosophy, etc.) that contribute to mental reproduction (entertainment knowledge) and in the form of traditional practices as aspects of education and socialization (practical knowledge). These four forms of knowledge are handed over to future generations and enriched by present generations through the course of the development of society. All humans contribute and benefit therefrom (although to different degrees under the given circumstances). Another form of knowledge is technological knowledge that is objectified in machines and practices that function as means for reaching identified goals so that labour processes are accelerated and the amount of externalized labour power can be reduced. Not all humans and groups benefit from the five types of knowledge to the same extent. Especially corporations consume a share above average. Educational, entertainment, and practical knowledge are aspects of the reproduction of manpower. Individuals and society perform these processes to a large extent outside of firms and labour time. Technological progress helps corporations to increase their productivity, that is, the ability of capital to produce ever more profit in even less time. Technological knowledge does not enter the production process indirectly as the other three forms of knowledge do; it is directly employed in the production process by capital. Technological knowledge is produced by society, but it is individually appropriated as a means of production by capital. One argument that some scholars employ is that corporations pay for technological progress in the form of machines, software, hardware, and so on that they buy as fixed capital. But the value produced by labour with the help of technology is much larger than the value of technology as such, and each individual item of technology is based on the whole history of technology and engineering that enters the product for free.

Another argument is that technological knowledge and progress are created in an industry that produces technology and in the research departments of corporations. This argument is deficient because a certain part of knowledge is produced in public research institutions and universities and each technological innovation is based on the whole state of the art of science, for which one does not have to pay and which is consumed by research departments and technology-producing corporations for free as an external resource.

The result of this discussion is that corporations consume the commons of society that consist of nature, inherited knowledge, educational knowledge, entertainment knowledge, practical knowledge, technological knowledge, and public infrastructures (labour in the areas of health, education, medical services, social services, culture, media, politics, etc.) for free. Hence, one important form of exploitation in the knowledge society is the exploitation of the commons by capital, which is also exploitation of the multitude and of society as a whole. But are capitalists and small employers not as well part of the multitude in the sense that they contribute to the production and reproduction of the commons in everyday life? There is no doubt that all humans contribute certain shares of unpaid labour to the production and reproduction of nature, knowledge, and services. But the capitalist class is the only class in society that exploits and expropriates the commons—it is the only class that derives economic profit and accumulates capital with the help of the appropriation of the commons. All humans produce, reproduce, and consume the commons, but only the capitalist class exploits the commons economically. Hence, this class should not be considered as a part of the multitude. With the rise of informational capitalism, the exploitation of the commons has become a central process of capital accumulation.

The immediate effects of surplus-value production in class relations are that the product belongs to the capitalist and not to the worker and that surplus-value "costs the worker labour but the capitalist nothing, and . . . becomes the legitimate property of the capitalist" (Marx, 1867, p. 731). If you do not produce cotton, the example mentioned by Marx (1867, p. 251) for defining surplus value, but knowledge, such as for example the Microsoft Windows Vista operating system, the decisive quality is that knowledge only needs to be produced once, can be infinitely reproduced at low costs and distributed at high speed. There is no physical wear and tear of the product, knowledge is not used up in consumption, it can be reworked and built upon. There are high initial production costs, but once knowledge as, for example, software is produced, it can be cheaply copied and sold at high prices. The constant and variable capital costs for reproduction are low, which is beneficial for sustained capital accumulation in the knowledge industries.

The situation again changes a little if knowledge is produced for new media and carried and distributed by it. A central characteristic of networked digital media is that the consumer of knowledge has the potential to become its producer. Alvin Toffler (1980) spoke of the emergence of the prosumer within the information society. Axel Bruns (2007, 2008) applied this notion to new media and speaks of produsers—users become producers of digital knowledge and technology. Philip Graham (2000) argues that hypercapitalism's immediacy and pervasiveness has resulted in the entanglement of production, circulation, consumption, material and non-material production, productive and unproductive labour, base and superstructure, forces and relations of production. Therefore value creation "becomes an immediate, continuous process" (Graham, 2000, p. 137). New media are simultaneously used for the production, circulation, and consumption of knowledge. They support cognition (thought, language), communication (one-to-one, one-to-few, one-to-many, few-to-one, few-to-few, few-to-many, many-to-one, many-to-few, many-to-many), and cooperation (peer production, sharing, virtual communities, social networking, cyberlove, online collaboration, etc.) by combining the universal digital machine of the computer with networking functions as structural principles (Fuchs, 2008b). In informational capitalism, the brain and its bodily mediations are enabled to engage in organic practices of economic production, surplus-value generation, co-production, communicative circulation, and productive consumption by new media. The production of knowledge is based on the prior consumption of the same, in co-production as well on communicative interchange as a coordinative mechanism. Consumption of knowledge produces individual meaning and incentives for further social production and communication. Circulation of knowledge is the consumption of bandwidth and technical resources and the production of connections.

For Marx, the profit rate is the relation of profit to investment costs: $p = s / (c + v)$ = surplus value / (constant capital + variable capital). If the users become productive, then in terms of Marxian class theory this means that they become productive labourers who produce surplus value and are exploited by capital, because for Marx, productive labour generates surplus. Therefore, the exploitation of surplus value in cases like Google, YouTube, MySpace, or Facebook is not merely accomplished by those who are employed by these corporations for programming, updating, and maintaining the soft- and hardware, performing marketing activities, and so on, but by these employees, the users, and the produsers that engage in the production of user-generated content. New media corporations do not (or hardly) pay the users for the production of content. One accumulation strategy is to give them free access to services and platforms, let them produce content, and to accumulate a large number of produsers that are sold as a commodity to third-party advertisers. Not a product is sold to the users, but the users are sold as a commodity to advertisers. The more users a platform has, the higher the advertising rates can be set. The productive labour time that is exploited by capital on the one hand involves the labour time of the paid employees and on the other hand all of the time that is spent online by the users. For the first type of knowledge labour, new media corporations pay salaries. The second type of knowledge is produced completely for free. There are neither variable nor constant investment costs. The formula for the profit rate needs to be transformed for this accumulation strategy:

$p = s / (c + v1 + v2)$ (s . . . surplus value, c . . . constant capital, v1 . . . wages paid to fixed employees, v2 . . . wages paid to users)

The typical situation is that $v2 => 0$ and that v2 substitutes v1. If the production of content and the time spent online were carried out by paid employees, the variable costs would rise and profits would therefore decrease. This shows that produsage in a capitalist society can be interpreted as the outsourcing of productive labour to users who work completely for free and help maximize the rate of exploitation ($e = s / v$, = surplus value / variable capital) so that profits can be raised and new media capital may be accumulated. If the wages paid to users converges towards zero, then the rate of exploitation $e = s / v$ converges towards infinity. Capitalist produsage is an extreme form of exploitation, in which the produsers work completely for free and are infinitely exploited.

Produsage in a capitalist society can be interpreted as the outsourcing of productive labour from wage labour to users who work completely for free and help maximizing the rate of exploitation ($e = s / v$, = surplus value / variable capital) so that profits can be raised and new media capital can be accumulated. This is a situation that converges towards infinite exploitation: $e = s / v$: $v => 0$ => exploitation=>infinity.

That surplus value generating labour is an emergent property of capitalist production, means that production and accumulation will break down if this labour is withdrawn. It is an essential part of the capitalist production process. That produsers conduct surplus-generating labour, can also be seen by imagining what would happen if they would stop using platforms like YouTube, MySpace, and Facebook: the number of users would drop, advertisers would stop investing in online advertising because no objects for their advertising messages and therefore no potential customers for their products could be found, the profits of the new media corporations would drop, and they would go bankrupt. If such activities were carried out on a large scale, a new economy crisis would arise. This thought experiment shows that users are essential for generating profit in the new media economy. Furthermore they produce and co-produce parts of the products, and therefore parts of the use value, exchange value, and surplus value that are objectified in these products.

Dallas Smythe (1981/2006) suggests that in the case of media advertisement models, the audience is sold as a commodity to advertisers: "Because audience power is produced, sold, purchased and consumed, it commands a price and is a commodity. . . . You audience members contribute your unpaid work time and in exchange you receive the program material and the explicit advertisements" (Smythe, 1981/2006, pp. 233, 238).

With the rise of user-generated content, free access social networking platforms, and other free access platforms that yield profit by online advertisement—a development subsumed under categories such as web 2.0, social software, and social networking sites—the web seems to come close to accumulation strategies employed by the capital on traditional mass media like TV or radio. The users who Google data, upload or watch videos on YouTube, upload or browse personal images on Flickr, or accumulate friends with whom they exchange content or communicate online via social networking platforms like MySpace or Facebook, constitute an audience commodity that is sold to advertisers. The difference between the audience commodity on traditional mass media and on the Internet, is that in the latter case the users are also content producers, there is user-generated content, the users engage in permanent creative activity, communication, community building, and content-production. That the users are more active on the Internet than in the reception of TV or radio content is due to the decentralized structure of the Internet, which allows many-to-many communication. Due to the permanent activity of the recipients and their status as produsers, we can say that in the case of the Internet, the audience commodity is a produser commodity. The category of the produser commodity does not signify a democratization of the media towards a participatory or democratic system but the total commodification of human creativity. During much of the time that users spend online, they produce profit for large corporations like Google, News Corp. (which owns MySpace), or Yahoo! (which owns Flickr), and other Internet firms. Advertisements on the Internet are frequently personalized; this is made possible by surveilling, storing, and assessing user activities with the help of computers and databases. This is another difference from TV and radio, which provide less individualized content and advertisements due to their more centralized structure. But one can also observe a certain shift in the area of traditional mass media, as in the cases of pay per view, tele-votes, talk shows, and call-in TV and radio shows. In the case of the Internet, the commodification of audience participation is easier to achieve than with other mass media.

Marx has anticipated the exploitation of produsers by arguing that as a result of the development of the productive forces a time of capitalist development will come, in which "general intellect", the "power of knowledge, objectified", "general social knowledge has become a direct force of production" (Marx 1857/58, 706). The productive forces would not only be produced in the form of knowledge, but also as "immediate organs of social practice, of the real life process". Marx here describes that in a knowledge society, social life becomes productive. That knowledge labour, such as the one performed online by produsers, is productive, then also means that under capitalist class relations it is exploited and that all knowledge workers, unpaid and paid, are part of an exploited class.

"By putting the means of production into the hands of the masses but withholding from those masses any ownership over the products of their communal work, the World Wide Computer provides an incredibly efficient mechanism for harvesting the economic value of the labor provided by the very many and concentrating it in the hands of the very few" (Carr 2009, 142f). Figure 10 shows the rapid growth of profits from Internet advertising in the United States. These profits amounted to 23.4 billion US$ in 2008, which make up 11.0% of the total U.S. advertising profits (data source: IAB Internet Advertising Revenue Report 2008). The online advertising profits were higher than the profits made by radio and cable TV advertising in 2008 and were only exceeded by profits in newspaper- and TV distribution-advertising (data source: IAB Internet Advertising Revenue Report 2008).

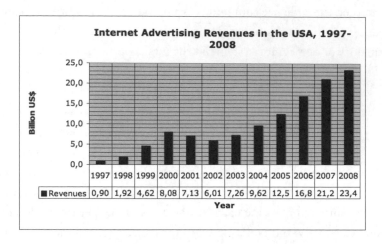

Figure 10: Internet advertising revenues in the United States, 1997–2008, data source: IAB
Internet Advertising Revenue Report 2008

Internet users come from all backgrounds. So for example the relative majority of YouTube users in the US is aged 18–34 (36%), 13% have obtained graduate
degrees. 49% of U.S. MySpace users come from lower income classes (< 60,000 US$
per year), whereas 58% of U.S. Facebook users have an upper income class background. 9% of U.S. Myspace users and 14% of U.S. Facebook users have graduated. 58% of U.S. Google users come from upper income classes. 56% of U.S.
MySpace users have attended no college or graduate school, whereas 42% of U.S.
Facebook users have attended college and 14% have graduated. 58% of YouTube
users, 73% of Facebook users, and 76% of Facebook users in the U.S. are aged 3–34
(all data by quantcast.com, accessed on July 18, 2009). Such data show that Internet
users have diverse backgrounds in terms of age, income, and education. The class
structure of the virtual world is not a reproduction of the class structure of the offline
world. The most decisive difference is that many more younger people produce
online than offline. Children, pupils, and students who do not have a regular paid
employment form the primary group of exploited produsers. Expressed cynically,
we can say that the Internet is today the primary space for the exploitation of child
labour. This example shows that it is necessary to go beyond the traditional class concept that considers only wage labour as productive and exploited, because there are
also many unpaid labourers who are necessary for the accumulation of capital
accumulation.

Conclusion

The aim of this chapter was to make a contribution to the debate on the role of class in informational capitalism. I first argued that the notion of informational capitalism is preferable to the one of cognitive capitalism because it is based on a subject-object-dialectic, whereas the concept of cognitive capitalism that has been introduced by autonomist Marxism is subjectivistic and idealistic. I also stressed that the claims that knowledge or information technology are the dominant qualities of contemporary society, economy, or capitalism are overdrawn because there are also other important phenomena such as globalization, financialization, and hyper-industrialism that shape contemporary society. Therefore the notion of informational capitalism should be used carefully and in a pragmatic way for characterizing those aspects of the economy that are information based. This is different from saying that society or the economy is dominated by information, knowledge, or information technology. I also analyzed in this chapter the relationship of class and information labour in informational capitalism based on Marxian class analysis.

If one considers knowledge not as a narrow but as a broad social category, then it becomes clear that it is not an economic category specific for a sector but also lies at the heart of class formation in informational capitalism. Knowledge forms part of the commons of society, it is a social product produced and consumed by all. All humans produce, reproduce, and consume the commons, but only the capitalist class exploits the commons economically. The multitude is an expanded Marxist class category that is used for describing the common labour class that produces the commons and is exploited by capital that appropriates the commons for free and subsumes them under capital in order to gain profit. The political demand underlying the argument that nobody is unproductive and that each human being is a productive worker producing and reproducing the commons of society that are appropriated by capital, is that capital should in return give something back to society in the form of taxes that are used for compensating society and its members for the theft of the commons by installing the common form of a guaranteed basic income.

Broadening the notion of class is necessary because the development of capitalism and the productive forces have increased the significance of non-wage workers. Therefore if Marxian class analysis is and wants to remain a political project, it needs to refine its notion of the potential agents of change. The proletariat "falls into a great number of constituent parts" (Thompson, 1960b, p. 24f). That more people are now "involved in the exchange of human services (welfare, education, entertainment and the like" shatters "traditional notions of the working-class as a fixed, unchanging category with a fixed consciousness and unchanging forms of expression" (Thompson, 1960b, p. 27). To broaden the notion of the proletariat is not a post-Marxist project applied to the economy. Post-Marxism sees universality as a totalitarian project (Laclau and Mouffe, 1985, p. 188) and argues for the primacy of a plurality of political subjects that are at best loosely connected. Laclau and Mouffe (1985) speak in this context of "the plurality of diverse and frequently contradictory positions" (1985, p. 84), "decentred subject positions" (1985, p. 87), the "plurality of political spaces" (1985, p. 137), the "rejection of privileged points of rupture and the confluence of struggles into a unified political space" (1985, p. 152), or the "polysemic character of every antagonism" (1985, p. 170). This chapter was specifically concerned with economic relationships, not with the relationship of the economic and the non-economic. Laclau and Mouffe have been primarily talking about the relationships of new social movements and the working class, but they have also pointed out that "workers' struggles are not universal, but have been numerous, and have assumed an extraordinary variety of forms" (1985, p. 167). Slavoj Žižek has in this context, in my opinion, correctly said that postmodernism and post-Marxism have, by assuming an "irreducible plurality of struggles", accepted "capitalism as 'the only game in town'" and have renounced "any real attempt to overcome the existing capitalist liberal regime" (Butler, Laclau and Žižek, 2000, p. 95).

Subordinating or equalizing the category of class to other antagonistic categories (gender, ethnicity, age, capabilities, etc.) poses the danger of burying the project and demands to establish participatory alternatives to the capitalist totality. All non-class antagonisms are articulated with class, whereas not all non-class antagonisms are articulated with each other, which means that all antagonisms of contemporary society have class aspects and are conditioned by class. Class is the antagonism that binds all other antagonisms together; it prefigures, conditions, enables and constrains, and exerts pressure on possibilities for other antagonisms (Fuchs, 2008b). At the same time, non-class antagonisms influence the class antagonism, so that complex dynamic relationships are present. If class is the super-antagonism of capitalism that does not determine or over determine, but conditions other antagonisms, then it is important to give specific attention to this category. The subdomains of the exploited class that were identified in this chapter can stand in antagonisms to each other, which in the actual world is frequently the case. So, for example, there are countries like Austria, where the majority of workers tends to vote for right-wing extremist parties and therefore politically supports racism and racist classism because they hope to improve their class position by achieving a downgrading of the class position of immigrant workers.

But given the possibility of the existence of internal antagonisms of the multitude, can there be a combined political project of the multitude that aims to overthrow capitalism? As Marx knew, a class-in-itself is not automatically a class-for-itself; there can be classes without class consciousness and without class struggles because defining the existence of a class based on the existence of a specific consciousness or practical political project is a philosophically idealistic, subjectivistic, and therefore also reductionistic move that negates Marxian analysis. The task is to construct political projects that aim at the connection of the multiplicity of subject positions that are immanent in the multitude and that have the potential to advance struggles that transcend capitalism and anticipate a participatory alternative to capitalism, i.e., grassroots socialism. Such projects can be organized around particular political demands (as, for example, the demand for a redistributive universal basic income that is financed by capital taxation, (Fuchs, 2008a) as part of a politics of radical reformism that creates frameworks that work within established institutions against these institutions. Workers' consciousness, demands, and struggles are not automatically progressive, but there can be no emancipation without abolishing the proletariat, which makes the task of advancing emancipatory proletarian struggles important. A widely given condition today is that proletariat is a "revolutionary class 'in-itself' but not 'for-itself', objectively but not subjectively" (Marcuse, 1969, p. 54).

Classes exist as objective economic groups that have certain subjective practices (in economic, political, and everyday popular settings) that to certain extents allow the class subjects to perceive their economic relationships as common or uncommon. Class as political class emerges if a class as a group perceives itself as a common economic and political entity, builds a common identity, and starts to act based on this entity. The subjective and the objective class dimension interact, class structures produce human practices that reproduce and (potentially) differentiate class structures, but there is no automatic guarantee that these practices acquire a political character, nor that they acquire an emancipatory political character. Classes owe "as much to agency as to conditioning" (Thompson, 1968, p. 8).

The political task is to create a political unity in plurality of the multitude so that the internal antagonisms are externalized and can by synergetically combining the strength of the now fragmented powers be directed against the capitalist class. An objective foundation for a political unity in plurality of the multitude is the experience of the lack of control of the commons and the lack of affluence that generates precariousness in one or the other sense. Such projects of creating unity in plurality are open and complex experiments without guarantees for success or failure, but at best, trial-and-error approaches that have learned from the lessons taught by political history. Fundamental social change might be triggered, but it cannot be determined, which also means that emancipation can only be the result of the self-activity of the proletariat. "It is the business of socialists to draw the line . . . between the monopolists and the people—to foster the 'societal instincts' and inhibit the acquisitive" (Thompson, 1960a, p. 8). Either the proletariat makes its own emancipation, and thereby creates grassroots socialism through its own destruction as class and the destruction of classes as such, or there can be no emancipation.

Informational capitalism is an antagonistic system that by trans-nationalization and informatization produces at the same time new potentials of class domination and class struggle (Fuchs, 2008b). Class domination can be observed in our everyday life, whereas class struggle from below is the exception from the rule, but nonetheless exists as examples, like the practice of file sharing that puts pressure on corporate interests shows. The forces of emancipation are only developed rudimentarily, and it is not determined how the future will look.

The multitude lacks the control of the commons of society, and all of its members lack the actual experience of affluence. The multitude is connected by its position in the production of the commons, by the confrontation with the expropriation and exploitation of the commons, as well as the lack of affluence, and the control of the commons. This exploitation of the commons also poses a threat of the destruction of the fundamental foundations of life itself (nature, health, education, etc.). These are common experiences that distinguish the multitude objectively and subjectively from the capitalist class that possesses the commons and the means that enable the class' own affluence by dispossessing the multitude and exploiting the commons in order to accumulate profit. The proletariat constantly creates and recreates spaces of common experience, such as the Internet, educational institutions, knowledge spaces, culture, etc., through their practices. These spaces and experiences are appropriated and thereby expropriated and exploited by capital in order to accumulate capital. Slavoj Žižek (2008, p. 428f; 2009, pp. 53–55) distinguishes three kinds of commons that are enclosed by capital so that destructive potentials are created: the commons of culture, the commons of external nature, and the commons of internal nature. "It is this reference to 'commons' which allows the resuscitation of the notion of communism: it enables us to see their progressive enclosure as a process of proletarianization of those who are thereby excluded from their own substance; a process that also points towards exploitation—for instance, that of anonymous 'knowledge workers' by their companies" (Žižek, 2009, p. 54).

References

Bakardjieva, M. (2005). *The Internet society. The Internet in everyday life.* London: Sage.

Beck, U., Giddens, A. & Lash, S. (1994). *Reflexive modernization.* Cambridge, United Kingdom: Polity.

Bell, D. (1976). *The coming of post-industrial society.* New York: Basic Books.

Berardi, F. (2009a). *Precarious rhapsody.* London: Minor Compositions.

Berardi, F. (2009b). *The soul at work.* Los Angeles: Semiotext(e).

Bhaskar, R. (1993). *Dialectic: The pulse of freedom.* London: Verso.

Bruns, A. (2007). Produsage: Towards a broader framework for user-led content creation. In *Proceedings Creativity & Cognition 6:* 99–106.

Bruns, A. (2008). *Blogs, Wikipedia, Second Life, and beyond. From production to produsage.* New York: Peter Lang.

Bühl, A. (2000). *Die virtuelle Gesellschaft des 21. Jahrhunderts.* Opladen: Westdeutscher Verlag.

Butler, J., Laclau, E. & Žižek, S. (2000). *Contingency, hegemony, universality.* London: Verso.

Carr, N. (2009). *The big switch.* New York: Norton.

Castells, M. (2000). *The rise of the network society. The information age: Economy, society and culture. Volume 1.* Malden, MA: Blackwell. Second Edition.

Dawson, M. & Foster, J.B. (1998). Virtual capitalism. In Robert W. McChesney, Eileen Meiksins Wood and John Bellamy Foster (Eds.), *Capitalism and the information age,* 51–67. New York: Monthly Review Press.

Drucker, P. (1969). *The age of discontinuity.* London: Heinemann.

Dussel, E. (2008). The discovery of the category of surplus value. In Marcello Musto (Ed.), *Karl Marx's Grundrisse: Foundations of the critique of the political economy 150 years later,* 67–78. New York: Routledge.

Dyer-Witheford, N. (2005). Cognitive capital and the contested campus. *European Journal of Higher Arts Education 2* (2005).

European Foundation for the Improvement of Living and Working Conditions- 2007. *Income poverty in the European Union.* URL (consulted January 2010): http://www.eurofound.europa.eu/ewco/surveyreports/EU0703019D/EU0703019D.pdf.

Fitzpatrick, T. (2002). Critical theory, information society and surveillance technologies. *Information, Communication and Society 5* (3): 357–378.

Fuchs, C. (2007). Transnational space and the "network society". *21st Century Society 2* (1): 49–78.

Fuchs, C. (2008a). Foundations and two models of guaranteed basic income. In Otto Neumaier, Gottfried Schweiger and Clemens Sedmak (Eds.), *Perspectives on work*, 235–248. Vienna: LIT.

Fuchs, C. (2008b). *Internet and society: Social theory in the information age*. New York: Routledge.

Fuchs, C. (2009). A contribution to the critique of transnational informational capitalism. *Rethinking Marxism* 21 (3): 387–402.

Fuchs, C. (2010a). Critical globalization studies: An empirical and theoretical analysis of the new imperialism. *Science & Society* 74 (2): 215–247.

Fuchs, C. (2010b). Critical globalization studies and the new imperialism. *Critical Sociology* 36 (6): 839–867.

Fuchs, C. (2011). *Foundations of critical media and information studies*. New York: Routledge.

Garnham, N. (2004). Information society theory as ideology. In Frank Webster (Ed.), *The information society reader*. New York: Routledge.

Giddens, A. (1984). *The constitution of society*. Berkeley: University of California Press.

Glotz, P. (1999). *Die beschleunigte Gesellschaft. Kulturkämpfe im digitalen Kapitalismus*. München: Kindler.

Golding, P. (2000). Forthcoming features: Information and communications technologies and the sociology of the future. *Sociology* 34 (1): 165–184.

Graham, P. (2000). Hypercapitalism: A political economy of informational idealism. *New Media & Society* 2 (2): 131–156.

Graham, P. (2006). *Hypercapitalism*. New York: Peter Lang.

Hardt, M. & Negri, A. (2000). *Empire*. Cambridge, MA: Harvard University Press.

Hardt, M. & Negri, A. (2004). *Multitude*. New York: Penguin.

Hardt, M. & Negri, A. (2009). *Commonwealth*. Cambridge, MA: Belknap Press.

Harvey, D. (1989). *The condition of postmodernity*. London: Blackwell.

Haug, W. F. (2003). *High-Tech-Kapitalismus*. Hamburg: Argument.

Jones, S. G. (Ed.). (1998). *CyberSociety 2.0*. London: Sage.

Laclau, E. & Mouffe, C. (1985). *Hegemony and socialist strategy*. London: Verso.

Lazzarato, M. (1996). Immaterial labor. In Paolo Verno, Michael Hardt (Eds.), *Radical thought in Italy*, 133–146. Minneapolis: University of Minnesota Press.

Luxemburg, R. (1913/2003). *The accumulation of capital*. New York: Routledge.

Lyotard, Jean-François. (1984). *The postmodern condition*. Manchester: Manchester University Press.

Machlup, F. (1962). *The production and distribution of knowledge in the United States*. Princeton, NJ: Princeton University Press.

Marazzi, C. (2008). *Capital and language*. Los Angeles: Semiotext(e).

Marcuse, H. (1969). *An essay on liberation*. Boston: Beacon Press.

Marx, K. (1857/58). *Grundrisse*. London: Penguin.

Marx, K. (1867). *Capital: Volume 1*. London: Penguin.

Marx, K. (1885). *Capital: Volume 2*. London: Penguin.

Marx, K. (1894). *Capital: Volume 3*. London: Penguin.

Marx, K. & Engels, F. (1848). Manifesto of the Communist Party. In *Selected works in one volume*, pp. 35–62. London: Lawrence & Wishart.

Mies, M. (1986). *Patriarchy & accumulation on a world scale*. London: Zed Books.

Mies, M., Bennholdt-Thomsen, V. & von Werlhof, C. (1988). *Women: The last colony*. London: Zed Books.

Negri, A. (1982). Archaeology and project. The mass worker and the social worker. In *Revolution retrieved. Selected writings on Marx, Keynes, capitalist crisis & new social subjects 1967–83*, 199–228. London: Red Notes.

Negri, A. (1991). *Marx beyond Marx*. London: Pluto.

Negri, A. (2008). *Reflections on empire*. Cambridge, UK: Polity.

Schiller, D. (2000). *Digital capitalism*. Cambridge, MA: MIT Press.

Sennett, R. (2006). *The culture of the new capitalism*. New Haven, CT: Yale University Press.

Smythe, D. W. (1981/2006). On the audience commodity and its work. In Meenakshi Gigi Durham and Douglas M. Kellner (Eds.), *Media and cultural studies KeyWorks*, 230–256. Malden, MA: Blackwell.

Stehr, N. (2002). *Knowledge & economic conduct*. Toronto: University of Toronto Press.

Thompson, E. P. (1960a). Revolution. *New Left Review* (3):3–9.

Thompson, E. P. (1960b). Revolution again! *New Left Review* 1(6):18–31.

Thompson, E. P. (1968). *The making of the English working class*. London: Penguin.

Toffler, A. (1980). *The third wave*. New York: Bentam.

Touraine, A. (1971). *The post-industrial society*. New York: Random House.

Van Dijk, J. (2006). *The network society*. London: Sage. Second Edition.

Vercellone, C. (2007). From formal subsumption to general intellect: Elements from a Marxist reading of the thesis of cognitive capitalism. *Historical Materialism* 15 (1): 13–36.

Virno, P. (2004). *A grammar of the multitude*. New York: Semiotext(e).

Virno, P. (2008). *Multitude between innovation and negation*. Los Angeles: Semiotext(e).

Weber, M. (1978). *Economy and society*. Berkeley: University of California Press.

Webster, F. (2002a). The information society revisited. In Leah A. Lievrouw and Sonia Livingstone (Eds.), *Handbook of new media*, 255–266. London: Sage.

Webster, F. (2002b). *Theories of the information society*. New York: Routledge.

Werlhof, Claudia von. (1991). *Was haben die Hühner mit dem Dollar zu tun? Frauen und Ökonomie*. München: Frauenoffensive.

Woolgar, S., ed. (2002). *Virtual society?* Oxford: Oxford University Press.

Wright, E. O. (1997) *Class counts*. Cambridge: Cambridge University Press.

Wright, E. O. (2005). Social class. In George Ritzer (Ed.), *Encyclopedia of social theory*, Volume 2, 717–724. Thousand Oaks: Sage.

Žižek, S. (2008). *In defense of lost causes*. London: Verso.

Žižek, S. (2009). How to begin from the beginning. *New Left Review* 57(3):43–55.

Part 2. Education and Labor in Cognitive Capitalism

CHAPTER FIVE

Cognitive Capitalist Pedagogy and Its Discontents

JONATHAN BELLER

The first section of this article is a reflection from 2007, originally published in Sina Najifi's extraordinary *Cabinet* magazine on the dynamics of the emergent attention economy. The argument is, in short, that both its cognitive-material dynamics and its negotiation of its meanings (all of them) presupposes the global south as a surface of inscription. In other words, the role of two billion people has become, from the perspective of global capitalism, to perform the labor of survival for the benefit of capital. One could be tempted here to write "*and nothing more,*" except for the fact that this radically dispossessed humanity serves the purposes of referent, ground and surface of inscription, for the articulation and accounting of postmodern value. Of course, the standpoint of capital does not exhaust the potential of the Global South, it is, however, a network of enclosure and expropriation.

The second section juxtaposes a reflection on Philippine digital cinema from 2008, in which the erasure of the Global South (or at least a part thereof) is made legible, first by a reconfiguration of the historical archive produced by indexical technologies and second by making explicit that historically produced poverty is today the substrate of representation par excellence.[1] It is hoped that these aesthetic, theoretical and political concerns can shape a discussion of both the stakes and the strategies of self-conscious pedagogical endeavors in a world that is today nothing if not pedagogical through and through. In post-Fordist production, everything intelligible serves as a template for a lesson; all scripts are programs. Amidst the myriad exploits, constant updatings of scores for the general intellect, and forms of dressage deployed at local and planetary levels, it is to be hoped, and indeed believed, that strategies to "escape the overcode," (Holmes, 2009) in Brian Holmes's injunction, are among the innovations that future pedagogy adapts. Life depends on it.

Paying Attention (2007)

With the increasing banality of globalization, a new attention to attention is emergent. Networks and film production companies dream up new ways to sell eyeballs to advertisers (as industry parlance has it), internetworks reconceive themselves as the media companies that they are (Yahoo!, Google), and "angel" investors pour hundreds of millions into social networking platforms (MySpace, Friendster). This is the attention economy, built upon the premise becoming conviction, becoming fact, that human attention is productive of value. How has it happened that whether conceived of as informal workers, content providers, gamers, consumers, prosumers, or audiences, we, the people of Earth, still have something that corporations want? Like clean air, attention is something that once could be had for free but is now being encroached upon as the next and perhaps final frontier. Attention is now a commodity, and a special kind of commodity at that.

That's a theory, at least. In the RealEconomik, as distinct from a theoretical analysis that would correlate a radical transformation of perception and the senses with historically unprecedented levels of global immiseration, Seth Goldstein, an entrepreneur, has lucidly formalized the new relationship between attention and capitalist production by starting an attention business that has two sides. These sides are economically, as well as dialectically linked. On the one side, there is the Attention Trust, dedicated, it is said on the Trust's website, to the protection of online users' attention. To protect our right to our own attention, the Trust offers free downloadable software that tracks and records registered users' web usage in order to make us aware of the value we create as we move through cyberspace (as data trail and as human time interfacing with machinery). Later, perhaps, the Trust will arrange to sell our attention for us. On the other side, there is Root Markets—an effort to securitize attention, that is, to bundle and sell attention on secondary markets. For this side of the business, Goldstein has teamed up with Lewis Ranieri, the principal innovator in the 1980s "revolution" that brought about the securitization of home mortgages. Through the institutionalization of standardized lending practices via statistical measures, including income, debt, and credit score, securitization allowed for massive numbers of home loans to be bundled in large packages and then sold on secondary markets as low-risk securities. Like Google's "Adsense," which auctions searchable terms to the highest advertising bids, Root Markets' business plan to securitize attention is among the emerging strategies for the computerized, parsing, bundling, and re-marketing of attention. Taken together, these various strategies for the capture of attention mark a significant mutation in the conceptualization, character, and monetization of what Marx called "productive" labor (labor that produces capital for its capitalist). The rise of the internet along with the market valuation of internet companies allows us to grasp this simple fact: as with previous if still extant labor markets, the commodity being sold in capitalist media is productive power itself.

Not too surprisingly, this (counter-)revolution in the expropriation of human "sensual labor" (Marx again) has a history. The gathering and organization of attention by mechanized, standardized media, which is visible in early, though still persisting forms, including coinage, printing, and lithography, really becomes a thing unto itself with the advent of cinema—the open book of the industrialization of the senses. Phenomena such as the cult of the celebrity or the fetish for the painted masterpiece are revealing—the celebrity is not an individual but a social relation characterized by the accumulation of attention, and similarly the masterpiece accumulates the value of all of the gazes that have fallen upon it—inasmuch as they illustrate an important aspect of the attention economy. The productive value of the gaze accretes in the organization of social being, i.e., publicity. This visual economy, the attention of spectators, produces the value, which is to say, the fact of, both the painted masterpiece and the media icon. From the practical function of cinema and allied visual technologies we may derive a mediatic model for the production and extraction of surplus value—one in which spectators work in deterritorialized factories (museums, newspapers, cinemas, televisions, computers) to produce value for media companies and those investors who have a stake in the fourth estate. The cinematic century posited that looking could be treated as value-producing labor; the digital age presupposes it.

Since the early 90s, pre-internet, I have been arguing that during the last century in cinema and other media technologies, capital—that is, leveraged exchange with productive labor for the purpose of profit—has undergone a metamorphosis, not just imperialism or globalization, but *cinematicization* (Beller, 1994). By the last decade of the twentieth century, it was possible to see that Marx's labor theory of value, in which workers gave capital more labor time than they were paid for (for Marx, this dissymmetrical exchange with capital was the source of all profit), was being superseded not by marginal utility theory (which comfortingly suggests that profit does not inhere in exploitation but from differentials of supply and demand), but by what I call "the attention theory of value." By abstracting the assembly line form (in French, the *chaine de montage*), and *introjecting* that form itself into the visual realm such that spectators' practice of connecting a montage of images moving in front of them was not just analogous but homologous to workers in a factory assembly line producing a commodity, cinema brought the industrial revolution to the eye. In an emerging interpenetration of the economic and the visual (in which the filmstrip became the assembly line of the visible world), spectators "assembled" the image-commodities, at once valorizing the cinema and producing continuously revised versions of the world and of themselves within a matrix of industry and profit. This new machine-body interface known as the cinema, acted directly on the imagination to harness attention as a force of social production. The visible world and the Imaginary (the unconscious) became technologically linked and constantly retooled to create an industrial technologization of the Imaginary that today has become generalized. Moving images, the utilization of which valorizes their media as well as modifies spectators, result in the continuous modification of a collective, variegated operating platform, that images the world and its relations in exchange for pleasure, social "know-how," and what-have-you. Thus "the image" creates the techno-social modifications necessary to engineer the adaptive forms of social cooperation that have become the pre-requisites for the preservation of capital and capitalist hierarchy.

One should emphasize that as with assembly-line production, in the cinema and mass media both raw materials and worker/spectators are modified in the process of making a commodity-image. People and their objects/images are modified along with everything else, from the bank accounts of capitalists, the economic scale of production, and the built environment, to behavior, the sensorium, and cognition itself. Without the screen, there would be no globalization. If, with respect to the dissolution of traditional societies under the onslaught of industrialization, all that is solid once melted into air, as *The Communist Manifesto* put it, in the twentieth century all that is solid melted into film . . . or more generally, into images, television, computers. Hence, "the society of the spectacle," as Guy Debord (1992) called late capitalism; hence "simulation," as Jean Baudrillard (1983) characterized the hyper-reality-effect of the ecstasy of communication; hence, "cyberspace" and "virtual reality."

Because the increasing penetration of the image into the life-world poses huge problems for language function (ultimately demoting and even short-circuiting its processes of making the world intelligible), one could (and should) link the techno-capitalist intensification of visuality to the intellectual history of discourse analysis that begins with linguistics and continues to psychoanalysis, structuralism, semiotics, deconstruction, post-structuralism, and post-modernism and culminates, as it were, with the famous disappearance of the referent ("being") from representation and the near-simultaneous decline of master narratives. These intellectual movements, all really within the province demarcated by the field of linguistics (which itself came into being with the advent of cinema, very likely as a result of the suspicion that language was simply one medium among others), are thus to be understood as representing various inflection points of the increasing failure of language (and therefore humanism) laboring under the intensive onslaught of visuality.

Most recently, we have the inflection point called "Reality TV," which for accuracy's sake should be written properly with a hyphen, *Reality-TV*, if for no other reason than the fact that this nomenclature signals the historically achieved inseparability of one term from the other. Today, it is possible to discern that media transformations not only affect the organization of perception, production, literary form, affect, subjective interiority, monetization, state power, the built environment (down to the molecular-genetic), and war but also that when taken together, this thoroughgoing reorganization of social relations on a planetary scale constitutes nothing less than a world-media system. Among other things, this system signals that we have entered into a period characterized by the full incorporation of the sensual by the economic. This incorporation of the senses, along with the dismantling of the word, emerges through the visual pathway as new orders of machine-body interface, vis-à-vis the image. All evidence points in this direction: that in the twentieth century, capital first posited and now presupposes looking as productive labor, and, more generally, posited attention as productive of value.

While the above paragraphs cram 100 years of cinema history, political economy, and mediatic transformation into a few sentences, the following paragraphs set themselves a more difficult task—to describe the present situation of labor in relation to capital, of bodies in relation to capitalized ambient social machinery, and to point towards some possibilities for the next 10 years or so: economic, cultural, aesthetic, and political. Attention has become indispensable to production, both as a conceit and a practice. While some commentators sound cautionary notes, others speak of the Goldrush. Internet theorists such as Michael H. Goldhaber (1997) and Georg Franck (1999) note that the competition for attention is the defining aspect of an increasing number of business practices. Goldhaber, while cautionary when it comes to issues concerning the proprietary rights to words being accorded to corporations and the unscrupulous mining of attention by email spam and the manipulation of hyper-links to alter search result hierarchies, notes the decline of the material economy and the emergence of a "new natural economy"—the attention economy (1997). This economy, it should be noted in passing, is about as natural as the nature depicted in Oliver Stone's *Natural Born Killers*, in which every human emotion as well as all aspects of the built environment, again down to the molecular level, have passed through a media-program economy. (Think: genetically engineered fruits, grains, vegetables, pesticides along with the public consent to utilize them as capitalist bio-software, i.e., programming, i.e., mediation, i.e., not nature.) Franck has an idea of "mental capitalism" and understands that mass media has always traded information for attention (1999). He (1999) observes a primary economy in which eyeballs are sold to advertisers and a secondary economy that is not directly monetized that he calls social crediting (in effect when attention is paid to others by peers, colleagues, fans, etc.). Both thinkers understand, as I do, that the emergence of the attention economy has its origins in prior modes of economic and perceptual organization and that it marks a monumental transformation in the production of value (Franck, 1999; Goldhaber, 1997).

However, what drops out of these accounts both here and in the blogosphere, which is all abuzz with attention to attention, is the question of the Third World, of the Global South, of the "planet of slums" as Mike Davis calls it, of the more than 2 billion people who live on less than two dollars a day (2004, pp. 5–34).

Planet of slums, an apt appellation. Right about now, we are crossing a planetary threshold: half of the world's population lives in cities. This number, more than 3.2 billion, "is larger than the total population of the world in 1960" (Davis, 2004). By 2020, the number of people living in slums will be more than 2 billion. A single mega-city like Mexico City or Mumbai will soon have a larger population than the estimated urban population of Earth at the time of the French Revolution. Not only those who occasionally allow themselves to wonder about the fate of this emerging world of near starvation, bare-life, and effective non-existence with respect to representation and political economy, but even almost all of those who passionately warn of the horror that exists and the horror to come, believe that the existence of these huge masses of people is somehow extra-economic.

While massive poverty is at times acknowledged to be caused by the contradictions of capitalism (particularly the structural adjustment imposed by the World Bank and the IMF in coordination with Euro-American foreign policy and military power in order to service debt), even most radical critics of capitalism believe that the existence of the slum dwellers, what Davis calls "the informal proletariat," is really outside of and external to capital's productive base. The slum people in Karachi, Jakarta, Maputo, Kinshasa, among hundreds of other cities, along with the rural poor whose traditional ways of life have been demolished by agribusiness and the money-system, and who provide, as it were, the raw materials for slums (in the form of those who migrate to cities), are, from the prevailing economic point of view across the political spectrum, extra people—so much slag thrown off by the world-system.

Economists are fond of pointing out that the entire African continent only accounts for about 1% of the world's economic activity: How many times have we heard that Africa could cease to exist and it wouldn't make any difference to capitalism? But, and here we must pause to wonder, what kind of economic operation is it when people's (indeed a continent's) sole function is to be rendered as data, statistics, information that can be rendered as "meaningless" or as "a potential threat to stability?" Isn't this a new moment of planetary organization when humans can, from an economic and representational point of view, be reduced only to the bodies that underlie information or a set of concepts or images—a new order of accounting? This data-crunching reduction and/or mantel of sheer invisibility, this brutal calculus that renders human biomass into a mere substrate for information, is symptomatic of the qualitative transformation of the cinematic mode of production into the world-media system now organizing attention on a global scale in two distinct registers: that of the enfranchised who are to "understand" and/or dismiss huge swathes of the planet in a few lines of symbols or in a couple of isolated images as they make their daily movements and also that of the radically disenfranchised, who must attend to this dissymmetrical order of representation through a continuous and lifelong struggle for sheer survival as they make their way through a life in which they count for next to nothing.

Like the more familiar relationship to the image of the first-world spectator, this latter relationship too must properly be cast as a new form of work: just being there, staying alive to be counted in the spectacle or not, to be constructed in the world-media system as an infinitesimally small bit of the reasons required to build walls around countries, fund new weapons programs and surveillance technologies, institute new adjustment programs, and launch political campaigns and wars in the high-intensity illumination of the spectacle. This is work, mere survival beyond the frame of representation, to become a standing reserve of information, just as it is also work for the global spectator who must be constantly enjoined to see and therefore produce the world and themselves in accord with capital's accounting. The human has become the medium for information; put another way, the medium is human, despite the fact that human potential is foreclosed by its function.

While the labor of looking and the labor of survival are represented above as being split between first and third worlds, or between the West and the Global South, the relationship is dialectical, a lived abstraction, and also pertains within single individuals. Aspects of the history and community that constitute us are flattered into activation by the spectacle, while subaltern aspects of our historical legacy (our affiliations, our subterranean histories, politics, and potentials) are repressed. The informatics machine that powers the spectacle, correlates data through the transaction that is the image: who—that is, what parts of us (considered as the species we are)—will become the bits that run the program and what parts the bits that the program runs on? Think of it this way: there is a little human inside the screen after all, billions of us actually, human bodies captured in the vast network of capital that exist only to be signified upon. This abstract, visibly invisible problem is, not so surprisingly, a particularly material economic problem, even if few people are paying attention to that fact. But many are paying with their lives, caught as they are in the crush of the global data-sphere as it machines its images and concepts, along with the very "globe" of globalization.

And it is no secret that in the production of instrumental images, a production within which the world's poor are not so gainfully employed, there is simultaneously a mass production of ignorance. There is an economics to this ignorance as well. The Bush administration has provided ample evidence about the profits that can be made with socially produced stupidity: Americans are stupid by design. Never, perhaps, have forms of ignorance that include carefully calibrated racism, historical, economic, and political blindness, and a sheer inability to analyze or even retain the simplest facts, been turned to such productive ends. This essential ignorance marks a deeper failure (which pays those who fail with the coin of success) on the part of our political, economic, and media theorist-practitioners to conceptualize the economic parameters of the media-environment. Philosophically speaking, it represents a higher level of intellectual failure, one that leaves the question of social justice, conveniently on the side of the unconceptualizable. Here we have the philosophical and political consequence of the mediatic capture and incorporation of understanding and imagination. As one of my own teachers once remarked, "Today we can more easily imagine the death of the planet than we can the end of capitalism." This formulation is not merely a rumination on politics or aesthetics, nor a simple refashioning of Walter Benjamin's analysis of the aesthetic under fascism, in which we can experience our own destruction as an aesthetic pleasure of the highest order; it is the outline of the social imaginary, fundamental to the regime of production, characteristic of and indeed constitutive of postmodernity.

Let it be registered then that the media have not just been organizing human attention; they *are* the practical organization of attention just as factories, agribusiness, the military-industrial complex, and the service sector are the practical organization of labor. Attention is channeled in media pathways that traverse both hardware and wetware. These pathways are themselves the historical compilation of body-machine interfaces: cinematization also means cyberneticization. Readers here will have internalized the protocols of mass media (shot, countershot; turn on the radio, drive; jack in; check your email) and what to do when they interface. Indeed all of us are attuned to their constant developments. Moreover, such developments are further expressions of *our* productive capacities. Today, labor and attention are inexorably intertwined—indeed attention may be grasped as the superset of human productive activity that contains traditional labor as one of its forms. All of the historically sedimented "dead" labor that has become capital accumulation must be constantly serviced if it is to remain profitable. Therefore the evolving matrix of human productive relations must be continuously reconfigured. This means that we invent the media; it is *our* needs, *our* desires, *our* practices, or rather as perfect an expression of these as is possible within a near-totalitarian matrix of capitalization, that carve out the social space of each new form of mediation *in advance of its arrival.* These "advances" are captured by capital's always profitable self-transformation and rendered productive of intensifying inequality—they are the viral penetration of the logistics of capital into the life-world that turns revolutionary desires (for self-realization, for survival) into the life-blood of a growing totalitarianism. As Aimé Césaire(2001) reminded Europe, it was third world labor that built Europe's great cities—even if the colonial workers whose labor was expropriated did not end up owning them. Rather, colonized peoples encountered and still encounter the first world wealth that they produced as something "hostile and alien." With the world wide web, all these prior vectors of capitalist exploitation still obtain, not only in the global assembly line of computers themselves, not only in the computer screen-mediated global debt servicing that powers finance capital and sets the agendas of nations, and not only because US taxpayers financed the development of the web when it was still a Pentagon project, but because the collectivity has built the screen/society and the web through our utilization of it, even if most of us do not own a single share of Google. Prudhoun's (2007) great dictum, "Property is theft," might find its current expression in this cry for the expropriation of the expropriators: "Google belongs to us."

The generalized gathering of human productive capacities under the complex regulation of the matrix of relations that constitute spectacular society simultaneously extract profit and manufacture "consent." With the rise of visuality comes the erosion of language and therefore certain kinds of reason. As I have suggested, "consent" includes both the organization of mass desire and sensibility, as well as the rendering invisible and thus effectively unconscious for the society of the spectacle, the situation and indeed existence of a huge portion of the global population. A third element in the paying of/for attention, an element implied by the economic and social capture of corporeal practice by vast networks of structured attention, has perhaps received its strongest formulation in the recent work of Paolo Virno. In *A Grammar of the Multitude*, Virno claims, more or less correctly I think, that capital has captured the cognitive-linguistic capacities of humanity (2004). These capacities, what Marx once called "the general intellect" and which were once part of the commons, have been subsumed for capitalist production. We speak, act, think, behave, and micro-manage ourselves and others according to the "score" that is the general intellect—in short, the protocols or grammar of capital. For Virno (2004), each of our acts becomes a kind of virtuoso performance of the score that orchestrates contemporary life under the regime of capital accumulation. This final subsumption of our cognitive-linguistic capacities by capital (and its huge industries dedicated to the production of signs) is the mark of the real subsumption of society by capital and the full economicization not only of culture but of what was once called "human." *That* humanity, whether dancing and wailing on our screens, repressed beyond their frames, or stammering in our heads is the specter haunting the society of the spectacle—in the world of paying attention, humanity has become its own ghost.

Iterations of the Impossible (2008)

One place to go seeking alternative 'distributions of the sensible,' as Rancière nominated the category of the aesthetic, might be digital cinema (2006). [I am talking about the Philippines now, and why not? Pedagogical questions will not be answered by staying safely within the confines of Euro-America, or by confining ourselves to the idea of school. Althusser (1971) already told us, with apologies to the heroic teachers who try to make a difference, that the purpose of schools are to produce "know-how" and subjects who work.] In speaking about digital cinema in the Philippines I do not mean to ignore the courageous anti-state, pro-masa documentary work done by groups such as Southern Tagalog Exposure or the alternative cinemas being made by indigenous groups such as Abatan Records and Indigenous Film Productions in the Cordilleras, a study of these types of efforts seems essential to have a more complete picture of Philippine visual culture, cultural production and struggle.[2] Here, however, I focus on the fact that in the past five years in the Philippines, nearly 100 feature-length digital films have been realized, along with countless shorts.

Indeed, commentators, and perhaps the filmmakers themselves, are beginning to speak of 'a third Golden Age of Philippine Cinema.'[3]

Recently I was asked by Jo Labanyi, director of the King Juan Carlos I of Spain Center at NYU, to comment on two digital films being screened by the center (it seems that Spain is becoming more interested in its former colonies).

The films were Raya Martin's *Maicling pelicula nañg y sañg indio nacional (O Ang Mahabang Kalungkutan ng Katagalugan)* (A Short Film about the Indio Nacional (or, The Prolonged Sorrow of Filipinos) and Khavn de la Cruz's *Idol*. Martin, a youth of 24, has made four feature films including his most recent, the 4'40" Now Showing, which at the time of writing was showing at Cannes, and Khavn (pronounced Khan, like Cannes) has made more than 25 features and seventy shorts, and at the ripe old age of 35 is already known as 'the father of digital cinema in the Philippines.' Khavn is also a composer, a Palanca-awarded writer, an accomplished musician, and front man for a punk-rock band, 'The Brockas' (the band is named after the cinema of great Lino Brocka, includes digital filmmakers Khavn, John Torres and Lav Diaz, and is regularly billed as 'the greatest band you never heard of').[4]

What is important to note from these 'underground' successes, in addition to the emergence of much talent at both digital filmmaking and self-promotion, is a kind of worldliness to these new undertakings that is analogous and yet counter to the aspirations of some of the more mainstream 'independent' digital cinemas. Independent films over the last year or two, such as Chris Martinez's recent Cinemalaya success entitled *100*, which chronicles the last three months in the life of a cancer-stricken woman, aspire to the universal (and also to commercial distribution) by suppressing aspects of traditional Filipino filmmaking that allowed the site-specific grit of daily life, an untranslatable local idiom, to emerge in the form of everything from 'low' production values of a certain kind, to sweat, to city sounds, and forms of speech, as well as from the generic point of view, melodramatic and realist plastic qualities and structures of feeling. *100*, offering a bucket list of things to do before the main character dies, prominently features a bourgeois apartment in one of Manila's new urban cores, characters whose clothes are always new and clean, and 'experiences' that 'everyone' might covet, such as gorging oneself on Häagen-Dazs, kissing a stranger on the street, or eating exotic Filipino dishes, food that is here produced as one more possible eating experience amid the universal desire for a sanitized consumption of global difference. In contrast, Martin's and Khavn's films have a worldliness about them that differs from the universality of commodified reception and bourgeois experience characteristic of the aspiration of their more market-driven counterparts. However, what is significant is that, in nearly all cases, the Philippines is imagined as a site for the operations of and encounters with globality.[5]

Martin's film, *Indio Nacional*, is divided into two sections: a digital prologue depicting in excruciating real time a portion of a sleepless night that lasts about fourteen minutes, and then a 16mm silent section of about seventy-five minutes, comprised of vignettes ostensibly shot circa 1890 and accompanied by piano music composed and performed by Khavn. Khavn's film *Idol* is a riotously troubling farce, also comprised of a series of vignettes, each shot in some multiply parodic relation to various film, television and art genres, during which the hero Bayani Makapili (whose name means Hero Villian) finds himself in a sequence of impossibly tight spots that prevent him from really getting the film going.

From these descriptions, I hope it is clear that both of these films are antifilms. Each film in its own way refuses various cinematic conventions regarding time, space, and narrative structure. Raya Martin's film of a history that, properly speaking, does not exist, is a film that never was; Khavn's film about the impossible aspiration to be a hero in a society, in which heroism is only possible on TV and in the movies, is a film that never could be.

Because we (should) now know that cinema is imbricated in the production and reproduction of what passes for 'reality,' and furthermore, that representations that promulgate historical imagination and disseminate narrative function are machines for the making of history, we can therefore see that each film stands in some antagonistic relation not just to film history, but to History. One useful comparison here might be to see these two films against the backdrop of what is sometimes called 'the Second Golden Age of Philippine Cinema' (Lino Brocka, Ishmael Bernal, Mike De Leon, Laurice Guillen, Marilou Diaz-Abaya, among others). This cinema, which flourished during Martial Law, found its strong (protest) form primarily in Social Realism (secondarily in melodrama), and drew its compositional principles from a synthetic approach of the relation to objectivity laid out by Mao in his talks at the Yenan Forum and somewhat differently by Lukacs (1981) in his analysis of realism (Tung).Specifically in the Philippines, typical provincial figures who for one reason or another associated with modernization can no longer sustain themselves in their traditional communities move to the metropolis in pursuit of survival, a better life and, of course, their dreams. In Manila, they strive for self-realization only to be destroyed by social forces beyond their control. These films were interested in the relationship between subjective aspirations and objective conditions, and showed the ways in which objective factors of colonialism, feudalism and capitalism combined with modernization to first overdetermine and then further delimit subjective potential. Thus, in many films, particularly Brocka's, there was effectively an incitement to revolution because it became clear that only by changing the character and organization of society itself could individuals realize their dreams.

Without going too much more deeply into that history, I want to note in passing another significant strain that arose in the Second Golden Age of cinema. This strain has to do with the reality of dreams themselves, that is, the poetic thematization of the subjective experiences and aspirations that were somehow disallowed by reality, and were thus to be de-realized by the conventions of social realism as a form of individual fantasy that had to be overcome, let go of, and abandoned. Ishmael Bernal's *Manila by Night* is probably the classic example here, of a film that allowed those dream elements to achieve enough density to transform the plastic quality of the cinema text, but you see the resurfacing of these narratologically out of place yet nonetheless potent crystals of fantasy elsewhere as well (Chito Roño). These crystals were Solaris-like eruptions of fantasmagoria within the fabric of a realist text that seem to float on the tide of realism as a kind of purposeless, but persistent iteration of the impossible, an expression of foreclosed dreams. These impossible elements, the aesthetic climax of *Manila by Night* that is willfully set apart from the narrative climax, or the provincial lovers' kiss in Roño's *Curacha* that stops a coup attempt, are foreclosed, as it were, by the movement of the Real itself and exist only in the interstices of the Real, or at least of Realism.[6]

It is, perhaps, as iterations of the impossible that the two digital films named above could be discussed. In very different ways they are efforts to represent and perform iterations of Filipino life foreclosed by History, which is to say that they are developments of spaces and aspects disallowed both by Realism and its Real, i.e. the Real (both content and concept) that pertains to a certain world-historical representational regime; the Real understood as the truth-effect/meta-physical anchor/discursive placeholder for presence of a certain modality of analysis that is itself being displaced by the historical repurposing of the functionality of the signifier.

The synopsis that accompanies Martin's film is as follows:

> Set in the 1890s brewing revolution of Filipinos against Spain, *Indio Nacional* is a collection of silent film actualities revolving around an indio, the common man, during the colonial times. The film sketches the difficult situations of a people previously excluded from historical considerations. . . . (*Indio Nacional*, promotional materials, on DVD case)

This is to say that, like the term 'indio' itself, which in an act of ongoing violence imposes an extrinsic nomenclature on a people (or in fact on peoples who may not have thought themselves together), official history and its representations, along with the representations that uncritically draw upon this history, exclude the various experiences of interiority, temporality, community, indeed of lifeworlds that in the long gesture of colonialism were mis-identified and/or erased. Thus *Indio Nacional* can be seen as a kind of impossible compensation, at once an experiment and a corrective to what has been, in effect, the commandeering of History and everything that the term implies. The collision with contemporary film genres, the effort to remake artifacts, which given the way things were could not have existed, is an effort to stave off the disappearance orchestrated by coloniality, imperialism and its history to date. This is why we have in Martin's words, 'the prolonged sorrow of the Filipino' (*Indio Nacional*). Regarding this prolonged sorrow, extending from Spanish colonialism to the present, we might connect this film to the American efforts to disappear Filipinos with methods that included killing between one-tenth and one-sixth of the population of the Philippines during the Philippine-American war, and to the US-backed Marcos effort to disappear the masses and their claims with the imposition of martial law, which included press censorship, militarization, hamletting and the 'salvaging' of thousands and also the current GMA administration's efforts to suppress the legitimate claims of the people, by falsifying election returns, reclassifying insurgents as terrorists, accepting hundreds of millions in 'military aid' for the U.S. global war on terror, and presiding over more than 900 extrajudicial killings at home during the past five years. Currently the repression is so intense and sovereignty so obviously illegitimate that numerous contradictory media adjustments are required daily to re-spin the government's position on nearly every issue. Indeed, the prevailing political atmosphere is less of repression and more of farce but no less deadly for all that. As if the proliferation of versions, the ecstasy of communication, had overtaken the function of repressive dictatorship in the sorrowful suppression of class struggle. Given the current hyper-state/capital-mediated atmosphere for representation in the Philippines, we can bring this struggle against disappearance into even sharper focus utilizing the following Bazinian comments from Martin in an interview with Mark Peranson published in *CinemaScope*:

> I become really excited whenever I see actualities and silent films. I think a silent film is how I really see cinema. It's an exact transportation of time and space, and that there's something about the purity of images, to see just the images themselves, moving, and understanding that what you're seeing was a real space in a real time. (Peranson, n.d.)

It is clear from these comments that what for Bazin constitutes the unique character of cinema, 'the object itself, freed from the conditions of time and space that govern it [since in reality, these change]' (1967), is for Martin nothing less than cinema's punctum. It is this prick of the Real, what Bazin saw as a 'decal or transfer' (1967) and what Martin calls the transportation of time and space, that has captivated him. It is also precisely here in this indexical aspect of photography that Barthes (1981) locates its unique essence, its noesis, what he calls the 'that has been' of the photograph. And it is this indexical aspect of those now older analogue new media, the gramophone and the cinema, that for Friedrich Kittler (1999) harbors what is nothing short of an evolutionary change for humanity in as much as, all of a sudden and for the first time in history, the archive can overcome 'the bottleneck of the signifier.' Prior to these technologies all aspects of the past that were not communicated through traditional culture and architecture had to pass through the symbolic, in short, had to be written down.

Thus we can see that Martin's *Indio Nacional* is an effort to return to a euphoric moment in the emergence of indexical technologies (before the rise of simulation) and instantiate the absent real of a subaltern history, times and spaces that because of the violence of circumstance were never allowed to impress themselves in the archive, that is, on representation, in any way whatever such that they might, now, pour forth. The shift from symbolic to indexical technologies, with their incessant harvesting of what Benjamin (1967) would call 'the optical unconscious,' indicates that in the Postcolony, even the Political Unconscious has been eliminated from the archive. This removal is more extreme than the analysis of the symptom or trace will remedy. Historico-technological process itself has repressed to the point of exclusion the appearing of ontological aspects of Filipino history, even as cipher or trace, and Martin has had to invent them.

This reading in which Martin simulates a reality in order to posit a Real that is more real than the Real, deeper as it were than the elisions and absences discernable in the form of or at the margins of the images that we do have, allows us to see that the invention of a reality that had to be there but has been suppressed in historical mediation is a kind of answer to the allegorical story told (in digital) during the sleepless night of the character in the prologue of *Indio Nacional*. In this story a young witness is asked by the figure of the nation itself to move a mountain seen in the distance and place it on top of the ruler-exploiters that the nation has just buried. If the silent 'actualities' that Martin creates in order to capture the space-time Real of the Katipunan-in-formation are understood as a response to this allegory, then it is as if the impossible yet essential Real is the restless unconscious that keeps us awake during the night of false history and that being forced to invent that impossible real, to restore the archive and therefore instantiate a History that is doubly repressed since it is not even legible in the margins of official, colonial history, may be the only way to move the mountain that will bury the historical oppressors (who are still upon us) once and for all. This treatment of the unconscious and the Real, which despite being at a higher level of remove (because doubly absent), is in spirit much closer to the Lacanian Marxism of Althusser and Jameson than it is to that of Lukacs and Mao, should be contrasted with the treatments offered in the Representational 'Realism' of films like *Anak* which take their reality for granted, and also with the Social Realism characteristic of the Second Golden Age, which sees reality as something to be uncovered, and, what's more, as something there to be uncovered. From Sarah Raymundo's (forthcoming) analysis of *Anak*, we might see that what I call the world-media system is the unconscious of the film and that it is to remain the unconscious-necessarily so if the film is to realize its narrative and aesthetic effects.

In social realism, the unconscious is more closely allied with the real relations of production, but it is presumed that through the careful intensification of the contradictions that inhere in the dominant ideology these real relations can be made narratively legible and therefore analytically discernable and strategically acted upon. The Real clearly has a different status in the digital moment, for the hindsight of the digital and the paradigm of the database allow us to grasp that the lacuna in narrative (History in the ellipses) and the lacuna of the archive do not occupy the same epistemological status. To understand the full import of this claim also means to recognize that the delinking of the Real from consciousness via the Lacanian schema of the symbolic (which defines the Real as that which eludes symbolization) was a historical phase in the marginalization of the Real, which was advanced (intensified) by the subsequent depresencing of being in Poststructuralism, and that, furthermore, these ostensibly autonomous theories were symptomatic of the mediated organization of global society as it achieved an increasing virtualization. They are theories appropriate to certain stages in the mediatic domination of social becoming. In other words, the displacement of realism by the digital allows for the understanding that the Real, as well as History, were simulations of the colonial media and the colonial archive.

It is interesting that Martin's new film, *Now Showing*, has at its centre remnants and remainders from the lost history of Philippine cinema. The film, about a young woman, Rita, who works in her parents' bootleg VHS/DVD rental shop, is split into two parts: the first a low-tech amateur section looking on the end of her childhood and the second a more polished section about her life as a disaffected young woman. Between these sections it situates a montage of deteriorated cinema fragments. We could compare this absence of images with Jacques Rancière's treatment of Godard's *Historie(s) du Cinema*, a film that is composed in significant part with images from the West's film archive (2006). Rancière understands Godard's utilization of historical clips as at once a kind of critique of lost opportunities and abrogated responsibilities, but also, precisely because these materials are used to posit an alternative to history, as a form of redemptive advance. If Rancière is correct in saying that, "History, properly speaking, is this relationship of interiority that puts every image into relation with every other" (2006), Martin may be understood to be asking, what are the consequences for a postcolonial nation such as the Philippines where, comparatively speaking, there are so few extant images? In a world saturated by images, and where some of the new aesthetico-political strategies are thought in terms of 're-mediation' and 'inter-mediation'—whereby one shifts the significance of images by shifting montage elements, contexts and platforms —Martin's character Rita (and the ten million like her) has little to work with in order to construct a history that might be hers (Bolter, 2002). With so few indigenous images to work with, how could a Filipino artist be a contemporary Godard? More importantly, what is the role of the filmmaker in the absence of an archive of her own? How could one constitute a subaltern history that cleaves closer to the agency of the colonized rather than merely being discernable from the unevenness of the colonial record? The archive perpetrated by imperial powers in an automatic, de facto and therefore 'natural' fashion during the 'ordinary' operation of their new recording devices is almost insurmountable. Particularly because, since with Foucault on the one hand and the contemporary analysis of the spectacle on the other, we can now see that violence was built into the sheer function or even absence of the apparatus because the organization of the visible world has become decisive for world history and because media technologies are never degree-zero political entities but are always already invested with the logic of their conditions of emergence and use. Thus, in addition to the well-documented racist, sexist and psychological exigencies that have been shown by scholars such as Malek Alloula and Vicente Rafael to pervade early photographs, we must also consider the form, that is, the very fact, of the archive itself (Alloula, 2006; Rafael, 2000). Therefore the attrition rate of the archive in colonial-postcolonial societies such as the Philippines (which, due, in short, to historically produced poverty, cannot afford to preserve even the indexical materials that did get made as the world-media system was being built) is extremely urgent. This attrition, combined with sheer absence, may even limn the Real. This Real is not to be found in the interstices of representation; it is neither repressed nor unconscious, nor even there to 'elude symbolization.' It is, in short, outside, and consequently, impossible.

If Raya Martin feels impelled to invent an outside to representation (displacing the unconscious of the archive, with an impossible unconscious of an archive that does not exist) as a way of bolstering the sensibility that the story of the Philippines is one of deferred justice, then Khavn de la Cruz seems to operate from the sensibility that representation is all and thus that there is no outside to representation and most likely no possible justice. It is in Khavn's work that we really can grasp the contemporary relationship between digitization, capitalization, narrative, representation and interiority. Elsewhere (in 'The Poverty of Farce'), I have analyzed

Idol in some detail, referring to the impossibility for the film to get a proper story going, the utilization of the 'Get ready to rock' FM-radio voice-over as a lubricating interlude between vignettes that ceaselessly demonstrate the failure of the film's hero/villain to live up to the ideas of the hero, and invoking Sianne Ngai's new aesthetic category of the stuplime (an ego-shattering accumulation of comic fatigues) to describe the film (Ngai, 2007). From the opening scene of the film, in which a mentally and physically challenged person is commanded by an offscreen voice to sing "Bayang Magiliw," the Philippine national anthem, we see that one of the topics of *Idol* is the idea of Command Performance. Because television heroism and televisual/cinematic conventions have so profoundly structured the imaginary (this is one of the great themes of the drama of *Idol's* principal character BayaniMakapili), audiences/social actors have internalized these scripts and use them to imagine their relation to reality and indeed to tactically organize their actions.

This insight of Khavn's is given a strong theoretical articulation in the work of Paolo Virno, who, in *Grammar of the Multitude*, convincingly argues that virtuosity has become a significant, if not the dominant, mode of valorization of late capitalist society (2004). For Virno, the meaning of what Hardt and Negri call 'the real subsumption of society by capital' is that we now perform virtuosically, according to the score of the general intellect that we have internalized and that scripts the various activities that we engage in both for our own survival and for the production and reproduction of society. For Virno, the effect of this expanded domain of production, which now covers the entire socius, is that capital has appropriated the last vestiges of the commons, i.e., language itself. In short, capital has captured the cognitive-linguistic capacities of humankind and nearly checkmated linguistic representation's liberatory potential. In passing it is worth pointing out that what is missing in Virno's striking account, aside from an acknowledgment of his (unconscious?) debt to Marxist feminism and theories of servile labour, is an understanding of the role of capitalized media in the expropriation of the linguistic commons. Real subsumption does not take place in the absence of capitalized media technologies; however, 'new left' beyond-Marx Marxism has 'advanced' with little attention to the materiality, gender-politics, or even geographics, in short, the material mediations, of the very transformations ('immaterial labor') it has abstracted. While this is a necessary polemic, we can see here, with respect to the Philippine context, the impossibility of utilizing the old generic forms because of the changed situation of representation that brings about the failure/obsolescence of the realist, and the heroic narrative urgently demands a new set of aesthetic categories, i.e., the stuplime, along with new insights into the meaning and possibilities of affect, viscerality and performativity.

In *Idol*, Khavn suggests that when aspiring for notoriety in accord with given cultural scripts, the common person's virtuosic performance is always also a failed performance. This gives performativity in the postcolony a farcical aspect and reveals Khavn's strategy of displaying the workings of power endemic to communication, now mediation. With the capitalization of the techno-visible and the expropriation of the linguistic commons, expropriation is endemic to 'communication,' which is to say that it is the very mediation of social logic. And since in the Philippines farce has become something like the meta-political reality a corrupt, small-power nation is also subject to the same performative failures as it tries to take on the mantle of dignified sovereignty in a situation in which, to maintain its sovereignty, it has to regularly resort to extrajudicial measures, such as political killings and the censorship produced by the allied chilling effect, that violate the conventions of reality. Because of the chill, and all that underlies it, in the Philippines, everyone knows the score and thus more or less willingly participates in the farce that passes under the signs of 'democracy' and 'rule of law.' The current investment of capital in signification and all the other mediations of the social renders these state-forms, along with heroism itself, impossible.

We also see from *Idol* the total imbrication of consciousness and cinematic convention. This dialectic between what once was called human being and media machines is manifest not only by the very organization, themes and structures of the impossible narrative, but also by the presence of 'critics' in the film whose comments necessitate the film's five and a half separate endings. In one, Bayani Makapili lifts himself up on his hands before dying in order to declaim twenty or so of the most famous lines from Philippine cinema, and in another, Bida (Bayana Makapili's very own idol, who came out of the TV in a moment of BayaniMakapili's desperation to help him) fails, because of a brown-out, to be able to jump back into the TV and is left half in and half out. This relic, a TV screen with Bida's legs and butt sticking out, is promptly taken to Christies' and auctioned off as art. Thus the film has not only a farcical notion of both high-and low-cultural production, but a completely cybernetic dimension to its understanding of human agency such that the distinction between bodies and machines is no longer discernable: media codes have overtaken the very structures of narrative, of the imagination, and of corporeal praxis. This cybernetic incorporation of codes into bodies and of bodies into codes speaks in turn to the larger metaphysical issues raised by the question of the digital itself, to the question implicit in 'This is not a film by Khavn,' 'Filmless Films' and 'Be Movies' that always appear in the opening titles of Khavn's digital works. For we are talking here about a transformation of the material substrate of representation itself, in which one cannot help but 'be movies' even as the older metaphysics of the cinema, and its analogical relation to the real, have been vitiated. This of course would mean that all statements that would ground themselves on the real have been rendered highly suspect if not impossible. Using *Idol* to illuminate metaphysical questions (Khavn would love this), one could say that it's media all the way down and that from now on the most intractable realities will have to make their way in the digital if they are to make their way at all. In another film Khavn seems to challenge and confirm this reading, which suggests that the situation of knowledge and action is heretofore always-already cybernetic.

I want to conclude here by speaking about, or rather 'near-by', as Trinh Min-ha might say,[7] Khavn's incredible film *Squatterpunk*. In some respects *Squatterpunk* is as simple and as monumental as Warhol's epic eight-hour film, *Empire*, composed of one continuous shot of the Empire State Building (shot at twenty-four frames per second but to be viewed at sixteen). However in Khavn's dialectical image, rather than allowing the immensity and duration of capitalist achievement to conjure directly from the substance of the viewer something akin to World History as the conditions of possibility for the image of the vertical mass that the viewer sees on the screen, *Squatterpunk* juxtaposes shots of squatter children living on the outskirts of Manila with a punk-rock soundtrack, in order to create the conditions for a new and profoundly complex experience.[8]

The children swimming through the dense and toxic garbage on some coast on the outskirts of Manila combine play and work as they gather plastic in their small nets in order to sell it for a few pesos to buy food. Meanwhile, Khavn's band knocks out its syncopated punk-rock track, sometimes stammering with percussive tweaks, sometimes providing an acoustic bath of feedback and static, and sometimes grinding out a series of chords and licks that build to an emotional plateau of dark euphoria. A voice, scarcely human, burbles here and there, and then disappears for long stretches. Meanwhile the kids ride a bike, roll a large metal ring down the unpaved street with a stick, run through the alley-ways that link their shanties, squat in a group to shit. Flies buzz about open sores on the legs and feet of one youth; aeons of garbage, forgotten truck parts, chain-link fence, broken pavement, old tires, rotting metal structures compose the landscape. The tireless children, some no more than 2 or 3 years old, pee anywhere, dance hiphop to karaoke, laugh while strumming guitars in a church, sniff plastic bags full of glue and lie stoned on the ground. Khavn's suppression of the soundtrack, that is, of the sounds that would have been recorded while the images were being made, is no more or less violent than leaving the camcorder machine to make the decisions about what a viewer should hear. Indeed by interfering with the normative operations of the digital machine, Khavn visits a set of difficult questions about the default operations of technology and the 'natural' or default formation of the digital archive. By showing the images in black and white, Khavn estranges the viewer from the ordinary mode of visual appropriation and harks back to documentary traditions. However, the combination of the banality and the aesthetic violence of the images as well as the obvious manipulations-the use of the red chroma key as the kids sniff glue, the high-contrast solarization effect that renders the grey bodies bright silver and the streets full black and the metal structures a sizzling white-all give the lie to the dominant strain of the documentary project: that one is getting (or ever could get) an unmediated objective look into reality. During all this, the viewer/listener is allowed their emotions: waves of boredom, horror, indifference, sadness, mild amusement and nausea, punctuated by humor, curiosity, awe, abjection, euphoria and disgust. These responses, as it turns out, are similar to those that give rise to punk rock itself and are, in fact, part of the whole aesthetic relationship that punk develops to alienation and disaffection in the capitalist metropole. But punk, as we know, also affects a kind of cultural cachet and participates, albeit as minimally as possible while still maintaining its visibility, in the legitimating realm of world culture. Put another way, Punk as a movement has been able to represent its experience and to own it. One recognizes then that its cultural function as a limit case, a rejection of bourgeois manners and sensibilities, an embrace of the corporeal, the cacophonous, the nonsensical, the anti-aesthetic and the abject, is at once a political position and a style-choice (it signifies a limit, but from the inside). And while the Punk ethos may approach the situation of the children in the film, who live outside the basic rules governing hygiene, childhood, domesticity and acceptability that have been minimally agreed upon by what passes as world civilization, it is nonetheless a comparatively mainstream and enfranchised social form. The children, although they exercise incredible agency and creativity, also occupy a political position, but this position is not a choice in any sense of the word. Through the solidarity and the disconnect between punk and squatterpunk, punk is thus construed as an aesthetic symptom, an expression of a deeper reality, a kind of world-historical sickness, that has at its core the subaltern, unrepresentable and indeed unfathomable condition, not just of some humans but of humanity in toto.

Who is the spectator/listener that takes all this in? Not, I think, one on whose bodies these images are grounded. These thoughts, like the film itself, are inscribed on those bodies. Nonetheless, just as the images Khavn produces are, in the first but also in the last instance, the conditions of possibility for the questioning and questionable aesthetic experience I am describing, these bodies, the garbage that feeds on the garbage of the third world, that itself lives on the refuse of the West, are the conditions of possibility for the viewer and for the reader, for all the meanings that will get made or not made, because the relations of global violence that inhere in the lives of these kids also inhere in the fabric of being that composes all of the other symbolic mediations imposed upon them, whether to think near-by or, as is more often the case, to make them disappear. I would say that it is these relations, this suppressed genetic material that underlies contemporary representation itself in as much as it thrives on and represses a world shattered by inequality and injustice, that are activated when we feel or understand something in the film. Thus the film not only effects the production of what Jameson, following Lukacs I think, called the concept of the social totality, it gives the concept an affective inflection that links it to the Real. However the meaning of this link is undecidable, and the derivation of objective knowledge from it is impossible.

It is for this reason that I am tempted to say that *Squatterpunk* could also be thought of as *Squatterpunctum*. In generating its dialectical image in which everything that has ever happened, colonialism, imperialism, globalization, "all the mediations of history," are palpably the conditions of possibility for the spectator's experience (and not just this particular experience), it manages to create in the contemporary universe in which digital media is now paradigmatic, the prick of the real. Barthes's two ways of photography, mad or tame, are relevant here. As he writes at the end of *Camera Lucida* (1981, p. 119), "the choice is mine, to subject its spectacle to the civilized code of perfect illusion, or, to confront in it the wakening of intractable reality." It is this wakening of intractable reality, the emergence of a reality at once extrinsic to representation and inherent in its capitalized computer electronics, of a reality that would vitiate all prior and future semiotics, the squatterpunctum, that informs my use of the impossible throughout this essay.

When I invoked "humanity in toto" a moment ago, I did so from the relatively informed perspective of post-humanism, or, rather, what would be post-post-humanism (from what Joel Dinerstein (2006), in critiquing mainstream post-humanism as a white liberal techno-fetishism, calls the pan-human, 'an emergent global identity invested in a creolized self-concept, and by extension a creolized world history'). The category of 'the human,' with its racist exclusions, its colonial and imperialist wars, its ethnocentric naturalisms, its genocides and concentration camps, has lost credibility and been on the wane in certain sectors for some time. Nonetheless, our aesthetic categories, our political imaginations, our narrative codes, and our media machines, all bear the impress of this historical construction, to such a degree that the disappearance of the human is seen by its mainstream expositors as a consequence and/or artifact of technological advancement and computation. 'The digital' as the summation and reification of world history may well mean the disappearance of the human; however, it has the impossible lurking somewhere behind, beyond, within or outside its simulation. Technocapitalist mediation, that is, virtualization, is for us not a matter of mere technology, but always-already contaminated with the radical inequality rife on planet Earth. This foreclosure, this impossibility of becoming, in short, the forestalling, of worldwide democracy, is techno-capital's, meaning to say, 'the digital's. . .' historical condition of possibility. With the understanding that 'the digital' may be among the most pernicious reifications of all time (right up there with 'the human'), today we must pursue the following thought: what would it take to stage the confrontation between the fully capitalized world of representation and the horizon of the impossible, such that the results were not merely convivial but transformational?

Such questions, questions that demand an alternate accounting for intermediated practices which otherwise are accounted for only in ways befitting of capital, necessarily inform a post-humanist, pan-human pedagogy in the age of cognitive capitalism. Otherwise, why bother asking about pedagogy at all?

Notes

1. This first section is from an article that was first published in 2007 as part of *Cabinet's* contribution to documenta 12 magazines, a worldwide editorial project linking over seventy periodicals as well as other media. See <www.documenta.de> for more information on documenta 12 and this project. The second section is from a 2008 article, 'Iterations of the impossible: Questions of digital revolution in the Philippines,' published in *Postcolonial Studies*,11:4,435–450.
2. For more on the censorship of 'rights,' see STE's website: www.stexposure.org/en/node/29.

3. Digital works break into two main groups, those of 'Independent Cinema' which, while not fully integrated into the major studio productions of Philippine Cinema, are sometimes made in cooperation with or distributed by these studios and are designed to have a commercial appeal, and those of 'underground' cinema, which, while not to be confused with the political underground in the Philippines, have a counter-cultural and non-commercial/artistic aura.

4. More recently, Khavn had a rock opera performed at the Cultural Center of the Philippines and launched two books, one of poetry and one of prose, at Magnet (with readings of his work by luminaries of the leftist culturati), a gallery near the University of the Philippines, and Ateneo, which often screens alternative cinema and features live performance and gallery shows with painters such as Manuel Ocampo. Khavn's reputation is growing as international festival organizers, bloggers and critics tirelessly compete to invent appellations for this artist: he has been called the 'Filipino Renaissance man,' 'one of underground digital cinema's best kept secrets,' 'the Lars Von Trier of the Philippines,' 'the enfant terrible of Philippine Cinema,' 'an ass-kicking rebel priest,' 'Philippine punk rebel,' 'the new Takashi Miike,' 'the Philippine counterpart of Peter Baiestorf,' and the 'Che Guevara of the Digital Revolution.' These citations are from one of Khavn's websites: www.kamiasroad.com/khavn/bio.htm.

5. For his five manifestos see: www.kamiasroad.com/khavn/writings.htm.

6. For a fuller discussion of this topic, see my *Acquiring Eyes: Philippine Visuality, Nationalist Struggle and the World-Media System* (2006), particularly chapter 3; 'Directing the Real,' (2002), and chapter 4, 'Third Cinema in a Global Frame.' (2001)

7. In her now classic deconstruction of the documentary form, *Reassemblage*, Trinh T Min-ha refuses to speak about the people of Senegal and instead chooses to 'speak nearby.'

8. In Warhol, the viewer is devoured by an all-negating time that destroys the viewer's subjectivity and very life but hatches and sustains the edifice of empire; in *Squatterpunk* the viewer is devoured by the inhumanity of humanity: the inhumanity of the viewer's own humanity, which must disavow its conditions of possibility and the humanity of those who have been rendered inhuman for the viewer to exist at all.

References

Alloula, M. (1986). *The Colonial Harem*. Minneapolis: University of Minnesota Press.

Althusser, L. (1971). "Ideology and Ideological State Apparatuses" in *Lenin and Philosophy and Other Essays*, trans. Ben Brewster, New York: Monthly Review Press.

Anak, directed by Rory B. Quinotos (2000).

Barthes, R. (1981). *Camera Lucida: Reflections on Photograpy*, trans. Richard Howard, New York: Hill and Wang.

Bazin, A. (1967). *What Is Cinema* (Hugh Gray, trans., Vol 1). Berkeley: University of California Press.

Beller, J. (1993). The Circulating Eye. *Communication Research*, 20, no. 2, pp. 298–313.

Beller, J. (1994). Cinema, Capital of the Twentieth Century, *Postmodern Culture*, 4, no. 3 (1994).

Beller, J. (2001). Third Cinema in a Global Frame. *Positions*, 9(2), pp. 331–368.

Beller, J. (2002). In Nicholas Mirzoeff, (ed.), Kino-I, Kino World: Notes on the Cinematic Mode of Production. *The Visual Culture Reader*. London and New York: Routledge.

Beller, J. (2002). Directing the Real. *Third Text, 45*.

Beller, J. (2006). *The Cinematic Mode of Production.* Lebanon, NH: Dartmouth and UPNE.

Beller, J. (2006). *Acquiring Eyes: Philippine Visuality, Nationalist Struggle and the World-Media System*. Manila: Ateneo de Manila University Press.

Beller, J. (2008). Iterations of the impossible: Questions of digital revolution in the Philippines. *Postcolonial Studies*, 11:4, pp. 435–450.

Benjamin, W. (1967). "The Work of Art in the Age of Mechanical Reproduction" in *Illuminations*, ed. Hannah Arendt, New York: Schocken Books.

Bolter, J.D. & Grusin, R. (2002). *Remediation: Understanding New Media*. Cambridge, MA: MIT Press.

Césaire, A. (2001). *Discourse on Colonialism*, New York: Monthly Review Press.

Davis, M. Planet of Slums: Urban Involution and the Informal Proletariat. *New Left Review*, no. 26, pp. 5–34.

Debord, G. *Society of the Spectacle*, Donald Nicholson-Smith (trans.), Cambridge: Zone Books, 1992.

Dinerstein, J. (2006). Technology and Its Discontents: On the Verge of the Posthuman, *American Quarterly,* 58(3), pp. 569–595.

Franck, G. (1999). The Economy of Attention. *Telepolis*, December 1999. Retrieved from www.heise.de/tp/r4/artikel/5/5567/1.html

Goldhaber, M.H. (1997). The Attention Economy and the Net. *First Monday*, 2, no. 4. Retrieved from www.firstmonday.org/issues/issue2_4/goldhaber

Hayles, K. *My Mother Was a Computer: Digital Subjects and Literary Texts*. Chicago: University of Chicago Press.

Holmes, B. *Escape the Overcode: Activist Art in the Control Society*, Zagreb: WHW; Eindhoven: Van Abbemuseum, 2009.

Idol, directed by Khavn de la Cruz, 2006.

Kittler, F. (1999). *Gramophone, Film, Typewriter*, trans. Geoffrey Winthrop-Young and Michael Wutz, Stanford: Stanford University Press.

Lukacs, G. (1981). "The Ideology of Modernism" in *Essays on Realism*, Cambridge, MA: MIT Press.

Ngai, S. (2007). *Ugly Feelings*. Cambridge, MA: Harvard University Press.

Peranson, M. (n.d.). A Short Interview with Raya Martin. *CinemaScope, 27*. Retrieved from www.cinemascope.com/cs27/int_peranson_martin.html.

Proudhon, J. (2007) [1840]. *What is Property?; or, An Inquiry into the Principle of Right and of I Government*. Dodo Press.

Rafael, V. (2000). *White Love and Other Events in Filipino History*. Durham, NC: Duke University Press.

Rancière, J. (2006). *Politics of Aesthetics*. London: Continuum International Publishing Group.

Ranciere, J. (2006). *Film Fables*, trans. Emiliano Battista. Oxford: Berg.

Raymundo, S. (Forthcoming). "In the Womb of the Global Economy: *Anak* and the Construction of Transnational Imaginaries," in a special issue of *positions* entitled *Vaginal Economies*.

Squatterpunk, directed by Khavn de la Cruz, 2007.

Virno, P. (2004). *A Grammar of the Multitude*. trans. Isabella Bertoletti, et al. New York and Los Angeles: Semiotext(e).

Weheliye, A.G. (2002). "Feenin": Posthuman Voices in Contemporary Black Popular Music. *Social Text*, 20(2), pp. 21–47.

CHAPTER SIX

Creative Economy
Seeds of Social Collaboration or Capitalist Hunt for General Intellect and Imagination?

ERGIN BULUT

Defining Creative Economy

The creative economy discourse in its crystallized and most recent form is based on the argument that we are now living in a world in which labor has been displaced from production and it is ideas that create value. The very book title of the most prominent champion of the discourse, John Howkins, reveals this fact: *The Creative Economy: How People Make Money from Ideas*. Designing the book as a bestseller, Howkins basically claims that in the 'new' economy, "people with ideas—people who *own* ideas—have become more powerful than people who work machines and, in many cases, more powerful than the people who *own* machines" (Howkins, 2001, p. x). Having advised various major corporations like Time Warner, IBM, Sky TV and other companies, Howkins defines creativity as such:

> Creativity is the ability to generate something new . . . It is a talent, an aptitude . . . It is present when we dream of paradise; when we *design* our garden, and when we start planning" (Howkins, 2001, p. ix, my emphasis).

Then, Howkins goes on to say that "ideas are not limited in the same way as tangible goods, and the nature of their economy is different" (Howkins, 2001, p. ix). So, first, we are told that creativity is a talent and then learn that ideas are not limited, so that anybody who is wise and lucky enough to happen to own these ideas and use them, makes money in the 21ˢᵗ century global capitalism. Even though Howkins concedes the fact that "creativity is not necessarily an economic activity" (Howkins, 2001, p. x), the book unsurprisingly deals with *this* aspect of the concept. After underlining the fact that many creative products qualify as intellectual property, Howkins classifies intellectual property as copyright, patents, trademarks, design, and the industries related to these four areas make up what he calls creative industries, whose "annual growth in the OECD countries through the 1990s was twice that of the service industries overall and four times that of manufacturing overall" (Howkins, 2001, p. xvi) and "worldwide, the creative economy was worth about $2.2 trillion in 1999 and is growing at 5% a year . . . and represents 7.3% of the global economy" (Howkins, 2001, p. 86).[1]

Another major figure in this sector of creative ideas is Richard Florida, who has written in a prolific manner on this issue. Echoing Howkins, Florida focuses on the idea of a creative class, which cities and regions around the world try to attract in order to maintain their competitive edge (Florida, 2000, 2005). Like Howkins, he argues that "human beings have limitless potential, and that the key to economic growth is to enable and unleash that potential" (Florida, 2005, p. 5). The idea of design is also in the center of Florida's writings that describe the trends in creative economy:

- The Creative Class is moving away from traditional corporate communities, working class centers, and even many Sunbelt regions to a set of places I call *Creative Centers*.
- The Creative Centers tend to be the economic winners of our age. Not only do they have high concentrations of Creative Class people, but they boast high concentrations of creative economic outcomes, in the form of innovations and high-tech industry growth.
- The Creative Centers . . . are succeeding largely because creative people want to live there.
- Creative people are not moving to these places for traditional reasons. The physical attractions that most cities focus on building—sports stadiums, freeways, urban malls, and tourism-and-entertainment districts that resemble them—are irrelevant, insufficient, or actually unattractive to many

Creative Class people. What they look for in communities are abundant high-quality experiences, an openness to diversify of all kinds, and above all else the opportunity to validate their identities as creative people (Florida, 2005, p. 36).[2]

Florida's 'Creative Class' corresponds to 30% of U.S. workforce,[3] and he defends his theory:

My theory recognizes creativity as a fundamental and intrinsic human characteristic. In a real sense, all human beings are creative and all are potentially members of Creative Class. It is just that 38 million people—roughly 30 percent of the workforce—are fortunate enough to be paid to use their creativity regularly in their work (Florida, 2005, p. 35).

Here, there are two problems I can briefly state and will focus later on. First, even though the core of this class seems to be comprised of high-status people with marketable skills, we are not given information about how power relations are differential among these people. In other words, the relationality among this 'emergent' class is left untouched. Second, why are they fortunate to be paid? If they are creative and their creativity is worth being paid in global capitalist relations of production, it is only natural that they are rewarded, even though, yes, Florida concedes the fact that everybody is creative. Then, what historical and socio-political context makes these people a part of the creative class, whereas other still intrinsically creative people are left out of this fortunate 30% of U.S. workforce?

Florida has also argued elsewhere that geography did not end and "regions are becoming more important modes of economic and technological organization in this new age of global, knowledge-intensive capitalism" (Florida, 1995, 2003). He has warned policy workers in the sense that universities should promote leveraging talent, rather than technology (Florida, 1999) if the United States doesn't want to lose its competitive human capital stock (Florida, 2004).[4]

Having spent quite a bit of time on the discourse of creativity, let us look at some of the critiques. Some scholars raised their doubts, not against the whole discourse, but rather the method:

rather than spend time calculating the impact or size of the creative economy, we should direct our analytical and policy energies toward better understanding how creative work and institutions are changing and what might be done to foster a more robust, more creative, and more diverse cultural life (Tepper, 2002, p.1).

Nevertheless, the contested meaning of creativity has aptly been dealt with, as well (Bröckling, 2006). Leaving my own critique to a later part of the essay, I would like to argue that the creative economy overall is not even new and has fed on various discourses around human capital and knowledge economy:

> In one sense these new studies of the 'creative economy' grow out of a long gestation of blended discourses that go back at least to the early literatures in the economics of knowledge initiated by Friedrich von Hayek and Fritz Machlup in the 1940s and 1950s, to studies of the 'information economy' by Marc Porat in the late 1960s, and to the sociology of postindustrialism, a discourse developed differently by Daniel Bell and Alain Touraine in the early 1970s. The creative economy also highlights and builds upon important ideas given a distinctive formulation by Paul Romer under the aegis of endogenous growth theory in the 1990s, and aspects of the emerging literatures concerning national systems of innovation and entrepreneurship that figure in public policy formulation from the 1980s. Indeed, the notion of the 'creative economy' sits within a complicated and interconnected set of discourses that rapidly succeed, replace and overlap one another. This set of literatures gave rise to the notion of the 'knowledge economy' that has dominated both national economic policy and development agendas since the early 1990s and has strong conceptual affinities with the creative economy (Peters, 2009, p.41).[5]

When discussing different accounts of creativity, Peters also argues that there are two different types. It's worth quoting at length the historical roots of the discourse around the buzzword creativity:

> The first I have called 'personal anarcho-aesthetics': it is the dominant model. This highly individualistic model emerged in the psychological literature at the turn of the 20th century from sources in German idealism and Romanticism that emphasized the creative genius at one with Nature and the way in which creativity emerges from deep subconscious processes, involves the imagination, is anchored in the passions, cannot be directed and is beyond the rational control of the individual. This account has a close fit to business, often as a form of 'brainstorming', 'mindmapping' or 'strategic planning', and is closely associated with the figure of the risk-taking entrepreneur. This fit is not surprising given that Schumpeter's 'hero-entrepreneur' springs from the same Romantic sources as the creative genius of the Romantic Movement. The second account I have called 'the design principle' and, by contrast to the first individualistic and irrational model, it is both relational and social. This second account is more recent and tends to emerge in literatures that intersect between sociology, economics, technology and education. It surfaces in related ideas of 'social capital', 'situated learning', and 'P2P' (peer-to-peer) accounts of commons-based peer production (Peters, 2009, p. 42).

Thus, we have seen so far that the fancy discourse around creative economy has been criticized by various people either for its method, for its contested nature or its historical roots. The next section of the paper will focus on certain features of 21st century capitalism that justify the emergence of creative economy discourse. It will basically try to address the following questions: What are the political economic conditions that give rise to the discourse of creativity? How has the nature of global capitalism shifted?

'New' Capitalism

It is undeniable and needless to posit that capitalism is not the same capitalism for which Karl Marx wrote brilliant analyses. Marx was not writing for a rigid capitalism, and he was saying that it is destined to expand, prone to crisis and reinvent itself in times of these crises (Thrift, 2006). So, then, what are the general shifts in global economy and the way capitalism operates? In his attempt to underline certain trends, George Liagouras provides certain clues about this. According to him:

- There is a transition from an energy-intensive to an information-intensive technical system, which is characterized by the concept of weightless economy.
- The dominant form of wealth is no longer the accumulation of goods but the proliferation and the amelioration of symbolic and relational systems.
- The information revolution is enforcing an amazing compression of time-space equation.
- Investment in intangible capital (R&D, training, software, and long-term marketing positioning) becomes more important than the mechanization of labour processes (Liagouras, 2005, pp. 21–23).[6]

Nigel Thrift has also written pages on the new direction capitalism has taken[7] and that is "to try to squeeze every last drop of value out of the system by increasing the rate of innovation and invention through the acceleration of connective mutation" (Thrift, 2006, p. 281).[8] Taking the co-existence of this new direction and primitive accumulation into account, Thrift uses the term *full palette capitalism* in which "knowledge and life become inextricable" (Thrift, 2006, p. 281). Now, the world is dependent upon "germs of talent": there is "an obsession with knowledge and creativity", "a desire to rework consumption so as to draw consumers much more fully into the process" and "an active engineering of the space of innovation" (Thrift, 2006, pp. 281–282). One of the interesting points he makes is related to the changing ways in which markets operate:

> Products and services are *not* basis of value. Rather, value is embedded in the experiences co-created by the individual in an experience environment that the company co-develops with the consumers (Prahalad & Ramaswamy; cited in Thrift, 2006, p. 290).

Elaborating on the issue of value, Thrift claims that "no longer can the value be restricted to labour at work. It encompasses life, with consumers trained from an early age to participate in the invention of more invention by using all their capabilities and producers increasingly able to find means of harvesting their potential" (Thrift, 2006, p. 295). According to him, "capitalism increasingly uses the whole biopolitical field as labour is redefined as what Marx in the *Grundrisse* called the 'general intellect' or as general social knowledge acting as a direct force of production organizing social practice" and value is to be rethought in three senses: economic, the activity of knowing and aesthetic activity (Thrift, 2006, p. 296).

Thus, it is clear that the weight of the traditional worker as we know him/her is shifting. Robert Reich has emphasized this in his *The Work of Nations* too and also once again reminded that routine and 'dirty' jobs, which are totally ignored by the champions of creative economy, still do exist (Reich, 1992).[9] And it is the new emergent sector and the type of worker (perhaps an outdated word) it requires that have increased in scale:

> It was the symbolic-analytical sector with all its research and *design* capabilities, as well as its flexibility, that determined leadership in the world economy. Hence *education* to this end was the goal of development . . . the paradigmatic worker in that economy is the symbolic-analyst, who is not just a recipient but a creator of culture and, in the process, of his/her own subjectivity. Unlike the proletariat of capitalist modernity who, even when highly skilled, was subject to the drudgery of mass production and management decisions over which s/he had little control, the new worker modelled after the symbolic-analyst is a closer approximation of the precapitalist artisan who has far greater control over the product and the process of production. Indeed, with the new controls over the process of production, this worker is more of an entrepreneur than proletarian, responsible for his/her performance (Dirlik, 1997).[10]

Indeed, the issue of being responsible for one's performance and the extent to which you are regarded as creative and talented become vital for survival:

The statement "you lack potential" is much more devastating than "you messed up." It makes a more fundamental claim about who you are. It conveys uselessness in a more profound sense. Just because the statement is devastating, organizations engaged in continual internal talent searches . . . The invidious comparisons between people become deeply personal. In this talent cull, those judged without inner resources are left in limbo. They can be judged no longer useful or valuable, despite what they have accomplished (Sennett, 2006, pp. 123, 129–130).

And when the issue of talent is at stake, education comes into play. Actually, education has always been central to growth and creation of value. When we look at the writings of Adam Smith, it becomes obvious that Gary Becker's human capital theory had its seeds in classical political economy. For instance, he argued in the first volume of *The Wealth of Nations* that wealth creation depends on "skills, dexterity and judgment with which its labour is applied."[11] It is also asserted that "Smith believed the development and use of human capital as of other resources to be closely associated with the degree to which the system of natural liberty, together with free competition, was allowed to prevail" (Spengler, 1977, p. 32).[12] In this respect, we can easily claim that Smith was not only a fountain for Gary Becker but also the proponents of creative economy, because the notions of liberty, creativity, lack of hierarchy and freedom obviously overlap in relation to creation of value and free market. Before we mention about the educational implications of the new capitalism from which the discourse of creative economy emerges, we have to take the changing nature of work and labor processes into account. This is vital to comprehend why education all of a sudden has moved to the top of the global policy networks.

Labor and Creative Economy

Recall the shifts I have sketched with regard to postindustrial society. Another significant feature of this phase of capitalism is the increasing amount of 'immaterial' labor. Here, what I mean by immaterial labor is the following: It is completely material in terms of value creation and exploitation. Nevertheless, it is different from that of industrial labor in the sense that there seems to occur a shift from manual skills towards cognitive skills.[13] As far as the debate regarding immaterial labor after Marx, we are provided the names of the following: Gabriel Tarde and Werner Sombart (Fortunati, 2007).[14] Nevertheless, the revival of contemporary debates about the issue revolves around Michael Hardt and Antonio Negri, Maurizio Lazaratto, the journal *Futur Anterieur*.[15] According to Lazzarato, for instance, immaterial labor "is defined as the labor that produces the informational and cultural content of the commodity. Informational content: related to big industry and tertiary sectors; skills involving cybernetics and computer control . . . Cultural content: kind of activities involved in defining and fixing cultural and artistic standards, fashions, tastes, consumer norms and more strategically public opinion" (Lazaratto, 2006). Hardt and Negri, on the other hand, elaborate on this issue in their thoroughly debated book *Empire*. The focus of these authors, in this book, was the changing nature of work, especially as the first world moved from a Fordist towards a Toyotist model. Within this historical moment in which "factories will maintain zero stock" (Hardt & Negri, 2000), the centrality of immaterial labor would increase. Hardt and Negri's conceptualization of immaterial labor involves three types of immaterial labor:

> one is involved in an industrial production that has been informationalized and has incorporated communication technologies in a way that transforms the production process itself . . . Second is immaterial labor of analytical and symbolic tasks, which itself breaks down into creative and intelligent manipulation on the one hand and routine symbolic tasks on the other. Finally, a third type of immaterial labor involves the production and manipulation of affect and requires (virtual or actual) human contact, labor in the bodily mode (Hardt & Negri, 2000, p. 293).[16]

Hardt and Negri's departure from a Marxian political economy can be understood in various respects. In the first place, they do not conceive labor power (variable capital) "as activated by and made coherent only by capital" and argue that "today productivity, wealth, and the creation of social surpluses take the form of cooperative interactivity through linguistic, communicational, and affective networks" (Hardt & Negri, 2000, p. 294). Secondly, they seem to ignore the fact that capital was conceived, by Marx, as a relation, rather than a thing. Nevertheless, my aim in this section of the paper is to use Hardt and Negri's useful but insufficient insights in order to point to the drawbacks in the discourse of creative economy.

First, some of the shifts Hardt and Negri underline are quite first world centric. In other words, these new circuits of capital "look a lot less immaterial and intellectual to the female and Southern workers who do so much of the grueling physical toil demanded by a capitalist general intellect whose metropolitan headquarters"

(Dyer-Witheford, 2001, p. 71). Second, as I will try to demonstrate shortly, it is questionable how immeasurable this labor is (Dowling, 2007). Third, as Dowling demonstrates, we have to think seriously about the potential of immaterial labor and creative economy discourse for a participatory economy and politics, let alone the elementary communism suggested by Hardt and Negri. To explicate this point, let me give some examples of the immaterial laborers from so-called creative industries. Then, I will talk about education, the issue of value and then conclude.

As I argued, value creation for the sake of value creation is central to creative economy discourse. When this is the case, "the extraction of value from immaterial labor, much like that occurring at the zenith of Fordism in the automobile factories of Turin or Detroit, is not a friction-free matter" (Brophy & Peuter, 2007, p. 179). Actually, one actually has to come to grips with the notion of friction and precarity as central to capitalism and "Fordism as exception" (Neilson & Rossiter, 2008).[17] One example in relation to this friction demonstrates the manifestations of precarious and flexible work in film industry (Christopherson, 2008).[18] Another example is from Hollywood, which focuses on the bonus features of DVDs which document behind-the-scenes, where the stunning work of stars are highlighted while "some forms of labor are under-represented" and "the realities of industrialized production in Hollywood are systematically erased and distorted" (Sullivan, 2007, pp. 69–70). Additionally, the workplace, as a site of production, is where creativity is not only implemented but also negotiated along with independence and job security, as it is shown in the case of Taiwan's film industry (Day, 2007). Whether production circles allow an individual to realize his/her creativity is also another matter of debate since research indicates that a significant amount of outsourcing takes place within advanced capitalist countries, where high-skilled workers are required for particular types of jobs and not many cultural differences exist (Mosco & Stevens, 2007). Precarity, as it is argued, is not only restricted to low-wage workers within creative industries, since "high-tech workers in the US have not escaped layoffs" (Rodino-Colocino, 2007, p. 211).[19] These data we have, of course, do not necessarily mean that knowledge workers do not struggle or resist (Zhao & Duffy, 2007). Nevertheless, they do provide useful insights regarding the two myths of creative economy discourse. One is that these examples demonstrate that labor is still central to value creation, as opposed to the myth that "the 'new economy' has transformed labor into an expression of creativity, leaving behind the alienated, public/private split characteristic of factory or office work of the 19th and early 20th centuries" (Kapur, 2007, p. 164). The second myth, as Kapur argues, is related to the stick, which means that unless you become innovative or hardworking, you are doomed to lose. Therefore, the discourse of social networking, participation, collaboration needs to be received cautiously since the figures regarding political economy require us to do so (Fuchs, 2008b).[20] The subsumption of labor is also a matter of concern in the sense that free time of 'prosumers' is channeled into production (Fuchs, 2008a). In other words, what is at stake is the production of new flexible subjectivities that are constantly alert to create value. Thus, the so-called democratic discourse of creative economy disguises the exploitative and estranging features that are intrinsic to capitalism, be it creative, knowledge or industrial. So, then, what is the role of education in cultivating these skills and subjectivities? What happens to the educational institutions and people employed in those places under these circumstances? I will briefly answer these questions in the next section and then conclude.

Education and Creative Economy

Despite the rhetoric around the notion of creativity, I have demonstrated that creative economy discourse is in tandem with what scholars have called knowledge capitalism (Peters, 2009). Thus, education becomes central to reproducing the labor power and neoliberal subjectivities in this phase of global capitalism. Within this picture, universities have undertaken an enormous role (Peters, 2003). As far as the productive role of academics and higher education institutions are concerned, the work of academics has become subject to "quantification, surveillance and standardization" (Angelis & Harvie, 2006; Harvie, 2000). Universities increasingly aim to respond to market demands and become entrepreneurial (Liesner, 2006) and a "form of academic capitalism" comes into being (Slaughter & Rhoades, 2004). As knowledge increasingly becomes a factor of production, the public character of education tends to fade away. There emerges a global divergence of policies around lifelong learning policies, vouchers privatization, "regulatory systems emphasizing accountability, uniform standards with very instrumental ends, and performance-based rewards" (Stromquist, 2002, p. 40). To put it in a nutshell, we can make the following arguments regarding education.

First of all, it is increasingly becoming a national and international market. Citizens are now becoming consumers who buy education plans and invest in themselves. Second, it is transformed institutionally in such a way to train the highly skilled, global workforce required by capital. That is, new types of schools are established where parents have a right to 'choose' between different education *services* offered to them. Third, and most importantly, I would argue, a new flexible subjectivity is constructed through both discourses and the realities of the labor market. This neoliberal ideology attributes "employment insecurity to a deficiency of human capital appropriate for information society" (Lewidow, 2002). Again, with reference to the notion of human capital, it is now the very brains of the human beings that are targeted or what Marx called general intellect in *Grundrisse*. In a passage known as the 'Fragment on Machines', Marx "suggests that at a certain point in the development of capital the creation of real wealth will come to depend not on the direct expenditure of labor time in production but on two interrelated factors: technological expertise, that is, scientific labor, and organization, or social combination. The crucial factor in production will become the development of the general powers of the human head" (Dyer-Witheford, 1999, p. 220).

Capitalism, through various crises it has undergone, especially in the 20th century, now has reached that stage. That the intellect and capacity of human beings have become a target manifests itself in workplaces and educational institutions such as universities. Students and academics' work are becoming objects of quantification, surveillance and standardization; payments are becoming related to performance, which in turn results in a situation where we face a world of education comprised of "research capitalists and proletarians, publications as capital and the accumulation of academic capital" (Harvie, 2000, p. 115). These are developments that refute the debates whether the work of teachers is productive or not (Harvie, 2008). How these conditions are experienced by different subjects is open to debate and the topic of another paper. Nevertheless, there is one thing that is obvious. Despite the increasing amount of 'immaterial' labor in a knowledge-based economy, capital's greed for value has not decreased; despite the discourse around flexibility and risk, rationality is still controlling the accumulation process and new subjectivities are aimed to achieve so as to meet the demand for surplus value. Thus, the ideology behind this discourse has to be unmasked and especially teachers and academics that identify with the national policy discourse have to ask: to what extent is the knowledge economy democratic and egalitarian? And how general is general intellect? (Dyer-Witheford, 1999).

Conclusion

In this chapter, I have analyzed the claims of creative economy for a more egalitarian and participatory social system. I have tried to demonstrate that it is imperative and reasonable to locate the emergence of these new discourses and practices in relation, not to a dull language fetishizing technology and development, but the constant desire to make profit, increase surplus value and productivity of the workforce. As it is aptly argued with reference to capitalists and entrepreneurs, that is what "drives them to adopt new technology and sometimes even to go to the expense of financing the research and development of new technology" (Allman, 2001, p. 70). In line with this, we witness that labor becomes a part of capital (Allman, 2001, p. 71),[21] and this is the very foundation of the assertion that creative economy/knowledge economy is 'different' from industrial economy. Nevertheless, there are many problems in this discourse. One of them is that the claim for creativity and knowledge, "an autonomy over and above society separates knowledge from labor" and "decapitates the worker" (Kapur, 2007, p. 166). Second, it ignores the stratification among creative workers in the sense that while the so-called creative class (designers, film makers, etc.) 'owns' its means of production, its work is only sustained by process workers who essentially follow its directions (Huws, 2003).[22] Moreover, we do not know how gender and race and power relations operate among the members of the so-called creative class. This discourse presents a shining picture of global capitalism and "reproduces the division between manual and mental labor and the agency to be creative—despite the contrary claims—is given to the First World or the privileged subject of the Third World" (Dirlik, 1997, p. 197). Thus, the ghettoization in so-called creative regions or green zonings in countries like Iraq are ignored. The discourse around creative economy is also problematic in the sense that it is highly elitist, though not representing elitism in the sense that of denying creativity to humanity. We are grateful to Richard Florida for acknowledging that we are creative too. Yet, the discourse is elitist in the sense that it attempts to theorize the cream of the crop of the society as if they are living in space where everything is carried out with intangible labor, and there are no goods and services that can come to terms with the five senses. And finally, it is highly ideological (yes, ideological) in terms of disguising the existence of working class. Despite the claims that the society is not consisting of the capitalists and workers, I would invite the owners of these claims to travel to parts of the world other than the global cities they frequently talk about and visit. As it is brilliantly argued, "if production does not seem to occupy a major place in our consciousness presently, it may be because, it has been moved elsewhere" (Dirlik, 1997, p. 209). In relation to this very same issue, Dirlik, because of his sharp and satirical critique, is worth quoting at length:

> Production at home, while it seeks to create the illusion of ever greater corporate openness, subjects the laborer to unprecedented supervision, depriving him/her not only of external but also of internal spaces, which is what "cultural engineering" is about. Whether or not we see production as an important aspect of contemporary life depends on how much of the capitalist totality we wish to see . . . Hence a president of the United States may enjoin American workers, without any hint of irony, to embrace productivity gains that may lead to a loss of jobs (1997, p. 209).

In this respect, what kind of creativity, participation and knowledge is allowed to operate is dubious. If we think, with an inspiration from Dirlik (1997, p. 210) that various activities and applications within so-called creative economy are texts that are produced with the collaboration of authors (managers) and readers (employees), one has to acknowledge "the origination and the goals of the text" (1997, p. 210).[23] Otherwise, no creative brain can escape the ironic trap to attach to ideals of progress and rationality while at the same time legitimate their 'democratic' academic work with reference to creativity, which is supposedly independent of rationality, hierarchy and power relations.

Notes

1. More from the book: More than 3.8 million Americans work in the core copyright industries, about 2.9 per cent of the total workforce. . . . More than 750.000 Britons describe themselves as working in the creative industries (Howkins, 2001, pp. 86–87). The fifteen sectors that are closely related to creativity, according to Howkins, are advertising, architecture, art, crafts, design, fashion, film, music, performing arts, publishing, research & development, software, toys and games, TV and radio, video games.
2. Before we move onto the critique of the discourse, here, I cannot help but ask the question: If that is the case, why doesn't this creative class—with all differential power relations among them—leave wherever they live (now that it is the era of interconnectivity) and settle with a bunch of creative people like themselves in a location where there is high speed internet, say a village in Turkey where there is transportation, food, means of communication? Is it this easy to dismiss tangible features of a neighborhood?

3. "At its core are the scientists, engineers, architects, designers, educators, artists, musicians, and entertainers, whose economic function is to create new ideas, new technology, or new content. Also included are the creative professions of business and finance, law, health care, and related fields, in which knowledge workers engage in complex problem solving that involves a great deal of independent judgment. Today, the creative sector of the U.S. economy, broadly defined, employs more than 30% of the workforce (more than all of manufacturing) and accounts for nearly half of all wage and salary income (some $2 trillion)(almost as much as the manufacturing and service sectors together. Indeed, the United States has now entered what I call the Creative Age." (Florida, 2004).

4. This article is available online at: http://cobe.boisestate.edu/Create!Idaho/images/US%20loo ming%20creqativity%20crisis.pdf. Florida has interesting comments that deserve mentioning. According to him, over time, terrorism is less a threat to the U.S. than the possibility that creative and talented people will stop wanting to live within its borders.

5. The critique presented by Peters regarding the design principle will be touched upon later in the essay.

6. Along with these, we should note that Liagouras concedes the fact that physical labor is far from being eliminated. Yet, he argues that the heart of the capitalist valorization process is situated now in the 'symbols-manipulating' workers and by this, he refers to not only the intensified use of cognitive resources in economic activity, but also to communicative and aesthetic ones (Liagouras, 2005, p. 23).

7. Even though he concedes the fact that primitive accumulation (dispossession and enclosure as part of a search for mass commodities like oil) as described by Marx still goes on around the globe (Thrift, 2006).

8. One can also argue that the idea of innovation is intrinsic to capitalism and has been also touched upon by Adam Smith, as well. In Book 1-Chapter 8 to *The Wealth of Nations*, he actually talks about innovation: It deserves to be remarked perhaps that it is in the progressive state, while the society is advancing to the further acquisition rather than when it has acquired its full complement of riches, that the condition of the labouring poor, of the great body of the people, seems to be the happiest and the most comfortable . . . the stationary is dull; the declining melancholy.

9. Reich identifies three types of jobs: routine, production jobs, in-person services and symbolic-analytic services. It is obvious that the last category is the one glorified by creative economy discourse.

10. The word here regarding the precapitalist artisan having more control is absolutely striking in that it reveals the romantic and optimist discourse of creativity as if it were not embedded processes of surplus value extraction and exploitation. Dirlik also here criticizes Reich for reproducing the mental-manual labor distinction as it played itself out between First World and Third World, respectively.

11. http://www.econlib.org/library/Smith/smWN1.html#B.I,%20Introduction%20and%20Plan %20of%20the%20Work

12. Spengler further asserts that Smith included human beings under "fixed capital" besides useful machines, profitable buildings, and improvements of land. According to Spengler, Smith was also making an analogy between skilled labour and expensive machine. The cultivation of this skilled labour, would depend on experience and education. Education, according to Smith, was priceless, since a society "derives no inconsiderable advantage from their instruction. The more they are instructed, the less liable they are to the delusions of enthusiasm and superstition, which, among ignorant nations, frequently occasion the most dreadful disorders. An instructed and intelligent people, besides, are always more decent and orderly than an ignorant and stupid ones" (Cubberley, 1920, p. 520).

13. This shift, along with the focus on cultivation and accumulation of human capital, should be understood with reference to the tendency of capitalism to develop productive forces.

14. Fortunati mentions Tarde's *Les Lois de L'imitation* (1890) and *La Logique Sociale* (1895) and states that he stressed the existence of other forces (or laws) acting on a socio-psychological level, such as imitation, the law of minimal effort, and innovation. In doing so he argued that the social teleology imposed by classical economists unaware of the true foothold of political economics was at fault for the omission of affections, and especially of desire, in analyses of valorization—spheres that were also neglected by subsequent Marxisms (Fortunati, 2007, p. 142). As far as Sombart is concerned, Fortunati refers to his *Modern Capitalism* where he argues the increasing centrality of immaterial labor to capitalism.

15. For a brief historical account of these names, see (Dyer-Witheford, 2001).

16. Their comments about this third type of labor is worth questioning, in terms of its immateriality, though, since this affective labor can be regarded as quite material in terms of how labor power is reproduced. Along with that, we have to acknowledge that the authors clarified this point in *Multitude: War and Democracy in the Age of Empire* by arguing that the labour itself is not immaterial. What is immaterial is the product or affects it creates (Hardt & Negri, 2004, p. 109)

17. Isn't it meaningful that primary school kids in Detroit are taken to the Henry Ford museum? In this respect, I tend to view Fordism not as a particular type of dead production style but an ideology, a lifestyle and a particular type of disciplining labor power. That is, Fordism was an "exception in the history of capitalism" as an attempt to restructure devastated economies, and also was a response to the threat by labor towards capital (Brophy & Peuter, 2007, p. 187). Moreover, it is aptly argued that labor precarity is as old as capitalism, and the secure Fordist worker image was never universal and rested upon the unpaid domestic work of women (Brophy & Peuter, 2007, p. 187).

18. Christopherson's article indicates that despite the increasing demand for media production, this basically pertains to low-budget features and extremely low-budget production for cable work. Moreover, she demonstrates that workers are pushed to maintain low labor costs and the strategies, as might be guessed, are flexibility and long working hours. Labor segmentation between men and women and between different ethnicities is another dimension Christopherson underlines.

19. Rodino-Colocino gives a number of 1.1 million job losses between 2001–2006 and mentions the demand for 80-plus hour weeks and underpayment.
20. Fuchs provides the following information: the total assets of the top six knowledge corporations were 1132.41 billion U.S. dollars in 2007 and are larger than the total African GDP.
21. Hence the meaning of terms like collaboration, participation and win-win situation.
22. Cited in Kapur, 2007, p. 167).
23. As it is reasonably argued, capitalism's beating heart is still commodity production, commodification and primitive accumulation (Thrift, 2006, p. 280) and value is the life-blood of capitalism (Rikowski, 2003).

References

Allman, P. (2001). *Critical Education against Global Capitalism.* London: Bergin & Garveyrave.

Angelis, M. D., & Harvie, D. (2006). *Cognitive Capitalism and the Rat Race: How Capital Measures and Affects in UK Higher Education.* Paper presented at the Immaterial Labor, Multitudes and New Social Subjects: Class Composition in Cognitive Capitalism, Cambridge.

Bröckling, U. (2006). On Creativity: A Brainstorming Session. *Educational Philosophy and Theory,* 38(4), 513-521.

Brophy, E., & Peuter, G. D. (2007). Immaterial Labor, Precarity, and Recomposition. In C. McKercher & V. Mosco (Eds.), *Knowledge Workers in the Information Society* (pp. 177-193). Lanham, Maryland: Lexington Books.

Christopherson, S. (2008). Beyond the Self-expressive Creative Worker: An Industry Perspective on Entertainment *Media. Theory, Culture & Society,* 25(7-8), 73–95.

Cubberley, E. P. (1920). *Readings in the History of Education.* Cambridge, Massachusetts: The Riverside Press.

Day, W. W. (2007). Commodification of Creativity: Reskilling Computer Animation Labor in Taiwan. In C. McKercher & V. Mosco (Eds.), *Knowledge Workers in the Information Society* (pp. 85-101). Lanham, Maryland: Lexington Books.

Dirlik, A. (1997). The Postmodernization of Production and Its Organization: Flexible Production, Work and Culture. In *The Postcolonial Aura: Third World Criticism in the Age of Global Capitalism* (pp. 186-220). Boulder, Colorado: Westview Press.

Dowling, E. (2007). Producing the Dining Experience: Measure, Subjectivity and the Affective Worker. *Ephemera,* 7(1), 117-132.

Dyer-Witheford, N. (1999). *Cyber-Marx: Cycles and Circuits of Struggle in High-Technology Capitalism.* Urbana and Chicago: University of Illinois Press.

Dyer-Witheford, N. (2001). Empire, Immaterial Labor, the New Combinations, and the Global Worker. *Rethinking Marxism,* 13(Fall/Winter).

Florida, R. (1995). Toward the Learning Region. *Futures,* 27(5), 527-536.

Florida, R. (1999). The Role of the University: Leveraging Talent, Not Technology. *Issues in Science and Technology*, 67(7).

Florida, R. (2000). *Competing in the Age of Talent: Environment, Amenities and the New Economy:* R. K. Mellon Foundation, Heinz Endowments.

Florida, R. (2003). Cities and the Creative Class. *City & Community*, 2(1), 3-19.

Florida, R. (2004). America's Looming Creativity Crisis. *Harvard Business Review, October.*

Florida, R. (2005). *Cities and the Creative Class.* New York, London: Routledge.

Fortunati, L. (2007). Immaterial Labor and Its Machinization. *Ephemera*, 7(1), 139-157.

Fuchs, C. (2008a). Book Review of *Wikinomics. International Journal of Communication*, 2, 1-11.

Fuchs, C. (2008b). *Qué es Información? (What Is Information?).* Paper presented at the First International meeting of Experts in Information Theories: An Interdisciplinary Approach, Spain.

Hardt, M., & Negri, A. (2000). *Empire.* Cambridge, Massachusetts: Harvard University Press.

Hardt, M., & Negri, A. (2004). *Multitude: War and Democracy in the Age of Empire.* New York: Penguin Press.

Harvie, D. (2000). Alienation, Class and Enclosure in UK universities. *Capital & Class*, 71(Summer), 103-132.

Harvie, D. (2008). Academic Labor: Producing Value and Producing Struggle. In T. Green, G. Rikowski & H. Raduntz (Eds.), *Renewing Dialogues in Marxism and Education: Openings* (Vol. 231-247). London: Palgrave Macmillan.

Howkins, J. (2001). *The Creative Economy: How People Make Money from Ideas.* London: Penguin.

Huws, U. (2003). *The Making of a Cybertariat: Virtual Work in a Real World .* New York: Monthly Review Press.

Kapur, J. (2007). "New" Economy/Old Labor: Creativity, Flatness, and Other Neo-Liberal Myths. In C. McKercher & V. Mosco (Eds.), *Knowledge Workers in the Information Society* (pp. 163-177). Lanham, Maryland: Lexington Books.

Lazaratto, M. (2006). Immaterial Labor. In P. Virno, S. Buckley & M. Hardt (Eds.), *Radical Thought in Italy* (pp. 133-151). Minneapolis: University of Minnesota Press.

Lewidow, L. (2002). Marketizing Higher Education: Neoliberal Strategies and Counter-Strategies. In *The Virtual University?* (pp. 227-249). Oxford: Oxford University Press.

Liagouras, G. (2005). The Political Economy of Post-Industrial Capitalism. *Thesis Eleven*, 81, 20-35.

Liesner, A. (2006). Education or Service? Remarks on Teaching and Learning in the Entrepreneurial University. *Educational Philosophy and Theory*, 38(4), 483-495.

Mosco, V., & Stevens, A. (2007). Outsourcing Knowledge Work: Knowledge Workers and Clients in the Social Service Sector. In C. McKercher & V. Mosco (Eds.), *Knowledge Workers in the Information Society* (pp. 147-163). Lanham, Maryland: Lexington Books.

Neilson, B., & Rossiter, N. (2008). Precarity as a Political Concept, or, Fordism as Exception. *Theory, Culture & Society*, 25(7-8), 51-72.

Peters, M. (2003). Classical Political Economy and the Role of Universities in the Knowledge Economy. *Globalisation, Societies and Education*, 1(2), 153-168.

Peters, M. (2009). Education, Creativity and the Economy of Passions: New Forms of Educational Capitalism. *Thesis Eleven,* 96, 40-63.

Prahalad, C. K., & Ramaswamy, V. (2004). *The Future of Competition.* Boston: Harvard Business School Press.

Reich, R. (1992). *The Work of Nations: Preparing Ourselves for the 21st Century Capitalism.* New York: Vintage Books.

Rikowski, R. (2003). Value—The Life Blood of Capitalism: Knowledge Is the Current Key. *Policy Futures in Education,* 1(1), 160-178.

Rodino-Colocino, M. (2007). High-Tech Workers of the World, Unionize! A Case Study of WashTech's "New Model of Unionism." In C. McKercher & V. Mosco (Eds.), *Knowledge Workers in the Information Society* (pp. 209-229). Lanham, Maryland: Lexington Books.

Sennett, R. (2006). *The Culture of the New Capitalism.* New Haven, Connecticutt & London: Yale University Press.

Slaughter, S., & Rhoades, G. (2004). *Academic Capitalism and the New Economy : Markets, State, and Higher Education.* Baltimore: Johns Hopkins University Press.

Spengler, J. (1977). The Invisible Hand and Other Matters: Adam Smith on Human Capital. *The American Economic Review,* 67(1), 32-36.

Stromquist, N. P. (2002). *Education in a Globalized World: The Connectivity of Economic Power, Technology, and Knowledge.* Lanham,Maryland, New York: Rowman & Littlefield Publishers.

Sullivan, J. L. (2007). Marketing Creative Labor: Hollywood "Making of" Documentary Features. In C. McKercher & V. Mosco (Eds.), *Knowledge Workers in the Information Society* (pp. 69-85). Lanham, Maryland: Lexington Books.

Tepper, S. J. (2002). Creative Assets and the Changing Economy. *The Journal of Arts Management, Law, and Society,* 32(2).

Thrift, N. (2006). Re-inventing Invention: New Tendencies in Capitalist Commodification. *Economy and Society,* 35(2), 279-306.

Zhao, Y., & Duffy, R. (2007). Short-Circuited? The Communication of Labor Struggles in China. In C. McKercher & V. Mosco (Eds.), *Knowledge Workers in the Information Society* (pp. 229-249). Lanham, Maryland: Lexington Books.

CHAPTER SEVEN

Learning to Immaterial Labour 2.0

Facebook and Social Networks

MARK COTÉ AND JENNIFER PYBUS

> Can one already glimpse the outlines of these future forms of resistance, capable of
> standing up to marketing's blandishments? Many young people have a strange crav-
> ing to be 'motivated', they're always asking for special courses and continuing educa-
> tion; it is their job to discover whose ends these serve, just as older people
> discovered, with considerable difficulty, who was benefiting from disciplines. A
> snake's coils are even more intricate than a mole's burrow.
> (DELEUZE, 1995, P. 182)

Facebook is undoubtedly the biggest and brightest new star of the media firmament.
There are now 500 million users and counting, making it the world's second most
popular website, behind only Google. More importantly, Facebook users log an
average of 60 minutes each day, by visiting the site an astounding 13 times from
when they wake up till they go to sleep (Facebook). The superlatives of Facebook
are not limited to the social and communicative realm. In early 2011, its market
value was pegged at almost $83 B (TechCrunch, 2011a). Given that Facebook has
only been open to the general public since the fall of 2006, it seems likely that its
social and political-economic significance will only increase in the foreseeable
future. Indeed, it is our contention that social networks like Facebook are not only
exemplary of what is increasingly known as the Web 2.0,[1] they are also paradigmatic of an emergent form of *immaterial labour*.

The progenitor of immaterial labour, Maurizio Lazzarato (1996), identifies one manifestation as an activity that produces the cultural content of the commodity—that is, "activities involved in defining and fixing cultural and artistic standards, fashions, tastes, consumer norms, and, more strategically, public opinion".[2] Our fundamental thesis is that what is transpiring on social networks like Facebook is a particular kind of immaterial labour—what we are calling *immaterial labour 2.0*—a more accelerated, intensified, and indeed inscrutable variant of the kind of activity initially proposed by Lazzarato or within the pages of *Empire*. Thus, our interest in social networks is in the social and cultural component of labour; where, above all else, users enthusiastically respond in the affirmative to the call: 'become subjects!' In other words, our inquiry regards how we 'work' amidst our myriad interfaces with Information and Communication Technology (ICT); how the digital construction of our subjectivity within such social networks is a constitutive practice of immaterial labour 2.0; and how 'learning to immaterial labour 2.0' is an integral process to the reproduction of cognitive capitalism.

For some, immaterial labour is an untenable dilution of the category of labour; flying in the face of the continued presence of material production, and the immiserating global diffusion of factory production.[3] However, we harbour no totalizing delusions that this has become the singular new form of labour; rather, we present it as a tendency that helps us understand the way in which capital has taken a cultural and subjective turn on the edges of its expanding borders. Indeed, the very notion of immaterial labour will seem nonsensical unless you are willing to consider the following: i) that there has been a conflation of production and consumption; ii) an elision of author and audience—especially in the new virtual ICT networks that increasingly mediate our everyday lives; iii) that there has been a process of convergence across formerly discrete media sectors; and iv) that therein, our communication and our cultural practices are not only constitutive of social relations but are also a new form of labour increasingly integral to capital relations. In short, we want to do two things: first, build upon and expand the concept of immaterial labour so that it can account for the modulations and variations present within networked formations like Facebook; and second, demonstrate that the pedagogical elements of immaterial labour 2.0 are integral to cognitive capitalism.

We propose immaterial labour 2.0 as a distinct new subset and addendum to Hardt and Negri's tripartite frame.[4] What the 2.0 addresses is the 'free' labour[5] that subjects engage in on a cultural and biopolitical level when they participate on a site such as Facebook. In addition to the corporate mining and selling of user-generated content, this would include the tastes, preferences, and general cultural content constructed therein. While this strongly resonates with the "labour that creates immaterial products, such as knowledge, information, communication, a relationship, or an emotional response" (Hardt and Negri, 2004, p.108), we want to further delineate the subjective composition of this labour. Immaterial labour 2.0 explicitly situates this subjective turn within the active and ongoing construction of virtual subjectivities across social networks. Furthermore, we wish to emphasize the role of affect as the binding, dynamic force that both animates those subjectivities and provides coherence to the networked relations. Finally, we posit such social networks as biopolitical networks, insofar as they articulate new flows through differential compositions of bodies—populations, as it were, whose capacities to live are extended through the particularities of their subjective networked relations.

What is Facebook?

Given its massive popularity, our introduction of Facebook can be brief. The tale of Harvard-undergraduate Mark Zuckerberg has become a legend of the new millennium. Within 24 hours of launching 'The Facebook' in 2004, a reported 1,200 people had joined. By the end of its first year, there were over 64 million active users (Phillips, 2007). Of the more than 500 million users today, some 200 million access Facebook via mobile phone, a number that has doubled since May 2010, bolstered by the 20 million mobile phone apps that are downloaded each day. Facebook's statistics also show that in total, users are on the site more than 700 billion minutes each month (2011). While logged on, the depth and breadth of user-generated content is remarkable. According to one source, in just "20 minutes on Facebook, over one million links are shared, two million friend requests are accepted and almost three million messages are sent" (Digibuzz Blog, 2010). It is therefore not so surprising that each month, the site yields some 30 billion pieces of content, including web links, news stories, blog posts, notes, and photo albums. In fact, the site's popularity is growing so much that an average 48 percent of youth who use the site in the United States now reports receiving their news from Facebook on a daily basis (Digibuzz Blog, 2010). Moreover, during New Year's Eve 2010, an astounding 750 million photographs were uploaded on the site in just two days (TechCrunch, 2011). What can unequivocally be drawn from these statistics is that people are actively using this site, feverishly archiving personal information, building up their profiles and for the most part, increasing their digital presence online.

What makes Facebook similar to its precursor MySpace is its abundant capacity for the proliferation of networked relations. Yet, while both represent "a vast cyberspatial public sphere, a place, in which one can 'hang out' with all one's friends" (Boyd, 2006, p.4), the interactive sociality that gets reproduced within Facebook's circuits is far more sophisticated. User profiles function as an important "site of *becoming*" and subjectivization. But unlike MySpace, where users simply post on other pages, link to bands and customize homepages, Facebook offers users "the newsfeed". This marks a quantum leap forward in social networking. The newsfeed is an intensely performative public sphere that sets the ontological conditions for 'intelligibility'[6], or rather a user's virtual existence and circulation. In short, a social network like Facebook—unlike MySpace—which allows users to become immediately recognizable and valorized publically through both the user, who updates her/his profile, as well as by those 'friends' who 'like' what they have read on the 'newsfeed', and who may choose to comment on or share a link. Within Facebook's user generated platform, identities are reproduced via the immediate feedback loops that get attached to every update, every link, or every photo that gets uploaded to someone's profile. The fact that its statistics show a consistent increase in user-generated content suggests that as the flow of the newsfeed intensifies, so too does the need for valorization or recognition therein. Whether this is because such moments of 'intelligibility' are ephemeral, is worthy of more study. Regardless, it is clear that users are 'learning' to be more and more productive, as evidenced by the overwhelming amount of content that gets generated. Further, the impetus to do so is unrelenting, given that the performative act of signifying and remaining present is so precarious. Failure to then continuously update and ultimately be a 'good cultural worker' means that one may cease to remain 'legible' (Butler, 2009). The newsfeed is perhaps, then, one of the most important biopolitical features on Facebook; a 'performative' virtual playground that drives the production of subjectivities on-line, while simultaneously acting as site of capture for the immaterial labour required for users to remain recognizable.

Biopower: Theorizing the 'Digital Body' of MySpace

Let us take a momentary step away from the particular practices of Facebook to consider other implications for this new composition of bodies—or network of friends. We have theorized this composition by making the claim that the immaterial labour exercised therein is a modality of biopower; here we will also suggest that the organizational form of social networks is also expressive of biopower. Unpacking this claim necessitates a brief overview of Michel Foucault's famous triptych of sovereign power-disciplinary power-biopower, specifically the latter two. This is especially important because each of those dispositifs of power is dependent upon a specific deployment of bodies. This is further important because our genealogy of immaterial labour links a particular Foucault to a particular Marxism.[7] This enables us to read cognitive capitalism's diffusion of production in the social factory as not only being exemplified in Facebook but as more generally resonant with the dispositif of biopower.

Organizationally, what most distinguishes disciplinary power from biopower is that the former fixes relations between individuals and various institutions; power is exercised over those individual bodies in order to attain capacities and aptitudes more adequate to the different and changing needs of the social body. Thus, discipline is enacted by individualizing techniques of power. As Foucault stated in a lecture in Brazil in 1976, later published as *Les Mailles du Pouvoir*, disciplinary power entails "how we surveil someone, control his conduct, his behavior, his aptitudes, intensify his performance, multiply his capacities, put him in his place where he will be most useful" (Foucault, 2001: 1009).[8] While this provides a greater flow in comparison to the rigidity of sovereign power, it remains discontinuous. In the memorable characterization by Deleuze: "Individuals are always going from one closed site to another, each with its own laws: first of all the family, then school ('you're not at home, you know'), then the barracks ('you're not at school, you know'), then the factory, hospital from time to time, maybe prison, the model site of confinement" (Deleuze, 1995, p.177). In other words, disciplinary societies spatially and temporally ordered things via discrete institutions, composing bodies in fixed, stable subjectivities, and in the process making them greater than the sum of their parts.

Such a dispositif of power, however, was inadequate to our ever-increasingly mobile and interconnected society: "[t]he mesh of the net is too large, almost an infinite number of things, elements, conducts, and processes would escape the control of such power." Hence they are supplemented by newer, more continuous networked relations of *biopower*, which is less onerous and more flexible, and "is exercised in the direction of economic processes" (Foucault, 2001, p. 1009). Since we are making linkages to the Autonomist Marxist concept of immaterial labour, we must stress that Foucault is not crudely reinscribing a causal economic base; indeed, he explicitly warns against falling into this habit "once again, in the spirit of a somewhat primitive Marxism" (Foucault, 2001, p. 1010). This wards off the mode of production as a totalizing causality lest the cohesive form of the terminal composition blind us to the heterogeneous trajectories of its constitutive elements. In this way, it is not that there is any incompatibility or total disassociation between capital and the dispositif of biopower. Rather, it is that there are myriad 'minor' elements with their own temporal-historical trajectory whose particularities would be effaced by such a perspective. One real implication of that addresses his conceptual relationship to Marx in an atypically candid manner, specifically in relation to his dispositifs of power. He emphasizes his reading of Marx where he locates a 'positive' conception of power very much in line with his own perspective in that the target of radical social change is the terminal form, as opposed to the dynamic elements that make any dispositif function in the first place.

Thus, following Foucault, we can look at the relationship to capital in the dispositif of biopower without reference to a determinant economic base. Here we can remember how Lazzarato (2000) emphasized the conflation in biopower of the *zoe* (natural life) with the *bios* (political life); similarly immaterial labour signifies the diffusion of a new labouring subjectivity into the biopolitical lifeworld. In more prosaic terms, we could say the diffusion of work into play, or more specifically, labour into communicative sociality. In short, the logic of capital increasingly flows through a widening swathe of otherwise discrete social relations and finds passage in different political and social techniques and practices—precisely what we are suggesting is at play in Facebook. Foucault himself repeatedly noted that an emergent capital had the urgent need for a new dispositif of power.

Biopower, then, is that which "uses this population like a machine for production, for the production of wealth, goods and for the production of other individuals" (Foucault, 2001, p. 1012). Regulating the flow of bodies in specific compositions would supplement the containment of disciplined juridical subjects in institutional spaces. "From the 18th century, life becomes an object of power" (Foucault, 2001, p. 1013). This marks the end of neither sovereign nor disciplinary power; juridical and normative practices continue to flourish—dispositifs are always overlapping, never totalizing. However, there is a new materiality (and embodied technology) of power expressed through networked relations in populations. It is in this manner that Foucault situates his study of sexuality: "a point of articulation between the discipline of individuals and bodies, and the regulation of populations . . . of primary importance for making society a machine of production" (Foucault, 2001, p. 1013).

Biopower,[9] then, marks a shift away from both the juridical body of sovereign body and the individual body of disciplinary power. It is the social body in its entirety, or the population, which becomes an object of regulation of power relations. It is because of the emphasis on the composition of bodies in a given population that social networks are a most adequate organizational form for biopower. To conclude, recall here the famous line uttered by Sean Parker/Justin Timberlake in the film *The Social Network*: "A million dollars isn't cool. You know what's cool . . . a billion dollars." Beyond its political economic prophecy for Facebook, this quote indicates the scope of biopower, so effectively manifested in social networks. Scale matters, both in terms of communicative and affective capacity and capitalist valorization. The sheer number of bodies enmeshed in Facebook—at 500 million and trending toward a billion—is just part of what makes it such an exemplary biopolitical network.

Learning to Immaterial Labour and Develop Affective Capacity

We posit Lazzarato's immaterial labour as a conceptual guide for understanding the contemporary practice of forging social networks. Thus we can read how the 'work' of updating one's profile "constitutes itself in immediately collective forms that exist only in the form of networks and flows" (Lazzarato, 1996). Circulating favorably within Facebook's public sphere—that is, its newsfeed—is paramount if one is interested in maintaining particular kinds of social and increasingly political and economic relations. What then motivates users to 'labour', or rather update their profile so regularly? Here we turn to Judith Butler to further extend the subjective turn of immaterial labour. We posit that this intense flow of sociality is driven, at least in part, by the desire to, as Butler argues, "count as a subject", and thus "become eligible for recognition" (2009, p. iv). She developed this conceptual frame to examine how power relations reproduce heteronormative gender relations and hence who can effectively assume the role of a legible subject in politics or before the law. We see Facebook as a conceptually linked space because it is intensely social and performative, inviting users to participate, to connect and hence to become 'recognizable' in its public sphere. The desire to then signify amongst networks of friends, establishes modes of intelligibility, through both the personal updates that a user uploads but equally, and more importantly, in how that information circulates and gets taken up by others in the form of tagging photos and updates, leaving comments, clicking the 'like' button, or the sharing of links. The newsfeed should therefore be conceptualized as a sphere of interdependence, that is, an ontological space grounded in the affective and constitutive relations of users. In this sense, it functions as a fluid and flexible site of identity (re)production.

Equally, amidst these circuits, there is "continual innovation in the forms and conditions of communication . . . [that] gives form to and materializes needs, the imaginary, consumer tastes, and so forth, and these products in turn become powerful producers of needs, images, and tastes" (Lazzarato, 1996). Such series of activities are not recognized in an orthodox conception of work, but they are at the heart of immaterial labour; they are also vital to the *raison d'être* of Facebook—to be valorized, to be recognized and to extend one's social network. Yet what are the 'flows' that enable these networks to get extended? Or rather how does sociality circulate?

As Jenny Sunden has argued, people keep going back to these sites in part because the border between the material and the virtual continues to erode. The computer screen that was once conceived of as a fixed window or a mirror in which people could see into, or rather see their own reflection within, has shifted. According to Sunden, it now functions as an 'affective surface', or rather a second skin that is capable of interfacing the body with other worlds and other people (2009). Moreover, given the portability of these virtual spaces, such as through the mobile phone, the digital profile should not simply be understood as a static repository of data but rather, as a social practice that enables subjectivization both in the virtual and the fleshy body. As such, the specific ways in which individual users gather signs together to create a "unity of meaning" allows us to understand the creative and communicative practices of immaterial labour that enumerate some of the particularities of that new 'economy of forces'.

How does that 'affective surface' mediate this new 'economy of forces' vis-à-vis immaterial labour? Recall here that Lazzarato leaned conceptually on Foucault, precisely because of the urgent need to propose a different kind of political economy, which is "neither the political economy of capital and work, nor the Marxist economic critique of 'living labour'" (Lazzarato, 2000), hence the more heterogeneous economy of forces. Therein are contestations between coordination and command, between the exploitation of 'surplus power' and formations of radically new collective possibilities, the likes of which were envisaged as far back as Marx (1973) in his visionary *Fragment on Machines*. We posit that the creative and communicative practices of immaterial labour enumerate what is novel in these new 'economy of forces'. Further, part of the 'surplus of power' produced—certainly that which is pursued with great avarice by capital—is affect itself—the very stuff that coheres and differentiates those myriad networks that express those myriad subjectivities.

Lazzarato recently touched on that affective realm, seeking to clarify misconceptions regarding immaterial labour:

> The activation, both of productive cooperation and of the social relationship with the consumer, is materialised within and by the process of communication. It is immaterial labour which continually innovates the form and the conditions of communication (and thus of work and of consumption). It gives form and materialises needs, images, the tastes of consumers and these products become in their turn powerful producers of needs, of images and of tastes. The particularity of the commodity produced through immaterial labour (seeing that its essential use-value is given by its value contained, informational and cultural) consists in the fact that this is not destroyed in the act of consumption, but enlarges, transforms, creates the 'ideological' and cultural environment of the consumer (Lazzarato, 2001).

Lazzarato is training our eyes on the subjective transformation as opposed to a specific physical capacity of a given labourer or, indeed, its particular affective components.[10] These social/affective elements are at the core of what we 'learn to immaterial labour' and why its pedagogical value is of general import. What we learn, amidst our quotidian immaterial labour, is how to extend, amend, and reproduce social relations in networked form that are also capital relations *non pareil*.

But again, capital relations are always already social relations. Social networks enable an exponential explosion of such social and economic relations. And what is also produced in these social and economic relations—indeed, what causes them to coalesce in the first place—is the production of affect. It is this affective trajectory that we argue passes through the heart of what is immaterial labour—a modality of work that diffuses production (in subjectivity and consumption) throughout the extremities of the social factory. Facebook demonstrates the extent to which this social factory has already become ensconced in youth-specific social relations. Indeed, it is both a liminal and constitutive part of the social factory. While its demographic has become unexpectedly broad ranging, a majority of Facebook users remain young adults between the ages 18–25 who comprise thirty percent of the site's active users, who are yet to fully or are just enter the labour market. One of the most fundamental tasks they learn is a kind of online personal brand management in a network comprised by multiple lines of valorization (both social and capitalist). Thus it is similar to, but different from, the *Learning to Labour* outlined in the classic study by Paul Willis some 30 years previous. At that time, English working class 'lads' were disaffected from an education system they were compelled to attend. Amidst their cultural practices in the resultant resistance—a line of flight away from school—they unwittingly reproduced their working class position in the labour market (Willis, 1977). But our passage toward biopower—what Deleuze (1995) also calls 'society of control'—not to mention our post-Fordist turn to the social factory, necessitates new ways for youth to learn to labour anew. One of the things that Facebook users must learn to more adequately construct, if they wish to be extended through a wider social network, is something both iterable and mutable, and expressive only in relation to others (both users and preferred cultural commodities). In short, they learn to produce their networked subjectivity on social networks, which offer an unprecedented milieu for myriad forms of circulation and valorization. It is, then, a polyvalent pedagogy. That is, this apprenticeship is not only socially 'profitable' for youth, it helps capital construct the foundations of a future of networked subjectivity and affect.

From the Audience Commodity to Immaterial Labour

There were concrete signs that social networks were central to the process of media convergence when back in 2004 Murdoch's News Corp spent more than half a billion dollars for MySpace. News Corp's traditional mass media empire of movies, newspapers and television already straddled the globe, aggressively pursuing audiences in the United States, the UK, Asia, South Asia, and Latin America, among others. The addition of MySpace signaled the paradigm shift that remains underway in the relationship between audiences and popular culture.

This convergence has been widely examined. Henry Jenkins (2006), for one, has intensely studied the cultural dimensions of convergence, highlighting new forms of agency and new practices among new media audiences. Relatedly, Mark Deuze (2006) has looked at the workplace, particularly how media, in newly convergent forms, have radically reconfigured the contours of work, especially in related cultural fields. So convergence has entailed changes in culture and changes in work, but what about changes in *cultural work*, via audiences? Jack Bratich (2005) helped make key linkages between more traditional audience studies and Hardt and Negri's conceptual touchstone the 'multitude'; this important theoretical gesture locates what was missing in much of early 'audience studies' research, namely an inherent constituent power. What Bratich deftly draws out is how audience 'power' is immanent to their very cultural and symbolic practices. It is via this red thread that we will further contextualize immaterial labour 2.0 amidst the shifting contours of contemporary media. Before doing so, let us briefly restate what hopefully has become clear: social networks like Facebook are not just new forms of communication but an increasingly important part of media in general.

Convergence resonates throughout our general claim regarding immaterial labour; namely that it is a rich concept to understand how the economy, media, culture, language, information, knowledge, and subjectivity are becoming increasingly inseparable in the reproduction of our contemporary social order. In other words, how communication and subjectivity—including the realm long considered 'mere consumption'—have become an active articulation of capitalist production. In short, like News Corp has done instrumentally in its pursuit of surplus value, we need to conceptually trace the shift from the *audience* as discrete, measurable quanta in the chain of production, circulation, consumption, to a dynamic, productive composition of bodies as aggregates networked in ICTs. One way of contextualizing this process of convergence is to consider what the political economist of communication Dallas Smythe called 'the audience commodity' (1980).

What seems curious today is how much the concept of the audience commodity was a novelty when it was first proposed amidst the famous communication blindspot debates of the late 1970s.[11] In 1980, Smythe wrote in *Dependency Road*, "presently we know very little about this strange commodity, the audience" (Smythe, 1981, p. 263). The basic thesis of the audience commodity is straightforward: "readers and audience members of advertising supported mass media are a commodity produced and sold to advertisers *because they perform a valuable service for the advertisers*" (Smythe, 1981, p. 8). In short, the audience is not a social category like class, gender or race; rather, it is economic, an aggregation of people linked to a particular market, be it for a cultural commodity (such as a TV program) or the commodities advertised therein. There is already a conceptual alert to biopower here—the audience is a population that must be managed if capital is to attain desired aptitudes and capacities. In Smythe's more Marxist terms, the audience is always already a market. It is because of this intrinsic functional position in the circuit of production and consumption that Smythe—ever the political economist—considered the audience commodity as a key entry point in the analysis of capitalist reproduction.

It is important to remember that Smythe, in part, was responding to the Frankfurt School's critique, which considered 'ideology' as the main commodity produced by the culture industry. He writes, "[f]or a variety of methodological and substantive reasons I do not find them particularly helpful . . . I mistrust such analysis because it seems static—ahistorical and tending to ignore the movement of the principal contradiction: people vs. capital" (Smythe, 1981, pp. 268–271). This latter comment is especially important to the genealogy of immaterial labour as it demonstrates an affinity to both Foucault and the Autonomists. Smythe found nothing novel in the notion that force was supplemented by the use of media in the service of the dominant class. From Smythe's perspective, the Frankfurt School's focus on the domination thesis meant overlooking the productive role audiences played in the production of surplus value and the general extension and intensification of capitalist markets into everyday life—a trend clearly continuing amidst cognitive capitalism. Likewise, because Smythe's concept theorises 'commodity output' as driven by the demand produced by the labor of the audience commodity, it problematizes the base-superstructure model in a way that renders it redundant. So despite some antiquated and problematic elements, one can admire Smythe's conceptual insight.

Nick Dyer-Witheford has also noted this linkage between Smythe and Autonomist Marxism, the theoretical crucible in which the concept of 'immaterial labour' was developed. In *CyberMarx*, Dyer-Witheford mentions Smythe within his analysis of the circulation of capital. In a footnote about the key role of audience 'labour' he reveals that "[i]n a personal conversation shortly before his death Smythe agreed his perspective converged with the Autonomist [. . .] analysis" (Dyer-Witheford, 1999, p. 271). We must be careful not to remake Smythe into an Autonomist—his understanding of the 'audience' is rather static and preformed, as they are passively bought and sold with no participation other than the movement of their eyeballs. Yet there remain strong parallels. Smythe writes "[f]or, in inventing the mass media and the mass audience as its principal protagonist, monopoly capitalism has created its chief potential *antagonist* in the capitalist core area" (Smythe, 1981, p. xvii). As he never tires of repeating, the principal contradiction of capital is 'people vs. capital'; likewise for Autonomists, the true dynamic of capitalism (and one of their key conceptual interventions) is the antagonistic relationship between labour and capital, with the former driving the latter.

Immaterial labour attempts to conceptually map major shifts that have occurred in labouring practices amidst post-Fordist globalization. One of many important differences with Smythe's audience commodity is the convergence of production and consumption—keeping in mind that Smythe's audience commodity was a corrective response to what he considered an excessive focus on 'consumption' via ideology. As Lazzarato notes, with the economy of immaterial labour, 'leisure time' and 'working time' are increasingly fused, making life inseparable from work. This is a key aspect of what Marx (1990) called 'real subsumption'—the absorption of capitalist logic and the dictates of surplus value through more and more of everyday life.

We by no means suggest that there are no longer 'audiences'; rather, that immaterial labour is a better conceptual lens to understand the qualitative shift in which culture, subjectivity, and capital come together in new networks of ICT. In short, the term 'audience' is not adequate for understanding participants in social networks like Facebook. Even if we modify audience with the adjective 'active,' it still fails to capture the shift in the process of capitalist valorization—or how surplus value is produced. This is one of Lazzarato's underlying reasons for conceptualizing immaterial labour in the first place. Part of the process of 'real subsumption' is capital seeking an unmediated form of command, not just over labour in the factory but in everyday life (similar to the form of command in which biopower is exercised). That is why, for post-Fordist capital, Lazzarato coins the slogan 'become subjects' (Lazzarato, 1996)—hence the subjective reading of capital. But this is not an uncritical celebration of the proliferating subjectivities of what was once called postmodernity. When looking at actual labouring practice, the subjects that you become must be compatible with the needs of contemporary capitalist reproduction. This is a pedagogical imperative of cognitive capitalism. Thus linguistic and communicative elements are so integral; they facilitate an expanded capacity for social cooperation, which is absolutely essential for more flexible production practices of cognitive capitalism.

But we cannot make a straight line to immaterial labouring practices in the social networks of popular culture here. Rather we must remember the Autonomist view of labour, which like Foucaultian resistance, always comes first. Even in the context of social networks, we must remember its origins in the cultural practices of early P2P file sharing like Napster. It is techniques of immaterial labour that allowed for the proliferation of such decentralized practices of virtual social cooperation, in the process radically altering potential kinds of interface with popular culture. Yet, this is not to make an argument for some kind of emerging consumer sovereignty. Indeed, one thing the immaterial labour thesis stresses is the higher level and intensity of antagonism that is created along the way—something borne out in practice with the forced closure of Napster and the subsequent proliferation of new and seemingly uncontainable forms of P2P practices like torrents. Lazzarato notes this fundamental contradiction in the workplace. Capital "is obliged ([in] a life-and-death necessity for the capitalist) not to 'redistribute' the power that the new quality of labor and organization imply" (Lazzarato, 1996).

We can see this playing out in the dynamic decentralized architecture of the internet, the distributed network in which computers with a shared protocol can communicate directly without a hierarchical mediary. This is not only a radically different media terrain than television, it is one animated primarily by immaterial labour. In short, we have shifted from the static world of the couch potato to the dynamic one of the blogger or the social network, busily updating, Tweeting, or checking in. Capital has paid attention to this and there is a shift in what is being valorized. With television, the audience commodity was an isolated and sedentary beast, an aggregation of individuals linked only through the show they watched each week. Its organizational form was also more static: a centralized network with the audience in a cluster of dead-end lines. With the internet—and specifically, social networks—it is about the dynamic immaterial labour that traverses and constructs the decentralized networks. In short, it is the links, the networks that people construct and participate in, that comprise not a new audience commodity but immaterial labour 2.0.

What is therefore required is a means to harness, to capture and to render productive, this immaterial labour. That is, an apparatus that begins to take form as a result of the immaterial labour of those who regularly update when they use social networking sites like Facebook. One way to conceptualize this modality of capture is by examining how Facebook actively encourages the circulation of sociality via the production of individuated digital archives or rather what we would like to refer to as 'digital archives of the self'.

The digital archive of the self, of feeling, and of profit

For Facebook, user-generated individuated archives are the lucrative lifeblood of surplus value and exchange. Indeed, the seemingly endlessly increasing market value of Facebook is entirely predicated on the willingness of users to upload their immaterial and affective labour. The (re)production of those 'digital archives of the self' is a deeply recursive process. For users, it is about the production and circulation of subjectivities; for Facebook, it is a political economic imperative. This is a fundamental point of tension at the heart of cognitive capitalism. But before delving further into how the digital archive functions profitably for social networks, we must necessarily attend to its techno-sociality. The social dimension of the archive, then, is ontological, ascribing an overtly mediated reality of unprecedented proportions and speed. What we learn in this techno-social realm is a more fluid understanding of presence vis-à-vis subjectivity, communication and the body. The manner in which we 'choose' to update our profiles and upload content connects us to a data flow that confounds the temporal and spatial borders demarcating our body. We find ourselves in a radically different ontological realm where our communicative and affective capacity attains an instantaneous and global reach while our material bodies remain stubbornly Newtonian, subject to hyper-locality and sluggish physical movement through time and space. This condition—what we like to call *(non)locality*—cannot be adequately described by older distinctions between the so-called material and virtual, such is the ontological force and quotidian diffusion of social networks.

Within this new ontology of the (non)local body comes new forms of intelligibility. Hence our earlier reference to Butler. We are particularly interested in the epistemological dimension that 'intelligibility' flags within the digital public sphere of Facebook's newsfeed. We can bring further conceptual depth and nuance to the 'digital archive of the self' when we recall that for Foucault, the initial distinction of the archive was as an epistemological frame. But in the case of Facebook, intelligibility is in the service of sociality. This too resonates with Foucault's latter use of the term archive, wherein it was more sociological and riven by asymmetrical power relations. After all, this intelligibility is the means by which subjectivities are to become and remain legible. This is far from a strictly rational process, whereby users rigorously 'read' their newsfeed and meticulously construct identikits of subjectivities. Instead, it is a deeply affective dynamic wherein the social dimension comes first, in turn driving the capitalist accumulation that results from immaterial labour 2.0. This affective ontology can be further explicated via Ann Cvetkovich's "archive of feeling," which is predicated on "an exploration of cultural texts as repositories of feelings and emotions, which are encoded not only in the content of the texts themselves, but in the *practices* [emphasis added] that surround their production and reception" (2003, p.7). Cvetkovich uses this to examine how affective sociality functions as a mechanism for the subjectivization of the queer subject. Specifically, she brings together different elements of queer public culture by including oral histories, performance and literature, as well as specific LTBG archives such as the 'Lesbian Herstory Archives' in Brooklyn, New York, and San Francisco's Gay and Lesbian Historical Society. What is unique about Cvetkovich's work lies not just in the important compendium of documents that comprise the archive, but rather in its attempt to capture 'lived experiences', which in turn leads to the production of lesbian public cultures. Such 'experiences' or practices are impregnated within the interstices of the archive's materiality, thereby filling the 'archive of feeling' with traces of affective sociality—indeed, a 'way of life'—which helps bring these 'queer publics' together. Thus, we are deploying the 'archive of feeling' to help us better understand how to theorize the affective sociality on a site such as Facebook, in particular the user generated content of the newsfeed. However, we are focusing our attention on those communicative practices that cohere networks of (techno)sociality; that is, those affective practices, which we posit as *the* central dynamic of social networks. Our proposed user-generated digital archive of the self, which circulates publically in the newsfeed, both coheres and fuels its reproduction by the continuous circulation and hence archiving of those lived experiences.

It is important to clarify how we are conceptualizing affect. Briefly, Sarah Ahmed suggests that affect occupies a new terrain of struggle that exists in between the subject and the social. Thus, on the one hand, it is something that gets generated from the inside of bodies and moves outward, connecting the individual to other bodies (2004). This is why we are also suggesting affect as a relational process that can propel bodies to 'act'. But importantly, affect is produced outside the body in a realm 'beyond representation.' Here, Ahmed raises important questions about how "emotions shape the very surfaces of bodies" on which they operate (2004, p. 4). This exteriorization relates to how we are 'affected' by the discursive frames that "align individuals with communities—or bodily space with social space"—and is, at least in part what coheres the social practices that exist on social networking sites. For Cvetkovich, it is the accumulation of these practices that inscribes culture into the archives. Such a perspective illuminates what we mean by the 'digital archive of the self.' This archive is first a communicative and affective practice; it is the very inscription of these cultural practices that drives the (re)production of the individuated Facebook profile and the aggregated newsfeed. Thus we see this archive as productive, a composition of what Lazzarato might call biopolitical practices. Here, we recall the central point of tension: our myriad subjectivities in permanent states of becoming and, concomitantly, where we learn to immaterial labour so well.

The digital archive of the self, is paradigmatic of new forms of social *and* economic relations. It is radically different from the modern, classical archive, which can be characterized as a read only, discretely housed and categorized grouping of material objects or documents. That is, static repositories of information, stored, and only irregularly retrieved. The digital archive of the self in social networks are user generated and user oriented. The information stored is always in process; even when it ceases to be part of an active flow, it remains both retrievable in its profile and aggregated across the social network. The digital archive of the self is permanently *in medias res, always* in the middle of being updated, linked to, in circulation, in transubstatiation from the social to surplus value.

This "constant updating is a direct consequence of the new paradigm of permanent transfer" and fits with how Foucault tried to characterize the evolution of the archive. That is, "not a monument for future memory but a document for possible use" (Laermans and Gielen, 2007). And while he was illustrating how larger structural apparatuses within the disciplinary society operate through the body, such as the dynamic archives of the prisoner, the child, or the madman, the logic can still be applied to a more individuated archive that mirrors Deleuze's modular logic. Yet, instead of the serpent we have a different kind of cyborg, or even better, a transductive body, as the human and technology increasingly meld in the information flow/archive.

Conclusion

We have suggested that the new social and communicative practices underlying social networks like Facebook are hallmarks of immaterial labour 2.0. In turn, both are integral to cognitive capitalism. In short, youth and adults, young and old are learning techniques and practices that are necessary for the transformation and continued growth of capitalist relations. But is that all? Is that the sole end of learning to immaterial labour 2.0?

Such concluding questions resonate with a more fundamental debate, which has raged for more than a decade now. There are myriad proponents, but two key positions are succinctly captured by Jodi Dean and Hardt and Negri. *Empire* and *Multitude* were both replete with hope for new revolutionary politics. Dean, however, is less sanguine about the political prospects amidst the broad subsumption of society to what she calls 'communicative capitalism.' Indeed, while her model builds upon Hardt and Negri, she differs in seeing a more corrosive effect of communication as a key modality of capitalist production. For her, communicative capitalism "undermines democracy" by only ever contributing to the production of surplus value for the corporate entities which stand to gain from the production and circulation of content. In short, the expansion of capitalist market relations is predicated on networked communicative practices that valorize the exchange value of messages over their content, or use value:

> The message simply [becomes] part of a circulating data stream. Its particular content is irrelevant. Who sent it is irrelevant. Who receives it is irrelevant. That its need be responded to is irrelevant. The only thing that is relevant is circulation, the addition to the pool (Dean, 2004, p. 275).

The user-generated content of Facebook's newsfeed, for example, is paradigmatic of this "circulating data stream." We have posited it as part of a digital archive of the self as comprising a digital ontology of becoming. But, following Dean, we also see it as clear evidence of communication as a "force of production." One need look no further than Facebook's Terms of Service for confirmation:

> You hereby grant Facebook an irrevocable, perpetual, non-exclusive, transferable, fully paid, worldwide license (with the right to sublicense) to use, copy, publish, stream, store, retain, publically perform or display, transmit, scan, reformat, modify, edit, frame, translate, excerpt, adapt, create derivative works, and distribute any User Content [remotely related to you].

These are heavy contractual chains binding a vast operational terrain for communicative capitalism. There can also be no doubt that they set out stringent terms for immaterial labour 2.0, subjecting the entirety of those expanded communicative and affective capacity to capitalist extraction. But there is something more. At the heart of immaterial labour, Lazzarato notes, is its liberatory potential—the creative and affective dynamic, which is captured, not created, by capital. So we can finish by going back to a basic conceptual maneuver made by Lazzarato (2000): unpacking the Foucaultian concept of biopower by distinguishing it from biopolitical production. If there is political potential here, it will be expressed in and through modalities of immaterial labour resonant with biopolitical production. Here we return to immaterial labour's elemental conceptual affinity between Foucault and autonomia—namely that *resistance always comes first*. In short, the collective dimension of our immaterial practices are neither determined by nor reduced to the relations of domination expressed in Facebook's terms of service (TOS). As Lazzarato (2000) notes, "Biopower is always born of something other than itself", as is immaterial labour 2.0, at least in its form that is readily transferable into surplus value.

A postscript then. Late 2010, early 2011 saw unexpected social and political movements across North Africa and the Middle East that were unprecedented in their usage of social media. It is illuminating how social media effected what we call a (non)local dimension to the uprising. That is, how they were deployed for both hyperlocal organizing and globally to extend support for and circulation of their struggle. In Egypt, 'el Face' as Facebook is called by local youth, has become extremely popular—in July 2010, there were 3.5 million users and as of February 2011, it spiked to more than five million (Coffee Today, 2011). Furthermore, in a country with severely truncated democratic public sphere, Facebook has facilitated access, inclusion, discussion and participation. As one young Egyptian woman noted, "It is such a release to go on Facebook. I feel so liberated knowing there's a place I can send my thoughts" (Herrera, 2011).

In June 2010, a young man exposed corruption by uploading photos of police sharing in the spoils of a drug bust; he was soon thereafter beaten to death in plain sight by those same Cairo officers. Within days, a Facebook page "We Are All Khaled Said" was started in hopes of bringing about justice. Eventually, the page administrators started a page in support of the "Day of Rage" to help mobilize the 25 January 2010 protest in Tahrir Square, which essentially continued until the Mubarak regime fell.

To be clear, we are not suggesting Facebook *caused* this revolution. What is clear, however, is that social media was mobilized, first to address specific concerns of police and government abuse, then to build an online community and finally to mobilize protest and broader political action. But there was widespread criticism amidst the uprising that Facebook's terms of service exposed key organizers in Egypt. Indeed, Wael Ghonim, an administrator of the Khaled Said site was identified and arrested by the Egyptian police soon after the Tahrir Square protests began. Facebook refuses to knowingly allow pseudonyms, making organizers like Ghonim easy targets for the authorities. In the words of Ethan Zuckerman, a senior researcher at Harvard's Berkman Center on Internet and Society, "Facebook has seemed deeply ambivalent about this idea that they would become a platform for revolutions. And it makes sense that they would be deeply ambivalent" (as cited in Watson, 2011). This ambivalence is undoubtedly befitting a private business valued at $83 billion.

Yet Ghonim is unequivocal in his views on Revolution 2.0 and the positive role of Facebook. He is on the record repeatedly praising Mark Zuckerberg, stating "[I want to] thank him, actually. This revolution started online, this revolution started on Facebook" (All Facebook, 2011). For Ghonim, it is clear that without 'learning to immaterial labour 2.0' there could not have been a revolution:

> Our revolution is like Wikipedia, okay? Everyone is contributing content, [but] you don't know the names of the people contributing the content. This is exactly what happened. Revolution 2.0 in Egypt was exactly the same. Everyone contributing small pieces, bits and pieces. We drew this whole picture of a revolution. And no one is the hero in that picture (*60 Minutes*, 2011)

It would be churlish to dismiss these comments just because Ghonim is also Google's head of Marketing for Africa and the Middle East. Equally, it would be a mistake to suggest this political triumph trumps social media's basic role in reproducing and extending cognitive capitalism. What remains open, however, is how innovative use of social media might create new forms of political action? Some in Egypt, Tunisia, Libya, and soon elsewhere have learned this lesson well. What remains open to question is to what extent others might learn how to reverse "biopower into biopolitics, the 'art of governance' into the production and government of new forms of life"? (Lazzarato, 1996).

Notes

1. O'Reilly (2005) uses this term to describe what many see the internet is becoming; that is, as second-generation networked services. For example Google would be a leading Web 2.0 entity as the efficacy of its search engine largely depends upon the collective activity of its users. Web 2.0 is what happens when the accretion of cultural knowledge, or the 'general intellect'—in networked relations—becomes the primary dynamic of the internet. Other Web 2.0 exemplars would be Twitter, tumblr, wikis (open user-generated content sites like Wikipedia) and geo-social networks like Foresquare. Finally, all variants of user-generated content, from content rating (Digg, Reddit), to user reviews (UrbanSpoon, YELP) to 'tagging' (Flickr, de.licio.us) are integral to this active turn in internet usage.

2. While the original source for Lazzarato's eponymous article is Hardt and Virno's (1996) *Radical Thought in Italy*, it has since been diffused throughout the internet. Perhaps the richest such source is the veritable treasure trove, the Generation Online site [www.generation-online.org], which has a vast array of articles from a very broadly defined Autonomist tradition and incisive materials on concepts ranging from 'immaterial labour' to 'biopower' to 'general intellect'.

3. Cf. Wright (2005). Wright is not only a thoughtful critic of the immaterial labour thesis, but his book *Storming Heaven* (2002) offers perhaps the best English-language overview of Italian Autonomist Marxism, the theoretico-practical crucible from which the very concept emerged.

4. Hardt and Negri's frame can be broken down as follows. The first form of immaterial labour refers to cerebral or conceptual work like problem solving and symbolic and analytical tasks. Typically, such jobs are found in the technological sector of the culture industry—i.e. public relations, media production, web design etc. What is key is that production shifts from the material realm of the factory to the symbolic production of ideas. The second component includes the production of affects. Herein affective labour refers to those forms that manipulate "a feeling of ease, well, being, satisfaction, excitement or passion" (Hardt and Negri, 2004: 108). Historically, this labour has been unpaid and has been commonly regarded as 'women's work'. Jobs in this field typically include those that produce services or care through the body. The third flags the way in which communication technology has been incorporated and transformed original industrial production (Hardt & Negri 2000: 293), thus referring to the way in which labour has become increasingly mechanized and computerized.

5. Tiziana Terranova (2004) impressively draws upon Autonomist theory, cybernetics, and information theory in her book *Information Culture: Politics for the Information Age*. Therein she develops a similar thesis that she called 'free labour'—namely, that free labour is a central feature of both the internet and informationalized economy.

6. The concept of intelligibility comes from Judith Butler's recent work, specifically from her article entitled 'Performativity, precarity and sexual politics.' The question of intelligibility is inextricably linked to legibility. We use this to speak about how users are able to reproduce and circulate their respective digital profiles.

7. For an introduction to this genealogy, cf. Coté (2003). Briefly, this is the Foucault of the mid-1970s who realized power was expressed in subjectivities and that the possibility of resistance always came before strategic relations of domination. This was the Foucault enthusiastically read by many Italian Autonomist Marxists, eventually taking form in the 'second-generation' Autonomist Lazzarato's concept of immaterial labour.

8. This article (literally translated as 'The Meshes of Power' or more elegantly as 'The Intricate Network of Power') is arguably one of Foucault's most significant never to be translated into English. It is of particular importance in this context because in it Foucault addresses his conceptual relationship to Marx in an atypically candid manner, specifically in relation to his dispositifs of power. He emphasizes his reading of Marx where he locates a 'positive' conception of power very much inline with his own. All translations are our own unless otherwise stated.

9. Quite relevant to our examination of immaterial labour is the lengthy consideration by Hardt and Negri of the way that "life itself becomes an object of power" (2000, pp. 22–41).

10. The constitutive role of affect in immaterial labour is stressed by Hardt and Negri: "[affective labour produces] social networks, forms of community, biopower [where] the instrumental action of economic production has been united with the communicative action of human relations" (2000, p. 293). The breadth and depth of affect vis-à-vis labour is an important site of inquiry. For example, Emma Dowling has made a compelling case for the importance of affect to traditional material forms of social networks in relation to service work in her essay "Producing the Dining Experience—Measure, Subjectivity and the Affective Worker." As well, Melissa Gregg studied the role of affect in home-based white collar work that utilizes new media technology. The varying scope of these studies suggests the importance of affect across all forms of labour, not least of all that of audiences/social networkers.

11. Cf. Jhally (1982); Livant (1979); Livant (1982); Murdock (1978); Smythe (1977); Smythe (1978).

References

60 Minutes. (2011). Wael Ghonim and Egypt's new age revolution. *CBS News Online*. Retrieved from http://www.youtube.com/watch?v=LxJK6SxGCAw

Ahmed, S. (2004). *Cultural Politics of Emotion*. New York: Routledge.

Alexa. (2011). Top sites. Retrieved January 15, 2011. Retrieved from http://www.alexa.com

All Facebook. (2011). Google's Wael Ghonim thanks Facebook for revolution. Retrieved from http://www.allfacebook.com/googles-wael-ghonim-thanks-facebook-for-revolution-2011--02.

Boyd, D. (2006). Identity production in a networked culture: Why youth heart MySpace. *American Association for the Advancement of Science*. Retrieved from http://www.danah.org/papers/AAAS2006.html

Bratich, J. (2005). Amassing the multitude: Revisiting early audience studies. *Communication Theory,* 15(3), 242–265.

Butler, J. (2009). Performativity, precarity and performativity. *AIBR. Revista de Antropología Iberoamericana,* 4(3), i-xiii.

Coffee Today. (2010). Facebook has seen its greatest number of users in Egypt. Retrieved from http://www.coffetoday.com/facebook-has-seen-its-greatest-number-of-users-in-egypt/9010790/

Coté, M. (2003). The Italian Foucault: Subjectivity, valorization, autonomia. *Politics and Culture,* 3. Retrieved from http://aspen.conncoll.edu/politicsandculture/page.cfm?key=259

Coté, M. (2005). The soft revolution: An emerging dispositif of creative resistance. Paper presented at *L'Échiquier du Présent: Généalogies de la Biopolitique,* Université de Montréal. Retrieved from http://wwwradicalempiricism.org/biotextes/textes/cote.pdf

Cote, M. & Pybus, J. (2007). Learning to immaterial labour 2.0: MySpace and social networks. *Ephemera,* 7(1), 88–106.

Cvetkovich, A. (2003). *An Archive of Feelings: Trauma, Sexuality, and Lesbian Public Cultures.* Durham, NC: Duke University Press.

Dean, J. (2004). The networked empire: Communicative capitalism and the hope for politics. In Dean, J. and Passavant, P. (Eds.), *Empire's New Clothes* (pp. 265–88). New York: Routledge.

Deleuze, G. (1995). Postscript on Society of Control. *Negotiations*: 1972–1990. New York: Columbia University Press.

Deuze, M. (2006). *Media Work,* London: Polity.

Digibuzz Blog. (2010). Facebook: Facts and figures for 2010. Retrieved from http://www.digitalbuzzblog.com/facebook-statistics-facts-figures-for-2010

Dowling, E. (2007). Producing the dining experience—Measure, subjective and the affective worker. *Ephemera: Journal of Theory and Politics in Organisation,* 7(1), 117–132.

Dyer-Witheford, N. (1999). *C--Marx: Cycles and Circuits of Struggle in High-Technology Capitalism.* Urbana: University of Illinois Press.

Facebook. (2011). Statistics. Retrieved on January 15, 2011, from http://www.facebook.com/press/info.php?statistics

Foucault, M. (2001). Les mailles du pouvoir. *Dits et Ecrits 2,* Paris: Gallimard, 1001–1020.

Gregg, M. and Seigworth, G. (2010). *The Affect Theory Reader.* Durham, NC: Duke University Press.

Hardt, M. and Negri, A. (2000). *Empire.* Cambridge, MA: Harvard University Press.

Hardt, M. and Negri, A. (2004). *Multitude: War and Democracy in the Age of Empire.* London: Penguin.

Herrera, L. (2011). Egypt's revolution 2.0: The Facebook factor. *Jaddaliyya.* Retrieved from http://www.jadaliyya.com/pages/index/612/egypts-revolution-2.0_the-facebook-factor

Jhally, S. (1982). Probing the blindspot: The audience commodity. *Canadian Journal of Political and Social Theory,* 6(1–2), 204–210.

Laermans R. & Gielen P. (2007). The archive of the digital an-archive. *Image [&] Narrative.* 17. Retrieved from http://www.imageandnarrative.be/inarchive/digital_archive/laermans_giel en.htm

Lazzarato, M. (1996). Immaterial Labour. *Generation Online*. Retrieved from http://www.-generation-online.org/c/fcimmateriallabour3.htm

Lazzarato, M. (2000). From biopower to biopolitics. *Generation Online*. Retrieved from http://www.generation-online.org/c/fcbiopolitics.htm

Lazzarato, M. (2001). Towards an inquiry into immaterial labour. *Makeworlds, 1*. Retrieved from http://makeworlds.org/node/141

Jenkins, H. (2006). *Convergence Culture: Where Old and New Media Collide*. New York: New York University Press.

Livant, B. (1979). The audience commodity: On the "blindspot" debate. *Canadian Journal of Political and Social Theory*, 3(1), 91–106.

Livant, B. (1982). Working at watching: A reply to Sut Jhally, *Canadian Journal of Political and Social Theory*, 6(1–2), 211–215.

Marx, K. (1973). *Grundrisse*. London: Penguin.

Marx, K. (1990). *Capital Volume 1*. London: Penguin.

Massumi, B. (2002). In M. Zournazi (ed.), Navigating movements: A conversation with Brian Massumi, *Hope: New Philosophies for Change*. New York: Routledge.

Murdock, G. (1978). Blindspots about Western Marxism: A reply to Dallas Smythe. *Canadian Journal of Political and Social Theory*, 2(2), 109–119.

Negri, A. (1999). Value and affect. *Boundary, 2*, 26(2), 77–88.

O'Reilly, T. (2005). What is web 2.0? Retrieved from http://oreilly.com/web2/archive/what-is-web-20.html

Phillips, S. (2007). A brief history of Facebook. *The Guardian*, 25(7). Retrieved from http://www.guardian.co.uk/technology/2007/jul/25/media.newmedia

Smythe, D. (1977). Communications: Blindspot of Western Marxism. *Canadian Journal of Political and Social Theory*, 1, 1–27.

Smythe, D. (1978). Rejoinder to Graham Murdock. *Canadian Journal of Political and Social Theory*, 2(2), 120–127.

Smythe, D. (1981). *Dependency Road: Communications, Capitalism, Consciousness, and Canada*. Norwood: Ablex.

Sunden, J. (2002). In Fornas et al. (Eds.), Cyberbodies, writing gender in digital self-presentations. *Digital Borderlands: Cultural Studies of Identity and Interactivity on the Internet*, pp. 79–111. New York: Peter Lang.

Sunden, J. (2009). Transformations in screen culture. *Screen Culture: JMK Seminar Series*. Retrieved from http://www.youtube.com/watch?v=UAMDJCmCUKk

TechCrunch. (2011). Facebook users upload a record 750 million photos over New Years. Retrieved from http://techcrunch.com/2011/01/03/facebook-users-uploaded-a-record-750-million-photos-over-new-years

TechCrunch. (2011a). Facebook now worth more than Yahoo and ebay. *TechCrunch*. Retrieved from http://techcrunch.com/2011/01/03/facebook-yahoo-ebay

Terranova, T. (2004). *Network Culture: Politics for the Information Age*. London: Pluto.

Virno, P. & Hardt, M. (eds.). (1996). *Radical Thought in Italy: A Potential Politics*. Minneapolis: University of Minnesota Press.

Virtanen, A. & Vähämäki, J. (2005). The structure of change: An introduction, *Ephemera*, 5(X). Retrieved from www.ephemeraweb.org

Watson, T. (2011). Facebook, Egypt and the social network. *My Dirty Life and Times*. Retrieved from http://tomwatson.typepad.com/tom_watson/2011/02/facebook-egypt-and-the-social-network.html

We Are All Khaled Said. (2011). Retrieved from http://www.facebook.com/elshaheeed.co.uk#!/els haheeed.co.uk?sk=info

Willis, P. E. (1977). *Learning to Labour: How Working Class Kids Get Working Class Jobs*. Farnborough: Saxon House.

Wright, S. (2002). *Storming Heaven. Class Composition and Struggle in Italian Autonomous Marxism*. London: Pluto.

Wright, S. (2005). Reality check: Are we living in an immaterial world? *Mute Magazine*, 2(1). Retrieved from http://www.metamute.org/en/node/5594

CHAPTER EIGHT

Pedagogies of Cognitive Capitalism:
Challenging the Critical Subject [1]

EMMA DOWLING

> But, if constructing the future and settling everything for all times are not our affair,
> it is all the more clear what we have to accomplish at present: I am referring to ruth-
> less criticism of all that exists, ruthless both in the sense of not being afraid of the results
> it arrives at and in the sense of being just as little afraid of conflict with the powers
> that be.[2]

Historically, universities have been both sites for the reproduction of power and privilege, as well as sites or conduits for the contestation and transformation of these power relations; in both instances, critical scholarship has been central, albeit in different ways or from different vantage points. Today, the university, when viewed as the training ground for cognitive capitalism's immaterial labourers, presents new challenges for the teaching of critical scholarship within its walls. On the one hand, the instrumentalised classroom seems to render critique and contestation risk factors for students under pressure to obtain the grades they need to ensure the return on their cognitive, emotional and financial investment, i.e., a degree qualification that has an exchange value in the labour market, thus furthering their 'employability'.[3] On the other hand, cognitive labour requires a capacity for critical thinking. Yet, what kind of criticality is this? What kind of 'critical subject' is the labouring subject of cognitive capitalism? Raunig (2008) has suggested that, "if today, we negotiate the position of the General Intellect, a collective and militant intellectuality in post-Fordist cognitive capitalism, this in turn means a new challenge for the various forms of critique." Indeed, the contemporary university is one of a multiplicity of sites upon which this negotiation is occurring. The current resistance against 'disaster capitalism's (Klein, 2008) plans for the dismantling of publicly funded education in the wake of the crisis, are part of this negotiation, not to say struggle. My contribution here is a reflection on my experiences of teaching in a Business School at a U.K. university.[4] Here, I am interested in two related questions: in what ways do students have to navigate the neoliberal university and what are the possibilities for an emancipatory pedagogical practice of self-valorisation, or what Spivak (2007) calls a "non-coercive rearrangement of desire."

Criticality remains central to the common understanding of what students, lecturers and researchers do in a university. This is echoed in the myriad of EU policy documents on higher education that demand not only creativity, innovation and entrepreneurship skills from graduates, but also the ability to "formulate judgements", "handle complexity" and conduct "critical analysis".[5] Nick Dyer-Witheford has suggested that today's universities are sites where the post-Fordist labour force "is sorted and socialized to the new information economy through increasingly vocational and technically orientated curricula that stress skills and proficiency at the expense of critical analysis and free thinking" (2005, p. 76).

Whilst I agree with this analysis, I wish to suggest that this observation requires refining. The neoliberal university does not necessarily do away with critical analysis or free thinking per se. As highlighted above, critical analysis remains a key component of educational policy. Consequently, it is necessary to discern how critical analysis becomes articulated as a technical or vocational skill, which in turn shapes what criticality and critique as an intellectual practice come to mean in this specific pedagogical context. Rather than obliterating criticality, my experience is that what happens is that critique and critical analysis become 'overcoded' (Deleuze and Guattari, 1987), in a way that gives them meaning within a matrix of power relations as governed by the institutional context of the neoliberal university and the imposition of the commodity form. The real subsumption of the university leads to two related moments of commodity production (and labour processes) that exist in a double-bind. Firstly, there is the (co-)production[6] of the student as commodity in a labour process that adds value to the labour-power of the student and also conditions the student as precarious labour. Secondly, the university is directly subsumed under the drive (and need for) profit, therefore managed as a business in and of itself. What are the mechanisms through which the capital relation overcodes and structures the pedagogical activities that take place within the university? Furthermore, what effects do these mechanisms have and how can they be challenged? Before turning my attention to these questions, I first discuss what it is that is meant, or what it is that can be meant, by terms such as critique, criticism, criticality or critical analysis.

The Meaning(s) of Critique

The etymological roots of the word critique or criticism lie in the Greek 'kritikos' or 'krinein', which means 'to discern', 'to distinguish' or 'to separate out'. The critic is engaged in an activity in which she discerns true from false, distinguishes between right and wrong, or separates out error, finds fault. Critique is an activity that involves decision, a decision through which meaning is given to something. Thus in the first instance, the critic seeks to make the object of her criticism intelligible, from which vantage point she validates and in turn may seek to find ways of improving something in order to overcome the errors she has identified. We can thus say that critique is about interpretation and it is about judgement. The critic asks questions of her object of critique: does it uphold the standards, norms or values that it espouses or is allegedly founded upon (the immanent critique)? Are there other criteria that stand outside or above the object of critique that should inform how it is judged (the transcendental critique)? Critique requires an object of critique, it is not a generalisable practice, which is a way of interpreting notions of someone *having critical skills* or *the ability to conduct critical analysis*. The critic is always critical *of* something, such as a particular institution, practice, norm, episteme or discourse (Butler, 2001; Foucault, 1997). Critique as judgement, according to Butler, is "a way of subsuming a particular under an already constituted category" (2001). Therefore, if critique is to be able to be a device for transformative practices, she argues that critique cannot simply remain an endeavour of 'fault-finding'. Instead, she argues that critique as an activity must involve the suspension of judgement, opening up the space to be able to ask questions and think something in ways that only become possible if critique is separated—even if this is only temporarily—from judgement. It is thus the process of critique as deconstruction can thereby allow for something new or different to emerge, not only on the level of the ideational, but as a concrete material practice.

Critique is the interrogation of received thought, both that which is articulated and that which remains unspoken in the gaps, occlusions, silences and tacit assumptions that accompany it. Moreover, critique necessitates an understanding of the relationship between knowledge and the materiality of social relations of power. Critical theories have sought to uncover how the status quo of power is materially secured and reproduced, as well as rendered objective, neutral or natural, i.e., legitimised. They have also demonstrated how certain political and economic arrangements affect those who are exploited or oppressed by them and have argued for an epistemological starting point that is able to question the kinds of knowledge and theoretical approaches that reproduce the status quo as objective and value-free (Frampton et al., 2005, 5) and are merely "problem-solving" (Cox, 1986, 205) without exposing the material interests, purpose and perspective that inform them, reproducing precisely the relations of power that their supporters benefit from. The archetypical question of critical theories has thus been, *'In whose interest?'* For Foucault, critique also involves a contestation of the status quo. For him, the problematic of critique lies in "the problem of certainty in its confrontation with authority"; whilst truth produces the subject, critique is desubjugation and the refusal to be governed in a particular way:

> Critique is the movement by which the subject gives himself the right to question truth on its effects of power and question power on its discourses of truth. Well then! Critique will be the art of voluntary insubordination [. . .] the desubjugation of the subject in the context of what we could call, in a word, the politics of truth.

If the Kantian critique was about probing the limits of the right to govern and the "legitimacy of historical modes of knowledge" (Raunig, 2008), then critique as the refusal to be governed in a particular way involves not only criticising that legitimacy and how it is inscribed in the institutions of society (the law, the state, social norms and conventions) but actively transgressing its limits in a refusal of governance.

How do these different forms of critique relate to the contemporary university and pedagogies of critique? My argument so far has been that the neoliberal university 'overcodes' criticality in particular ways; as I have already insinuated, there is a tendency for critique to be articulated as a generalisable practice of the development of the technical skill of 'criticality' of cognitive labour. To understand how this comes about we have to understand how neoliberalism—and neoliberal governance—function. Neoliberal governance denotes a new era of supposed 'co-management of common affairs', an ideological projection (that celebrates the end of ideology and the 'truth' of the market) of governance as a benign process infused with a commitment to efficient and technocratic management. Governance is a process that fixes antagonistic relations through rule-making on the one hand and that functions as a depoliticising mode of subjectivation invoking the rationale of efficiency and 'good governance' in the reproduction systemic imperatives, the social relations of capital. The observation Pavlich makes is succinct in this respect:

> As the privileges of modern disciplinary truth regimes erode, so critique is increasingly assembled around images of system performance. If such developments erode disciplinary critical grammars, they also nurture a new breed of 'critics'—those who speak out in order to enhance, improve and expand the efficient management, or performance, of existing systems. Their critiques are designed less to challenge the founding rationales of systems than to fine-tune, or finesse, the technical elements of given configurations.(2005, p. 99)

However, it would be all too easy to counter-pose critique as the enhancement of system performance to critique as the contestation and transformation of the status quo. As an (autonomist) Marxist analysis reminds us, capital recuperates and renders productive not only the creative capacities of living labour but also the struggles for liberation. Moreover, the processes that I am describing here constitute sites of struggle, where both the governance and the disruption of these labour processes occur. In the remainder of this chapter, I turn to the mechanisms by which and the effects of how the capital relation informs university education.

Modes of Subjectivation in the Neoliberal University

When I ask my students why they are at university, most of them answer that they are studying so that they can get a better job than they otherwise would have done without a degree. They almost never answer that they are at university to learn, to pursue their interest in a particular field of knowledge, or even, to develop any particular skills. Whilst this kind of instrumentalised approach to university education is perhaps more prominent in certain subject areas than others (and indeed more likely to be the case at non-elite institutions), this is a tendency across the board and will only increase in light of the new wave of restructurings that will see the cost of going to university increase for the individual student, thus raising the stakes in terms of the need to maximise employability, and the closure or downsizing of many subject areas and departments deemed 'unviable' in terms of the market logic imposed upon the university itself (unable to attract sufficient revenue) and notions of 'employability' as attuned to business and industry. It is important to be aware of how the emphasis is not on the skills the students hope to learn but on the degree qualification they come out with at the end. This is what the students understand as the key that (they hope) will open the door to secure employment. I have never had a student complain to me that they have not been able to sufficiently develop their critical literacy skills or their ability to communicate complex ideas to their peers, even less, that they have not been able to sufficiently develop their reading of a particular theorist or event. However, I regularly encounter stressed students wishing to discuss with me the mark I gave them for a particular assignment. It would be too easy to simply see this as a short-hand way of talking about the form and content of their degree programme, the mark awarded as correlated to level of knowledge and skill. But this is not what is going on. Many times, the student wishes to discuss their mark with me not because they think that I have given them a mark that their work did not deserve but because the mark I gave them brings down their average, thus lowering the exchange value of their degree qualification (I am regularly told by the students that their degree is 'worth nothing' if it is not at least a '2:1'). Therefore, their return on investment is measured in terms of the successful completion of the degree, where the higher the overall mark, the better, and where if it falls below a certain degree classification, it has a diminishing rate of return. The student is fearful of her precarious status and the volatilities of the labour market that await her upon completion of her degree, compounded by the inordinate levels of debt that she has to take on in order to be at university in the first place. Nonetheless, as a neoliberal subject (Read, 2009), she strives to be an entrepreneur of herself, investing in her cognitive skills and her capacity to endure risk and uncertainty, wanting to better herself in order to be able to sell her labour power—posed not as labour but as 'human capital'—at a higher price than she may be able to without the university degree and in competition, of course, with her peers.

Spivak reminds us of the importance of an attention to silence when she states that,

> Logic allows us to jump from word to word by means of clearly indicated connections. Rhetoric must work in the silence between and around words in order to see what works and how much. The jagged relationship between rhetoric and logic, condition and effect of knowing, is a relationship by which a world is made for the agent, so that the agent can act in an ethical way, a political way, a day-to-day way. (1993, p. 181)

Enquiring into the silences of the classroom has allowed me to work in precisely such silences between and around words. One of the silences that I have encountered in the classroom has been a very literal silence, the inability or unwillingness of students to speak in class and engage in a discussion of the material at hand. During one seminar, after having endured silence after silence, following a series of questions on my behalf regarding the key text the students were supposed to have read for that particular week, I asked the students present why nobody was speaking and why everyone sat staring straight ahead of them or playing with their mobile phones. There was a wave of embarrassed mutterings and uneasy smiles, followed by further silence. I decided to sit it out and we sat for a good few minutes together in silence. After a while, one student raised her hand. She explained to me that the reason nobody spoke was because there was no mark for participating in the seminars of my course, therefore, it was not 'worth' contributing to the discussion because it did not 'count' for anything. Despite my dismay at this attitude to learning, I decided in the following year to give a mark for participation in class. This did not make the pedagogical environment any better; now, the students began to worry about the mark for participation: it became another issue for them to worry about and be fearful of not achieving.

It is not only the student who is continuously subjected to measure, the lecturer's teaching practices are also subjected to forms of measure and control. In the United Kingdom for example, the National Student Survey (NSS)[7] is a satisfaction survey that each third-year undergraduate is encouraged to complete (interestingly, at present, response rates are actually quite low and students do not seem to be that concerned with participating in the survey, which has prompted a major advertising campaign to get students to fill in the online survey). The NSS quantifies the overall 'student experience' of individual universities and university departments, in turn pitting them against each other by competition through rankings, which in turn are used to performance-manage staff through the figure of 'the student as customer'. Mechanisms of governance through which the subjectivities of the student and lecturer are produced: the student as the obedient willing worker fearful of their individual future and the lecturer as the enforcer of the current regime of governance, equally under pressure to hit key performance indicators (KPIs), targets imposed as 'measures of success' that become the standards as to what and how much can be demanded of workers and the condition of continued employment. The problem here is not evaluation or feedback per se, in and of itself a useful conversation between students and lecturers. The issue is how such measures are conducted, in what ways and to what end, where it is necessary to interrogate education as both mediated and constituted by forms of measure that serve as mechanisms of control that have disciplining functions, whilst the use value of the lecturers' labour is 'objectively' established through specific processes of measurement that served to quantify its corresponding exchange value, subjecting it to the calculating eye of capital and its interest in the exchange value that can be potentially generated, in turn affecting how the labour process of teaching and learning is organised.[8]

Challenging the Critical Subject

A critical pedagogy must begin from a practical critique of the way that the institution of the university organises the field of knowledge and teaching to conform with the demands of capital. Decentering the modes of neoliberal subjectivation within the university setting means connecting critique and critical analysis to the experiences of students in how they are subjected to debt, competition and cost-benefit calculations, and their self-understanding as 'human capital'. This means however, that the pedagogical problematic cannot be posed as an opposition between (critical) analytical and vocational education and must be posed from the position of the antagonism of labour. Moreover, in the struggle over measure, this requires a pedagogy that entails a collective transformative practice of refusal of the subjectivities produced by governance and a transgression of the current relationship between student and lecturer on these terms. Such pedagogy begins from an under-standing that as subjects we have an "experience of the lived multiplicity of posi-tioning" (Blackman et al., 2008, p. 6) that constitutes knowledge in ways that intersect at the moment of the material experience of social life. However, there is an irony here. The current emphasis of positing the 'student experience' or 'student-centred learning' as a quantifiable 'measure of success' or KPI lies precisely in how it becomes abstracted to conform with the demands of capital at the expense of an actual increase in the autonomy of the student and their social experience of learn-ing. 'Experience' (as subjectivation) thus becomes a site of struggle for self-valorisation as an emancipatory pedagogical practice.

Experience serves to rupture the ideological accounts that power-holders give of themselves and of the system that they wish to maintain and reproduce, because the actual lived experience of what such accounts seek to obscure lays bare the dis-juncture. Secondly, experience is the encounter of the subject with the social world; it thus forms the epistemological point of departure for making sense of social real-ity and one's subject position, where the complexity of the world connects to our lives through experience. Thirdly, experience enables us to begin from the actual lived experiences of those subjected to a ruling regime and is thus grounded in a grass-roots perspective that can explain how a ruling regime is actually lived and con-stituted, such that the processes of legitimation and the construction of particular class interests as general or as 'objective', can be uncovered and put centre-stage in the analysis. Focusing on experience also provides the possibility for analysing how the reproduction of capital functions not only through ideology as a discursive or symbolic technology of power but also as a mode of subjectivation that is not a form of external command but is embedded in the everyday lives and engagements with the production and reproduction of livelihood and of labour power.

An experience is an event through which one has been affected, providing both knowledge and transformation. Benjamin suggests two different connotations of the term *experience* in German, as on the one hand, *Erlebnis* (to live something) and on the other, *Erfahrung* (to go through and make sense of something). The distinction between these different types of experience is informative of the varying ways in which social life is perceived and processed. Benjamin uses this differentiation to express different registers of perception and understanding of experience. *Erlebnis* is connoted as a form of 'standardised', 'denatured' life, an assimilation of isolated spectacular forms of stimuli to the body and mind, or simple information about things that are happening (Benjamin, 1961, 166). Benjamin contrasts *Erlebnis* with *Erfahrung*. *Erfahrung* designates experience dependent upon comprehension and reflection. Thus, an *Erfahrung* is a comprehensible experience that requires an integration into memory through reflection. *Erfahrung* in Kluge and Negt's work denotes the movement between that which is experienced in a number of conscious, subconscious, sensory and embodied ways, and the process by which the deployment of cognitive faculties that are linked to memory, language, discourse and articulation, subjects come to make sense of their encounters in the world and integrate it into an understanding of them (1972, p. 8). For Benjamin, Kluge, and Negt, the embodied, affective[9] experiences matter in affect how they are lodged in our unconscious and produce both action and knowledge. The libidinal drive is paramount as the motivation for knowledge.[10]

The difference between an *Erlebnis* and an *Erfahrung* becomes even more evident in Kluge and Negt's treatment of *Erfahrung* as movement. Grounded in the etymological root of the German word *fahren*, which means *to drive* or *to go*, *Erfahrung* is something that we move through, which is different from an understanding of experience as a trial or experiment, as is the etymological root of the word in English (Hansen, 1993, vxi).[11] Whilst Kluge and Negt's understanding is not a Benjaminian one in the sense of making a clear distinction between *Erlebnis* and *Erfahrung*, it is evident that in both theorisations, experience as *Erfahrung*, as a form of (social) movement, a process in which we go through something, is central. In both renderings, it is experience as collective social experience, an experience of both production and of the reception of the appearance and the validity of social life as it is organised, that is understood as *Erfahrung*, a de-centering of the subject and the establishment of new social relations as a process of transformation (Foucault, 2001, p. 242)

Distinguishing amongst different kinds of experience makes it possible to designate the openings for self-valorisation as a pedagogical practice. What happens through the imposition of measure is that the 'student experience' becomes over-coded as *Erlebnis*, the objectification of an experience, a severing of collective social experience, as a form of capture and of control through the imposition of the commodity form. This is different to experience as *Erfahrung*, the experience of learning as a process of transformation. An *Erlebnis* is an affective stimulation that is not integrated into experience as *Erfahrung*; without a process of reflection, this is a stimulation that is isolated from the realm in which it could affect, remaining "in the sphere if a certain hour of one's life" (Benjamin, 1961, p. 159). An experience as *Erfahrung* is something one emerges from transformed, having gone through a process of learning, or having encountered new ways to relate to oneself and to one's environment. It is a return to the everyday, a return in which one is transformed. The differentiation of experience as *Erlebnis* and *Erfahrung*, and the clarification of *Erfahrung* as social experience of learning and of subjectivation is key. Going through something, a process, an event, and feeling and experiencing it for oneself and together with others, consequently understanding—or trying to understand—what ramifications that has for critical analysis, in the sense that knowledge production is understood as a social activity, where "the exploratory activity that constitutes thinking is a discussion carried out not only in the imagination, but on a social scale" (Kluge and Negt, 1972, p. 23) and involves a form of knowing that is embodied and affective.

Affect, Cognition and Pedagogy

The concept of affect is an attempt to articulate the intensities that are sensed and perceived by the body. Affect draws attention to a 'sub-stratum' of non-verbal, non-cognitive communication between bodies, as one of the dimensions or registers of human relations. It is an attention to the inter-, or better transactions that occur between and among bodies prior to and in excess of how they are cognitised or verbally expressed as feelings. Affect as a philosophical, psychoanalytical and neuroscientific concept is connected to the relationality of 'sense' and describes physiological shifts or transmissions of energy, mood or intensity. The anti-Cartesian philosophy of Benedict Spinoza (1677/2001) and Friedrich Nietzsche (1886/2005) inform contemporary studies of affect. Affect is not emotion. Affect is a "subjectively registered embodied experience" and emotion is a "cultural or discursive articulation of bodily response"(Redman, 2009, p. 53). Both affect and emotion are thus social, but what distinguishes them is that emotion is cognitised or (whether internally formulated or actually expressed) verbalised feeling, a 'match' of affect in words (Brennan, 2004, p. 3). Neither affect nor emotion is individual, but there is a subtle distinction with respect to ownership, expressed in the distinction between the individual and the personal. Massumi (2002, p. 212) suggests that the difference between affect and emotion is that emotion is qualified; it is a personal intensity, where affect is unqualified and thus not ownable. The moment that I register a sensation and experience it as an emotion, it becomes personalised. It is 'my' emotion even if how I formulate the experience is socially and culturally contextualised. Affect exists before personal interpretation takes place (Burkitt, 1997, p. 42). Affect thus describes how individuals are affected by their environments as "receivers, interpreters of feelings, affects, attentive energy" (Brennan, 2004, p. 87). The emphasis is on the social and collective aspects of human existence as bodies that act upon other bodies (Spinoza, 1677/2001) and produce sensation. The implications are a more radical deconstruction of methodological individualism than has taken place so far in the study of emotions, because of an ontological shift away from the individual subject as the 'owner' of emotions in a complex process in which "the discursive and the felt experience of being in the world exist in relations that are contingent, variable and mutually constitutive" (Burkitt, 1997, p. 42). Affect thus circulates in the collective actual and virtual relationalities in which we exist. To be attracted, repelled, to be excited or depressed, to be swept up in something, to be compelled to take a particular action or not, to sense moods and levels of energy, are affective processes. What is apparent here is the importance of movement, of changing levels of intensity, as a way in which the body registers affect, or 'intensity in flux' (Massumi, 2002). Feelings are the experience of a circulation of such intensities, putting subjects in relation to one another in a way that radically decentres the subject as "simultaneously embodied and social" (Burkitt, 2002, p. 53).

Affect is material. In the philosophical and psychoanalytical literature, the materiality of affect is understood in terms of embodiment, where bodies act upon bodies and affect one another. The affective register is located between bodies but experienced through bodily responses and actions. The emphasis is on acknowledging and being attentive to these levels of pre-conscious or unconscious sensing in which body language, body movements, tone of voice, facial expressions and attention to atmospheres registered by the body. Affect itself has no materiality: it is the bodies that register and receive affect that have a materiality to them, a capacity to act, to affect or be affected. Bodies thus do not just receive and interpret affect. Bodies produce affect in their relationality with other bodies. To 'affect' or to be 'affected' is about the increase or diminution of bodily propensity; it is about the increase or diminution of power as it takes place in action in relation to the world around us.[12] Therefore, Clough (2007, p. 3) defines affect as

> a substrate of potential bodily responses in excess of consciousness, and, following Spinoza, as the bodily capacities to affect and be affected, or the augmentation or diminution of a body's capacity to act, engage and connect.

Affect is therefore "probabilistic" (Clough, 2009) because capacity is a potentiality, potential because it does not determine human activity, but denotes a power to "affect the world around us as well as be affected by it (Hardt, 2007, p. xii). It is 'pure capacity' (Massumi, 2002, p. 16) because it is precisely not the capacity of one body but the capacity that is generated through the desires and drives which affect produces in relation to other bodies. If affect is about those elements of human (and other) relations that are pre-conscious or non-conscious, then the question is raised of how we make sense of affective sensations. Affect seems to preclude its own analysis, given that analysis requires a conscious process of sense-making, of evaluation, and is communicated through language. What is the relationship between affect and cognition? This is not only a question that surfaces with an interpretation of contemporary capitalism as 'cognitive', which omits how affect and communicative capacities beyond a simple demarcation of its cognitive dimensions are equally rendered productive for capital accumulation in contemporary 'biocapitalism' (see also the editors' introduction). This is also a question for a pedagogical practice that is engaged in teaching critical-intellectual skills.

What are the possibilities of an affective cognition and of how we make sense of the affective register? Clough (2009, p. 49) argues that,

> any method of attending to affect will necessarily become entangled with an immanent dynamism, with the potential for individuation. A method attending to affect necessarily is performative, having become entangled or assemblage with affect's capacity of self-informationality. [. . .] it also cannot simply be a matter of interpretation, meaning, signification or representation. Method cannot help but produce affective resonance, attunement, that is, the intensifying or dampening of affect.

What this means is that affect cannot represent itself or be represented in its potentiality for becoming in the undoing and remaking of bodies, where the body is in itself an event for affective resonance (Manning, 2010, p. 120) beyond self-referentiality and the individual as the starting point for analysis. In these terms, an affective cognition would not be possible and is rendered to the level of the performative in which the engagement with affect, as the capacity to affect and be affected, is itself the expression of the comprehension of affect. Does this mean that the discursive explanation of affect is always suboptimal on its own terms? Brennan (2004) suggests that there is the possibility of 'discernment' through which the affective experience finds a vocabulary that is expressed as feeling, i.e., it is personalised. Therefore, we leave the terrain of the affective and necessarily must do so as affect becomes conscious. The concept of affect seeks to capture precisely the kinds of processes and circulations as moments of co-production that are prior to consciousness and thus exceeds phenomenological accounts of experience that focus on the individual subject. However, what I wish to propose is that if indeed affect is pre-conscious, then bringing together affect and cognition denotes the possibility of integrating affective experience into comprehension as an emancipatory practice, suggests how an affective cognition could be fashioned. This becomes evident when we understand the will to knowledge is in itself an affective drive. The moment of experience is one of movement, a "dialectical movement which consciousness performs on itself" (Kluge and Negt, 1972, p. 52). This dialectical movement of consciousness on itself points to how the integration of an affective experience is a process of movement, a transformation that is an embodied form of knowing. Affect and cognition are thus not mutually exclusive, but remain different processes of sense-making that become integrated through attention and enable a form of knowledge production that is transformative. Thus, we are looking for vocabularies of affect that are not merely discursive and for a form of discernment as critical practice that is rooted in experience and is attentive to drives, desires and affect. Affect and cognition do not stand opposed to one another, where affect constitutes a form of 'data collection' of sensed experience and cognition constitutes the 'sense-making' of the data; instead, an attention to affect allows for an understanding of the interrelationship between experience, subjectivity and (critical) analysis and sense-making.

Conclusion

In teaching, I mostly encounter students torn between two perspectives: either they are caught up in a positivist world of ideological projections posing as objective truth and neutral fact or they have been exposed to a critique of the status quo and interrogate the nexus of power, knowledge and material interests, yet the pendulum swings to the other side where 'everything is subjective' and 'everyone has their own individual opinion'. Whilst post-positivism has made claims to impartiality, objectivity and universalisability that obfuscate the power relations that are thus reproduced problematic (although certainly not obsolete). At the same time, such advances have put in place criticality, deconstruction, subjectivity and perspective as antidotes to the false presumptions of positivism in ways that have rendered notions of diversity and difference, or postmodernism as a form of radical relativism, desirable solutions to the problem of power/knowledge. Such approaches remain premised upon a neglect of the material realities of the social relations of capital as a contradictory class relation. Based on my experience of teaching at a university in the UK, I have sought to inquire into the relationship between the recent round of neoliberal restructurings of university education, the teaching of critical scholarship as subsumed under capitalist valorization and the possibilities for critical and emancipatory pedagogies. My intention has been to provide a discerning analysis of the central role that notions of education as the development of critical faculties have in contemporary neoliberal educational policies. I have sought to show how criticality thus becomes overcoded within the University, it is given meaning within a matrix of power relations as governed by the institutional context of the neoliberal university and the imposition of the commodity form. In other words, the question of what a critical pedagogical practice is must make the connection to an analysis of how the neoliberal university is governed and governmentalised. If critique is indeed the contestation and transformation of the status quo, then education as the development of critical skills must begin from the question of the antagonism of labour and the affective experiences of subjectivation, not as isolated immaterial workers but as situated within a global wage hierarchy that begins in the classroom.

Notes

1. For provocations, conversations and insights on the questions I address in this chapter, I thank Estelle du Boulay, Janna Graham, Nic Beuret, Elise Thorburn, Denise Ferreira da Silva and Michal Osterweil.

2. From Marx's letter to Arnold Ruge, Deutsch-Französische Jahrbücher, September 1843; many thanks to John Hutnyk.

3. Defined by the EU Commission as "the ability to gain initial employment, to maintain employment, and to be able to move around within the labour market." [http://www.ond.vlaanderen.be/hogeronderwijs/bologna/actionlines/employability.htm]. How this employability (i.e., a capacity to be employed) is to be determined relies upon statistical figures of actual graduate employment and the involvement of business and industry in higher education policy that together are taken as measures of increased capacity.

4. See also Harney (2009).

5. See for example, 'The framework of qualifications for the European Higher Education Area', Bergen Conference of European Ministers Responsible for Higher Education 19–20 May 2005 [http://www.ond.vlaanderen.be/hogeronderwijs/bologna/documents/QF-EHEA-May2005.pdf]

6. I am designating this as a co-production to highlight how there are multiple agents involved with producing the student as commodity. In particular, I argue that it is incorrect to view the relationship between the student and lecturer as one that is based on a simple model of customer and service provider, instead, any analysis must recognise how both are actively involved in the labour process (on the co-production of services in post-Fordism, see also Lazzarato, 1996).

7. See http://www.thestudentsurvey.com

8. On cognitive capitalism, measure and academic labour, see also Harvie and De Angelis (2009).

9. Neither Benjamin nor Kluge and Negt use this term explicitly, but what they are expressing is affect.

10. This has resonances with the work of Nietzsche, Foucault, Deleuze and Guattari, although these are not Kluge and Negt's interlocutors.

11. Interestingly, the Argentinian *Colectivo Situaciones* referenced in the section on militant research are also attentive to experience and its different manifestations. Aside from this focus on lived experiences as the important terrain of inquiry, they also have an understanding of the importance of experiment, as the trial and error of finding new ways of being (cf. the translators' preface to Colectivo Situaciones, 2007, p. 73), of constructing new social relations, which cannot be determined in the abstract but needs to be lived as a mode of becoming. This is similar to the Zapatista understanding of social change as a process in the making, not as predetermined by an articulated political programme, captured in their practice of 'preguntando caminamos' (walking we ask questions). Here experience is extended to connote not only past or present actual lived experiences but also future new lives together in the process of building new and different social relations.

12. This is similar to Foucault's definition of power, as action upon action (2001, p. 340).

Bibliography

Benjamin, W. (1961).*Illuminationen.* Berlin: Suhrkamp Verlag.

Blackman, L. &Venn, C. (2010). Affect. *Body & Society*, 26 (1): 7–28.

Brennan, T. (2004).*The Transmission of Affect.* Ithaca, NY: Cornell University Press.

Burkitt, I. (1997). Social Relationships and Emotions. *Sociology* 31(1): 37–55.

Butler, J. (2001).*What is Critique? An Essay on Foucault's Virtue.* I Retrieved from http://eipcp.net/transversal/0806/butler/en

Clough, P. (2009).The New Empiricism, Affect and Sociological Method. *European Journal of Social Theory* 12(1): 43–61.

Cox, R. (1986). In R. Keohane (ed.), Social Forces, States and World Orders: Beyond International Relations. *Theory, Neorealism and Its Critics.* New York: Columbia University Press.

De Angelis, M. & Harvie, D. (2009)."Cognitive Capitalism" and the Rat-Race: How Capital Measures Immaterial Labour in British Universities. *Historical Materialism*, 17(3): 3–30.

Deleuze, G. & Guattari, F. (1987). A Thousand Plateaus—Capitalism and Schizophrenia, trans. Brian Massumi. London: Continuum.

Caffentzis, G. (2005).Immeasurable Value? An Essay on Marx's Legacy.*The Commoner*, 10: 87–114.

Dyer-Witheford, N. (2005). 'Cyber-Negri: General Intellect and Immaterial Labour', in S. Murphy and A. Mustapha (eds.) *The Philosophy of Antonio Negri—Resistance in Practice.* London: Pluto Press.

Dyer-Witheford, N. (2005). In G. Cox. and J. Krysa (eds.), *Cognitive Capitalism and the Contested Campus, Engineering Culture—On the Author as Digital Producer.* New York: Autonomedia.

Foucault, M. (1977). In S. Lotringer and L. Hochroch (eds.), What Is Critique?*The Politics of Truth: Michel Foucault.* New York: Semiotext(e).

Frampton, C., Kinsman, G., Thompson, A.K. and Tilleczek, K. (eds.).*Sociology for Changing the World.* Halifax: Fernwood Publishing.

Hansen, M. (1993). Foreword, in O. Negt and A. Kluge, The Public Sphere and Experience. Minneapolis: University of Minnesota Press, pp. ix–xliii.

Hardt, M. (1999). Affective Labour. *Boundary*, 2 26 (2): 89–100.

Harney, S. (2009). Extreme Neoliberalism—An Introduction. *Ephemera*, 9 (4): 318–329.

Klein, N. (2008). *The Shock Doctrine—The Rise of Disaster Capitalism* London: Picador.

Kluge, A. & Negt, O. (1973). Oeffentlichkeit und Erfahrung—zur Organisationsanalyse von buergerlichen proletarischen Oeffentlickeit. Suhrkamp: Frankfurt am Main.

Manning, E. (2010). Always More Than One: The Collectivity of a Life. *Body & Society*, 16 (1) 117–127.

Marx, K. (1843). Letter from Marx to Arnold Ruge, Deutsch-FranzösischeJahrbuecher. Retrieved from http://www.marxists.org/archive/marx/works/1843/letters/43_09-alt.htm

Negri, A. (2009). In S. Shukaitis, D. Graeber and E. Biddle (eds.), The Logic of the Inquiry— Militant Praxis as Subject and Episteme.*Constituent Imagination—Militant Investigations, Collective Theorization.* Oakland, CA: AK Press.

Pavlich, G. (2005). Experiencing Critique, *Law and Critique,* 16: 95–112

Scott, J. (1991). The Evidence of Experience. *Critical Enquiry,* 17: 773–797.

Smith, G. (2005). In C. Frampton, G. Kinsman, A.K. Thompson and K. Tilleczek (eds.), *Political Activist as Ethnographer, Sociology for Changing the World.* Halifax: Fernwood Publishing.

Spivak, G. (1993). *Outside in the Teaching Machine.* New York and London: Routledge.

Spivak, G. (2007). *Other Asias.* Oxford: Blackwell.

Raunig, G. (2008). *'What Is Critique?' Suspension and Recomposition in Textual and Social Machines* (trans. Aileen Derieg). Retrieved from http://eipcp.net/transversal/0808/raunig/en

Read, J. (2009). A Genealogy of Homo-Economicus: Neoliberalism and the Production of Subjectivity, *Foucault Studies,* 6: 25–36.

CHAPTER NINE

Creativity as an Educational Problematic within the Biopolitical Economy

ALEX MEANS

The changing role of the university is bound up with the broader shift from an older industrial economy to an emerging Creative Economy. The past few decades have been one of profound economic transformation. In the past, natural resources and physical capital were the predominant drivers of economic growth. Now, human creativity is the driving force of economic growth.

-RICHARD FLORIDA et al., "THE UNIVERSITY IN THE CREATIVE ECONOMY"

Creativity has emerged over the last decade as a prominent theme in business, academic, and state policy discussions. Deployed under an umbrella of neologisms—"creative economy," "creative class," "creative age," "creative citizenship," "creative industries", and "creative cities"—creativity has been positioned as a key capacity for addressing the overlapping economic, technical, social, and environmental challenges of the 21st century. The rhetoric of creativity has also become prevalent within educational debates where it has been geared toward promoting governmental, curriculum, and research initiatives aimed at spurring technological innovation, entrepreneurialism, and economic expansion over the coming decades.[1] From transnational organizations like the Word Bank, the Organization for Economic Cooperation and Development (OECD), and the United Nations, to mega-billionaire corporate philanthropists like Bill Gates, to academics and journalists such as Richard Florida and Thomas Friedman, creativity has arrived as a dominant frame in which to imagine educational change in secondary and higher education that is responsive to an advanced capitalism increasingly reliant on intellectual property and immaterial labor as engines of financial valorization.

It is now widely recognized by academics, policy makers, and economists that knowledge and creativity have become primary drivers of economic value within the global economy. As such, many argue that educational systems must become responsive to these trends. For some, the "creative economy" signals the possibility of greater openness in educational systems and the development of more fluid and democratic educational structures modeled on network and digital infrastructures that can promote enhanced cooperation in knowledge production and the broad based development of mass intellectuality. This chapter suggests that trends within educational management and policy present distinct barriers for realizing such possibilities. It mobilizes autonomist conceptions of "cognitive capitalism," "biopolitical production," and the "common" as an analytic grammar for thinking creativity as a material and discursive force at the center of current educational conflicts over knowledge, social stratification, and subjectivity. Drawing examples primarily from the North American context, I suggest that extant efforts to manage creativity in secondary and higher education are ultimately unstable, revealing what the Edufactory collective has referred to as the "double crisis" in education. This refers to the erosion of the social purposes of education conjoined with emergent conflicts and crises within the creative and communicative circuits of immaterial labor and value as they intersect with educational processes. Ultimately, creativity rests at a key axis of contestation between state-corporate power and the possibility of imagining and calling into being alternative democratic and sustainable futures rooted in the common—representing a struggle both of and for education.

System Crisis and the Rise of the Creative Economy

Capitalism is eminently creative. It is a system based on unlimited expansion and the necessity to perpetually overcome its own internal and external limits. New outlets for profit have to be continuously found in order to ensure the generation and reinvestment of capital surpluses through forms of "creative destruction" in the opening of new markets; the geographic and institutional management of spaces, bodies, and flows; and the seamless invention and integration of new models of financial innovation. While capitalism is inherently creative it is also intrinsically prone to instability and crisis. Continued instabilities in global markets, sovereign debt crises, and widespread austerity measures stemming from the 2008 collapse of the U.S. "subprime" housing bubble can be understood as a systemic crisis organizing new limitations and possibilities for capital. As David Harvey notes, "financial crisis serve to rationalize the irrationalities of capitalism. They typically lead to reconfigurations, new models of development, new spheres of investment, and new forms of class power" (2010, p.11).

The current crisis is rooted in the transition from the industrial-Fordist model of national production in the 1970s to post-Fordist globalization in the 1980s and 1990s. This has extended the reach and organizational power of the market into ever more domains of life and led to a broad expansion of global corporate profit making driven by a wave of privatization, wage repression (outsourcing, automation, free trade/labor zones, precaritization, etc.), informational and communicative processes, and speculative innovations and semiotic manipulations in the financial markets. Combined with the rise of a deregulated "shadow-banking" sector, these developments have led to myriad structural deformities and a ripple of bubbles and busts— East Asia 1997, Silicon Valley 2000–2001, Argentina, 2001—culminating in the Wall Street crash in 2008 and the destabilization of Western Europe across 2009–2010. The result has been deepening inequality and insecurity. Millions have lost their homes and livelihoods. Unprecedented wealth has been upwardly redistributed as publics have been left holding the bag—systemic risk, debilitating debt, and historic social disinvestments. While the architects and cheerleaders of neoliberal globalization claimed that unbridled information-driven capital would usher in a new era of "friction-free" exchange in a "flatter" world, everywhere we turn we seem to be confronted with new walls, hierarchies, and points of conflict.

Out of this milieu, creativity has emerged over the last decade as a central theme in debates over state restructuring and institutional and economic planning. The "turn" to creativity and the "creative economy" can be understood to share a complicated genealogy with ideas associated with the "knowledge economy" and "information revolution". This includes perspectives on the "post-industrial society" articulated Alain Touraine (1971) and Daniel Bell (1973); the management theories of Peter Drucker (1968); Alvin Toffler's (1984) "Third Wave" studies; the "knowledge society" popularized in the 1990s by Nico Stehr (1994); Robert Reich's (1991) analysis of postindustrial work, and more recent analysis of digital network capitalism such as in Yochai Benkler's (2006) seminal *Wealth of Networks*. While diverse in orientation and content, theories of the "knowledge economy" have tended to share certain consistencies in efforts to describe and imagine an informational phase of capitalist development characterized by more fluid and decentralized organizational forms, techno-scientific knowledge, and diffusions in information technologies and postmodern regimes of work, finance, and culture across the globe.

The rise of the "creative economy" shares much common ground with knowledge economy theory. Since the late 1990s, business and policy makers have asserted the value of fostering what have become known as the "creative industries" (CI) defined by a much discussed 1998 Creative Industries Task force set up in the United Kingdom by Tony Blair as "those industries which have their origin in individual creativity, skill and talent and which have a potential for wealth and job creation through the generation and exploitation of intellectual property". The term "creative economy" has been used more recently by both John Howkins (2001) in his book *How People Make Money from Ideas,* and in a series of books by Richard Florida (2002), most notably *The Rise of the Creative Class,* in order to describe the increasing centrality of creative energies, ideas, and modes of work for economic development in spheres such as regional and urban planning, commodity production and circulation, workforce development and entrepreneurship, institutional and networked restructuring, media, finance, and digitalization.

Across these various sectors creativity is typically positioned as an engine to expand economic innovation and wealth creation. In an economy where new sources of value and capitalist expansion have been heavily premised on privatization, intellectual property, and speculative finance, creativity becomes a key resource for the invention of new markets, products, and patterns of work and institutional management. On the one hand, creativity can be understood as a rhetorical figure in the deepening naturalization and enforcement of political commitments to unfettered global capitalism. Former Microsoft CEO Bill Gates (2008), for example, has named "creative capitalism" as a force to unite both corporate expansion and altruism so as to ameliorate poverty and climate change through the further extension and intensification of market forces, competition, and global consumerism. On the other hand, however, elements of the "creative thing" cannot be reduced to such delusional thinking. Not only do the circuits of creative activity often defy or even in some cases directly challenge neoliberal economism, but also they contain resistant grounds for generating spaces and circulations of cooperation and social democratic invention outside the disciplinary specter of capitalism and the state.

The "creative economy" can be read as a site of tension in the evolution of a global capitalism encountering new constraints and points of conflict. Undeniably, amidst intersecting economic, ecological, and political crises, creativity and innovation are indeed essential for realizing more sustainable and equitable futures. This raises fundamental questions, however. How can we understand the dynamics of creativity as a force of valorization and conflict within the contemporary moment? How does education as central node in the circuits of creativity and knowledge production factor in these processes particularly within the fields of educational policy and governance? How might an analysis of educational spheres help us to answer the most pressing questions of all: What kind of creativity? In whose interest? To what ends?

Towards an Analytic Grammar of Creativity

One of the most dynamic analyses of the role of creativity within neoliberal political economy and culture has come from the Italian post-*operaismo* or "autonomist" line of thought. This has offered a kind of alternative genealogy and conceptual grammar from which to approach the knowledge society and creative economy theses.

The autonomists have argued that over the last four decades of globalization, capital has mutated into a "cognitive" phase. This reading of "cognitive capitalism" is derived loosely from Marx's comments found in a section of the *Grundrisse* titled "Fragments on Machines". Here Marx speculates that technological developments contain the potential to pass a threshold whereby collective intellectual and communicative processes—the "general intellect"—overtake industrial labor as the primary driver of production and surplus value. As he puts it, this occurs when "general social knowledge has become a direct force of production" and "the conditions of the process of social life itself have come under the control of the general intellect and have been transformed in accordance with it" (1973, p. 706). Carlo Vercellone has thus argued that the "hypothesis" of cognitive capitalism "cannot be reduced to the mere constitution of an economy founded on knowledge". As Marx's formulation implies, it is rather "the formation of a knowledge-based economy framed and subsumed by the laws of capital accumulation" (2007, p.14).

Cognitive capitalism signals the transformation of capital into a productive force at the level of language, ideas, and social relations. In this schema, capitalist valorization and labor become increasingly organized around immaterial factors—the generation and circulation of ideas, images, codes, and affects. Hardt and Negri have called the intersection of economic valorization and immaterial activity "biopolitical production"—a term they derive from Michel Foucault's analysis of modern systems of power and social regulation. They argue that biopolitical production has meant that "capitalist production is aimed ever more clearly at the production of not only (and perhaps not even primarily) commodities but also social relationships and forms of life" (2009, p. 133). Here the object of production increasingly tends toward the production of a subject; that is, the forms of cooperation and sociality conducive to generating and coordinating immaterial and affective relations within the biopolitical economy. "This means, of course, not that the production of material goods, such as automobiles and steel, is disappearing or even declining in quantity but rather that their value is increasingly dependent on and subordinated to immaterial factors and goods" (Hardt and Negri, 2009, p. 132).[2] As capital becomes increasingly organized and coordinated through social and immaterial labor, traditional distinctions between work and leisure, authorship and ownership, production and consumption blur. This can be seen, among other places, in the expansion of web 2.0 platforms such as Twitter, Facebook, Flickr, Google, and YouTube, where users generate free user content that is then mined for marketing purposes and the further research and development of new products and lifestyle services.[3]

As biopolitical production becomes a dominant force of production, surplus value increasingly depends on the exploitation and expropriation of the creative and communicative circuits of culture—or what can be said to form the "common". In his conversations with Antonio Negri, Cesare Casarino has defined the *common* in distinction to the *commons*. Whereas the *commons* has traditionally referred to the representational sphere marking the state management of public wealth and resources, the common, in contrast, is understood as an infinite and non-representational force of communicative production, "namely, a common intellectual, linguistic, and affective capacity along with its appertaining forms of realization, circulation, and communication—or, in short, thought, language, and affect, in both their potential and actual aspects" (2008, p. 12). Casarino observes that while the common is increasingly extensive with capital, it is always in a position of partial exteriority and autonomy from it–"capital requires the common but the common does not require capital".

As Carlo Vercellone (2007) and other economists have pointed out, within the biopolitical economy capital is increasingly charged with the expropriation of value as "rent"—"the becoming rent of profit". This expropriation of rent may take the form of primitive accumulation or what David Harvey (2005) calls "accumulation by dispossession": the privatization of "fixed" assets like schools, transportation systems, hospitals, as well as natural resources and biogenetic materials. However, what is increasingly at stake is the capture of value directly on the basis of the common. Hardt and Negri have argued that this represents a key axis of struggle and crisis within the biopolitical economy. They observe that as the general intellect becomes a primary source of value, production is increasingly autonomous from capitalist command. Ideas, particularly within digital networks that allow for instant and infinite reproducibility, do not conform to the normal laws of production or scarcity. Moreover, ideas often become more powerful as they are freely shared and individuals enter into cooperative arrangements of communication and collaborative exchange. Thus as capital attempts to exert control over the common in order to extract value, it tends to become a fetter to creativity and immaterial labor. Put differently, in its efforts to control and capture immaterial value as rent and to privatize knowledge as property, capital mobilizes apparatuses of organization, measurement, and discipline that paradoxically undermine the creativity and productivity of the common (Hardt and Negri, 2009).

The common can be understood as the immanent terrain of creativity. In this sense, creativity is what is proper to the common—a shared capacity for social invention and collaboration that is embedded within yet always exceeds capital. Creativity thus represents an axis of struggle and a stubborn surplus within the communicative vectors of capitalist exploitation and expropriation. As capital seeks to exert control and to expropriate and capture the fruits of human creativity on the basis of the common, it risks stifling creativity and thus the well of valorization and innovation itself. As Michael Hardt has argued, this is the emerging internal contradiction inherent to biopolitical capital: "as the common is corralled as property, the more its productivity is reduced; and yet expansion of the common undermines the relations of property in a general and fundamental way" (2010a, p. 136).

Mapping the Double-Crisis in Education

If we take autonomist hypotheses seriously, calls for creativity within educational contexts become revealing of multiple overlapping conflicts and tensions. These conflicts speak to what the scholarly and activist collective Edu-factory (2010) has referred to as the "double crisis" in education. On the one hand, this refers to the evolving crisis of educational systems resulting from the neoliberal erosion of their historical, cultural, and democratic referents. On the other hand, it refers to the crisis specific to immaterial labor and value particularly as they intersect with educational organization and policy. Both sides of the double crisis represent conflicts over the common, between economic reason on one hand and the vitality of the general intellect on the other.

Drawing on the Edu-factory's analysis we might suggest that the double-crisis can be understood through four interrelated frames. First, it is *global*. It is articulated and experienced in highly differentiated ways within and between transnational, national, regional, and metropolitan contexts. Educational sectors are in the position of reacting to as well as shaping new global economic and political realities including the mediation and transformation of borders and institutions, temporalities of work and culture, and new articulations of centers/peripheries and inclusions/exclusions. Second, it speaks to new *strategies of management* as educational sectors have increasingly adopted and even in some cases pioneered their own market-based organizational forms aimed at the control of knowledge production. Within this schema, lines between the public and private blur as corporate and educational synergies generate new systems of measurement, curricular and research standards, and labor controls so as to enhance and drive the generation and capture of economic value. This has coincided with qualitative shifts in the value of knowledge within educational spheres and a dominant emphasis on the privatized input and output binaries of human capital theory and its singular focus on entrepreneurialism and economic competition. Third, the double crisis is *economic* and *ongoing*. The persistent realities of labor precaritization and widening chasms in social inequality along with widespread disinvestments in social projects including public schools and universities at all levels, points to the continued salience of the global economic crisis and speaks to its durability. This has made *adaptation* to crisis and its duel basis in deregulated bubble economics and social austerity a lasting form and a *new technique of governance*. Fourth, and on this later point, the double crisis is driving new arrangements of *power* and *stratification* that are constructing new hierarchies and conflicts within and across the "planetary educational market" (Edu-factory, 2010).

While the Edu-factory project concentrates their analysis on the university, I would like to suggest that the double crisis also resonates with secondary educational transformation in distinct ways. In what follows, I situate creativity in secondary and higher education within the context of the double crisis at the level of social stratification, knowledge, and subjectivity.

Searching for Creativity in Secondary Education

In the fall of 2009, *New York Times* columnist Thomas Friedman wrote a piece entitled "The New Untouchables" in which he suggested that an "educational breakdown on Main Street" stood as an absent cause of the U.S. recession stemming from the 2008 financial meltdown. Surveying the realities of a present and future labor market rooted in mobile networks of global production, the rise of China and India as strategic competitors, and the centrality of immaterial labor in driving economic growth, he suggests that without a "reboot" of the educational sector, many if not most American workers will be left behind in the current transition. For Friedman, the educational challenge of the 21st century is to produce workers who possess "the imagination to make themselves untouchables"; that is, subjects who can invent the new markets and employment niches of the future. He states that, "schools have a doubly hard task now—not just improving reading, writing and arithmetic but entrepreneurship, innovation and creativity" (Friedman, 2009).

Friedman is far from alone here. Recent books like *Out of Our Minds: Learning to Be Creative,* by Ken Robinson, and Daniel Pink's *A Whole New Mind: Why Right-Brainers Will Rule the World* express similar views, arguing that educational systems must promote imagination and creativity in the interest of economic growth and development. This conjuncture of creativity and labor has not been lost on the corporate world either. For instance, the Partnership for 21st Century Skills is a U.S.-

based educational advocacy group made up of a consortium of corporate entities and leaders from the media, technology, and education sectors such as AOL Time Warner, Apple, CISCO Systems, Dell, Microsoft, Walt Disney, Oracle, McGraw Hill, Pearson, and many more. They argue for the implementation of a series of market-driven 21st century skills in education such as "creativity, innovation, critical thinking and financial, economic, business and entrepreneurial literacy" (21st Century, 2010).

On the surface, these calls for more creativity, entrepreneurialism, and innovation appear to recognize and support substantial investments in secondary education. If the creative economy demands fresh thinking about workforce capacities and open and dynamic institutions, then it might follow that the rhetoric of creativity would push for experimentation and a more expansive view of schooling. If capital is increasingly charged with extracting value from the common—that is, from mass intellectuality and communicative and immaterial processes—it would seem logical that calls for creativity and innovation would present a substantive challenge to a narrow industrial model of schooling based on stratified, centralized, and instrumentally rationalized forms of school organization and curriculum. One would imagine that schooling for the creative economy would want to draw on, harness, and develop human capabilities while promoting greater autonomy and equity. The reality has been somewhat different.

Taking the United States as our example, we should first point out that national anxieties over education and global economic competiveness are far from new. They became particularly salient during the Cold War and more recently have intensified under the twin emergence of globalization and neo-liberalization in the 1980s—the Reagan era task force and report entitled a "A Nation at Risk" offering perhaps the paradigmatic statement on concerns over post-industrialization and educational performance in the global economy. Here informative distinctions can be made between the liberal Keynesian rationalities that marked educational planning during the Cold War and the last three decades of neoliberal policy incursions into the educational sphere. The Cold War era was marked by a strong federal commitment to increased public funding, expanded access, and commitments to cultural development and knowledge. While embedded within a clear-cut Fordist division of labor and racialized social hierarchy, investments in education combined with anti-poverty programs and a strong public ethos nonetheless enabled marked educational and economic advancement at all levels of society. In contrast, as Michael Hardt (2010b) has noted, "if the launch of Sputnik made the United States smarter, the attacks of September 11th, perceived as the primary challenge to the national position in this period, only made the country more stupid". The War on Terror combined with the neoliberal revolution and extensive right-wing involvement in educational policy have manifested in the profound retrenchment of educational investment, equity, and access. This has led to deepening cuts in funding to public schools and universities accompanied by a narrowing of educational focus co-extensive with corporate and military technical demands.

Since the 1980s, in the sphere of U.S. secondary education policy, there has been an intensive and extensive path toward market integration and corporate manage-rialism. First, this has meant widespread privatization efforts in the form of vouch-er initiatives, charter schools, and even limited experiments in for-profit secondary education.[4] Second, along with privatization, the management of U.S. schooling has been captured by technocratic logics that have sought to bring market-based strate-gies of accountability and institutional "efficiency" into schooling at all levels. This has included the broad-based standardization of curricula, the proliferation of auditing and evaluation mechanisms that tend to limit the professional autonomy of teachers, and an across-the-board emphasis on the rote learning of "basic skills" conjoined with incessant high-stakes testing. These policies crystallized under George W. Bush's No Child Left Behind legislation and are currently being expand-ed and intensified under the Obama administration through policies such as "Race to the Top" where, as Ken Saltman has noted, "billions in public dollars are being dangled in front of states to induce them to expand privatized and managerialist school reform . . . that imagine historically neglected schools as private enterpris-es that need to be subject to the "creative destruction" of private markets" (2010, p. 3).

Far from promoting educational investments rooted in creativity and the gen-eral intellect, these policies have been more likely to "drain the common" than to nurture and expand it (Hardt and Negri, 2009). First, in practice, neoliberal edu-cation policies have tended to extend and intensify the worst aspects of industrial schooling while pioneering new mechanisms of technocratic management impli-cated in deepening social stratification and inequality. Privatization has enabled the transfer of public assets over to publicly unaccountable corporate entities while emphasis on testing and basic skills have led to the narrowing of curriculum, the de-professionalization of teachers, the marginalization of liberal arts subjects, and the transformation of public education into a three-tiered system: a small number of exclusive public and private schools to serve the rich; a middle tier to train a large-ly white and increasingly insecure cadre of future middle class service workers and managers; and a rung at the bottom of the racial and socioeconomic hierarchy form-ing little more than testing warehouses and/or potential markets for educational speculators. To take one example, the 400,000 students in the Chicago public schools, almost 90% of whom are either African American or Latino/a and more than 88% live at or below the federal poverty line, typically receive half the fund-ing per year than their mostly white middle class suburban counterparts receive. This means, for instance, that a group of "6,413 students who started elementary school in Evanston in 1994 and graduated from high school in 2007 had about $290 million more spent on their education than the same number of Chicago Public Schools students" (Lowenstein et al., 2008). Furthermore, the schools they attend are often in dismal states of repair, have bloated class sizes, are subject to strict scripted forms of curricula, and are increasingly materially and symbolically conjoined to the criminal justice system through the ubiquitous presence of armed police and state surveillance. Research suggests that neoliberal policies combined with the economic crisis and concurrent austerity measures are exacerbating these inequalities and deepening already vastly uneven educational opportunities along the lines of space, race, and class.

Second, the rhetoric of creativity does not generally extend beyond market rationalities or practices, representing a myopic vision of knowledge, creativity, and subjectivity. Let's go back for a moment to Thomas Friedman who has been an unapologetic cheerleader for the neo-liberalization of secondary education for the last two decades. While tending to ignore the sociopolitical divisions and decisions that determine economic opportunities in the first place, Friedman argues that education embrace creativity in order to produce subjects capable of gaming competitive global labor markets. There are multiple problems here. For starters, Friedman assumes that a hyper-deregulated global capital is and should be the only game in town and thus consigns workers to a future that subordinates social life and the environment to a vulgar race to the bottom. Further, Friedman and other neoliberals tend to either ignore or dismiss the social dimensions of creativity, falsely equating creative value with a reductive economic vision of entrepreneurialism, technical knowledge, and subjectivity. This narrow reading of creativity lends itself to education policies that stifle the development of social capacities and ways of being by promoting hierarchical, privatized, and disciplinary management strategies in educational contexts. Friedman's call for creativity as economic ideology blinds him to the fact that the neoliberal education reform recipes that he has consistently supported *consistently fail on their own terms*: they do not produce the kinds of imaginative and social capabilities required to promote sustainable prosperity in the biopolitical economy, nor do they advance the cause of expanded equity, autonomy, and democracy. In short, they poison the common.

Managing Creativity in Higher Education

In 2010, the University of Toronto embarked on a landmark $200 million dollar architectural expansion of its Rotman School of Business. Slated to house a much ballyhooed "Integrative Thinking Center" along with the "Martin Prosperity Institute," Rotman's own creativity guru in residence Richard Florida claims that "the new building will reflect the 'new way to think' that is the basis of our approach, providing students, researchers, staff and the local community with a springboard to harness their creative capabilities". This serves the larger mission of Rotman: "reinventing management tools and frameworks for a creative society" (RotmanWeb).

Like its counterparts across North America and beyond, the University of Toronto has openly embraced the image of the university as hub and driver of global economic competition and corporate innovation. With the Rotman expansion we can see how creativity speaks to a reinvention of management that places business at the heart of a project to reframe the value and focus of knowledge and creativity in the university. In the case of the University of Toronto, while money has been poured into business and technoscientific programs and research, the university has simultaneously cut funding for a number of important humanities and social science programs and has even proposed disestablishing or amalgamating a number of programs such as Educational Philosophy and History, the Department of East Asian Studies, the Centre for Ethics, the Centre for International Studies, and the Centre for Diasporic and Translational Studies, along with the prestigious Centre for Comparative Literature founded by Northrop Frye.

This is representative of how the university has responded institutionally to its role as a crucial node in cognitive capital's circuits of value. The contemporary university provides a key training and disciplinary ground for future knowledge workers and a key public infrastructure for generating and capitalizing on intellectual property and for subsidizing corporate technological innovation. While it has hardly been seamless, out of the deregulatory and "new managerial" fever of the 1980s and 1990s has emerged what Nick Dyer-Witheford (2005) has referred to as "Corporate U". This is a university largely re-configured in the image of the corporation and organized in accordance with corporate interests and economic imperatives.

In his book *How the University Works*, Marc Bousquet incisively documents the recalibration of higher education's institutional and administrative norms under the neoliberal logic of "total quality management". This has fed the radical casualization of university labor and erosion of the tenure system; the proliferation of standardization, audits, and evaluations; the rise of cost-cutting online and distance "learning"; enhanced corporate university partnerships and the sinking of vast sums of money into bio-tech, pharmaceutical, energy, and military/defense research. Programs without direct application to industry have been cut while budgets and resource allocation have become increasingly linked to economic outcomes. Within this schema students are increasingly configured as either cheap sources of expendable labor or as consumers encouraged to pursue higher education as a form of credentialing—a skills-for-jobs transfer. Professors or at least those 25%-30% still fortunate enough inhabit a tenure track, are imagined as the ultimate immaterial workers, less public intellectuals than entrepreneurial information "technicians" and "producers". Meanwhile university administrations increasingly leverage their position to lower operating costs, attract corporate dollars, and capitalize on copyright, licensing, and intellectual property. This has occurred at the same time that public funding to universities has been steadily declining while administrations have presided over extensive and exclusionary tuition hikes, passing on the costs of their new business parks and sports facilities and their own ballooning salaries through massive increases in student debt.

Christopher Newfield has highlighted the apparent contradiction between these trends and the demands of the creative knowledge economy. He asks why it is that leaders in the United States and in other wealthy countries are "containing and cheapening the research and educational systems on which they say the future of their economies depend?" Isn't this counterproductive for the creative economy and knowledge capitalism? Newfield offers a sophisticated response to this question. He argues that cognitive capital is defined by a "productive contradiction" between the expropriation of rent from the common and the "full knowledge that it is forcing knowledge out of its creative collective habitat". Drawing on the management theory of Thomas Stewart, Newfield argues that cognitive capital has devised systems of knowledge management (KM) that enforce strict multilayered controls over knowledge production and knowledge work. These systems rely heavily on complex arrangements of stratification within and between higher education and industry in order to ensure the generation and value of proprietary knowledge even at the expense of placing limits on creativity and innovation. For instance, there are roughly 7 million STEM (Science, Technology, Engineering, Mathematics) jobs in the United States. This is a notoriously stratified sector that includes armies of precarious "permatemps" and "cognitariat" workers that perform most routine programming and clerical tasks without job security, benefits, or living wages. This leaves a select few to perform the hard core creative work required for capitalization projects. Moreover, with 2.3 million higher education degrees awarded each year in all fields, over a 30-year period (the length of a typical career), the university system produces roughly 10 times more graduates than are required in the technical workforce. "The issue for knowledge industries then, is *not* how they can create armies of knowledge workers. The issue is the opposite: how can they limit their numbers and manage their output?" (2010, p. 12).

Under these conditions, Newfield suggests that the tension between the creative economy and the neoliberal management and defunding of public higher education comes into focus:

the contradiction exists only if we assume that today's leaders of the knowledge economy actually seek a mass middle class, desire high standards of living for the vast majority of their population, and believe that the knowledge economy needs armies of college graduates. If instead, we posit that the political and business leaders of the knowledge economy seek a smaller elite of knowledge-based star producers, then the unceasing cheapening of public higher education in the U.S. and elsewhere makes more sense. (2010, p. 11)

In his book, *Unmaking the Public University*, Newfield expands these insights by outlining their cultural underpinnings. He details how the rise of the post-industrial knowledge economy in the 1980s and 1990s corresponded to an intensification of right-wing attacks on the university. These attacks on campus politics, multiculturalism, postmodernism in the humanities, and affirmative action have ultimately eroded support for robust public funding and broad commitments to equitable access to high quality public higher education. This was made possible largely by an insurgent market fundamentalism in public life, which worked to generate white middle-class resentment against the supposed advantages accrued to minority populations in the wake of the Civil Rights movement. This has been disempowering to the majority while contributing to the naturalization of race and class inequalities—justified, of course, by the rough justice of the market. Newfield states that "the culture war strategy was a kind of intellectual neutron bomb, eroding the social and cultural foundations of a growing, politically powerful, economically entitled, and racially diversifying middle class, while leaving its technical capacities intact" (2008, p. 6). The culture war can thus be viewed as an "economic war," in the sense that it was successful in eroding the capacities to understand and reflect on rapidly changing historical conditions in non-market terms, and thus to advance a political framework from which to protect and advance the cause of economic and social development for the majority. Ultimately, as Newfield argues, this has contributed to the erosion of the cultural foundations of the university and its role in promoting social development, creativity, and equality.

Coda: Creativity beyond the Double Crisis

Even if factory and society were to become perfectly integrated at the economic level, they would nevertheless continue to be in contradiction at the political level.
                                        —MARIO TRONTI, "THE STRATEGY OF REFUSAL"

What we can observe in both secondary and higher education is that the concept of creativity is marked by instability and contradiction. Invocations to unleash creativity and innovation in educational contexts appear to stand in tension with the realities of the reorganization of education along the lines of privatization, audits and testing, standardization, and the marginalization of the social sciences and the humanities—processes that place limits on knowledge production and the free and cooperative exchange of ideas. Christopher Newfield has made a compelling case that this tension can be explained at least partially by raising the question of whether the political elite does in fact desire a highly educated and creative workforce at all—preferring instead a small and manageable core of highly skilled workers. There is certainly a broad spectrum of evidence regarding deepening social stratification and insecurity across educational and employment sectors to support this conclusion.

An accompanying hypothesis might be that neoliberal educational management and policy has tended to mistake or misrecognize the educational capacities necessary for the biopolitical economy, confusing entrepreneurial and technocratic knowledge and subjectivity for multifaceted and cooperative forms of innovative potential and creative value. If indeed, cognitive capitalism tends to increasingly generate value from social processes on the basis of the common, and these processes are increasingly autonomous from capital and reliant on creativity, then the paradox emerges that I have tried to provisionally trace out in this chapter whereby tendencies in educational management and policy place restrictions and limitations on creativity, and hence, on capital's own drive to immaterial value. This is indicative of what the Edu-factory has identified as the double crisis: the erosion of the social and democratic mission of education due to the intensive and extensive application of economic and technocratic reason, and the attendant crisis in capitalist labor and value as it intersects with these processes.

There is another explanation to consider here, however, and it is one that I think is particularly important when considering the liberatory and indeed creative power of education as a social and democratic force. Perhaps ultimately, linking creativity back to educational and social investments, expanded and equitable access and broad, open, and interdisciplinary commitments to knowledge production beyond reductive forms of economic reason and control is just too risky for capital. The kinds of educational innovations that hold the potential to promote greater social intelligence and more creatively inclined subjects capable of meaningful democratic participation in the world raises distinct problems for the neoliberal project especially in light of its all too evident recent failures. Broad-based investments in creativity, human and social development, and cooperation contain the potential to not only raise and circulate basic questions about the legitimacy and sustainability of current economic and political systems, but also to inspire forms of intellectual and political engagement that contain the potential to challenge hegemonic forms of management and domination by capital and the state.

The subordination of creativity to neoliberal reason highlights fundamental tensions concerning the value of knowledge and the democratic role of education. Rather than a social good thought necessary for promoting sustainable and democratic cultures, knowledge is reduced to a commodity—a form of property valued only as far as it functions to enhance corporate profit making. Similarly, creativity is largely positioned as an economic capacity to be tamed through educational and corporate management rather than a common oriented to social collaboration and democratization. Politically it seems that the central question becomes: how do we begin to nurture those autonomous aspects of the common in educational spheres and beyond in order to build capacities toward subordinating political economy and technical knowledge to the common as opposed to the other way around? Certainly, this is the possibility invoked by the now familiar rallying cry, "*We won't pay for your crisis!*", uttered by countless students, educators, workers, and citizens at protests across North America, Europe, South America, North Africa and beyond, in response to further cuts to education and its continued reduction to neoliberal imperatives and forms of management. It appears that education is increasingly at the center of struggles for what the future is going to look like: a future of broadly shared prosperity and sustainability, made possible through social democratic cooperation and creativity or one marked by continued sociopolitical marginalization, insecurity, and crisis for the majority.

Notes

1. See Michael Peters et al., *Creativity in the Global Knowledge Economy* for a collection of essays on this theme
2. There is considerable debate over materiality vs. immateriality within cognitive capitalism. For an insightful exchange on this question see Michael Betencourt "Immaterial Value and Scarcity in Digital Capitalism" and Arthur Kroker, Simon Glezos, and Michael Betancourt, "The Future of Digital Capitalism".
3. For more on this topic see Tiziana Terranova, "New Economy, Financialization and Social Production in the Web 2.0".
4. For a detailed discussion of these issues see Kenneth Saltman's *Edison Schools* and *Capitalizing on Disaster*.

References

Bell, D. (1973). *The coming of post-industrial society: A venture in social forecasting*. New York, NY: Basic Books.

Benkler, Y. (2006). *The wealth of networks*. New Haven, CT: Yale University Press.

Betancourt, M. (2010). Immaterial value and scarcity in digital capitalism. *C-theory.net*, Retrieved from: www.ctheory.net/articles.aspx?id=652.

Bousquet, M. (2008). *How the university works: Higher education and the low wage nation*. New York: NYU Press.

Casarino, C. (2008). *In praise of the common: A conversation on philosophy and politics*. Minneapolis: University of Minnesota Press.

Drucker, P.F. (1968). *Frontiers of management*. New York: Truman Talley Books.

Edu-factory Collective. (2010). The double crisis: Living on the borders. *Edu-factory Journal*, Zero Issue: Retrieved from www.edufactory.org

Florida, R. (2003). *The rise of the creative class: And how its transforming work, leisure, and everyday life*. New York: Basic Books.

Florida, R., Gates, G., Knudsen, B., & Stolarick, K. (2006). The university and the creative economy. Retrieved from www.creativeclass.com/rfcgdb/articles/University_andthe_Creative_Economy.pdf

Friedman, T. (2009). The New Untouchables. *New York Times*. Retrieved from www.nytimes.com/2009/10/21/opinion/21friedman.html

Gates, B. (2008). Making capitalism more creative. *Time Magazine*. Retrieved from www.time.com/time/business/article/0,8599,1828069,00.html

Hardt, M. & Negri, A. (2009). *Commonwealth*. Cambridge, MA: Harvard University Press.

Hardt, M. (2010a). The common in communism. In Costas Douzinas. & Slavoj Zizek (Eds.) *The idea of communism*. New York: Verso.

Hardt, M. (2010b). US education and the crisis. Retreived from www.edu-factory.org

Harvey, D. (2005). *The new imperialism*. London: Oxford University Press.

Harvey, D. (2010). *The enigma of capital: And the crises of capitalism*. London: Oxford University Press.

Howkins, J. (2001). *The creative economy: How people make money from ideas*. New York, NY: Penguin.

Kroker, A., Glezos, S. & Betancourt, M. (2010). The future of digital capitalism. *C-theory.net*, Retrieved from www.ctheory.net/articles.aspx?id=657

Lowenstein, J. K., Loury, A. K. & Hendrickson, M. (2008). Wildly disparate funding. *The Chicago Defender*, Retrieved from www.chicagoreporter.com/index.php/c/Web_Exclusive/d/Wildly_Disparate_Funding

Marx, K. (1973). *Grundrisse*. New York: Penguin.

Newfield, C. (2008). *Unmaking the public university: The forty-year assault on the middle class*. Cambridge, MA: Harvard University Press.

Newfield, C. (2010). The structure and silence of the cognitariat. *Edu-factory Journal*, Zero Issue: Retrieved from www.edufactory.org

Partnership for 21st Century Skills. Retrieved from www.21stcenturyskills.org

Peters, M., Marginsn, S., & Murphey, P. (2008). *Creativity and the global knowledge economy*. New York: Peter Lang.

Pink, D. (2005). *A whole new mind: Why right brainers will rule the world*. New York: Penguin.

Reich, R. (1991). *The work of nations: Preparing ourselves for 21st century capitalism.* New York: Vintage.

Robinson, K. (2001). *Out of our minds: Learning to be creative.* West Sussex, United Kingdom: Capstone Publishing.

Rotman Web. (2010). Retrieved from www.rotman.utoronto.ca/expansion/newbuilding.htm

Saltman, K.J. (2003). *The Edison schools: Corporate schooling and the assault on public education.* New York: Routledge.

Saltman, K.J. (2007). *Capitalizing on disaster: Taking and breaking public schools.* Boulder, CO: Paradigm.

Saltman, K.J. (2010). Facing corporatization and the myths of charter schools. Unpublished paper presented at the 2010 American Educational Studies Association Conference. Denver, CO.

Terranova, T. (2010). New economy, financialization and social production in the web 2.0. In Fumagalli, A. & Mezzadra, S. *Crisis in the global economy: Financial markets, social struggles, and new political scenarios.* Los Angeles: Semiotext(e).

Toffler, A. (1984). *The third wave.* New York: Bantam Books.

Touraine, A. (1971). *The post-industrial society. Tomorrow's social history: Classes, conflicts and culture in the programmed society.* New York: Random House.

Tronti, M. (2007). The strategy of refusal. In Lotringer, S. & Marrazi, C. (Eds.) *Autonomia: Postpolitical politics.* Los Angeles: Semiotext(e).

Vercellone, C. (2007). From formal subsumption to general intellect: Elements for a Marxist reading of the thesis of cognitive capitalism. *Historical Materialism,* 15, 13–36.

Witheford-Dyer, N. (2005). Cognitive capitalism and the contested campus. *European Journal of Higher Arts Education,* Issue 2.

CHAPTER TEN

For Fun, For Profit, For Empire:

The University and Electronic Games

TOBY MILLER

In a First Wave economy, land and farm labor are the main "factors of production." In a Second Wave economy, the land remains valuable while the "labor" becomes massified around machines and larger industries. In a Third Wave economy, the central resource—a single word broadly encompassing data, information, images, symbols, culture, ideology, and values—is actionable knowledge
  —A MAGNA CARTA FOR THE INFORMATION AGE (DYSON et al., 1994)

Blackwell is what his creators call an interactive virtual character—a life-sized, 3-D simulation of a person whose mission is to help train real soldiers. He inhabits FlatWorld, a kind of theme-park version of a war zone run by the University of Southern California's Institute for Creative Technologies. At a time when Hollywood is often tagged by those on the political right as a liberal bastion, ICT teams the military and the entertainment biz for defense projects, funded by a five-year, $100 million grant from the Pentagon—the largest the university has ever received
  —JAMES HEBERT (2005)

As per this volume's concern with "cognitive capitalism," since the 1970s, "knowledge workers" have been recognized as vital to sustaining the economies of the Global North, thanks to information-based industries that guarantee endless gains in productivity and the purest of competitive markets (Bar with Simard, 2006). To Cold War futurists such as former National Security Advisor Zbigniew Brzezinski (1969) and cultural conservative Daniel Bell (1977), converged communications and information technologies promised the permanent removal of grubby manufacturing from the First World to the Third and continued U.S. textual and technical power, provided that the blandishments of socialism and negative reactions to global business did not create class struggle; hence former U.S. Secretary of State and master of the dark art of international relations Henry Kissinger's consulting firm advising that the United States must 'win the battle of the world's information flows, dominating the airwaves as Great Britain once ruled the seas' (Rothkopf, 1997, p. 47).

In the words of lapsed-leftist cultural theorist and President of the European Bank for Reconstruction and Development Jacques Attali (2008, p. 31), a new 'mercantile order forms wherever a creative class masters a key innovation from navigation to accounting or, in our own time, where services are most efficiently mass produced, thus generating enormous wealth.' This gives rise to a putative 'aristocracy of talent' (Kotkin, 2001, p. 22), defined through the discourse of progress, informatization, and the "creative industries." Multiple meritocrats allegedly luxuriate in ever-changing techniques, technologies, and networks. Labor is acknowledged in this brave newness, provided that it is abstracted from physical, dirty work (Mattelart, 2002). As of 2007, college graduates in the United States earned 83% more than people who discontinued their studies after high school. And people with postgraduate qualifications gained 159% more. This was in accordance with the transformation of the United States from an industrial to a post-industrial country, with increasing numbers of jobs in services and culture in place of manufacturing (Henwood, 2010; Newfield, 2008). The international interests of these aristos also remain well served: by 2009, a new division of international labor had secured industrial outsourcing to keep costs down, and textual/technological hegemony remained in the First World: fewer than 7% of Africans and 20% of Asians were connected to the Internet (internetworldstats.com/stats.htm).

One of the most influential ideas guiding media and cultural studies is that the latest media technologies redefine the social and cultural relationships that earlier media helped shape. Old media that cannot carry certain new content are displaced by new media delivering higher-potency versions of old content through vastly enlarged channels. Each medium supposedly defines a particular way that social or symbolic interactions take place by extending human senses and communication throughout a manufactured environment. Much of the field buys into individualistic fantasies of reader, audience, consumer, or player autonomy—the neoliberal intellectual's wet dream of music, movies, television, and everything else converging under the sign of empowered fans. The New Right of media and cultural studies invests in Schumpeterian entrepreneurs, evolutionary economics, and "creative industries" with unparalleled zest. It's never seen an "app" it didn't like, or a socialist idea it does, as per futurists like Alvin Toffler, cosignatory to 1994's *Magna Carta for the Information Age* excerpted above, who coined the concept of 'the cognitariat' to describe the new creative class (1983).

On the other hand, progressive media and cultural studies buy into the corporate fantasy of control—the political economist's arid nightmare of music, movies, television, and everything else converging under the sign of empowered firms. Michael Hardt and Antonio Negri graphically, romantically (and inaccurately) refer to the exchange of information, knowledge, and emotion by computer as 'immaterial labor' (2000, pp. 286, 290–92). They have, more helpfully, re-disposed Toffler's idea of the cognitariat: Negri (2007) uses it to describe people mired in contingent media work who have heady educational qualifications and a grand facility with cultural technologies and genres. I find that typology quite suggestive, for all its flawed origins and emphases.

The cognitariat plays key roles in the production and circulation of goods and services by creating and coordinating media technologies and texts as:

- artists, comprising musicians, directors, writers, and journalists
- artisans, including sound engineers, editors, cinematographers, and graphic designers
- impresarios, connecting proprietors and executives to artists
- proprietors and executives, controlling employment and investment, negotiating with states and
- audiences and consumers, paying for content, interpreting it in order to give media meaning, and eliding real barriers of entry to media production through their dubious anointment as producer-consumers (prosumers).

These groups operate within institutional contexts:

- private bureaucracies, controlling investment, production, and distribution across the media
- public bureaucracies, offering what capitalism cannot, while comporting themselves in an ever-more commercial manner
- small businesses, run by charismatic individuals, and
- networks, fluid associations formed to undertake specific projects.

But the prevailing ideology of capitalist futurism that underpins the idea of the cognitariat requires correction. As Marcuse predicted seventy years ago, far from liberating all and sundry, technological convergence has intensified managerial coordination from above (1941). Writing in this critical neo-Marxist tradition, and *contra* Cold Warrior futurists, Herbert Schiller (1976, pp. 8–9, 16) recast cultural and technological convergence as the 'infrastructure of socialization,' designed to spread from rich capitalist countries into poor, post-colonial regions. It synchronized the interests of dominant strata in both core and periphery via common 'business cultures,' 'institutional networks,' organizational models, and modes of communication and cultural production.

The cognitariat forms at the complex interstices of capital, education, and government. Universities and their ilk are vital centers for training it. As Andrew Ross has shown, the contemporary university is split between *l'art pour l'art*, the desire for profit, and the need to obey the state. Sometimes these forms of life co-exist harmoniously; sometimes they do not (2010). This relates to the fact that the university is simultaneously and unevenly subject to governmentalization and corporatization (Miller, 2003, 2007, and 2009). In light of that background, this chapter offers a capsule history of the U.S. research university and an account of the present conjuncture, with an exemplification of this complicity in the creation of militaristic electronic games, which embody the fantasy world outlined by Bell, Brzezinski, Attali, Toffler, and their futuristic friends.

The Capsule

The classic U.S. model of higher education aims to equip students with a liberal inclination that respects knowledge *of* a topic and *for* a purpose, rather than simply knowledge *by* a particular person. The model places its faith in a discourse of professionalism, not charisma. In other words, it makes people believe in openly available knowledge, rather than secret magic. This is secular, and a good thing. But liberalism also uses the concept of human capital—that there should be a mutual investment of time, money, and training by both society and subject to create a corps of able-minded employees and willing patriots, schooled by a docile professoriat. To that end, we have seen the advent of higher education as an industry, with students as investors. How did this state of affairs come to pass?

Since the 1830s, when the first waves of white-settler European immigration across classes began, U.S. higher education has generated practices and knowledges for use by the state and business and sought to integrate the population. From the 1850s, when the country began its industrial take-off, the emergent *bourgeoisie* sought partnerships with tertiary education to develop a skilled workforce (Miller, 2003).

Universities flowered at the turn of the 20th century. Corporations began to place more and more faith in applied science via electromagnetism, geology, chemistry, and electricity. And by the twenties, Harvard had a business school, NYU a Macy's endorsed retail school, and Cornell a hotel school. The two World Wars provided additional pump-priming and premia on practicality from the federal government. The large research schools actually expanded their capacity during the Depression, and the shop was really set up to cater to corporate and military research and development in the late 1950s via the Cold War (Miller, 2007).

Today, governmentalization and commodification have merged in their concerns and methods. Congress provides more than a billion dollars in direct grants to universities, apart from the peer-reviewed funds available through the National Science Foundation and the National Institutes of Health. Corporations, by contrast, gave U.S. schools about US$850 million in 1985 and US$4.25 billion a decade later. This development dates from the extraordinary Bayh-Dole Act of 1980, which permits non-profit educational institutions to own and commercialize inventions, provided that the state can use them as it sees fit. Prior to the Act, research schools collectively accounted for about 250 patents a year. Now, the figure is close to 5,000. In 1999, the top 100 research schools received US$641 million in royalties, up by almost US$500 million in just four years (Newfield, 2003, 2004, and 2008).

The idea of working in the public interest has been compromised through amendments to state laws throughout the country that have quietly exempted publicly funded scientists from conflict-of-interest responsibilities that apply to, for example, refuse workers and personnel officers. Consider medicine. The pharmaceutical industry's proportion of U.S. health research grew from 13% in 1980 to 52% in 1995. Marketing, not medicine, decides how to develop a new compound once it has been uncovered, asking the following questions: will it be announced as a counter to depression or ejaculation; will it be announced in journal x or y; and which scholars will be chosen to front it and produce consensus over its benefits? Major advertising agencies that work with pharmaceutical corporations have subsidiaries that conduct clinical trials. Scholarly legitimacy is a key part of this merchandising. Pfizer describes academic publication as a means 'to support, directly or indirectly, the marketing of our product' (as cited in Moffatt and Elliott, 2007). Medical education and communications companies provide ghostwriting services, paid for by corporations, that deliver copy to academics and clinicians—then pay them for signing it. One in ten papers in leading medical outlets are the work of ghosts, and an astounding 90% of articles published in the *Journal of the American Medical Association* derive from people paid by pharmacorps, which pressure medical journals to print favorable research findings in return for lucrative advertising copy (Miller, 2008).

Turning away from research, we can see a tendency across the entire degree-granting sector of transferring the cost of running schools away from governments and towards students, who are regarded more and more as customers, who must manage their own lives by investing in human capital.

In the last four decades, the proportion of students from the bottom quarter of national income obtaining degrees rose from 6% to 9%; for the top quarter of the income stakes, that number grew from 55% to 95%. This is because the price of attaining an educational edge has become prohibitive. Since 1980, the consumer price index has gone up 179%; for attending college, the figure is 827%. What used to cost a quarter of middle-class family income each year now costs well over half (Henwood, 2010; Newfield, 2003, 2008).

According to the coin-operated right-wing think tanks that set up their stall against secular higher education, this is because federal subsidies have made it easy for universities to raise prices and because faculty salaries have increased. The first explanation is part of their reflexive reaction to anything at all where democracies respond to voters' desires. The second account is empirically falsifiable: pay for full-time professors since the early 1990s is just a wee bit ahead of inflation, and precarious sessional teaching has become a norm everywhere—the reality of life in the cognitariat for most of its denizens. Of course, universities have added needless numbers of managers, but even that folly doesn't account for cost hikes. The truth lies in the fact that fancy private universities are offering so many saunas, super-colliders, and screens in order to attract top students. And in the case of public schools, there have been massive declines in state funding. In 1980–81, the three levels of government accounted for 48.3% of funding, whereas the proportion was 38% in 1995–96. This trend towards reliance on tuition doubled student debt between 1992 and 2000. By 2005, state investment in public-university students was at its lowest level in a quarter of a century, and tertiary education's overall proportion of public appropriations declined from 6.7% to 4.5% between 1975 and 2000 (Henwood, 2010; Miller, 2007; Newfield, 2008).

This dual faculty-student financial dependence on private sources is twinned with what we might call the mimetic managerial fallacy, a process whereby governments and university administrators construct corporate life as their desired other. This not only makes for untimely influences on the direction of research and teaching, but on the very administration of universities, which are increasingly prone to puerile managerial warlock craft superstitions about "excellence," "quality control," and "flatter structures." (I guess the latter refers to a California parking lot after an earthquake.) Academic institutions have come to resemble the entities they now serve, as colleges are transformed into big businesses/government secretariats. Major research schools, particularly private ones, are also landlords, tax havens, and research-and-development surrogates.

The mimetic managerial fallacy also leads to more and more forms of surveillance. Regional accrediting institutions vouching for the quality of U.S. degrees have been in place for well over a century. But since the 1970s, we have seen ever-increasing performance-based evaluations of teaching conducted at departmental and decanal levels, rather than in terms of the standard of an overall school. Today, such methods are used by 95% of departments. These systems frequently link budgets to outcomes, in keeping with the prevailing beliefs of public-policy mandarins—their restless quest to conduct themselves like corporate elves *manqués*. As successive superstitions came along—the 1990s variety was Total Quality Management—administrators fell in line with these beguiling *doxa*. Along the way, faculty-student ratios worsened, and reporting, surveillance, and administration grew in size and power (Miller, 2009). Many of us who have actually worked for business and government know what laughably inefficient institutions they can be—but then, those who watch academics do research and teaching from the perch of administration frequently have *ressentiment* in their eyes and underachievement on their *résumés*, kicking down even as they kiss up.

Electronic Games

How do these relationships that universities have with futurism, governmentality, and commodification connect to electronic games? The latter provide telling examples of university complicity with projects of state and commerce, in ways that largely elude the Pollyannaish approaches favored by the prelates of game studies.

Most of us probably think of electronic games in one of two ways. Either they are the newest means of rotting the brains of the young, or they are exciting new educational forms that will improve learning. In terms of the role that research universities should play in them, we perhaps imagine that scholars evaluate the potential harm caused in real life by players of violent first-person shooters alongside the potential benefit of conflict-resolution gaming or peaceful virtual worlds. We might even think about those wacky folks over in creative industries making their own games as part of the entrepreneurial spirit of small business that is supposedly enabled by their work in universities.

Games in the university bind art to science as never before. The grand bifurcation that put science at the physical and symbolic top of the campus and the arts at the bottom, with no interaction, is jeopardized. Computing applications to narrative and art, and *vice versa*, are well known to professors from computer science to dance. Faculty at opposite ends of the university write the same codes, analyze the same narratives, go to the same parties, take the same drugs, and sleep with the same people. Fun in the cognitariat! And in the United States, there is a much more powerful link between electronic games and universities that brings science and art together. It's called the military.

Meanwhile, there is a binary in game studies, which situates at one antinomy an omniscient, omnipotent group of technocrats plotting to control the emotions and thoughts of young people around the world and turn them into malleable consumers, workers, and killers; and at the other, all-powerful desiring machines called players, whose wishes are met by producers (Tobin, 2004). New media *savants* are fond of invoking pre-capitalist philosophers, dodging questions of state and capital by heading for aesthetics. High art and high technology broker high neoliberalism thanks to ludology (ignoring the work of professional associations such as The Association for the Study of Play or the North American Society for the Sociology of Sport) and narratology, returning to the non-materialist, non-medium-specific work of literary studies (ignoring the media studies parlayed by the International Association for Media and Communication Research or the Union for Democratic Communication). Drawing on the banal possessive individualism of neoclassical economics, reactionary game analysts study virtual environments to understand 'whole societies under controlled conditions' (Castronova, 2006), neglecting or caricaturing the discourses of history and ethnography.

These dominant discourses fail to account for the fact that the first electronic game, *Tennis for Two*, was produced at the U.S. Department of Nuclear Energy (Consalvo, 2006), a hint that the material underpinning to electronic play has a serious history that must be uncovered. The political economy of the global gaming industry is essentially a rather banal repetition of Hollywood—domination by firms that buy up or destroy small businesses and centralize power in the metropole; the decimation of little bedroom concerns in favor of giant conglomerates; a working mythology of consumer power; and massive underwriting by the state through militarism and universities (Kerr and Flynn, 2003; Miller et al., 2005).

We need to follow Vincent Mosco when he reminds us that once the utopic rhetoric of new communications technologies and cultural genres has been played out, the real work begins, the moment when the 'mythic period' of alarm and fantasy has given way to banality, when every move is neither hailed nor derided, but silently normalized (2004, p. 19). Otherwise, we are left with the same tired choice: 'the freedom to choose after all the major political, economic, and social decisions have already been made' (2004, p. 60). These areas of analysis are just as important as the apolitical, ahistorical tendencies that characterize hegemonic games analysis, albeit with notable exceptions (Consalvo, 2006; Lenoir, 2003; Mirrlees, 2009). The history of the university and electronic games shows us what happens when these lessons are not heeded.

In 1996, the National Academy of Sciences held a workshop for academia, Hollywood, and the Pentagon, on simulation and games. The next year, the National Research Council announced a collaborative research agenda in popular culture and militarism. It convened meetings to streamline such cooperation, from special effects to training simulations, from immersive technologies to simulated networks (Lenoir, 2003, p. 190; Macedonia, 2002). Since that time, untold numbers of academic journals and institutes on games have become closely tied to the Pentagon. They generate research designed to test and augment the recruiting and training potential of games to ideologize, hire, and instruct the population. The Center for Computational Analysis of Social and Organizational Systems at Carnegie-Mellon University in Pittsburgh promulgates studies underwritten by the Office of Naval Research and the Defense Advanced Research Projects Agency (DARPA). DARPA is blissfully happy to use its US$2 billion annual budget to examine, for instance, how social networking of the *America's Army* game can uncover 'top America's Army players' distinct behaviours, the optimum size of an America's Army team, the importance of fire volume toward opponent, the recommendable communication structure and content, and the contribution of the unity among team members' (Carley et al., 2005). And it refers to Orlando as 'Team Orlando' because the city houses Disney's research-and-development 'imagineers'; the University of Central Florida's Institute for Simulation and Training; Lockheed Martin, the nation's biggest military contractor; and the Pentagon's Institute for Simulation and Training.

In Los Angeles, the University of Southern California's Institute for Creative Technologies (ICT) was set up in 1998 to articulate faculty, film and television producers, game designers, and the Pentagon. It was formally opened by the Secretary of the Army and the head of the Motion Picture Association of America, and started with US$45 million of the military's budget, a figure that was doubled in its 2004 renewal. ICT uses military money and Hollywood muscle to test out homicidal technologies and narrative scenarios—under the aegis of film, engineering, and communications professors (Deck, 2004; Silver and Marwick, 2006, p. 50; Turse, 2008, p. 120).

Companies such as Pandemic (part-owned by that high-corporate moralist, Bono) invest. ICT also collaborates on major motion pictures, for instance *Spider-Man 2* (Sam Raimi, 2004), and its workspace was thought up by the set designer for the *Star Trek* franchise. The Institute produces Pentagon recruitment tools such as *Full Spectrum Warrior* that double as 'training devices for military operations in urban terrain': what's good for the Xbox is good for the combat simulator. The utility of these innovations continues in combat. The military is aware that off-duty soldiers play games. The idea is to invade their supposed leisure time, weaning them from skater games and towards what are essentially training manuals. It even boasts that *Full Spectrum Warrior* was the 'game that captured Saddam,' because the men who dug Hussein out had been trained with it. And electronic games have become crucial tools because fewer and fewer nations now allow the United States to play live war games on their terrain (Andersen, 2007; Burston, 2003; Harmon, 2003; Kundnani, 2004; Stockwell and Muir, 2003; Turse, 2008, p. 122, 119).

To keep up with the Institute's work, why not listen to podcasts from *Armed with Science: Research Applications for the Modern Military*, which you can download at the Defense Department's web site <science.dodlive.mil>. You'll learn how the Pentagon and USC are developing *UrbanSim* to improve 'the art of battle command,' as part of Obama's imperial wars. It's described as a small shift from commercial gaming: 'instead of having Godzilla and tornados attacking your city, the players are faced with things like uncooperative local officials and ethnic divisions in the communities, different tribal rivalries,' to quote an Institute scholar in the pod (March 3, 2010 edition).

For its part, the Naval Postgraduate School's Modelling, Virtual Environments and Simulation Academic Program developed a game called *Operation Starfighter*, based on the film *The Last Starfighter* (Castle, 1984). The next step, the aforementioned *America's Army*, was farmed out for participation by George Lucas' companies, inter alia. It was launched with due symbolism on the 4th of July 2002—dually symbolic, in that Independence Day doubles as a key date in the film industry's summer roll-out of features. The military had to bring additional servers into play to handle 400,000 downloads of the game that first day. *Gamespot PC Reviews* awarded it a high textual rating and was equally impressed by the 'business model.' Five years after its release, it was one of the ten most-played games on line. *America's Army* has millions of registered users. Civilian developers regularly refresh it by consulting with veterans and participating in physical war games. Paratexts provided additional forms of promotional renewal. The website, Americasarmy.com/community, takes full advantage of the usual array of cybertarian fantasies about the new media as civil society, across the gamut of community fora, Internet chat, fan sites, and virtual competition. And the game is formally commodified through privatization—bought by Ubisoft to be repurposed for games consoles, arcades, and cell phones and turned into figurines by the allegedly edgy independent company Radioactive Clown. Tournaments are convened, replete with hundreds of thousands of dollars prize money, along with smaller events at military recruiting sites. With over 40 million downloads and websites by the thousand, its message has travelled far and wide—an excellent return on the initial public investment of US$19 million and US$5 million annually for updates. Studies of young people who have positive attitudes to the US military indicate that 30% of them formed that view through playing the game—a game that sports a Teen rating; a game that forbids role reversal via modifications, preventing players from experiencing the pain of the other; a game that is officially ranked first among the Army's recruiting tools ("AA:SF," 2008; Power, 2007, pp. 279–80; Turse, 2008, pp. 117, 123–24; Lenoir, 2003, p. 175; Nieborg, 2004; Turse 2008, pp. 118, 157; Craig, 2006; Shachtman, 2002; Thompson, 2004). Meanwhile, virtual blowback is underway, with Al Qaeda reportedly learning tactics by playing these games and developing counters of their own (Power, 2007, p. 283) and the artist Joseph DeLappe creating counter-texts on-line by typing the details of dead soldiers into the game under the moniker 'dead-in-Iraq' (unr.edu/art/DELAPPE/DeLappe%20Main%20Page/DeLappe%20Online%20MAIN.html).

Gaming and universities are clearly connected through 'technological nationalism' (Charland, 1986). They have formed a symbiotic ideological and material relationship with what is also, by the way, the globe's leading polluter—the U.S. Department of Defense. Military uses of electronics, information technologies, games, and special effects link universities to the Pentagon's orgiastic use of fossil fuels, destruction of terrain and infrastructure, radiation, conventional pollution, buried ordinance, defoliants, land use, anti-personnel mines, carcinogenic chemical deposits, and toxic effluents. Despite the Pentagon's latter-day claim that it is 'going green,' the Department remains the world's largest user of petroleum (Corbett and Turco, 2006; Jorgenson et al., 2010; Leaning, 2000; Shachtman, 2010).

University scholars involved with these delightful paymasters would do well to read some scientific history. In his testimony to the U.S. Atomic Energy Commission, the noted physicist J. Robert Oppenheimer, who led the group that developed the atomic bomb, talked about the instrumental rationality that animated the people who created this awesome technology. Once these scientists saw that it was feasible, the device's impact lost intellectual and emotional significance for them. They had been overtaken by what he labeled its 'technically sweet' quality (United States Atomic Energy Commission, 1954, p. 81).

Just such techno-saccharine is the lifeblood of instrumental pleasure and exhilarating utopia. "Technically sweet" qualities animate innovation, adoption, and the mix of the sublime—the awesome, the ineffable, the uncontrollable, the powerful—with the beautiful—the approachable, the attractive, the pliant, the soothing. In philosophical aesthetics, the sublime and the beautiful are generally regarded as opposites. But game technologies have helped bring them together for denizens of the ICT and their friends across campuses.

Conclusion

The current conjuncture is one of chaos for U.S. higher education. The businesses and governments it seeks to serve and emulate are revealed to be naked and saggy, even as the promises of futurism seem to be deliverable via the cognitariat.

This is a turning point in educational history, when pages are torn from a playbook, and lives are torn asunder. Dedicated scholars who made the decision to join the ranks of the gentried poor rather than follow mammon, find that the supposed trade-off—that they might pursue research secure in the knowledge that their basic welfare was guaranteed—no longer applies.

That said, the tremors that are undulating across corporate agendas and governmental methods may enable us to combat them. Commodification and governmentality need to be identified, problematized, and turned against themselves in any struggle for progressive education. We must shift into reverse the mimetic managerial fallacy by implementing collaborative (not competitive) and learned (not leeched) forms of work. Utilizing accountability to reveal corporate power over intellectual production, or pointing out to students the negative realities of a consumer address, can be fruitful. As per the brave actions taken by professional bodies in anthropology and—belatedly—psychology against their co-optation by the Bush and Obama war machines (aaanet.org/pdf/iraqtorture.pdf; apa.org/releases-/editorial-bray.html), we should shame universities for their role in electronic-game militarism, even as we acknowledge that this has its origins in the crass commercialism of a system in crisis feeding from the death roll of a discredited empire. The task is massive, and it will require people with progressive politics to collaborate as never before.

Works Cited

"AA:SF Tops 9 Million User Mark!" (2008, February 10). Retrieved from americasarmy.com/intel

Andersen, R. (2007). Bush's Fantasy Budget and the Military/Entertainment Complex. *PRWatch.org*. Retrieved from prwatch.org/node/5742

Attali, Jacques. (2008). This is not America's Final Crisis. *New Perspectives Quarterly, 25*, no. 2: pp. 31–33.

Bar, François, with Caroline Simard. (2006). In Leah Lievrouw and Sonia Livingstone (Eds.), From Hierarchies to Network Firms. *The Handbook of New Media: Updated Students Edition.* Thousand Oaks Calif.: Sage.

Bell, Daniel. (1977). The Future World Disorder: The Structural Context of Crises. *Foreign Policy, 27*: 109–35.

Brzezinski, Zbigniew. (1969). *Between Two Ages: America's Role in the Technotronic Era.* New York: Viking Press.

Burston, Jonathan. (2003). In Daya Kishan Thussu and Des Freedman (Eds.), War and the Entertainment Industries: New Research Priorities in an Era of Cyber-Patriotism. *War and the Media: Reporting Conflict 24/7.* London: Sage Publications.

Carley, K., Moon, Il-Chul, Schneider, M. & Shigiltchoff, O. (2005). *Detailed Analysis of Factors Affecting Team Success and Failure in the America's Army Game.* CASOS Technical Report.

Castronova, Edward. (2006). On the Research Value of Large Games: Natural Experiments in Norrath and Camelot. *Games & Culture: A Journal of Interactive Media, 1*, no. 2: 163–86.

Charland, Maurice. (1986). Technological Nationalism. *Canadian Journal of Political and Social Theory*, 10, no. 1: 196–220.

Consalvo, Mia. (2006). Console Video Games and Global Corporations: Creating a Hybrid Culture. *New Media & Society* 8, no. 1: 117–37.

Corbett, C. J. & Turco, R.P. (2006). *Sustainability in the Motion Picture Industry*. Report prepared for the Integrated Waste Management Board of the State of California. Retrieved from personal.anderson.ucla.edu/charles.corbett/papers/mpis_report.pdf

Craig, K. (2006). Dead in Iraq: It's No Game. *Wired*. Retrieved from wired.com/gaming/gamingreviews/news/2006/06/71052

Deck, A. (2004). Demilitarizing the Playground. *Art Context*. Retrieved from artcontext.org/crit/essays/noQuarter

Dyson, E., Gilder, G., Keyworth, G. & Toffler, A. (1994). *Cyberspace and the American Dream: A Magna Carta for the Knowledge Age*. Version 1.2. Progress and Freedom Foundation. Retrieved from pff.org/issues-pubs/futureinsights/fi1.2magnacarta.html

Hardt, M. & Negri, A. (2000). *Empire*. Cambridge, Mass.: Harvard University Press.

Harmon, A. (2003, April 3). More Than Just a Game, But How Close to Reality? *New York Times*. Retrieved from nytimes.com/2003/04/03/technology/more-than-just-a-game-but-how-close-to-reality.html

Hebert, J. (2005, November 6). Band of Brothers. *San Diego Union-Tribune*. Retrieved from legacy.signonsandiego.com/uniontrib/20051106/news_lz1a06ictech.html

Henwood, D. (2010). I'm Borrowing My Way through College. *Left Business Observer*, 125. Retrieved from leftbusinessobserver.com/College.html

Jorgenson, A.K., Clark, B. & Kentor, J. (2010). Militarization and the Environment: A Panel Study of Carbon Dioxide Emissions and the Ecological Footprints of Nations, 1970–2000. *Global Environmental Politics*, 10, no. 1: 7–29.

Kerr, A. & Flynn, R. (2003). Revisiting Globalisation through the Movie and Digital Games Industries. *Convergence: The International Journal of Research into New Media Technologies*, 9, no. 1: 91–113.

Kotkin, J. (2001). *The New Geography: How the Digital Revolution Is Reshaping the American Landscape*. New York: Random House.

Kundnani, A. (2004). Wired for War: Military Technology and the Politics of Fear. *Race & Class*, 46, no. 1: 116–25.

Leaning, J. (2000). Environment and Health: 5. Impact of War. *Canadian Medical Association Journal*, 163, no. 9: 1157–61.

Lenoir, Timothy. (2003). In Robert Latham (Ed.), Programming Theaters of War: Gamemakers as Soldiers. *Bombs and Bandwidth: The Emerging Relationship between Information Technology and Security*. New York: New Press.

Macedonia, M. (2002). Games, Simulation, and the Military Education Dilemma. *The Internet and the University: 2001 Forum*. Boulder, Colo.: Educause.

Marcuse, H. (1941). Some Social Implications of Modern Technology. *Studies in Philosophy and Social Sciences*, 9, no. 3: 414–39.

Mattelart, A. (2002). An Archaeology of the Global Era: Constructing a Belief, trans. Susan Taponier with Philip Schlesinger. *Media Culture & Society*, 24, no. 5: 591–612.

Miller, T. (2003). Governmentality or Commodification? US Higher Education. *Cultural Studies* 17, no. 6: 897–904.

Miller, Toby. (2007). In William T. Greenough, Philip J. McConnaughay, and Jay P. Kesan. (Eds.), The Governmentalization and Corporatization of Research. *Defining Values for Research and Technology: The University's Changing Role.* Lanham, MD.: Rowman & Littlefield. 189–209.

Miller, T. (2008). *Makeover Nation: The United States of Reinvention.* Cleveland: Ohio State University Press.

Miller, T. (2009). "Governmentality and Commodification: The Keys to Yanqui Academic Hierarchy." *Towards a Global Autonomous University.* Ed. The Edu-Factory Collective. New York: Autonomedia. 72–79.

Miller, T., Govil, N., McMurria, J., Maxwell, R. & Wang, T. (2005). *Global Hollywood 2.* London: British Film Institute.

Mirrlees, T. (2009). "Digital Militainment by Design: Producing and Playing *SOCOM: U.S. Navy SEALs.*" *International Journal of Media and Cultural Politics* 5, no. 3: 161–81.

Moffatt, B. & Elliott, C. (2007). Ghost Marketing: Pharmaceutical Companies and Ghostwritten Journal Articles. *Perspectives in Biology and Medicine* 50, no. 1: 18–31.

Mosco, V. (2004). *The Digital Sublime: Myth, Power, and Cyberspace.* Cambridge, Mass.: MIT Press.

Negri, A. (2007). *Goodbye Mister Socialism.* Paris: Seuil.

Newfield, C. (2003). The Value of Nonscience. *Critical Inquiry* 29, no. 3: 508–25.

Newfield, C. (2004). Jurassic U: The State of University-Industry Relations. *Social Text* 79: 37–66.

Newfield, C. (2008, October 31). Public Universities at Risk: 7 Damaging Myths. *Chronicle of Higher Education*: A128.

Nieborg, D. B. (2004). In Thomas Eberle and Willy Christian Kriz (Eds.), America's Army: More Than a Game. *Transforming Knowledge into Action Through Gaming and Simulation.* Munich: Sagsaga.

Power, M. (2007). Digitized Virtuosity: Video War Games and Post-9/11 Cyber-Deterrence. *Security Dialogue* 38, no. 2: 271–88.

Ross, A. (2010). The Corporate Analogy Unravels. *Chronicle of Higher Education.* Retrieved from chronicle.com/article/Farewell-to-the-Corporate/124919

Rothkopf, D. (1997). In Praise of Cultural Imperialism. *Foreign Policy* 107: 38–53.

Schiller, H. I. (1976). *Communication and Cultural Domination.* New York: International Arts and Sciences Press.

Schactman, N. (2002, July 4). "Shoot'Em Up and Join the Army." *Wired.* Retrieved from wired.com/gaming/gamingreviews/news/2002/07/53663

Shachtman, N. (2010). Green Monster. *Foreign Policy* Retrieved from foreignpolicy.com/articles/2010/04/26/green_monster?page=full

Silver, D. & Marwick, A. (2006). In David Silver and Adrienne Massanari (Eds.), Internet Studies in Times of Terror. *Critical Cyberculture Studies.* New York: New York University Press. 47–54.

Stockwell, S. & Muir, A. (2003). The Military-Entertainment Complex: A New Facet of Information Warfare. *Fibreculture* 1. Retrieved from journal.fibreculture.org/issue1/issue1_stockwellmuir.html

Thompson, C. (2004). The Making of an X Box Warrior. *New York Times Magazine*, August, 22.

Tobin, J. (2004). In Joseph Tobin (Ed.), Introduction. *Pikachu's Global Adventure*. Durham, N.C.: Duke University Press.

Toffler, A. (1983). *Previews and Premises*. New York: William Morrow.

Turse, N. (2008). *The Complex: How the Military Invades Our Everyday Lives*. New York: Metropolitan Books.

United States Atomic Energy Commission. (1954). *In the Matter of J. Robert Oppenheimer. Transcript of Hearing Before Personnel Security Board.* Retrieved from honors.umd.edu/HONR 269J/archive/Oppenheimer.html

CHAPTER ELEVEN

Algorithmic Capitalism and Educational Futures

MICHAEL A. PETERS

The word *algorithm* comes from the name of the 9th century Persian Muslim mathematician Abu Abdullah Muhammad ibn Musa Al-Khwarizmi. The word *algorism* originally referred only to the rules of performing arithmetic using Hindu-Arabic numerals but evolved via European Latin translation of Al-Khwarizmi's name into *algorithm* by the 18th century. The use of the word evolved to include all definite procedures for solving problems or performing tasks.

—*HISTORY OF ALGORITHMS AND ALGORITHMICS*
http://www.scriptol.com/programming/algorithm-history.php

Khwarizmi, Abu Jafar Muhammad ibn Musa al- (**d. ca. 850**)
Mathematician, astronomer, and geographer. Synthesized extant Hellenic, Sanskritic, and cuneiform traditions to develop algebra, a term derived from the title of one of his books (containing the term al-jabr, meaning "forcing" [numbers]). Introduced Arabic numerals into the Latin West, based on a place-value decimal system developed from Indian sources. The word algorithm is derived from a Latin corruption of his name.

OXFORD ISLAMIC STUDIES ONLINE

http://www.oxfordislamicstudies.com/article/opr/t125/e1305

Introduction: Algorithmic trading and cloud capitalism

The Report of the Staffs of the CFTC and SEC to the Joint Advisory Committee on Emerging Regulatory Issues "Findings Regarding the Market Events of May 6, 2010"[1] begins:

> On May 6, 2010, the prices of many U.S.-based equity products experienced an extra-ordinarily rapid decline and recovery. That afternoon, major equity indices in both the futures and securities markets, each already down over 4% from their prior-day close, suddenly plummeted a further 5–6% in a matter of minutes before rebounding almost as quickly (p. 1).

The Report provides a compelling account of that turbulent day: 'At 2:32 p.m., against this backdrop of unusually high volatility and thinning liquidity, a large fundamental trader (a mutual fund complex) initiated a sell program to sell a total of 75,000 E-Mini contracts (valued at approximately $4.1 billion) as a hedge to an existing equity position' (p. 2). The report indicates that liquidity crises ensued because a large trader used an automated execution algorithm ("Sell Algorithm") that was programmed to trade large volume (E-Mini contracts) with regard only to volume rather than price or time and the Sell Algorithm was executed rapidly in the period of 20 minutes, resulting in one the three largest single-day price movements in the history of the stock market. Under the heading 'Lesson Learned' the Report suggests that 'under stressed market conditions, the automated execution of a large sell order can trigger extreme price movements, especially if the automated execution algorithm does not take prices into account. Moreover, the interaction between automated execution programs and algorithmic trading strategies can quickly erode liquidity and result in disorderly markets.' The report also goes on to comment on the way May 6 market volatility is a 'reminder of the inter-connectedness of our derivatives and securities markets' and the 'nature of the cross-market trading activity'. The report concludes, 'Of final note, the events of May 6 clearly demonstrate the importance of data in today's world of fully-automated trading strategies and systems. This is further complicated by the many sources of data that must be aggregated in order to form a complete picture of the markets upon which decisions to trade can be based.'

Algorithmic capitalism and its dominance of the market increasingly across all asset classes has truly arrived. Rob Iati (July 10, 2009) writing for *Advanced Trading* asserts:

Algorithms account for more than 25% of all shares traded by the buy side today—a number steadily rising for several years now. However, the incredible capabilities offered by technology have given meteoric rise to a relative few high-frequency proprietary trading firms that now wield far greater influence on the markets today than most people recognize. The familiar names of Lehman, Bear and Merrill are being replaced by less familiar ones like Wolverine, IMC and Getco . . . high-frequency trading firms, which represent approximately 2% of the 20,000 or so trading firms operating in the U.S. markets today, account for 73% of all U.S. equity trading volume.[2]

Iati indicates that value of high-frequency algorithmic trading relies on 'a real-time, collocated, high-frequency trading platform . . . where data is collected and orders are created and routed to execution venues in sub-millisecond times.'

Algorithmic capitalism is an aspect of informationalism or informational capitalism or 'cybernetic capitalism', a term that I prefer because it speaks to the genealogy of postmodern capitalism and recognizes more precisely the cybernetic systems, similarities among various sectors of the postindustrial capitalist economy in its third phase of development—from mercantilism, industrialism to cybernetics—linking the growth of the multinational info-utilities (e.g., Googgle, Microsoft, Amazon) and their spectacular growth in the last twenty years, with developments in biocapitalism and the informatization of biology, and fundamental changes taking place with algorithmic trading and the development of so-called financialization.

It is in this context that we can talk of 'cloud capitalism' that is recentralizing the Net and creating large-scale monopolies in the knowledge economy, on a vastly larger scale than anything imagined possible in the industrial era. For example, take Google's project of digitizing millions of books that will make its digital library bigger than the Library of Congress. By doing so, as Charles Leadbeater (2010) argues, "Google will acquire huge power over the future of publishing. It will be able to head off potential competition from other databases of digital books." As he goes on to explain: "Google is the first and most successful exponent of a new kind of economic power: cloud capitalism." He suggests that the internet that the cloud capitalists want to give us is quite different from that of the "information superhighway" or "cyberspace":

> In cloud computing, our data—emails, documents, pictures, songs and software—will be stored remotely in a digital cloud hanging above us, always there to access from any device: computer, television, games console, hand-held and mobile. We should be able to draw down as much or as little of the shared cloud as we need (http://www.guardian.co.uk/technology/2010/feb/07/cloud-computing-google-apple).

Leadbeater raises questions about the way cloud capitalism aims at complete control that ultimately excludes other databases while maximizing revenues and the capacity of clouds to hold vast amounts of data on us that occludes the interests of citizens and eludes the control of governments. We might see 'cloud capitalism' as an aspect of a wider phenomena of cognitive or cybernetic capitalism.

Cybernetic and cognitive capitalism

Cybernetic capitalism is a system that has been shaped by the forces of formalization, mathematization and aestheticization beginning in the early twentieth century and associated with developments in mathematical theory, logic, physics, biology and information theory. Its new forms now exhibit themselves in finance capitalism, informationalism, knowledge capitalism and the learning economy with incipient nodal developments associated with the creative and open knowledge (and science) economies. The critical question in the wake of the collapse of the global finance system and the impending eco-crisis concerns whether capitalism can promote forms of social, ecological and economic sustainability.

'Cybernetic capitalism' is a term we use in order to distinguish a group of theories, or, better, positions, on the Left that attempt to theorize the nature of the *new* capitalism (Peters, Britez & Bulut, 2010). We group these contributions as largely sociological and Left-leaning, characterizing them in terms of what they share with and how they differ from the Marxist theory of industrial capitalism. Using a kinship with Marxism we can generate the following rough groupings of recent work that we have systematically categorized as:

1. Informational capitalism
2. Cultural capitalism
3. Cognitive capitalism
4. Finance capitalism
5. Biocapitalism

There are strong overlaps and conceptual connections among these five broad categories and also some interesting differences within them. They are systematically related phenomena that grow out of the same forces of increasing *formalization, math ematicization* and *aestheticization* that have been in operation since the beginning of the twentieth century but that began to coalesce and impact after WWII with the development of cybernetics and a group of theories that developed to explain linear and nonlinear dynamical systems (catastrophe, chaos, complexity). These relationships and particularly the way in which they profile education is the concern for this chapter. We have categorized, referenced and discussed aspects of cybernetic capitalism in a series of other papers (Peters, 2010; Peters, Britez & Bulut, 2010; Peters &Britez, 2010; Peters & Venkatesan, 2011a, 2011b).

Cognitive capitalism is another label for a range of contemporary capitalism that represents a change in the regime of accumulation and new modes of knowledge production that highlight immaterial or digital production. The production of intangible goods and services that conflates the traditional categories of political economy blurring the boundaries between consumption, information, cognition, and communication issued from the pervasive use of new information and communication technologies. As Franco Berardi Bifo (2010) in 'Cognitarian Subjectivation' argues:

> Recent years have witnessed a new techno-social framework of contemporary subjectivation. And I would like to ask whether a process of autonomous, collective self-definition is possible in the present age. The concept of 'general intellect' associated with Italian post-operaist thought in the 1990s (Paolo Virno, Maurizio Lazzarato, Christian Marazzi) emphasizes the interaction between labor and language: social labor is the endless recombination of myriad fragments producing, elaborating, distributing, and decoding signs and informational units of all kinds. Every semiotic segment produced by the information worker must meet and match innumerable other semiotic segments in order to form the combinatory frame of the info-commodity, semiocapital (http://worker01.e-flux.com/pdf/article_183.pdf).

This new semiocapital, Bifo argues, puts neuro-psychic energies to work. It is a theme that has been thematized also by Warren Neidich (2009) who credits Lazzarato and reads it back onto Deleuze's 'societies of control'.

> In the words of Maurizio Lazzarato, "In the societies of control, power relations come to be expressed through the action at a distance of one mind on another, through the brain's power to affect and become affected, which is mediated and enriched by technology . . . The institutions of the societies of control are thus characterised by the use of technologies acting at a distance, rather than of mechanical technologies (societies of sovereignty) or thermodynamic technologies (disciplinary societies). . . . First, in the transition from the Disciplinary Society to the Society of Control and onward to what Lazzarato refers to as noo-politics, the focus of power and the technology at its disposal is not directed toward the materiality of the body but, instead, its psychic life, particularly its memories and attention, recognising that the mind and the body are inextricably linked through voluntary and involuntary, somatic and autonomic, striated and smooth conditions . . . (p. 186).

He extends this idea to develop a new focus of sovereignty—a kind of neural plasticity as a generator of fields of difference produced by post-Fordist deregulation. He goes on to argue that 'these new forms of the social as a multiplicity, formulated in the conditions of post-Fordist labour, produce the conditions of the dynamic, manifold, and metastable brain and mind.' Biopower and algorithmic syn-optic power produce new forms of informational transnationalism within capital-ism while producing also new forms of resistance. Who would have thought the political uses of Facebook, a technology that began as a rating platform of female students within U.S. privileged universities could also serve as a contagion of rebel-lion against dictators in the Muslim world in places like Tunisia, Egypt and Yemen?

Clearly, if something like what Lazzarato and Bifo indicates is an accurate description of conditions for labor under post-Fordism, then education—school, community colleges and universities—is the sites for the proliferation of cognitive capitalism and also resistance to it. As Neidich (2006) succinctly summarizes in an earlier paper 'The Neurobiopolitics of Global Consciousness'

> [Where] the disciplinary society is constructed through a dissemination of social com-mand by diffuse networks of machinic assemblages . . . that regulate each subject's cus-toms, habits and productive practicethe society of control operates within the domain of intensive cultural apparaticharacterised by the Riemannian spaces, rhizomatic log-ics and folded temporality induced by the multiplicity of flows that characterise our global world post-internet (pp. 222–23).

Deleuze makes a classification of three specific kinds of power: sovereign power, disciplinary power and 'control' of communication and views the third kind of power as becoming hegemonic, a form of domination that, paradoxically, is both more total than any previous form, extending even to speech and imagination. According to Deleuze (1989a, b) we now live in a universe that could be described as meta-cinematic and his classification of images implies a new kind of camera con-sciousness that determines our subjectivities and perceptions selves. We live in a visu-al culture that is always moving and changing and each image is always connected to an assemblage of affects and forces.

The New Logic and Culture of Social Media[3]

In the Oscar-winning *The Social Network*, Mark Zuckerberg, the founder of Facebook, is portrayed as someone who rips off an idea from two Harvard student colleagues (the Winkleboss twins) who want to create a virtual community and exploit the brand of Harvard. The film is directed by David Fincher, featuring Jesse Eisenberg, Andrew Garfield and Justin Timberlake among others, based on a screenplay by Aaron Sorkin who adapts Ben Mezich's (2009) *The Accidental Billionaires*. Mezich subtitles the book *The Founding of Facebook, A Tale of Sex, Money, Genius, and Betrayal* and insists that while written as in the narrative style it is not a work of fiction. As he says in the 'Author's Note': '*The Accidental Billionaires* is a dramatic, narrative account based on dozens of interviews, hundreds of sources, and thousands of pages of documents, including records from several court proceedings' (p. 1). The film has won critical acclaim yet while called *The Social Network* really focuses on the personality of Zuckerberg (perhaps unfairly) and the resulting lawsuits rather than on the social phenomenon of Facebook beyond the fact that it starts as a mechanism for rating the attractiveness of female students at Harvard. Perhaps this is philosophical enough? The movie begins in 2003 when Zuckerberg hacks into residence halls to download details and photos, and while he is punished for this act, the idea of a social networking site is born, and he soon devotes himself to exploiting the idea and building the network. We witness the building of a vast network as the idea is financed and the network grows, finally shifting to a site in the Silicon Valley. The oft-quoted observation that 'with 600 million users Facebook is the fourth largest country in the world', really misses the point about globalization and networks that are now no longer geographically based. As some technology writers pointed out, the film was 'anti-social', 'anti-geek' and misogynistic—Zuckerberg himself ironically is portrayed as someone almost autistic in his anti-social behavior—yet highlighted the intellectual property issues that established, as Larry Lessig has pointed out, the idea of the social network is not patentable and that the code written for Facebook (where the real innovation is) was Zukerberg's.

Facebook was launched in 2004 as a social network service. It is estimated that over 40% of the U.S. population has a Facebook account and that in one month in October 2010 Facebook had over 135 unique visitors. Facebook's value has been estimated to be $41 billion and has become the third largest U.S. web company after Google and Amazon. Along with Microsoft and eBay these web companies increasingly define the new landscape of cybernetic capitalism. Facebook employs some 1,700 people in twelve countries and heads the list of over 200 social networking sites (excluding dating online websites).[4] The focus of these social networks run across the spectrum of social activities: websites for sports, gaming, nationalities, ethnic groups, mothers, Afro-Americans, green and social activists, investment groups, communities, sex groups, photo-sharing, movies, colleges and schools, religious-based groups, alumni associations, charity, travel and so on. Indeed, a list of social networking sites reveals well over 200 social networking sites[5] with some established as early as 1995 predating the establishment of Facebook by almost a decade. Many like Academia.edu, Classmates.com, TeachStreet, Tuenti, and LinkedIn are specifically professional and educational sites; others focus on business.

In "An Anthropological Introduction to YouTube", Michael Wesch (2008) indicates that YouTube produced more hours of broadcasting in six months than ABC has since it began broadcasting in 1948, that is, YouTube adds 9,232 hours every day, the equivalent of 200,000 three-minute videos, without producers and most of the material is new.[6] YouTube was launched in 2005. Wesch (2007) in his video "Web 2.0 . . . The Machine is Using Us"[7] argues the Web 'is no longer just about information; it's about connecting people' and user-generated organization, distribution and commentary (blogging) of material so that we are living in a whole different mediascape based on the understanding media means *mediating* human relationships, not content, especially among the 18–24 age group, which is emblematic of a 'participatory culture' of drag and drop editing, and remixing, sometimes as many times as 2000.

The language of the new social media is easily programmable given that its algorithmic character and its numerical coding allows for the automation of many of its functions including media creation. New media are variable and interactive and no longer tied to technologies of exact reproduction such as copying (Manovitch, 2000). They are part of a wider paradigm and system that Castells (2000) calls 'informational capitalism', which is a new technological paradigm and mode of development characterized by information generation, processing, and transmission that have become the fundamental sources of productivity and power. More and more of this information that is the raw material of knowledge capitalism is increasingly either image-based or comes to us in the form of images. We now live in a socially networked universe in which the material conditions for the formation, circulation, and utilization of knowledge and learning are rapidly changing from an industrial to information-and media-based economy. Increasingly the emphasis has fallen on knowledge, learning and media systems and networks that depend upon the acquisition of new skills of image manipulation and understanding as a central aspect of development considered in personal, community, regional, national and global contexts.

These mega-trends signal both changes in the production and consumption of symbolic visual goods and also associated changes in their contexts of use. The radical concordance of image, text and sound, and development of new information and knowledge infrastructures have encouraged the emergence of a global media networks linked with telecommunications that signal the emergence of a Euro-American consumer culture based on the rise of edutainment media a set of information-utility conglomerates.

Jonathan Beller (2006) argues that cinema and other media formations including the internet as media platform, are deterritorialized factories in which spectators work or perform value-productive labor. The cinematic mode of production (CMP) is an exploitation of the sociality that characterizes a spectator economy. The question is whether we have already moved beyond spectatorship and the spectator economy to one now centered on new social media and a social mode of production that requires collaboration and co-creation as a matter of participation and entry.

The logic of free software as it underwrites social media has breathed new life into new facets of culture from music to politics, engendering what Kelty (2008) calls a recursive public—one that is *vitally concerned with the material and practical maintenance and modification of the technical, legal, practical, and conceptual means of its own existence as a public* (p. 3). In this new social media culture the individual imagination is harnessed in forms of hypertextual forms of multi-creation that tie the expressive to politics and to democratic action, transforming and reshaping the deterritorialized community as one a global polis with shifting and temporary alliances mobilized for particular causes and social movements and political events.

Commons-based peer production is also an economic system of text and image production facilitated by the infrastructure of the Internet that encourages collaboration among individuals who share information, knowledge or cultural goods often without relying on the market pricing or corporate bureaucracies to coordinate their common enterprise. This might be true of open social media that has come to characterize open science and open education, but not all social media is open in this sense. Indeed. Only a tiny proportion of social media is open and the difference between commercialization and non-commercialization is a critical question that goes to the heart of education. Some argue that open science demonstrates an 'exemplar of a compound of "private-collective" model of innovation' that contains elements of both proprietary and public models of knowledge production (von Hippel & von Krogh, 2003; von Krogh & von Hippel, 2003). Yet others maintain that the expansion of a patenting culture undermines the norms of open science (Rhoten & Powell, 2007; Peters & Roberts, 2011).

As code for greater political and economic freedoms the concept of openness symbolizes the development of a myriad of open public global spaces that serves as host for new forms of international collaboration in research, scholarship, innovation, creativity and expression. The movement toward greater openness represents a change of philosophy, ethos, and government and a set of interrelated and complex changes that transform markets altering the modes of production and consumption, ushering in a new era based on the values of openness: an ethic of sharing and peer-to-peer collaboration enabled through new architectures of participation. These changes indicate a broader shift from the underlying industrial mode of production—a 'productionist' metaphysics—to a postindustrial mode of consumption as use, reuse, and modification where new logics of social media structure different patterns of cultural consumption and symbolic analysis becomes a habitual and daily creative activity. The economics of openness constructs a new language of "presuming" and "produsage" in order to capture the open participation, collective co-creativity, communal evaluation, and commons-based production of social and public goods. Information is the vital element in the "new" politics and economy that links space, knowledge, and capital in networked practices and freedom is the essential ingredient in this equation if these network practices are to develop or transform themselves into 'knowledge cultures' (Peters & Besley, 2006).

In terms of economic and political systems much also has been written recently about openness as a new hybridized mode of production. Thus, openness has emerged as an alternative mode of *social* production based on the growing and overlapping complexities of open source, open access and open archiving and open publishing. It has become a leading source of innovation in the world global digital economy increasingly adopted by world governments, international agencies and multinationals as well as leading educational institutions. It is clear that the Free Software and 'open source' movements constitute a radical non-propertarian alternative to traditional methods of text production and distribution. This alternative non-proprietary method of cultural exchange threatens traditional models and the legal and institutional means used to restrict creativity, innovation and the free exchange of ideas. In terms of a model of communication there has been a gradual shift from content to code in the openness, access, use, reuse and modification reflecting a radical personalization that has made these open characteristics and principles increasingly the basis of the cultural sphere.

The fundamental distinction between social media and industrial media is that the former is a platform for social interaction and the new web-based technologies that are highly accessible, scalable, and user friendly turning communication into dialogue and promoting the exchange of user-generated sharable content. This new media ecology contrasts strongly with the old one-way broadcast industrial media that is tied into a transmission model and is rarely dialogical or interactive although industrial media do now try to make concessions to the new demand for interactivity via blogs, emails, and associated websites.

Web 2.0 technologies enhance creativity, communications, secure information sharing, collaboration and functionality of the web based on openness (open standards, open platforms), innovation, and evolution of web-culture communities. The applications of technologies of openness to education are still in their infancy (Peters & Britez, 2008) and the logic of new open systems outstrips that of our educational institutions built for the industrial age. These web 2.0 technologies (web as platform) are based on new architectures of participation and collaboration, promote social media and social networking, and increasingly encourage wiki-collaborations based on the 'wisdom of the crowd' (Surowiecki, 2004) and mass innovation (Leadbeater, 2009).

These new communications technologies are based on the economics of file-sharing that promote mass customization and the personalization of services (Peters, 2009) based on the co-production of knowledge goods and services where the user is increasingly seen as as co-designer or co-creator integrated into the value creation process. The growing interconnectedness of the Web has also passed into a new phase that Tim Berners-Lee calls 'linked data', an aspect of the 'semantic web' used to describe a method of exposing, sharing, and connecting data.[8]

There is a set of emerging open-knowledge ecologies that can be briefly noted and sketched by observing that MIT adopts OpenCourseWare in 2001[9]; the Budapest OA statement[10]; National Institute of Health (NIH) adopts an open access policy requiring every scientist who receives an NIH research grant and who publishes the results in a peer-reviewed journal to deposit a digital copy of the article in PubMed Central (PMC)[11], the online digital library maintained by the NIH; the Ithaca Report *University Publishing in a Digital Age* (2007)[12] says both the 'creation of new formats made possible by digital technologies . . . will enable real-time dissemination, collaboration, dynamically updated content, and usage of new media' and 'alternative distribution models (institutional repositories, pre-print servers, open access journals) have also arisen with the aim to broaden access, reduce costs, and enable open sharing of content' (p. 4); and, Harvard mandates open self-archiving (Feb. 14, 2008).[13]

The fact is that there are some major moves towards openness policies in regard to adoption of open source, open access, open archiving and open publishing.[14] Yet the openness of the Internet runs deeper and can be described in terms of an overlapping set of characteristics: *open standards*–TCP/IP, HTML, HTTP, interoperability, open processes, end to end principle, no centralized control; *open source software*—extended development community, alterable source code, flexible, personalizable; open access to networks; *open spectrum*—new source of wireless Internet broadband; *open availability of information*—free distribution of digital goods threatens intellectual property regime; DMCA, DRM; *open governance*—extraterritoriality, multilateral, self-regulation. All of these characteristics are in the process of development and emergence and educational and pedagogical possibilities are also still open to development, manipulation and control.

The Googlization of Education

One post in response to Siva Vaidhyanathan's 'The Googlization of Higher Education' succinctly summarizes the argument and recognizes the high stakes involved:

> The official mission of Google is "to organize the world's information and make it universally accessible". That is also the goals of colleges throughout the world. As institutions increasingly surrender information organization and technology functions to Google, is the academy surrendering its function and goals to a private corporation?[15]

Interestingly, the official mission does not say "to make inordinate profits off the backs of others" yet

In a companion paper "The Googlization of Universities" Siva Vaidhyanathan (2009) begins:

> The relationship between Google and the world's universities is more than close. It is uncomfortably familial. Google has moved to establish, embellish, or replace many core university services such as library databases, search interfaces, and e-mail servers. Its server space and computing power opened up new avenues for academic research. Google Scholar has allowed non-scholars to discover academic research. Google Book Search radically transformed the vision and daily practices of university libraries. Through its voracious efforts to include more of everything under its brand, Google fostered a more seamless, democratized, global, cosmopolitan information ecosystem. But it also contributed to the commercialization of higher education and the erosion of standards of information quality.

He documents the googlization of students, of scholarship, of book learning and of research to argue that universities must reverse the terms of the relationship to impose their values. It's a theme that Vaidhyanathan (2011) follows up with *The Googlization of Everything* that addresses three questions: What does the world look like through the lens of Google? How is Google's ubiquity affecting the production and dissemination of knowledge? and how has the corporation altered the rules and practices that govern other companies, institutions, and states? He writes:

> Google dominates the World Wide Web. There was never an election to determine the Web's rulers. No state appointed Google its proxy, its proconsul, or viceroy. Google just stepped into the void when no other authority was willing or able to make the Web stable, usable, and trustworthy. This was a quite necessary step at the time. The question is whether Google's dominance is the best situation for the future of our information ecosystem.

Vaidhyanathan (2011) argues that Google is a Web search-engine service, "But as the most successful supplier of Web-based advertising, Google is now an advertising company first and foremost." He suggests that currently major search engines do not 'read' for meaning, they are purely navigational and while the industry pursues semantic search, which takes into account contextual meanings of search items, semantic analysis is still not advanced enough to take away Google's market position. One of the most significant arguments against Google is what economists call the free rider problem, and Vaidhyanathan (2011) claims that Google rides for free on the creative work and investment of others; he reports that even Rupert Murdoch has complained of Google's ability to monetize the Web. And he also mentions the political interference of YouTube since its acquisition in 2006.

Perhaps most tellingly, Vaidhyanathan (2011) challenges the neoliberal presumption that market forces can best solve problems and suggests that

> It had its roots in two prominent ideologies: techno-fundamentalism, an optimistic belief in the power of technology to solve problems . . . , and market fundamentalism, the notion that most problems are better (at least more efficiently) solved by the actions of private parties rather than by state oversight or investment.

And he goes on to argue:

> Our dependence on Google is the result of an elaborate political fraud, but it is far from the most pernicious result of that fraud. Google has deftly capitalized on a thirty-year tradition of "public failure," chiefly in the United States but in much of the rest of the world as well. Public failure is the mirror image of market failure. Markets fail when they can't organize to supply an essential public good, such as education, or have no incentive to prevent a clear harm to the public, such as pollution. Market failure is the chief justification for public intervention.

Vaidhyanathan's argument here is one ultimately against neoliberalism in relation to global public knowledge goods, but the theory of cognitive capitalism provides us with a 'stage' theory of the changing nature of capitalism that helps us better to understand the logic of knowledge capitalism that operates on the basis of arrhythmic logics to expand a universe of information accessibility while changing the nature of the regime of accumulation and creating giant global info-utilities that make their profits off the back of the creative endeavors of others at the same time posing as corporations dedicated to the commonweal. Educational futures require a global transnational public investment in infrastructures that stands against both the monopolization and privatization of knowledge and education.

Notes

1. See http://www.sec.gov/news/studies/2010/marketevents-report.pdf. Release September 30, 2010. Acronyms are CFTC: Commodity Futures Trading Commission; SEC: Securities & Exchange Commission.
2. See http://advancedtrading.com/algorithms/showArticle.jhtml?articleID=218401501.
3. This section draws on Peters & Roberts (2011) and Peters (2010).
4. See the full list at http://en.wikipedia.org/wiki/List_of_social_networking_websites.
5. See the list provided at http://en.wikipedia.org/wiki/List_of_social_networking_websites. See also the top 500 sites at http://www.alexa.com/topsites.
6. See http://www.youtube.com/watch?v=TPAO-lZ4_hU.
7. See http://www.youtube.com/watch?v=6gmP4nk0EOE.

8. See the Web Design Issues Note by Berners Lee at http://www.w3.org/DesignIssues/Linked Data.html; see the whitepaper at http://virtuoso.openlinksw.com/Whitepapers/html/VirtLin kedDataDeployment.html; and Berners-Lee on the next Web at TED (video) at http://www.ted.com/index.php/talks/tim_berners_lee_on_the_next_web.html.
9. See http://ocw.mit.edu/OcwWeb/web/about/history/.
10. See http://www.soros.org/openaccess.
11. See http://www.pubmedcentral.nih.gov/.
12. See http://www.ithaka.org/ithaka-s-r/strategy/Ithaka%20University%20Publishing%-20Report.pdf.
13. See Peter Suber's note on this event at http://www.earlham.edu/~peters/fos/newsletter/03–02–08.htm.
14. See Foundations of Openness: Evaluating aspects of openness in software projects, A collaboration between Waugh Partners & OSS Watch (2008), Oxford at http://pipka.org/blog/2008/07/23/the-foundations-of-openness/; see also OpenTechnology at http://tomw.net.au/moodle/ and Foundations of NOpen (Australia) at http://brianna.modernthings.org/article/103/foundations-of-open-australia-2020-local-summit.
15. See http://blog10.facultyacademy.org/2010/04/19/the-googlization-of-higher-education/.

References

Beller, J. (2006). *The Cinematic Mode of Production*. Dartmouth, NH: University Press of New England.

Deleuze, G. (1989a). *Cinema: The Movement Image*, trans. Hugh Tomlinson and Barbara Habberjam. Minnesota: University of Minnesota Press.

Deleuze, G. (1989b). *The Time Image*, trans. Hugh Tomlinson and Robert Galeta. Minnesota: University of Minnesota Press.

Peters, M.A. (2010). Three Forms of Knowledge Economy: Learning, Creativity, Openness. *British Journal of Educational Studies*, 58 (1): 67–88.

Peters, M.A. &Venkatesan, P. (2011a). Biocapitalism and the Politics of Life, *Geopolitics, History and International Relations*, 2(2).

Peters, M.A. & Venkatesan, P. (2011b). Bioeconomy and the Third Industrial Revolution in the Age of Synthetic Life, *Contemporary Readings in Law and Social Justice*, 2(2).

Peters, M.A., Britez, R. & Bulut, E. (2010). Cybernetic Capitalism, Informationalism, and Cognitive Labor, *Geopolitics, History and International Relations*, 1 (2): 11–40.

Peters, M.A.& Britez, R. (2010).Ecopolitics of the 'Green Economy': Environmentalism and Education. *Economics, Management and Financial Markets*, 4 (3): 1–15. Reprinted in *The Journal of Academic Research in Economics*, 2010, vol. 2, issue 1 (May), pages 21–36. Retrieved from http://econpapers.repec.org/article/shcjaresh/

Vaidhyanathan, S. (2009). The Googlization of Universities. Retrieved from http://www.nea.org/assets/img/PubAlmanac/ALM_09_06.pdf

Vaidhyanathan, S. (2011). *The Googlization of Everything (And Why We Should Worry)*. Berkeley: University of California Press.

CHAPTER TWELVE

The Limits of Autonomy
Cognitive Capitalism and University Struggles

ALBERTO TOSCANO

The vicissitudes of the crisis that began in 2008 have cast euphoric pronouncements about the knowledge-based economy, which had already lost much of its sheen with the dot.com crash, in a new, ambiguous light. The aftershocks on the university have not been slow in coming. The 'Bologna process' vision of a university dedicated to the 'generation, transmission, and exploitation' of knowledge and 'mobilising the brainpower of Europe' (as cited in Sevilla, 2010, pp. 19, 25) has certainly not gone away. But it has been recoded, especially in the United Kingdom, to reverse the expansion of the university and to undo the notion that the arts, humanities and social sciences are incubators of the kind of 'creativity' and 'innovation' that were trumpeted in the nineties and noughties as the driving forces of a post-industrial economy. The instrumentalisation of scarcity and austerity for the sake of a further reassertion of class power entails the end of that neo-liberal transition that saw the mass content of the sixties university maintained in increasingly privatised and financialised forms. Among the 'assets returning to their rightful owners' is the right to education itself.

Crisis has also meant that, contrary to the view of a knowledge society founded on the molecular cooperation of creative individuals (or 'singularities'), governments have returned to a very classical understanding of what knowledge as a productive force involves: STEM (science, technology, engineering and mathematics). Accordingly, the state will only fund those kinds of knowledge that translate either into fixed capital or into highly skilled and specific competencies. The general intellect, pulverised into millions of calculating and competing human capitals, strategising about the uses of indebtedness, can fend for itself. We are thus witnessing both a massive devaluation and dispossession of certain forms of intellectual work and a re-centring, albeit in a much-mutated scenario, of the state's attentions onto forces of production as traditionally understood.

This is a scenario that poses pressing analytical and political questions for the paradigm of cognitive capitalism and for any reflection on the link between knowledge, production, labour and struggle.[1] The critical role of the university in the stratagems of capital and the workers' struggles that made possible the emergence of cognitive capitalism is evident in its most theoretically sophisticated and precise formulation. Carlo Vercellone paints the mass university as both the product and the site of a crisis of the real subsumption of labour that had characterised an expansive Fordism. It is its product to the extent that the imperative 'to incorporate the totality of society, by means of the generalisation of the wage relation and of exchange-value' and to maintain the consumption norm, requires, in great part because of the class struggles that criss-cross it, 'the socialisation, on the part of the state, of certain costs of the reproduction of labour-power' (Vercellone, 2007, p. 25).

The mass university is functional to the designs of both the state and private managers of this real subsumption, but at the same time it very rapidly generates a powerful criticism of those designs themselves not just in terms of the hiatuses between the modernizing project and its institutional reality (critique of authoritarianism and elitist selection), but as a questioning of the control of labour-power itself (critique of technocracy, of the instrumentalisation of academic disciplines, of the relationship between the university and the labour market). It is the functional containment of mass intellectuality, that contradictory requirement of Fordist industrial capitalism, which in many respects fails with the emergence of the student movements of the sixties: 'the "democratisation" (although partial) of education is one of the factors at the origin of the diffusion of knowledges and of the crisis of the first dimension of real subsumption' (Cohn-Bendit, Duteuil, et al., 1969, p. 377). While born out of the dynamics of industrial capitalism, the post-war university is also forced to sap the three ways in which this capitalism economically regulated knowledge: 'the social polarisation of knowledges, the separation between intellectual and manual labour, and a process of the incorporation of knowledge into physical capital' (Lebert and Vercellone, 2006, p. 24). Along with the contestation of the scientific management and organisation of labour (Taylorism and its by-products), and the expansion of the social cost of the reproduction of labour-power via welfare, the mutations of the university have played a signal role in the 'social crisis of the Fordist wage-relation', by constituting 'a diffuse intellectuality as the outcome of the phenomenon of the "democratisation of instruction" and the raising of the general level of education. It is this new quality of labour-power that has led to the increase in immaterial and intellectual labour and to the questioning of the forms of division of labour and technical progress that belonged to industrial capitalism' (Lebert and Vercellone, 2006, p. 30).

Vercellone, here in keeping with an *operaista* reading that sees the excess of cooperative living labour over its measure, rather than the colossal potentialities of science embodied in dead labour,[2] as the lesson of the *Grundrisse*, reads in Marx a premonition of the explosive function that mass education would have in the transition of the 1970s[3]: 'It is important to emphasise that the point of departure of the analysis of the general intellect refers to a preliminary transformation of the intellectual quality of living labour, or to the education of a diffuse intellectuality' (Vercellone, 2007, p. 27). Whereas others will read the development of the 'social individual' to which Marx refers in terms of the accumulation, centralization and alienation of the productive powers of man, in Vercellone it signals the increasing centrality of cooperative powers that are only *formally* subsumed by capital, albeit in a formal subsumption that is obliged entirely to reinvent the instruments that characterized its pre-industrial incarnations (e.g., rent).

Indeed, the *Grundrisse* is interpreted in a manner diametrically opposed to those who focus on the supremacy of science and technology as fixed capital: 'the essential dimension of this mutation is found in the conflicts that have led to a new qualitative preponderance of the knowledges of living labour over knowledges incorporated in fixed capital and in corporate organisation' (Vercellone, 2007, p. 32). Even more starkly: 'The principal source of value now resides in the knowledges incorporated and mobilized by living labour and not in capital and material labour' (Vercellone, 2007, p. 31). Transposing this interpretation of the *Grundrisse* onto the current phase and conjuncture, and thus periodising the relationship between knowledge and struggles over production, means reading the emergence of the mass university qua apparatus of real subsumption as creating the very conditions for a crisis. This crisis is in turn managed by trying to exert external, 'parasitic' control on expressions of 'the autonomy of living knowledge' (Vercellone, 2007, p. 33) that are no longer encompassed by capital and its strategy, which nevertheless continues to 'attempt to enforce the law of value artificially' (Vercellone, 2007, p. 34).

The thesis of cognitive capitalism—alongside associated concepts of immaterial labour, the autonomy of living labour, biopolitics, commons and precarity—has gained considerable prominence in recent attempts, especially in Italy, to provide politically efficacious theoretical mappings of recent struggles around the university. In straddling political proposition and socio-economic analysis, activism and theory, Francesco Raparelli's *La lunghezza dell'Onda. Fine della sinistra e nuovi movimenti* provides an illuminating document for a reflection on the pertinence of the cognitive capitalism thesis to current university-based movements against marketisation, austerity and debt. Crucial to Raparelli's argument (but also to collective experiments in 'movement theory' like *edu-factory, Uninomade, Uniriot* and so on) is the connection between the supposed autonomy of living labour in context of contemporary capitalism and the political practice of truly appropriating that autonomy, namely in experiences of *autoformazione* (self-education) in and against the neoliberal university. Needless to say, the wish to ground the strategy of a collective project in an analysis of the mutations of capitalism and its apparatuses of control is laudable, but how plausible as a starting point is the thesis of the autonomy of living labour under cognitive capitalism?

Raparelli states that 'Today the common is ever more the condition of the capitalist valorisation of labour: independence of productive cooperation, downward shift of ideational and decisional functions, centrality of communication, relational character of the performance of labour, diffusion of knowledges and temporal and quantitative extension of processes of formation, these are today the material and social conditions of the production of wealth' (2009, p. 130). While we may dispute whether 'wealth' is produced by diffuse, intellectual, immaterial and communicative cooperation, 'value', at least as it translates into capitalist imperatives and strategies, seems not to transit primarily or necessarily via the forms of labour that Raparelli identifies. Though in certain sectors that are by no means representative, and we could also argue, not hegemonic, the capture of activities not directly subsumed or organised by the firm can play an important role, it is very difficult to discern the 'independence of productive cooperation', for instance, in the occupational areas that have recently seen by far the greatest expansion in employment, namely health and social work, and real estate and business services.[4] The contradictions attendant to the subsumption of labour, especially insofar as they involve the state's fiscal and planning role in the reproduction of labour-power and of the capital-relation, are here bypassed all too quickly in an understanding of precariousness that presents it as the political way of disciplining a living labour that is already enmeshed in relationships of creativity and cooperation. 'Precariousness is the form of government of labour-power in the new productive scene. The more that labour-power incorporates functions of command, ideation and knowledge, the more its level of autonomy and independence increases, the more it is necessary for capital to artificially define new measurements and new hierarchies' (Raparelli, 2009, p. 73).

More than a relationship to the labour-market, dictated by the imperatives of profitability in not particularly buoyant economies, or by the out-and-out restoration of class power, precariousness is here envisaged as a tool to repress what seem to be incipiently communist relations: 'What creates must be destroyed because its creation is ever more common, ever more independent, ever freer' (Raparelli, 2009,

p. 74). But if all value stems from the autonomous, proto-communist interactions of 'singularities' of living labour, what of the contradictions faced by a capital that both needs creativity and is obliged, politically, to stifle it? Raparelli provides a kind of answer when he states that 'the more labour is precarious and autonomous *formally*, though directed *in substance*, the more surplus-value grows' (Raparelli, 2009, p. 86). But this assertion opens the path to what could be a devastating counter to the political translation of the thesis of cognitive capitalism, to wit that between a substantial autonomy (of the kind that we might equate with emancipation) and the formal autonomy of much outsourced, self-employed or precarious labour, there is no transition, just homonymy.

The political problem lies precisely with the *premise* of autonomy. It is one thing to argue that the mutations in the organisation of labour and in the state's framing of the reproduction of the capital-labour relation have led to a shift in the mechanisms that subsume labour under capital, it is quite another to read this passage solely or primarily through the lens of the affirmation of an autonomy of living labour. This would in fact imply, rather perversely, that the loss of rights and security of labour is the result of a strange victory of labour over capital, forcing it to give labour greater domains of autonomy. In other words, that the dismantling of the welfare state is a belated effect of the proletariat's own attack on it as a device for perpetuating its real subsumption. Now, while one cannot gainsay the struggles of workers and others against the forms of discipline and domination that accompanied the Fordist compact between 'big labour, big business and big government', equally, to treat resistance as the driving motor in this process, and to continue to do so in the present, is to posit a continuing social power (that of workers' autonomy) where political power has been long defeated. The thesis of the primacy of resistance can lead to a strangely masochistic narrative, where workers fought against the contract—viewed as an exchange of freedom and autonomy for security and protection—and the social pact of Fordism 'was broken under the blows of struggles and the demand for freedom' (Raparelli, 2009, p. 105),[5] while the effect was a precariousness in which only the privileged gain glimpses of autonomy. And *which* desire, freedom and autonomy are we talking about? Ones compatible with neoliberalism or at odds with it? And weren't many of the political struggles of the sixties and seventies ones around *needs* and around *security*, which were precisely *not* being provided to the majority, rather than simply *against* the state as agent of reproduction?

Without necessarily adopting the argument that we in fact live in the most intense phase of real subsumption,[6] of total commodification, it can nevertheless be argued that the autonomy that is only formally subsumed by capital is itself a very formal autonomy, one whose concrete determinants (from lack of health coverage to the expansion of working time, from the intensity of self-exploitation to the instrumentalisation of personal relations for profitable ends) are to the benefit of states and capitalists increasingly averse to burdening themselves with the reproduction of labour-power. In other words, we should ask *which* labour-power has become ever more autonomous because of the predominance of communicative knowledge and affective relations as sources of value under contemporary capitalism. In my view, by and large—that is to say outside of enclaves or forms of emancipated commonality stolen from the rhythms and imperatives of capitalist valorisation— what we face is an autonomy-within-heteronomy. This is the autonomy of the consumer and the social entrepreneur, whose desire and creativity is by definition *competitive*. Where the likes of Raparelli see an emergent common of singularities, I am struck by the competition of individuals (or groups) who, while they rely on the use of seemingly non-commodified relations (family, friendship, comradeship, intimacy), do so in forms antithetical to the 'common'. Isn't the *formal* notion of autonomy and independence here immensely limited and devoid of any critical take on the social forms within which it takes place—that is, in situations in which it is not so much the creation of new social relations but the identification of expedients that will allow one, or one's cooperators, to *compete* for (artificially) scarce resources?

It is precisely the imposition of competition—whether directly by the bottom line of profit or indirectly by various forms of measurement and 'New Public Management'—which is sidelined by a certain variant of the thesis of cognitive capitalism, perhaps because it doesn't give due significance to the existence of plural *capitals*, and to the fact that what primarily defines contemporary cognitive workers is not cooperation but competition, whether in the public or private sectors. There are of course domains of anti-competition, but these are wrested from an environment that is still defined by a overwhelming requirement to compete—whether between academics, hackers or consultants. What's more, without a matching capacity to gain some power and control over state resources, and to curtail the autonomy of capital, independent 'institutions of the common' and forms of self-education run the risk of *compensating* for the withdrawal of the public, without fundamentally challenging the strategies of capital.[7]

As Raparelli himself underscores, the imposition of managerial practices of measurement, and their aggressive homogeneisation across Europe via the Bologna process and its image of university governance, fetter the common (Raparelli, 2009, p. 118). And yet *how* we understand these processes is crucial. Are state and capital colluding to capture autonomous circuits of cooperation, or are they, as I would contend, in great part *inciting* them? 'Parasitism' is in my opinion the wrong term for the relations of power and the forms of valorisation that underlie contemporary forms of measurement and precarisation. Anybody acquainted with the current practices around (European) research and funding, will easily observe that, while undoubtedly taking advantage of relations and capacities produced outside of the wage-relation and outside of the workplace proper, research grants *generate* networks where there were none, putting to work relations that would otherwise have taken very different guises. To posit that commons are here produced autonomously and *then* become objects of parasitism is to schematise a much less linear and far more ambiguous situation. As De Angelis and Harvie note, in a trenchant and insightful treatment of the struggles over measurement within the university sector: 'In higher education, as elsewhere, production depends upon access over a common pool of resources, i.e. the commons. But some of these commons are not *given*: they must be produced by the academic labourers themselves. The ways and forms in which commons are produced depend on the balance of forces between clashing values and measuring processes' (De Angelis and Harvie, 2009, p. 27).

Ongoing shifts in modes of measurement and funding regimes, as well as in national education policies, also problematise the idea of the 'centrality of production by means of language and affects, informational technologies and the extension of cooperative processes' (Raparelli, 2009, p. 64). Though they surely involve language, informational technologies and cooperation, and in some unspecified sense affect too, the STEM subjects that many governments are now investing in, deeming them central to production, do not so easily fit the images of reticular spontaneity that dominate accounts like Raparelli's. If we consider the rather large outlays in R&D by technology and pharmaceutical companies, is it possible for instance to argue that: 'Contemporary capital is a parasite or a rentier and the only way it's found to continue to exploit labour is precariousness and the continuous humiliation of labour's capacities' (Raparelli, 2009, p. 16)?

The more euphoric notes struck by Raparelli's book are tempered in the work of Gigi Roggero, whose comparative research into the mutations of the university on both sides of the North Atlantic nonetheless operates with similar theoretical coordinates. Roggero rightly indicates the ambivalence of any cognitive turn: 'Far from any naïve progressivism, which establishes an arbitrary causal nexus between intellectualisation of labour-power and its imminent liberation, the cognitivisation of labour also means a cognitivisation of measurement and exploitation, a cognitivisation of class hierarchy, wage regulation and the division of labour' (Raparelli, 2009, p. 36). The centrality of knowledge thus translates into a centrality of struggles over knowledge, over its measurement, its valorisation, its uses. But this also means that, to the extent that this relation is also a struggle, we cannot treat it axiomatically or metaphysically in terms of the primacy of one of its poles, be it capital or labour. The danger of a certain 'vitalist' version of the thesis of cognitive capitalism lies in arguing that somehow—despite the fact that concretely it may find itself incessantly on the back foot—living labour has the initiative, because of its excess over capital's capacities for measurement and capture. For Roggero, 'excess' is characteristic of cognitive labour and is to be linked to the 'crisis of the law of value'. But this is to imply that the imposition of measurement, of 'completely arti-ficial units of time' (Roggero, 2009, p. 16), is in some sense a weakness of capital. This is too tidy a tale of the passage from a truly grounded measurement to an arti-ficial one, from 'normal' exploitation to capture and parasitism. I am more persuad-ed by the argument, advanced by De Angelis and Harvie, that measure is always an object of struggle, that we do not pass from a normal to a parasitic form of exploita-tion. In this respect, the political and economic dimensions of the struggle over mea-sure cannot be easily sundered:

> Products', both material and 'immaterial', only become commodities if they can be com-mensurated on the basis of quantities of human labour in the abstract. Otherwise, they remain so many tonnes of wheat or barrels of oil, or such and such a number of schol-arly articles. The 'law of value' is wholly dependent for its continued operation upon measure against some universal equivalent. Thus, capital's constant struggle to impose and reimpose the 'law of value' is always a simultaneous struggle to impose (a single, universal) measure. It may well be true that producing subjects produce both material and immaterial products that *they* value in forms and ways that are outside and beyond capital's own measures. But it is also the case that capital—via its army of economists, statisticians, management-scientists and so forth—struggles to measure immaterial 'out-puts' in its own terms (profi t, effi ciency, competitiveness and so on). In so doing, cap-ital helps shape the forms immaterial labour, just as it shapes the form of material labour. (2009, p. 27)

In this respect measurement is always in a sense in 'crisis', and, though univer-sities, together with other dimensions of public services (most significantly health), are institutions that feel most severely the disjunction between 'arbitrary' measure-ments and the more-or-less immanent values that accrue to certain types of activ-ity (say, in realising that a book resulting from a life-long labour of research can 'count' as much or less than a wholly unoriginal article), this does not mean that the sheer proliferation of measurements, and their subtle or coercive imposition, is as such a sign of capital's weakness. The presupposition that capital is *reacting* to the excess of living labour seems to substitute a kind of socio-economic metaphysics for the marked absence of potent forms of collective power that could organise and express antagonism against capital. Indeed, one could even turn the argument around: rather than politically capturing, through measurement, some kind of pro-ductive excess, practices of measurement (think of the ways in which the 'impact' of university research is quantified) often *simulate* very ephemeral notions of productivity.

This is not insignificant at a moment when the economic imperatives restruc-turing universities revolve around the contribution of indebted students, the exten-sion and intensification of lecturers' labour-time and the emphasis on the traditional 'productive' virtues of the 'hard' sciences—and forms of measurement, from league tables to national student surveys, that give a Foucaultian twist to familiar strategies of labour discipline and management. The types of 'New Public Management' that Roggero very skilfully analyses, and which comprise the competitive allocation of resources, principles of customer satisfaction, comparison made possible by accreditation or auditing, and the transformation of internal university governance, do not require for their understanding that we posit an excess of cooperation 'upstream', which these controlling devices would then capture. The subsumption is here far more real, and the power much more productive: these forms of management do not capture an autonomous power of cooperation, they in many ways generate, format and incite it. Though it may rely on relations and resources that exceed the corporate university's powers (but this excess can most often be coded as a 'positive externality'), 'cooperation' is not something that takes place autonomously; it is an institutional and economic imperative (sometimes, to be fair, a rather baffling one: what are all these costly networks really productive *of*?).

Most forms of decommodified creativity, collectivity and cooperation, do not constitute a positive excess that is captured and measured *ex post facto*, they are negations or withdrawals from imposed relations of valorisation, or, perhaps most frequently in the university, relatively cynical participations in simulations of impact and productivity. In other words, they are forms of activity which, rather than affirming their productivity, try to fight against their character as (living) labour, that is as an activity whose parameters are in the final analysis determined by forms of value that give the lie to the idea of a lived cooperative autonomy in the present. Many of the analyses of the university that take their bearings from the thesis of cognitive capitalism thus tend implicitly to accept a conception of productivity that only makes sense from the standpoint of capital. In other words, instead of criticising the very form of value within which intellectual and other activities are measured and exploited, they seem to argue, in a very strange re-edition of a dogmatic historical materialist argument, that there are forces of production (cognitive ones in this case) that exceed the current relations of production (as dictated by intellectual property, New Public Management, Research Excellence Frameworks, etc.).

The danger in this argument, and in the way that the political demands that emerge from it (guaranteed wage, new welfare, etc.) are formulated, is that it seems to rely on the need to affirm that forms of knowledge, cooperation and commons antithetical to capital are in fact productive; what's more that their production is in excess of capital's parasitic capacities, which is why the latter has to politically employ precariousness as a form of control. But 'productivity' is an intra-capitalist concept, and it might very well be the case—as seems to be demonstrated by certain shifts from the humanities to the sciences in funding, for instance—that certain forms of the cooperation of living labour, however 'creative', are ultimately unprofitable, and therefore expendable, from the viewpoint of capital.[8] Though basing anti-systemic drives in the real tendencies of capital and in the contemporary forms of class composition is an important facet of a non-idealist method, it is misleading to posit that the shift to a formally subsumed cognitive capitalism means that non-capitalist relations are somehow germinating in the present. Immanence is not prefiguration.

Anticipating criticisms in this vein, Roggero sharply notes the importance to *denaturalise* knowledge, that is not to treat it as something that exceeds capital's valorisation by its very essence. Knowledge is not 'a *commons*, in the sense that it is already given and in existence, but it becomes common in the production of living labour and in the organisation of autonomy from the capital-relation' (Roggero, 2009, p. 103). One can second this statement, while simultaneously objecting to the notion that this autonomy is indeed being produced in any consequential way at present or that it is indeed in excess of the capital-relation. For reasons that may be too banal to state (above all the impossibility of reproducing one's labour-power outside of the wage-relation or of dependence on the state or on private institutions or individuals), while there are realities *antagonistic* to the capital-relation, there are no forms of life or knowledge simply *autonomous* from it.

In this respect, the theoretical debate within the Italian and European student regarding the class composition and economic situation of students brings into relief some of the stakes of cognitive capitalism as an analytical-strategic thesis. Where cognitive capitalism, in giving primacy to autonomous cooperation and an excessive and diffuse intellectuality, treats the student immediately as a 'cognitive producer' (Roggero, 2009, p. 16), iregardless of her inclusion in determinate relations of exploitation, critics coming from a more 'classical Marxist' position have argued that the current situation is one that sees the full realisation of analyses first produced in the sixties and seventies regarding the proletarianisation of the student body, with graduates working jobs that previously only required a high-school degree, and the intellectual/mental labour market witnessing a vast spectrum of employment situations for the same degree of qualification and skill, and increasingly less control over one's workplace and situation. For this latter perspective, rather than a component in a broader metropolitan apparatus of capture of the excess of living knowledge, the contemporary university is fundamentally geared towards the formation of precarious workers for an increasingly exploitative labour-market. It is within this perspective that the forms taken by the devaluation of knowledge can also be understood as logics of instrumentality, standardisation and speeded-up turnover in keeping with a university, which is ingreat part not geared to the capturing of cooperative excess but to the reproduction of labour-powers adequate to underpaid, over-exploited and low-skilled work, as well as to the generation of indebted subjects. The excess identified in the cognitive capitalism thesis is here to some extent recoded as a kind of immiseration, as the 'deskilling of mental labour' (Calella, 2008, p. 74),[9] as 'the time of education is transformed into a Taylorised time which seem to have the sole function of disciplining: to work, to flexibility, to pre-cariousness' (Sevilla, 2010, p. 16).

In other words, from this perspective, what we see is not the formal subsumption of the cooperation-in-excess of living labour under academic capitalism, but its real subsumption:

> To think that the contents and modes of intellectual production enjoy a creativity that is autonomous from the overall process of reproduction of capital and that capitalism limits itself to reabsorb in a parasitic manner the value autonomously produced by the cognitariat is a pious illusion—and not a *pia fraus*, because it risks having a mystifying effect. On the contrary, the processes of reform of the university and the very transformation of the figure of the educational worker simply make more evident how capitalism increasingly materially organises educational labour itself, determining in an ever more explicit and direct way its times, modes and contents. Culture, education and research are not goods autonomously created and then appropriated by capital, in the contemporary university they are already produced as commodities. (Arruzza and Montefusco, 2008, p. 95)

Universities thus become 'public agencies for the precarisation of labour' (Calella, 2008, p. 72).[10] The emphasis is here not on living labour, but on labour-power as a commodity that is shaped and reproduced, among other institutions by the university. In this perspective, students are precarious workers not *a priori* but in terms of their actual forms of employment. But they are above all a 'commodity-in-formation', moulded by the type of learning on offer, by credits, devalued degrees, modularisation, lack of control, speed-up, constant evaluation, and so on. Politically, rather than appropriating autonomy or producing a common that is already latent in the excess of living knowledge and labour, the proposal here is a fundamentally 'negative' one, that of 'attempting to block the production of oneself as a future precarious worker' (Calella, 2008, p. 78).

The occupation of the sociology faculty at Trento in 1968 gave rise to a text that nicely anticipates such reflections. It is worth quoting at some length:

> The university is one of the productive institutions in the current social system understood as a commodity system. It produces a particular type of commodity: *man* precisely understood as a commodity, as qualified or to-be-qualified labour-power, as graduated or graduating. The aim of such a productive institution (the university) is to place this commodity (the student-graduate) on the labour-market so that it be *sold* there, and to insert it in the overall cycle of social reproduction so that it be *consumed* there. (Movimento studentesco, 1968, p. 51)

The text goes on to note the varying degrees of 'finish' that such commodities may receive (some may be 'under-worked' [*semi-lavorate*], like the dropout, or sold below their value, like the PhD student working at a check-out counter, some again may become 'commodities producing commodities', i.e., lecturers), but also to point presciently to the devolution of the burden of reproduction onto the commodity itself, something increasingly true in a current context where the social costs of education are privatised and personalised through debt: 'The commodity itself is made to pay for process of valorisation at work in the university (taxes, books, expenses, accommodation, food . . .). The social necessity of a certain quantity and quality of qualified labour-power is thus dumped onto the private costs of individuals' (Movimento studentesco, 1968, p. 37). This process is particularly marked today in what has become a kind of master-signifier of the current wave of competitive restructuring, 'employability' (Calella, 2008, p. 75; Sevilla, 2010, p. 154).

This term, with its conjunction of capacity and futurity, brings out what is in some respects the common stake in the debate pitting advocates of the student as cognitive labourer and proponents of the thesis of the student as a precarious-commodity-in-production—a debate, we should note, which for all of its theoretical differends shares much in terms of the phenomenology of the present. This stake is the question of time or of the relationship between the time of capital accumulation and the time of politics. Indeed, the strongest argument for the idea of the student as already a cognitive labourer is made by Roggero precisely in terms of the ways in which the proliferation of debt as a device of capture and control virtually inserts the student in the labour-market even if she has no direct role within it (Roggero, 2009, p. 124). Precariousness is indeed, like the dark side of employability, a term linking capacity and time, which through financialisation and the monetary calculation of risk, becomes a potent norm constraining future action (Roggero, 2009, p. 125). The student-consumer formatted by the Browne Review, the catechism of the current counter-revolution-without-a-revolution in UK universities, is precisely a subject wholly determined by an instrumental relationship of financial calculus balancing the deferred purchase of skills and knowledges in the present against future income (http://www.bis.gov.uk/assets/biscore/corporate/docs/s/10–1208-securing-sustainable-higher-education-browne-report.pdf). However, while there is indeed a 'conflict between autonomy and subordination', I think a confrontation with the discourses and practices of the most recent wave of crisis-marketing of the university suggests that this conflict is not precisely the one posed in the terms of cognitive capitalism, that is 'between the heterogeneous and full temporality of the production of living knowledge and the imposition of the homogeneous and empty temporality of capital and measure' (Roggero, 2009, p. 128). In a context where the idea that one is the entrepreneur of one's own human capital is an anxiety-laden lived experience, that is, where the commodity that is labour-power thinks of itself constantly as a commodity, without this implying any Lukácsian revelation, it is better to start from inside the heteronomies of the university as a productive institution than from the autonomy of a living labour ,which would somehow maintain its distance from competition, commodification and abstract labour. Distorting the previous quotation, we might indeed say that an attempt to disarticulate the reproduction of the capital-relation within university struggles will involve pitting, against the full and homogeneous temporality of a capitalism, whose practices of measurement and discipline reach very deep into subjectivity, and make the attainment of autonomy not a premise but a difficult if worthy objective, a kind of empty and heterogeneous time, that is a negation of one's own constitution as a commodity.

Notes

1.   It is worth noting that the theme of the productivity of knowledge, which has determined so many of the readings of the *Grundrisse* and its 'Fragment on Machines' in the *operaista* tradition and beyond, was already an open object of contention in '68. Thus, before qualifying and correcting himself in later works, Ernest Mandel wrote: 'What the student rebellion represents at a vaster social and historical scale is the colossal transformation of the productive forces that Marx predicted in the *Grundrisse*: the reintegration of intellectual labour into productive labour, with the intellectual capacity of men converted into the principal productive force of society'. 'The New Revolutionary Vanguard', Black Dwarf 2 (1969), as cited in Sevilla, p. 153. Alongside considerations of the revolutionary potentials internal to the contradiction between such forces and the relations they were subjected to (above all, the increasingly anachronistic imposition of the wage-form), was a repudiation of the celebratory ideology of the knowledge society. Thus, writing against Alain Touraine, the young insurgent sociologists at Nanterre wrote: 'it is false to oppose the nineteenth and twentieth centuries. It is not true "that knowledge and technical progress are the motors of the new society". Knowledge and technical progress are subordinated to the struggles between firms for profit (or, which is the same, for monopolistic hegemony), and to the military confrontation between East and West' (Cohn-Bendit, 1969).

2.   The contrast here is especially with Moishe Postone, *Time, Labor and Social Domination: A Reintepretation of Marx's Critical Theory*, Cambridge: Cambridge University Press, 1996.

3.   As he writes: 'for Marx, the development of mass education was one of the essential conditions which would have permitted wage-labourers to accumulate a 'technological, theoretical and practical' knowledge adequate to the level attained by the capitalist development of the social and technical division of labour and, at the same time, to undertake its supersession' (27).

4. According to the European Labour Force Survey, the former category grew 81.7% and the latter 100.3% between 1992 and 2002. As emphasised by Kevin Doogan, from whom I take these statistics, these shifts in the labour market highlight the prevalence (in private and public sectors) of 'reproductive' activities, but also, of increases in long-term employment (in the two aforementioned categories, the increases in long-term employment are higher than in employment as such, namely 101.0% and 124.8%). See Doogan, p. 179. Doogan's comments on the move towards 'earning and learning' are much less persuasive, especially when he argues all too optimistically against arguments about the precarisation of student labour, and with little reflection on the disciplining and alienating character of service and retail work, that the 'incumbents are temporary, but their temporary part-time employment helps to complete an education which will enhance their labour market standing in the long run' (p. 164).

5. Raparelli, p. 105. This perception, while having some plausibility in light of the 'autonomist' component of (anti-)labour struggles in Italy, is singularly unconvincing in domains like the UK or US in the 1970s and 1980s.

6. This argument can be drawn among others, from the intellectual production of the group Théorie communiste. See the very useful survey and critique, which also takes in Negri and Jacques Camatte, in Endnotes, 'History of Subsumption', *Endnotes 2* (2010), pp. 144–48.

7. The more revolutionary moments in Raparelli's reject this perspective of a compensatory enclave, but their political prescriptions are all-too-rhetorical: 'self-education in cognitive labour can occupy the University and transform it into an institution of the common [but] the central problem is that of getting one's hands on the metropolis, to overthrow its productive articulations and to render the production of knowledge functional to the construction of freedom, to the egalitarian organisation of production and to the government of the common' (8). Similar problems are presented by Roggero's conception of 'autonomous institutionality' (108).

8. In this regard, when Roggero notes (p. 16) that 'the production of living labour' is to be understood as both 'the constitution of living labour' and as 'its productive power [potenza], not only for capital but also autonomously', I would note that a true critique of capitalist valorisation would demand that we posit a discontinuity between 'productive power' as understood from the side of capital and productive power in the horizon of some kind of autonomy of living labour.

9. Calella, p. 74. The political perspective of Calella, Arruzza and Montefusco, and Sevilla is a broadly Trotskyist one, in which some of the earlier analyses of Mandel resonate.

10. Calella, p. 72. See also Sevilla, who writes that in the current dispensation: 'One studies in order to learn to be precarious, available for any job' (p. 150).

Works cited

Arruzza, C. & Montefusco, A. (2008). 'Come perdere l'aureola. Vademecum per la ricerca precaria', in VV.AA., *L'onda anomala. Alla ricerca dell'autopolitica*. Roma: Edizioni Alegre.

Calella, G. (2008). 'Università-fabbrica e studenti-merce', in VV.AA., *L'onda anomala. Alla ricerca dell'autopolitica*, Roma: Edizioni Alegre.

'Capitalism Measures Immaterial Labour in British Universities', *Historical Materialism*, 17, 3 (2009): 3–30.

Cohn-Bendit, D., Duteuil, J.P., Gérard, B., & Granautier, B. (1969). 'Why Sociologists?', in Cockburn, A. & Blackburn, R. (Eds.), *Student Power: Problems, Diagnosis, Action*. London: Penguin/New Left Review.

De Angelis, M. & Harvie, D. (2009). '"Cognitive Capitalism" and the Rat-Race: How

Doogan, K. (2009). *New Capitalism? The Transformation of Work*, Cambridge: Polity.

Dyer-Witheford, N. (2005). 'Cognitive Capitalism and the Contested Campus', in G. Cox and J. Krysa (Eds.), *Engineering Culture: On 'The Author as (Digital) Producer*. New York: Autonomedia.

Lebert, D. & Vercellone, C. (2006). 'Il ruolo della conoscenza nella dinamica di lungo periodo del capitalismo. L'ipotesi del capitalismo cognitivo', in C. Vercellone (Ed.) *Capitalismo cognitivo. Conoscenza e finanza nell'epoca postfordista*, Roma: manifestolibri. *Endnotes.* (2010). 'History of Subsumption', *Endnotes* 2, 130–52.

Modugno, E. (2010). 'I conflitti svelati nella società della conoscenza', *il manifesto*, 31.

Moulier Boutang, Y. (2007). *Le Capitalisme Cognitif. La Nouvelle Grande Transformation*, Paris: Éditions Amsterdam.

Movimento studentesco (ed.), (1968/2008). *Documenti della rivolta universitaria*, Bari: Laterza.

Raparelli, F. (2009). *La lunghezza dell'Onda. Fine della sinistra e nuovi movimenti*, Milano: Ponte alle Grazie.

Roggero, G. (2009). *La produzione del sapere vivo. Crisi dell'università e trasformazione del lavoro tra le due sponde dell'Atlantico*, Verone: ombre corte.

Sevilla, C. (2010). *La fábrica del conocimiento. La universidad-empresa en la producción flexible*, Madrid: El Viejo Topo.

Vercellone, C. (2007). 'From Formal Subsumption to General Intellect: Elements for a Marxist Reading of the Thesis of Cognitive Capitalism,' *Historical Materialism*, 15, 1: 13–36.

CHAPTER THIRTEEN

In the Ruined Laboratory of Futuristic Accumulation:
Immaterial Labour and the University Crisis

NICK DYER-WITHEFORD

Introduction

In 2009 and 2010 a cycle of student uprisings spread across the most advanced sectors of capitalist society, ignited by university cutbacks that followed state bailouts of the financial sector meltdown. The preconditions for the revolt, in particular the increasing dependence of universities on a precarious academic workforce, had however been building for a long time. The talk that provided the basis for this chapter was delivered at a conference 'Beneath the University the Commons', organized by graduate students from the University of Minnesota in Minneapolis in April 9–11, 2009, a conference that was itself part of this cycle of struggle, and occurred after the campus rebellions in the United States and preceding the European wave, which was already building in the actions of Greek students and would within a year include revolts in Italy, Spain, France and the United Kingdom.

Futuristic Accumulation

In the *Economic and Philosophic Manuscripts* of 1844 the young Marx observes that scientific activity, even when apparently pursued in isolation, is a manifestation of "communal activity, and communal mind" (1964, p. 137). The collective character of science and technological innovation are repeated themes in his later work, from the "fragment on machines" in *Grundrisse* (1973, pp. 690–712), with its famous allusion to "general intellect", to *Capital's* account of "all scientific work, all discovery and invention" as "universal labour" brought about "partly by the cooperation of men now living, but partly also by building on earlier work" (1981, p. 199). The benefits of this collective effort are, he adds, "generally the most worthless and wretched kind of money-capitalists" who "draw the greatest profit from all new developments of the universal labour of the human spirit and their social application by combined labour" (1981, p. 199). I term this expropriation of general intellect and universal labour "futuristic accumulation."

Futuristic accumulation is the commodification of publicly created scientific knowledge, which via copyright and patent, is privatized as intellectual property for the extraction of monopolistic technological rents. The term is intended to suggest both an analogy and contrast with "primitive accumulation" (Marx, 1977, pp. 873–940), the process by which agrarian populations were, by enclosure, dispossessed from common lands to become a proletarian workforce. This sets the scene for capitalism's 'normal' operations of extended reproduction, in which the daily business of extracting surplus value from workers goes on through the buying and selling of labour power. Primitive accumulation, far from being a historical, once-only event, is an ongoing, renewed aspect of capital, increasingly salient in the era of neoliberalism, where the violent uprooting of agrarian populations into urban slums, supplying the workforce or reserve army of the unemployed for new manufacturing in Asia (especially China), Latin America and Africa is integral to the making of a factory planet (*Midnight Notes*, 1992).

By futuristic accumulation, however, I want to indicate a related but distinct process, by which capital does not so much dispossess people from existing territories but rather expropriates them from emergent domains of production created by the operations of technoscience. The two major examples are digital and biological—cyberspace and genetics. Enclosure here takes the form of the property rights in technological innovations, which vests ownership of genetic code, digital communication and other newly created fields of scientific activity in privatized owners, enabling the extraction of a stream of rents from these discoveries.

What I term futuristic accumulation is what Luis Suarez-Villa (2009, p. 10) in his recent study of techno-capitalism calls "experimentalism". It brings with it a systematized orientation of research to the extraction of value, deploying analytic templates, incentives, and a "permanent state of urgency." It involves, Suarez-Villa says, an acceptance of planned obsolescence; a blurring of boundaries between basic science and technological application; networks of "contact, diffusion and transaction" social institutions of legitimation and individual subject formation (2009, p. 28). The scale of these processes is, he suggests, "mega"- that is "all encompassing"; they "increasingly set the agenda for entire societies," with an "intrusive reach" and "scope and range" greater than, say, the nineteenth-century factory or twentieth-century mass production (2009, p. 16), but, "like its predecessor, dynamizing the accumulation of capital by concocting means to seize it in ever faster and larger quantities" (2009, p. 19). According to Suarez-Villa commercial experimentalism now directs the emergence of "critical masses of knowledge and . . . infrastructure" in "fields that become emblematic of the twenty-first century", including "every area of biotechnology, proteomics, genomics, biopharmaceuticals, and biomedicine, the nascent field of nanotechnology and all its innumerable future medical and mechanical applications, molecular computing, bioinformatics, and . . . biorobotics" (2009, p. 10).

These new enclosures are intimately related to old enclosures and extended reproduction; it is by biogenetic enclosure capital destroys peasant farming practices. And through communications protocols it commands the modularized work processes spread out along global supply chains. Futuristic accumulation is also integrally related to rampant financialization, in part both because it is on cybernetic instruments that finance capital depends for its risk calculation and modeling, but more so because it depends on speculative investment by techno-scientifically oriented venture capital—a process that underlay the dot.com boom and bust of 2001 that set the scene for today's larger crisis. But futuristic accumulation is also something new, for through its processes capital lays claim to and directs the future of life itself—the constitutive elements of our species-becoming.

The University Laboratory

What does it mean to call the university the laboratory of futuristic accumulation? In a way it is quite obvious, and literal. The major North American universities are the sites of some of the most significant research facilities—laboratories—in the world, laboratories absolutely integral to major techno-scientific innovations; think of the pivotal role of MIT and Stanford in the development of computing or of the more diffuse but equally decisive contribution of North American universities to the corporate direction of biotechnology research (Kenney, 1986; Loeppky, 2005). This construction of the university-system as a massive platform for innovation, as part of 'big science' is relatively new; it has its origins in the Second World War, and subsequent Cold War mobilization of science, with military funding playing a lead role.

The systemic linkage of this research capacity to capital is, however, more recent, arising directly out of the struggles of the 1960s and 70s. The concept of deploying a massive infusion of technoscience and innovation to break down or bypass the resistances of the mass worker and new social subjects–to move beyond the

factory, or the social factory to the planet factory—is key to the concept of an information society promoted by policy-savants such as Daniel Bell, Peter Drucker and
Zbigniew Brzezinski in the 1970s, and it becomes a keystone to the reconstruction
of the post-secondary education system from that period on. Capital's drive to hege-
monize academic research has not been a tidy process; universities are institutions
with their own specificities and genealogies, from the archaic feudalisms of academic hierarchy to neo-communist practices of basic science, and it is in the unevenness and contradictions of this process that we can find some other hopeful
opportunities. Nevertheless there has been constructed an apparatus that assembles
doctrines, disciplines, and subjects into a distinct and dominant formation; neoliberal economic policy, high technology research laboratories, and academic laborers.

It is unnecessary to rehearse at length the mechanisms of this process, because
we confront them directly, or at least see them out of the corner of our eye, every
day of our academic existence. The corporately funded research project, the spin-
off company, the research park, the incubator, the requirement 'business partners',
the emphasis on patents and IP, are all part of the landscape we inhabit. If one was
to choose a single salient recent example it might be the famous deal between British
Petroleum and UCLA Berkeley for an on-campus corporately staffed bio-fuels institute (Herper, 2007). Equally familiar are the various forms of corruption that go with
these relations—the revoking of academic appointments for those critical of corporate science, the creation of spurious journals to hype pharmaceutical products,
the occasional outright concoction of profitable research results . . . all this is
known, though it deserves to be better known. At the same time there is a risk, by
attending too much to the high-profile scandals, of missing the forest for the trees;
the main issue is not the uncovered examples of corporate pressure on university science (and what is uncovered is, we can be sure, only a fraction of the whole); nor is
the crucial concern even direct intervention by corporations by funding research (in
fact, directly funded corporate university research is still a relatively low proportion
of the whole). The point is not so much that corporations are funding research,
strategic and influential as such funding is. It is, rather, that capital siphons off for
free a massive reservoir of socially funded knowledge, because in a system where the
means of production are privately owned, the only way to practically realize the fruits
of scientific research is through the process of commodification.

Cyborg Subjects, Communal Research Base

Research capacities might seem arcane to those engaged in struggles about tuition
fees and classroom cutbacks. But as laboratories for futuristic accumulation universities are not only research sites where quantum computing and the immortality

enzymes are investigated. They are also the institutions where the subjects necessary to discover and operate these inventions are trained, graded, winnowed and selected. Just as primitive accumulation was an accumulation not just of territories, but of a proletariat, so futuristic accumulation is an accumulation not just of technologies, but of the workforce those technologies require, a cognitariat whose training for employment is, like the creation of technologies themselves, often substantially subsidized by the public or paid for by the subjects themselves. This process extends beyond the sciences and engineering; schools of media and communication, for example, socialize of subjects for an environment saturated by digitalization.

One problem with this process—a problem which is in fact the condition of possibility for a talk such as this—is that in the formation of such "cyborg" subjectivities, as Donna Haraway (1985) famously made plain, contradictions arise. Capital can't help creating subjects that make unwelcome discoveries. In a sense, innovation requires a modicum of unpredictability. It can't help this process taking swerves, going in contrary directions and making connections outside set paths, forging new assemblages. Let us consider, very briefly, three examples. The first is from computing science, a digital crucible for energies that flow directly into one of the most striking occasions, not of futuristic accumulation, but of futuristic commons, namely open source innovation. The second is in the life sciences, where, while one path has flowed into the instrumentalities of commodified genetic engineering, another has opened up to explosions of discovery about ecological commons and the consequences of their destruction: climate science, a high technology university project, is now one of the bases of a global movement against biospheric degradation. A third example comes from the social sciences, where the university has become a site not only for the preservation of intellectual strains from the struggles of the' 60s and 70s but also for the generation of new lines of radical thought including those attuned to the new conditions of commercialized biopower.

To mention these deviations from capital's research agenda is of course to instantly invite comment on the insufficiency and susceptibility to capture every single one. These criticisms are true; but such capture, cooption, and harnessing implies a resistance that, whether it comes first, second or third has proven hardily perennial, a contestation whose outcome is not completely decided in advance. It is indeed only thus that we can understand why the academy, even as it appears to us as colonized by biocapital, is also seen by the conservative right as an extraordinarily dangerous matrix of liberalism. Techno-capital wants the commonness of cooperative intellectual labour, operating to some degree outside the constraint of the corporate laboratory. The reliance of the planet factory on the university laboratory is an exemplification of what Paolo Virno (2004) calls "the communism of capital"—the dependence of post-Fordist regime on extreme socializations of production and communication whose outcomes exceed its control. This is the paradox of the corporate university, which is at once, in its major form, the laboratory of a futuristic accumulation and nonetheless also has a minor iteration as a research centre of communization. This coexistence of commodified and communizing elements in the university also helps explains why the present crisis poses us a dilemma.

The Crisis: Ruination

The deal that North Americans were offered by the corporate-university was this: become our cyborgs, and the rest of the world will be your slaves. Ascend the ladder of techno-knowledge, accept the acculturation, gadgets, grafts and implants that make your living labour merge with dead labour of machinery, learn how to stream network data and cultivate stem cells, and not only will you be lifted out of the grind of industrial work, but—even though your real wages may not rise—you will become the beneficiaries of the endless consumer goods pouring on from the *maquiladoras* and the Pearl River, supplied by uprooted peasants only too happy to accept your place on the relocated assembly lines, over whom you will enjoy the irrevocable ascendancy given by your position in endlessly rising line of high technology innovation.

Now, however, futuristic accumulation has turned back on its own laboratory. The immediate cause is the catastrophe of high-risk, high-tech financialization, which has not only sunk the endowments and investments of the research universities under water, but also required a bailout whose generalized expense is bankrupting public education. Universities have a responsibility for the crisis, not only by their general subservience to and dissemination of neoliberal economic doctrine, not only by the flagship status assigned to the many business schools (dubbed after the event "academies of the apocalypse") (James, 2009), whose role as "temples of the cult" of management orthodoxies has been called in question even by conservative critics (Hopper & Hopper, 2009, p. 165), but also more specifically by their cultivation of "the quants" (Patterson, 2010)—the mathematically modeling risk modelers whose CDOs, derivatives and mortgage-backed securities caused banks to implode. Not only is Chicago School economics an academic construct but so too are instruments such as the Black-Scholes algorithm for derivatives. In the years immediately before the crash, one quarter of graduates of the California Institute of Technology and thirty per cent of those from MIT went into the financial sector (Bannon, 2009).

The financial crisis, however only catalyzed a longer term structural malaise in which the university is also implicated. Capitalist accumulation depends on the creation not just of waged laborers but of surplus populations, dependent on the wage but unable to find a job, whose numbers serve to press down the wages and conditions of the employed. This logic was set in motion during the phase of primitive accumulation by the massive displacement of agricultural laborers, and maintained, first on a national and then on a global level, in capital's expanded reproduction by the maintenance of a reserve army of the unemployed. Futuristic accumulation too follows this logic: one of the consequences of the vast expansion of post-secondary education in North America and Europe has been the gradual establishment of a huge pool of surplus researchers, instructors and laboratory assistants, drawn from the ranks of graduate students, whose prospects for permanent academic employment are scandalously low: America reportedly produced more than 100,000 doctoral degrees between 2005 and 2009 (*Economist*, 2010, p. 157). And this is before the full weight of cutbacks resulting from the economic crash has been felt.

Behind the immediate budget crisis of the North American university lies the longer term destabilization of the American middle class, for whom not only stock market losses but also employment insecurity and stagnant real wages are making the financing of post-education increasingly difficult. I said that the public rationale for the high-tech, corporate academy rested on a dialectic of cyborgs and slaves. The universities claim that they would enable North Americans to find high-technology jobs implied manual labour is off shored to Asia and elsewhere. From the 1990s however it has become apparent that immaterial labour is itself being off shored, not only assembly line jobs but also informational jobs—first data processing and call centers, then asset management and design move to India, China and elsewhere.

Seven years ago, Dion Dennis (2003) noted that "US knowledge workers were being displaced "via one their own instrumentalities, the construction of high-speed communication networks", and forecast that the export of white-collar jobs would combined with university cutbacks to produce an implosion of American living standards." Over the coming decades, Dion predicted, several million white-collar jobs, from financial services to hardware and software computer design, would be permanently exported to "a younger, talented and low-cost global workforce" in East Asia and other points in the developing world. Prophetically, Dion suggested that as U.S. states suffer from revenue shortfalls, burgeoning college and university enrollments, post-secondary institutions would display large tuition increases, bundled with mounting class size, reduced course availability, and shrinking financial and infrastructural resources. The result would be "the digital death rattle of the American middle class, and an escalating and intensive restratification of the American class system." Today, that rattle is very loud, and it can be clearly heard in the halls of academia: a recent article in the *Chronicle of Higher Education* reports that business schools in Huston are outsourcing TA work to Bangalore (June, 2010).

Futuristic accumulation is undermining the centers from which it was disseminated, as the global wage-slaves refuse to stay in place. The North American and European university is becoming a victim of the capitalist crisis, which academia–in its dominant registers—incubated. Thus we arrive in the predicament that—with a bow to Bill Readings' *The University in Ruins* (1997)—I call the ruined laboratory of futuristic accumulation; decreasing funding for public colleges and universities, rising tuition, layoffs, cut backs and closings of programs, increases in class sizes and teaching loads. Against this characterization of academic "ruin" it might be objected that the global economic meltdown, far from spelling devastation to the corporate-oriented in fact serving it quite well—providing the occasion to charge higher fees, restructure curricula and recalibrate admissions to make its apparatus increasingly attuned to desperate competitors in a tight labor market willing to indenture themselves to employers via massive student loans, and to affluent education seekers searching out boutique-business oriented credentials. This is true; in many ways the crisis has become a classic occasion for application of neoliberal "shock doctrine" (Klein, 2008) to the reorganization of post-secondary education. What *is* ruined in this process, however, is the legitimacy of the university system's claims to equalitarian accessibility and to any vestigial degree of autonomy from market forces and corporate priorities.

The theme of the ruined laboratories is a familiar one; it is a classic moment in the "experiment-gone-wrong" story, of which the sorcerer's apprentice tale is one of the most famous. But if we want to think this metaphor through, it is not with a Disney-esque happy ending, in which everything gets put back in to place. Rather we want to invoke more contemporary versions, such as the SkyNet laboratory of the *Terminator* films, or *Blade Runner*'s Tyrell Corporation biotech studios, overrun by its own mutant creations—with the twist, perhaps, that we ourselves, or at least those involved in campus strikes and occupations, are amongst the rogue replicants. In this situation, after the initial moment of rebellion amongst the ruins, there is the question of what to do, of strategic direction; a question that becomes a dilemma because of the ambivalent nature of the university, containing both regressive and progressive elements, as both a laboratory for neoliberalism and a communal research base, an institution whose deterioration we can't simply celebrate with gleeful anti-capitalist schadenfreude because, as teachers and students we are part of it, caught up in the wreckage, the wreckage, moreover, of something that, once, seemed like a good idea—higher education. In this situation, to push the overwrought metaphor one more time, the rogue replicants stand in the ruined laboratory and discuss what to do; some want to rebuild it in a benign form; others say, "No, no, run away into the woods, something worse is about to happen."

Two different perspectives appear in response to the crisis: radical reformism and terminal secession. In the radical reformist scenario, defense of access to public education and of security for those who teach in it is tied to a call for the reconstruction of the institution—for a positive agenda of new knowledge generation, one that recognizes the discrediting of the neoliberal episteme to which academia has been harnessed. This is a program of demands for connecting universities less to the corporate sector and more to the public sector and community and labour groups; for an institutional recognition in business schools and economics of the failure of Freidmanite doctrines; for academia to assume a leading role in emergency response to ecological and energy crises; and for an internationalization that serves as an agency not of capitalist globalization but of a different concept of species collectivity, in which reduced consumption by the rich provides ecological room for a continued rise in living standards for the poor. It is a call for, not "Corporate U", but "Planet U" (M'Gonigle and Searle, 2006).

It is easy for critical critics to debunk such neo-utopian projects, but one can reference an example from a thinker no one can accuse of wearing rose-colored glasses, the Marxist urbanist Mike Davis. In a recent article entitled "Who Will Build the Ark?" Davis stages a "mental tournament between analytic despair and utopian possibility" (2010, p. 29). After first confronting in the starkest of terms the scale of the bio-crisis signed-off on by the failure of the Copenhagen climate talks, Davis argues for the need for to address the double disaster of climate change and planetary slums by a radical project of urban design, a movement in which "collaborations between architects, engineers, ecologists and activists can play a small but essential role in making an alter-monde more possible." In such a project a crucial role would be played by the creation of an "intellectual space where researchers and activists" meet to advocate "the necessary rather than the merely practical" and "to fight for 'impossible' solutions to the increasingly entangled crises of urban poverty and climate change, or become ourselves complicit in a de facto triage of humanity" (2010, p. 45). This is an agenda for a radically reformed—not to say remade—university.

Such a program requires a linkage to wider struggles not simply to defend but expand public sector and communal provisions against the privatizing processes of futuristic accumulation. The most likely direction would be a green jobs strategy, focused on a massive adoption of alternative energies, new transport systems and urban redesign. This would be a reformist move, for a new deal based on the equivalent of a environmental global Marshall Plan (an attempt to leverage capital's urgent need for a new regime of accumulation in a progressive direction. Whether or not it was *radical* reformism would depend on the degree to which it included demands for forms of public ownership—both large scale and local—over these resources, or, instead, surrendered the leadership to subsidized private capital. These alternatives are a matter of contestation. How far such an agenda might outrun what Gopal Balakrishnan (2009, p. 21) terms a "narrow project of capitalist restoration" into deeper commoning possibilities would depend on the strength of struggles of below. Such a strategy assumes that the crisis is at once chronic enough to force capital to the table but not so acute as to remove all room for long-term social movement mobilization, for example, through war or a break down in civil order.

The other current—'terminal secession'—has a different analysis of the present situation. It sees it not so much as a crisis, with the implied possibility of capitalist recovery, as a catastrophe in which the planet factory is disclosed as a system with "no future." These are the times of capitalism's "imminent collapse" (The Invisible Committee, 2007, p. 105). Prospects for better institutions, including better universities, are nil. It is too late. We are now in an end game or, rather, realize, finally, that an end game is has been playing for some time. The options are stoppage—to accelerate and exhibit the catastrophe—and the creation, either as a withdrawal, or as an offensive action, of autonomous communal spaces. Terminal secessionism has a variety of sources with different inflections. In North America, much of it flows from ecological critique—and in particular post-carbon and transition towns' movements. In this optic, though the economic meltdown reflects profound instabilities, the real problems arise not so much with recession as with the resumption of growth; capitalism roars back to life only to slam into the wall of peak oil, peak food, peak everything. In Europe, there's a different line, directly involved in student movements in France, Greece and Britain, which, while it includes ecological disaster in its perspective, looks more at deepening unemployment, precarity, alienation and exclusion, a state of incipient civil war: *The Coming Insurrection*, the pamphlet from the French journal *Tiqqun*, is an exemplary document of this tendency, which, in turn influenced the *Communiqué from an Absent Future*, the bulletin of the California university occupation movement:

> The collapse of the global economy is here and now. . . . But social programs that depended upon high profit rates and vigorous economic growth are gone. We cannot be tempted to make futile grabs at the irretrievable while ignoring the obvious fact that there can be no autonomous "public university" in a capitalist society (Research and Destroy, 2009).

These two tracks seem to run in different directions. They are activated by different groups, with distinct political genealogies, organizations and characteristic subjectivities. They are predicated on differing analysis of the scope, speed and outcome of capital's current convulsions. There are evident pitfalls for both; co-option and marginalization. Each might be making massive mis-estimates of the current conjuncture, reformers in terms of overestimating the capacities of union and civil society organizations, and secessionists in terms of failing to foresee the likely outcome of an actual civil war situation, particularly in a nation such as the United States, riddled with heavily armed right wing militias.

There are also, however, ways in which the two apparently divergent strains could run parallel or even reinforce on another. Marxist and anarchist traditions have understood reformist struggles as a type of training, or as one nineteenth-century anarchist put it, a gymnasium for revolutionary activism, nautilus machines for radicalizing subjectivities. Conversely, every reformist struggle has depended on the fear struck by those willing to go further. More speculatively, one can see a public sector strategy that builds resources for the local, dispersed and resilient communal spaces and resources required to meet a worsening crisis and secessionism that defends the bases from which those resources can be siphoned. The last massive capitalist recession, that of the 1930s, saw the emergence of "popular front" organizations. In the 2010s, when the crisis of capitalism is manifestly a crisis of species-being, of the wresting of the need for collective and distributed social planning adequate to the era of anthropogenic ecological transformation, what is required is, to take a phrase from Scottish science fiction writer Ken Macleod (2003), a "human front"—providing we understand this not as a struggle to preserve some mythic essentialized human nature but as an advancing front laying claim to expanding capacities for life and creativity to be shared in common. To rediscover the commons beneath the ruins of the laboratory of futuristic accumulation requires also the discovery of commonalities in different struggles—that is the communist project (Marx and Engels, 1964, p. 80).

References

Balakrishnan, G. (2009). "Speculations on the Stationary State." *New Left Review*, 59: 5–26.

Bannon, L. (2009). "As Riches Fade, So Does Finance's Allure." *Wall Street Journal*: 18 Sept., A1.

Davis, M. (2010). "Who Will Build the Ark?" *New Left Review* 61: 29–46.

Dennis, D. (2003). "The Digital Death Rattle of the American Middle Class." *C-Theory. Net*, Nov. 18: http://www.ctheory.net/articles.aspx?id=402

Economist. (2010). "The disposable academic." *The Economist*, 18 Dec, 156–158.

Edu-Factory Collective (Eds.). (2009). *Toward a Global Autonomous University: Cognitive Labor, the Production of Knowledge, and Exodus from the Education Factory.* New York: Autonomedia.

Haraway, D. (1985). "Manifesto for Cyborgs: Science, Technology, and Socialist Feminism in the 1980s." *Socialist Review* 80: 65–108.

Herper, M. (2007). 'BP's Biotech Bet' *Forbes.com*. 3 July. http://www.forbes.com/2007/07/03/bp-genomics-energy-biz-sci-cx-mh_0703green_bp.html

Hopper, K., & Hopper, W. (2007). *The Puritan Gift: Reclaiming the American Dream amidst Global Financial Chaos.* New York: I.B. Taurus.

Invisible Committee. (2007). *The Coming Insurrection.* New York: Semiotext(e).

James, A. (2009). "Academies of the Apocalypse?" *The Guardian*: 7 April, 10.

June, A. W. (2010). "Some Papers Are Uploaded to Bangalore to Be Graded." *The Chronicle of Higher Education*. 4 April.

Kenney, M. (1986). *Biotechnology: The University-Industrial Complex*. New Haven, Conn.: Yale University Press.

Klein, N. (2008). *The Shock Doctrine: The Rise of Disaster Capitalism*. New York: Picador.

Loeppky, R. (2005). *Encoding Capital: The Political Economy of the Human Genome Project*. London, Routledge.

Macleod, Ken. (2003). *The Human Front*. London: Gollancz.

Marx, K. (1964) *The Economic and Philosophical Manuscripts of 1844*, ed. D. Struk, trans. Martin Milligan. New York: International Publishers.

Marx, K. (1973). *Grundrisse. Foundations of the Critique of Political Economy*, trans. M. Nicolaus, New York: Vintage Books.

Marx, K. (1977). *Capital: A Critique of Political Economy, Volume 1*, trans. Ben Fowkes, New York: Penguin.

Marx, K. (1981). *Capital: A Critique of Political Economy, Volume 3*, trans. Ben Fowkes. New York: Penguin.

Marx, K., & Engels, F. (1964). *The Communist Manifesto*. New York: Washington Square Press.

M'Gonigle, M. & Searle, J. (2006). *Planet U: Sustaining the World, Reinventing the University*. Gabriola Island, BC: New Society Publishers.

Midnight Notes. (1992). *Midnight Oil: Work, Energy, War, 1973–1992*. New York: Autonomedia.

Reading, Bill. (1997). *The University in Ruins*. Cambridge, Mass: Harvard University Press.

Research and Destroy. (2009). *Communiqué from an Absent Future*. Retrieved from http://wewanteverything.wordpress.com/2009/09/24/communique-from-an-absent-future/

Schneider, F. & Kirchgässner, G. (2009). 'Financial and World Economic Crisis: What Did Economists contribute?' *Public Choice* 140 (3–4): 319–327.

Suarez-Villa, L. (2009). *Technocapitalism: A Critical Perspective on Technological Innovation and Corporatism*. Philadelphia: Temple University Press.

Paolo, V. (2004). *A Grammar of the Multitude*. New York: Semiotext(e).

Patterson, S. (2010). *The Quants: How a New Breed of Math Whizzes Conquered Wall Street and Nearly Destroyed It*. New York: Crown Business.

CHAPTER FOURTEEN

The Confinement of Academic Freedom and Critical Thinking in a Changing Corporate World:

South African Universities

TAHIR WOOD

Introduction

The question of academic freedom has recently become a topical one in South Africa (Hall, 2006, Waghid, 2006, Bentley, et al. 2006, Duncan, 2007), not for the first time, but obviously it has posed itself in a new way in the post-apartheid era. There are two aspects to this. The first is the sense of a general sea change in higher education, which is described variously as the decline of traditional academic values, as a decline of liberal humanism, as a rise of managerialism, or as the impact of neoliberalism, neoconservatism or globalisation. There is a widespread sense that universities and their ethos are changing in fundamental ways, so that institutional values of academic freedom, such as freedom of expression on the part of academics or the relative autonomy of the university as an institution that fosters critical thinking are being alarmingly eroded.

The second notable aspect is the proliferation of disciplinary procedures involving academic staff that have occurred at a number of universities in the last decade, and which have led to some antagonisms within these institutions and some soul searching within the higher education sector. There is a sense that one is not always free to speak one's mind, especially to criticise, and that this represents an encroachment upon the academy of certain values and practices that have in the past been more characteristic of the corporate sector (Duncan, 2007; Southall and Cobbing, 2001).

I will neither explore all aspects of the debate nor review all of the recently expressed points of view. Rather I will attempt to explain the evolution of one important source of pressure upon the academy that is helping to redefine its purposes: the imperatives affecting the broader society that are associated with productivity and innovation. While productivity and innovation are sometimes treated by academic authorities as absolute and unalloyed goods and as cast-iron arguments for uncritical partnerships with the private sector, I will draw attention to certain dangers inherent in such assumptions and attempt to reassert the importance of criticism and dissent within academia at the present time. This entails specifically dealing with academic freedom as the freedom to question and criticise the ways in which universities are being positioned in relation to the broader world of work. Having done this, I will present a notion of practical reason that may be something of a guide for the academic in the present circumstances.

Regarding the local socio-economic context for these debates, one should perhaps mention that the growth model of social development, epitomised in South Africa by GEAR (Growth, Employment and Redistribution policy), came about through a dovetailing of state and corporate interests. In other words, these two sets of interests are not necessarily antithetical as some writers (e.g. Bentley et al., 2006) might want to suggest. The practical question that arises is what the university's role, and indeed the role of the individual academic, should be in relation to such public-private strategies of development. GEAR, as described by Chikulo was designed to achieve

> high rates of economic growth, to expand the private sector, to improve output and employment, achieve fiscal reform and encourage trade and investment. Furthermore, GEAR sought to achieve redistribution and improvement in basic living conditions as a result of generally, revitalised economic performance. GEAR rests on the assumption that the expansion of the private sector would have a substantial impact on the economy, whilst the role of the state would largely be a facilitative one . . . In order to facilitate economic growth and the expansion of the private sector, the government undertook to reduce state spending and the budget deficit; reduce corporate taxes and relax foreign exchange controls. It further pledged to control inflation; promote privatisation, and encourage wage restraint: all goals which are prescribed as universal panaceas for 'development' by the Bretton Woods institutions such as the World Bank and IMF. . . . (2003, no pagination)

But authors such as the above, and others cited below, have shown that some favourable effects in terms of foreign investment and macroeconomic stability were not accompanied by the main intended goals of the strategy. Growth has been modest, averaging around half of the projected 6%, while joblessness and inequality have actually increased.

More recently, South Africa has joined the other nations in the global recession starting with a 6.4% contraction in the first quarter of 2009, together with the disastrous increase in joblessness that this has brought to an already dire employment situation (SouthAfrica.info, 2009). The global recession is perhaps a topic for another occasion, as is the role of universities and their graduates in innovations such as the design of systems, software, mathematical models and financial instruments that, whatever else they have done, have not helped to pull back the world's economy from its worst recession since the Great Depression. Of more direct relevance for our present purposes is rather the fact that research in South Africa post-1994 has revealed that the relatively jobless growth mentioned above was actually accompanied by some impressive productivity gains (Banerjee et al., 2006; Fryer and Vencatachellum, 2003; Kingdon and Knight, 2004, 2005; Rodrik, 2006; Wakeford, 2003; Wood, 2007). The inescapable implication is that gains in productivity resulting from innovation do not *necessarily* translate into a general social good.

Mike Davis (2006) has shown that a rapidly expanding urban poor now live on the peripheries of the world's cities rather than in inner city areas, often in close proximity to garbage dumps, a trend that, like migrant labour itself, was spearheaded in South Africa. And the squalor that he describes on a global level is found concentrated in South Africa, which has one of the highest rates of unemployment and of urban slum development in the world, and it is the country with the highest income inequality in the world, bar none, this *despite* the productivity gains (Economic Policy Institute, 2006).

Notwithstanding the scale of the global scientific enterprise today and the investments in it, both private and public–there are around 10,000 recognised universities worldwide–it seems that this collective intelligence has not been able to slow down the recent progress of global immiseration. Can one then entertain the hope that partnerships between these universities and the private sector will in themselves make a difference, when it is under the economic leadership of the corporate sector that these maldeveloped wastelands have come about in the first place?

The point here is that panaceas representing the shared wisdom of states, corporations and certain of the guiding doctrines of both cannot be accepted uncritically, and universities are precisely those institutions that must think critically about the social problems of the day. Further, below I will examine very carefully this notion of critical thinking.

Two notions of academic freedom

Hall (2006) discusses two distinct views of academic freedom. The first is the notion of an untrammeled pursuit of truth by an *autonomous* community of scholars, for example the view associated with T.B. Davie in the 1950s: 'our freedom from external interference in a) who shall teach, b) what we teach, c) how we teach, and d) whom we teach' (as cited in Hall, 2006, p. 371). This is described as the classical liberal position on academic freedom. But if one interrogates it, for example by asking how many scholars should make up this community, or specifically which sorts of truth they should be pursuing, it becomes apparent that these are impossible questions to answer without reference to external factors. And these are precisely the sorts of questions that higher education constantly asks itself. The mere fact that academics are sustained by the taxes of working people, as well as the tuition fees that are also paid by working people, should require us at least to qualify any such notion of absolute autonomy.

Hall presents an alternative to this, a 'conditional autonomy' that 'acknowledges the legitimate role of the state in steering the public higher education system, while also recognising the rights of individual institutions to autonomous governance over their central business of research, teaching and learning' (2006, p. 374). It is argued that 'accepting conditional autonomy is an effective defence of academic freedom' (Hall, 2006, p. 374). Yet despite this, it is recognised that the question of the *free speech of the individual* within the academy still remains.

Perhaps unsurprisingly, Hall reports that this issue is 'unresolved' at his own institution. He uses the example of an academic who advocates racism; should such an individual's freedom of expression be upheld? If it is claimed that academics have the right and perhaps the obligation to speak out on matters of public interest, why should someone who actually believes that races, sexes, cultures or creeds are unequal be prevented from articulating such views? One could argue that such people should be encouraged to express their views, even against the constitution, so that they can be openly countered in public rather than have such opinions festering on in secrecy, only to erupt occasionally in violence or other forms of humiliation and abuse, as has happened on occasion. But be that as it may, the difficulties in contextualist or conditionalist positions of the kind proposed by Hall are clearly associated with the determination or negotiation of acceptable boundaries and limits. The present article is also concerned to explore the boundaries and limits to academic freedom, not so much in terms of whether individuals should be allowed to express retrograde or discredited opinions, but rather in relation to other issues that have started to become more worrying than those.

Freedom under threat

Jane Duncan (2007, no pagination) has written of the 'proletarianisation of the professoriate' and how 'the labour relations dispensation that applies in broader society–with all its recent problems–is being imported into universities'. The question posed here is not so much whether professors should or shouldn't be treated the same as workers elsewhere in society, but rather why there is at this time such a preponderance of disciplinary measures being taken against them, when this sort of approach to university staff relations used to be relatively uncommon. Duncan discusses some recent instances in detail, including several cases of actual dismissal for criticism of university management, and the answer she gives relates to the corporatisation of the university:

> When a university is corporatised, power becomes 'sucked up' to the top, and is often centralised in the person of the Vice Chancellor. The university becomes a brand in the commercial sense. Substantial notions of accountability to the academic project are replaced by narrow notions of accountability to administrators and managers; in fact, in the entrepreneurial university model, management *is* the university. Criticism of the management amounts to criticism of the university, and therefore damage to the brand. Disciplinary measures against those who bring the brand into disrepute become an essential part of brand management. (Duncan, 2007, no pagination)

Why have universities become 'brands'? An answer may be given in terms of the funding that universities are allocated by the state relative to the income that they are able to generate by other means. The former is restricted by austerity measures of governments, increasingly so since the 1970s, while the latter is meant to be expanded through an increase in entrepreneurship on the part of the university and its professors. In fact it is becoming part of the job description of a professor that he or she should have the ability to raise funds from donors or from contracts. Often academics themselves are on short or medium-term contracts, whose renewal depends partially on success in fundraising. Here we are reminded of the condition of many precarious workers under the general regime of post-Fordism (Wood, 2005, 2007). Concerning this international reorganisation of higher education, Nick Dyer-Witheford explains that it

> arose from a dovetailing of two sets of interests: the state's and the corporate sector's. Governments, beset by the 'fiscal crisis of the state' (in fact largely induced by a corporate tax rebellion), were keen to cut costs; business, on the other hand, wanted more control over the troublesome but increasingly valuable education sector. Over the late 1970s and 1980s, funding for university education in most capitalist countries was cut. Tuition fees and student debt loads rose sharply. Programmes seen as subversive or simply inutile to industry were slashed. (2007, p. 46)

So there is a new convergence between the state with its fiscal crises, the corporate sector, and the purposes of higher education. Cutting funding to universities pushes them further into the arms of industry and commerce, whose problems they must help solve. However, this obviously does not quite settle the question of academic freedom. After all, it could be argued that we do not really have a narrowing of the possibilities for critical analysis and free enquiry, but rather a situation in which academics are choosing *freely* to implement a more commercial role for the university. As Barnett puts it: 'Now, academic freedom appears to be becoming the right to exploit the exchange value inherent in academics' knowledge' (2004, p. 63).

Note also that it is not necessary, for my purposes, to embrace the hypothesis that a change in university financing is now 'behind' each and every case of restriction of freedom. I am arguing for something that looks rather less like a conspiracy theory than this: a recognition that funding and its sources can be responsible for the creation of a generalised *climate of ideas*, one in which the possibility of calling into question the state-university-corporate consensus may be effectively proscribed.

Academic freedom and critical thought

In what does critical thought consist? I would like to concur that: 'A community engaged in the search for knowledge enacts critical thinking. *The justification for academic freedom lies in the activity of critical thinking* [emphasis added]' (Angus, 2007, p. 67).

Let us agree then that stimulating critical thinking is an inherent part of what it is that universities are meant to do. However one can undoubtedly come up with very different definitions of critical thinking, for example:

1. the capacity for original thought in the application of knowledge to problems in industry and commerce
2. the capacity to reflect on and to question the value or validity of all received knowledge in pursuit of the good life

Definition (a) reflects a mode of thought that we might call 'instrumental reason'. Reason in this view is a tool to reach certain goals, not to determine which goals are the right ones to have. Critical thinking in this sense is meant to be good for the profit-making sector, from which certain benefits will surely flow back into the university. But we have seen that the ways in which this sector has solved its problems in recent decades, with the help of universities, has often not translated into the general social good. No doubt university graduates in the United States and elsewhere were involved in designing the sophisticated instruments whereby sub-prime mortgage debts could be repackaged and sold. Why should they be accused of not engaging in critical thinking according to definition (a)?

A common argument for capitalist innovation, for example from the biotechnology industry, which extends deep into the academy, is that it increases productivity, for example in agriculture, leading to a possible lowering of food prices. But people who have no income because they are themselves excluded from productive activity do not benefit from a marginal lowering of food prices. The South African data already cited does not show increased employment flowing from productivity gains. Thus the good flowing from this form of 'critical thinking' tends to be a highly restricted one, benefiting a few immensely, others indifferently, and a great many others not at all. In time, this supposed 'critical thinking' may even become a positive impediment in the way of alternative thinking. This outcome seems likely, since we have seen how technical solutions, tightly managed from above, turn out to be solutions only to problems of successive capitalist crises, rather than brakes on the progress of generalised immiseration.

The problem with definition (b) is obviously quite different; this could be described as an 'ivory-tower' approach to critical thinking. The problem here lies in its idealist and quietest nature, in its very disjunction from the kind of critical thinking represented by (a). Like certain liberal academic views of academic freedom, it is simply not worldly enough, and the danger associated with it is that critique as a whole might be discredited as a woolly minded indulgence.

In the philosophical tradition that goes back to Kant and beyond, the questions about what one should do, i.e., what one's goals in life should be, have been termed 'practical reason'. They are questions of ethics, politics, morality and law. Without wanting to engage directly with this vast philosophical field, I can nevertheless suggest here that opposing instrumental reason to practical reason is not a helpful approach to the matters under discussion. Yet this is typically what happens. It is a move which impoverishes both notions, firstly by emptying instrumental reason of any real ethical substance, secondly by reducing practical reason to the status of an abstract universal divorced from actual means and ends. Far from wanting to keep one's idea of the social good isolated from, say, technological rationality, one would surely prefer that the question of technology should rather be situated firmly within the question of the social good, the question of what sorts of things are worth doing. If there is a general purpose for the university today then surely it is this integrative task of reconciling the notions of instrumental and practical reason that have become so disparate since the Enlightenment, a disparity that has, in this age of pollution, climate change and seemingly endless war, come to threaten humanity and its habitat. Thus when writers such as Faure et al. (1972) and especially Barnett (2000a, 2004) pose the question of education as *being* rather than knowing, there is a double significance to this word choice. At stake is not only the subjective question of how one should be, i.e., as an individual, but also the ontological question of the human being itself: under what sorts of conditions humanity may manage to survive and thrive.

It seems to me that what is required therefore is the worldliness and problem-solving attitude of critical thinking (a), combined with the ethical sensibility of critical thinking (b). If instrumental reason could be recovered as an inherent part of a more encompassing notion of practical reason, then this would constitute a mode of problem-solving, political thought that has only been glimpsed before in academic history and constitute a new 'realisation' of the university (Barnett, 2004, p. 67). But its emergence could be blocked by punitive restrictions on the freedom within universities to question received managerial wisdom. How does this relate to the current situation of the academic?

Let us recognise first that the university must deal with a certain contradiction in its situation. The fact that it obtains revenue from the corporate sector makes it less than independent (the same principle applies to its funding from the state), yet it must continue to strive for a degree of independence from both. As a way of understanding this practically, I think we need to see a number of difficult mediating roles within the university. One of these is the mediation by academics of the relationship between the students and their future employers. One would not want to support uncritically all and any demands that those employers might make on one's students (!). Yet, at the same time, serving the interests of one's students means unavoidably that they must be helped to find convergences with the interests of their future employers, as part of their preparation for work. So students must themselves be inculcated with the consciousness of what it means to add value to an enterprise, whatever it might be, while *at the same time* retaining the critical notion of a broader good, one that extends beyond the profit, making capacity of the enterprise and which may in some instances even be antithetical to it. Here we surely sense profound implications for academic practice and for the nature of the university curriculum.

Similarly in research, academics know that the sorts of applied research demanded by the corporate sector actually depend on the basic, curiosity-driven research that those same corporate partners may actively wish to discourage or marginalise. Here again they must mediate in this contradiction and defend the relative autonomy of academic work, if knowledge is not to descend to the worst sorts of pragmatism. An analogy may be drawn with some other institutions of society, the judiciary for example. Such an institution, if it is to have any credibility at all in society (something not to be taken for granted), must retain a certain professional independence from the government and vested interests, even though its existence is directly supported by the state and it is indirectly supported by corporate taxes.

Such professionalism is the only space for an autonomy that might retain a vestige of recognition from the capital-state nexus, and it must be fought for internationally, so that *the* question mentioned by Angus is still thinkable in the university context:

> The question, 'What is a social good?' must be raised both in universities and outside them. This is the connection between the democratisation of the university and democratisation of society. Without it, academic freedom in the corporate university is just a wizened, empty shell capable only of justifying the freedom of researchers to accept the large grants proffered by private interests. (2007, p. 73)

Now these sorts of conclusions may be sharply contrasted with conclusions that are being reached by other authors. For one South African example one might consider the following:

> My contention is that the university does not have to relinquish its pursuit of criticality and democratic participation if 'steered by the requirements of the labour market'. Why not? . . . I have made an argument for achieving democracy in a sphere of marketisation, if higher education is considered as a public good that allows space for the development of relations of trust, individual autonomy and democratic dialogue. Similarly, even if the university needs to develop human capital for global competitiveness and the establishment of a democratic citizenry (which are neo-liberal concerns), then higher education institutions need to restructure according to an organisational discourse which resonates with the language of inclusion, social cohesion and increased participation . . . For instance when a faculty has to develop an academic programme which aims to prepare students for participation in a global economy and a democratic society, I cannot imagine how this can be done without the deliberative engagement of academic staff, as well as giving consideration to students' voices. (Waghid, 2006, pp. 379–80)

It is remarkable how this passage is structured via a linking of democracy with a series of items throughout, such as 'marketisation', 'global competitiveness', 'human capital' or 'participation in a global economy', redolent as these terms all are of garden-variety neo-liberal thinking. Equally striking is the sense of an imperative that is reinforced throughout by formulations such as: 'steered by the requirements of the labour market'; 'the university needs to develop human capital'; 'a faculty has to develop an academic programme'. It seems that academics *have to* do certain things, and once they have accepted such an imperative, willingly or unwillingly, then they have complete freedom to do them. Many academics today would no doubt regard this as being an accurate description of their situation. But it is precisely the freedom to criticise such imperatives as these, and even to resist them entirely on occasion, that is being affirmed in the present article, and one really does have to wonder about the meaning of the term 'criticality' used in the first sentence above.

To take another example, Bentley, Habib and Morrow suggest that 'institutional autonomy and academic freedom need to be constructed through the contestation of empowered stakeholders, which itself is a product of a messy process of higher education reform and entrepreneurial academic practice' (2006, p. 30). Well perhaps, but it is suggested here that this approach is insufficiently critical of current 'entrepreneurial academic practice', to put it mildly. The ideas on entrepreneurship expressed by these authors appear naïve when they recommend almost uncritically that opening up 'other income streams (apart from student fees) to support their institutions' activities . . . is seen as an opportunity, where necessary, to speak with an independent voice' (2006, p. 26). They do at least concede that 'a number of cases have emerged there where, for instance, academic research has been compromised by institutions' relationships with business corporations' (2006, p. 28).

Nevertheless the idea that entrepreneurship is the best (or perhaps only) guarantor of academic freedom is sustained by these authors throughout, apparently on the grounds that there appears to be a correlation in the South African case between successful generation of non-state and non-fee income and academic freedom, even though they themselves note that 'this is a striking correspondence rather than direct proof of a connection' (Bentley, et al., 2006, p. 27). Furthermore, the argument they present suggests that academic freedom is defined *only* as freedom from direct state interference, whereas I have taken pains to show in this essay that direct state interference is not the only source of unfreedom in academia.

Bentley et al. do not concede that the potential for compromised academic freedom may turn out to be as great in the link with the private sector as it is in the link with the state. Nor do they express any thought that disciplinary cases against academics may sometimes be linked with a managerial anxiety concerning public relations with corporate partners in mind or that such cases may in fact be central to concerns about academic freedom. Thus they miss the import of certain comments made by Jonathan Jansen that they themselves cite, to the effect that 'an equality of empowered stakeholders [holds] the danger of an alignment amongst some of them against those who [have] a direct and permanent stake in the academic enterprise' (2006, p. 29).

If one names these two different sets of stakeholders as corporations and academics respectively then the nature of Jansen's warning comes very close indeed to what has been argued here. And we begin to see a dangerous generality in the notion of 'stakeholder'. Are all stakeholders custodians of the university and its future possibilities? Are they all equal in that sense? The answer given here is that they are not; academics collectively should be seen as custodians of the university in a way that private corporations cannot and must never be, even if the latter are, unavoidably, among its clients, or even, in some cases, its philanthropic benefactors.

Conclusions

The question of freedom of speech in universities cannot be disconnected from the question of freedom in general. Unfreedom inside the university has its correlates outside. This article has attempted to show how the character and range of external alliances being developed by the academy are the key to its future role in society and perhaps even a key to the future sustainability of society itself.

While I find myself in agreement with the conclusions of Southall and Cobbing (2001, p. 35) that university managers should be accountable to those they manage and that academics need to be better organised so as to be able to resist at least the most egregious forms of university authoritarianism, I do not think these measures on their own will ultimately be enough. They are in need of a strong supporting rationale that is widely accepted and around which support can be organised, in other words an academic ethos founded on an adequate notion of practical reason. Unless higher education can be defined in such a way as to steer it towards a more balanced notion of its *purpose* than the recent waves of managerialist enthusiasm (in which the fate of a university is seen as almost entirely dependent upon the profitability of its corporate partners) then there is little hope for a climate conducive to independent critical thinking.

The threats to academic freedom today are part and parcel of more general threats to the human species and its habitat. The gravity and the increasing prominence of such threats should lead one to take issue with Barnett (2000a, 2004) when he questions the existence of any central narrative or guiding set of values for the university, or indeed any shared ethos amongst the multifarious academic disciplines, and posits in their place only fragility and uncertainty. Leaving aside the difficult question of how fragility and uncertainty can exist with nothing else, we should perhaps agree rather with Protagoras that *man is the measure of all things* (ignoring the gender bias in this formulation just for the moment) and that the future flourishing of humanity and its habitat, in spite of the frightening thought of a loss of human being itself, is the central justification for the academic enterprise and the freedoms that it must embody.

One should therefore not look only for freedom in the hyper-subjectivity of 'individuals having to take onto themselves responsibility for continually reconstituting themselves through their lifespan' (Barnett, 2000b, p. 258)(notwithstanding certain exhilarating aspects of this way of thinking) but also look to new politico-epistemological alliances and new visionary pedagogies beyond neo-liberalism that they may bring, in an appropriate response to the march of unfreedom in academia.

References

Angus, I. (2007). Academic freedom in the corporate university. *In*: M. Coté, R.J.F. Day, and G. de Peuter (eds.), *Utopian pedagogy*. Toronto: University of Toronto Press, 64–75.

Banerjee, A., Galiani, S., Levinsohn, A. & Woolard, I. (2006). Why has unemployment risen in the new South Africa? Unpublished manuscript. Retrieved from http://www-personal.umich.edu/~jamesl/Treasury_10_06_labor.pdf

Barnett, R. (2000a). *Realizing the university in an age of supercomplexity*. Buckingham: Open University Press.

Barnett, R. (2000b). Supercomplexity and the curriculum. *Studies in Higher Education*, 25 (3), 255–265.

Barnett, R. (2004). The purposes of higher education and the changing face of academia. *London Review of Education*, 2 (1), 61–73.

Bentley, K., Habib, A. & Morrow, S. (2006). Academic freedom, institutional autonomy and the corporatised university in contemporary South Africa. Research report. Council on Higher Education, South Africa.

Chikulo, b.c. (2003). Development policy in South Africa: a review. *DPMN Bulletin*, 10 (2). Retrieved from: http://www.dpmf.org/images/south-africa-devt-policy-chikulo.html

Davis, M. (2006). *Planet of slums*. London: Verso.

Duncan, J. (2007). The rise of the disciplinary university. Harold Wolpe Memorial Lecture, University of KwaZulu Natal. Retrieved from http://www.fxi.org.za/content/view/85/1/

Dyer-Witheford, N. (2007). Teaching and teargas: The university in the era of general intellect. *In*: M. Coté, R.J.F. Day, and G. de Peuter, eds. *Utopian pedagogy*. Toronto: University of Toronto Press, 43–63.

Economic Policy Institute. (2006). Retrieved from http://www.epi.org/content.cfm/webfeatures_snapshots_20060419

Faure, E., Herrera, F., Kaddoura, A., Lopes, H., Petrovsky, A.V., Rahnema, M. & Ward, F.C. (1972). *Learning to be*. Paris: UNESCO.

Fryer, D. & Vencatachellum, D. (2003). Coordination failure and employment in South Africa. TIPS / DPRU Forum. Retrieved from http://www.tips.afrihost.com/research/papers/pdfs/690.pdf

Hall, M. (2006). Academic freedom and the university: Fifty years of debate. *South African Journal of Higher Education*, 20 (3), 370–378.

Kingdon, G. & Knight, J. (2004). Race and the incidence of unemployment in South Africa. *Review of Development Economics*, 8 (2), 198–222.

Kingdon, G. & Knight, J. (2005). Unemployment in South Africa, 1995–2003: Causes, problems and policies. Unpublished manuscript retrieved from http://www.isser.org/1%20Kingdon_Knight.pdf

Rodrik, D. (2006). Understanding South Africa's economic puzzles. CID Working Paper no. 130. Center for International Development at Harvard University.

SouthAfrica.info (2009). Retrieved from http://www.southafrica.info/news/business/33972.htm

Southall, R. & Cobbing, J. (2001). From racial liberalism to corporate authoritarianism: The Shell affair and the assault on academic freedom in South Africa. *Social Dynamics*, 27 (2), 1–42.

Waghid, Y. (2006). Academic freedom, institutional autonomy and responsible action: A response to Martin Hall. *South African Journal of Higher Education*, 20 (3), 379–382.

Wakeford, J. (2003). The productivity-wage relationship in South Africa: An empirical investigation. TIPS / DPRU Conference, Johannesburg.

Wood, T. (2005). You are subjects! Higher education and the general intellect. *Journal of Education and Work*, 18 (3), 341–353.

Wood, T. (2007). Lifelong learning, academic development and the purposes of higher education. *Journal of Education*, 42, 83–106.

Afterword
The Unmaking of Education
in the Age of Globalization,
Neoliberalism and Information

CAMERON MCCARTHY

Introduction

For those of us who work as educators, the joining of reflection on cognition and capitalism in this volume opens up a critical aperture in our self understanding of the academic enterprise, the role of intellectual labor, and the fate of late-modern subjectivity in the light of the radically corrosive uses of knowledge and information in the age of globalization. How are we to understand these developments as they pertain to the reorganization of knowledge in the education context in which globalization and neoliberalization are fully triangulated and self-translated frameworks of reference for a kind universalistic commonsense? What are we to make of these developments in education where, we, as scholars and practitioners, often thoughtlessly, separate what we do from the flow of the dynamic currents of history and the present? Let me expand on this then in what follows.

As a consequence of the new driving logics of globalization and the information age articulated most profoundly in the workings of "flexible capitalism" (Bauman, 2000, 2009; Schiller, 2003; Sennett, 1998, 2006, 2008), all late-modern institutions, all late-modern forms of association and affiliation are coming under the banner of new identities. These dynamics associated with global capitalism (the rapid and constant dispersal of cultural and economic capital across national boundaries, the intensification and rapidity of movement and migration of people across borders, the amplification of electronic mediation and the work of the imagination of the great masses of the people) reveal themselves in what scholars such as Zygmunt Bauman and Richard Sennett describe as a general lightness of being or liquidity of all social relations and social arrangements of late-modernity. Whether one is talking about the general trend of multinational corporations such as Adidas, Nike, Reebok, Microsoft and others towards what Naomi Klein (2009, 2007) calls "immateriality," as advertising, branding and R&D displace the emphasis on inventories of products as the primary emphasis of these juggernaut commercial institutions; whether we are talking about the new international division of labor in which the production, distribution and circulation of goods and services are being coordinated over enormous distances, numerous nations and markets; whether we are talking about new synchronicities of culture, the disembedding of forms of life and meaning of style from one setting and their transplantation to a next; or whether we are talking about what Richard Sennett (2008) sees as the decline of theodicy, meaning, and the control over craft in all forms of late-modern labor processes, intellectual and bureaucratic labor and the organization of knowledge not accepted, the relentless logic of the recasting of the modern world is proceeding and accelerating at a blinding pace.

These contemporary transitions have taken place in a context where the relations between government, society, the individual and the market have undergone profound transformations. Resulting from this shift—characterized by many as a neoliberal one—new discursive relations and practices emphasizing individual freedoms, autonomy and choice have emerged (Bansel, 2007). These new discursive practices can be understood as a response to both the shortcomings of what many critics have considered as an overprotective Welfare State (or "nanny state") and the persuasive and widespread claims about the inevitability of globalization and of workplace changes (Davies & Bansel, 2007). In this context, characterized by what Clarke (2007) refers to as the subjugation of the social, post-welfare state subjects are expected (and constructed) to willingly be responsible for their own well-being. Envisioned in government policy documents and practices, as well as in academic texts, labor-market rhetoric and education and training materials as international citizens of a global economy, which requires them to be up-to-date and take advantage of the numerous possibilities at their disposal, post welfare-state subjects are positioned as socially and economic mobile. As Bansel (2007) argues,

> this mobility is lived at the site of subjectivity, social location and work. Discourses of stable personalities with suitability for specific types of employment and of jobs or careers for life are displaced by the discourse of the mobile portfolio worker. Mobile portfolio workers are constituted as likely to have multiple careers for which they will need to be reeducated or retrained. As portfolio workers they accumulate skills, knowl-

edges and experiences that ensure not only their mobility, but also their flexibility, as they shift through multiple careers in the knowledge economy, supported through often self-funded lifelong learning. Flexible workers not only shift careers and the subjectivities that accrue to them but are also adapted to working conditions that demand increasing flexibility in terms of contracts, hours of work, rates of pay, casualization, levels of responsibility and so on (p. 288).

Furthermore, the flexible, or better yet, the entrepreneurial subjects of 21st century capitalism are expected not only to adapt incessantly to the constant changes in education and work, but also to create productive activity, not just to participate in it (Nairn & Higgins, 2007). In this way, as Robertson and Dale (2002) claim, the risk of precariousness and failure implicated in any entrepreneurial work resides now on the individual rather than on an external institution or organization. Although some authors have rightly pointed out that at a time when the "entrepreneur" has turned out to be a dominant and privileged subject (Du Gay, 1996), becoming an entrepreneurial self may contribute to the construction of a recognizable identity and a sense of social belonging (Nairn & Higgins, 2007). One cannot overlook the tensions between those discourses emphasizing the freedom to choose, endless opportunities, improved lifestyle and social mobility and the realities of a job market where choices are limited, opportunities are constrained and social mobility promises remain unfulfilled for many. These discourses position the individuals as the locus of success or failure: based on their self-discipline, hard-work, ambition, personality and efforts, they will either fail or succeed procuring for their well-being. Success (or failure) is conceived in their narratives as individual driven, not as socially constructed. Missing in these discourses is any consideration of the differential and inequitable positions of subjects in terms of economic, social and cultural capital, age, gender, class, race, ethnicity and sexual orientation. These discourses are based in the assumption that all subjects are equally positioned to identify, mobilize, and create productive or successful choices.

Although this type of discourse—intrinsically neoliberal in my view—is imbued with unquestioned presuppositions regarding "freedom" and "self-determination," one cannot fail to notice its normative nature. In relation to this, it is being argued that, under global capitalism, neoliberal technologies and practices work to shape docile subjects who are closely governed but who conceive themselves as inherently free (Rose, 1999). Similarly, Griffin (2007) claims that neoliberal discourse "structures and communicates appropriate types of and limits to human behavior and acceptable social aspirations" (p. 223). As Davies and Bansel (2007) put it, this type of discourse contributes to shape a new ethics of the subject: "Individuals are linked to society through acts of socially sanctioned consumption and responsible choice in the shaping of something called a 'lifestyle'" (Davies & Bansel, 2007, p.

252). In this narrative, the subject is unambiguously middle class, a wholehearted consumer of goods and investments (material and symbolic). Furthermore, Griffin (2007) argues, this dominant discourse relates "successful" behavior "almost exclusively with a gender identity embodied in dominant forms of heterosexual masculinity" (p. 220). She illustrates this by reference to World Bank discourses, which in her view, foster development policies and practices designed in accordance with gendered hierarchies of meaning, representation and identity. Besides, although the mainstream discourse of global capitalism presents itself as color-blind under the guise of racial justice, authors like Duggan (2003) claim just the opposite: it is "saturated with race" (p. xvi). Dominant neoliberal discourses rely on race-neutral language to support the argument that race is no longer a factor in life opportunities and achievement (especially in the U.S.). As Davis (2007) argues, "by rejecting race, formerly racialized 'others' can be fully incorporated as consumptive citizens with no racial barriers to their participation in the economy. Neoliberalism, then, willfully misconstrues and dismisses the reality of racism as a powerful explanatory factor in analyzing persistent racial inequities" (p. 350). How are these inequalities concealed? According to Davis (2007), neoliberal discourses operate "relocating racially coded economic disadvantage and reassigning identity-based biases to the private and personal spheres" (p. 349). By privatizing the discourse on race (i.e., defining racial problems as private ones), a color-blind logic allows people to maintain individualistic interpretations of racial inequalities (Quiroz, 2007) and, thus, reinforces the invisibility of white privilege.

Within this context of global capitalism under neoliberalism, the educational enterprise cannot be separated from other institutional and cultural aspects of the body politic. We must consider education as a critical flashpoint of neoliberalizing logics that is articulated to the problem of social integration of modern subjects into twenty-first century life—a context in which modern institutions, after Deleuze, seem to be imploding from systems complexities, contradictions and dysfunctions lodged in the socius and in the new teeming globalizing realities.

Some educators have understood this as the late-modern antithesis between movement and stasis, wherein the world outside keeps churning—driven forward by globalization—and our education system, by contrast, retreats while holding onto curricular guidelines of the past. This is what Dennis Carlson (2002) warns us about in his insightful book, entitled *Leaving Safe Harbors*. He admonishes educators to move out of the "safe harbors" of settled educational practices and philosophies in order to better address the challenges posed to schooling by the dynamics associated with globalization and multiplicity. In this important book, Carlson offers a proper riposte to the atrophy of critical theoretical reflection in the fields of education and the social sciences generally and bellwether ringing in the popular press that ushered in the new millennium: "The era of big theory is over," declared one

New York Times . With great assurance and self-satisfaction, she continued, "The grand paradigms that swept through the humanities departments in the 20ᵗʰ century—psychoanalysis, structuralism, Marxism, deconstruction, postcolonialism— have lost favor or have been abandoned. Money is tight. And, leftist politics with which literary theorists have traditionally been associated have taken a beating" (Eakin, 2003, p. 9). One is reminded, here, of a similar hand ringing and a similar denunciation of the amorphous Left in the *New York Times* in the late' 70s by the senior anthropologist, Marvin Harris. It was the occasion of the American Anthropological Association's Annual Meeting. On the eve of that meeting, Harris suggested, in an op-ed piece written for the *New York Times*, that anthropology was being "taken over by mystics, religious fanatics, and California cultists; that the meetings were dominated by panels on shamanism, witchcraft and 'abnormal phenomena'; and that 'scientific papers based on empirical studies' had been willfully excluded from the program" (Ortner, 1994, p. 372). The *New York Times*, the newspaper that the late Edward Said liked to call the "newspaper of record" has made it its business to periodically prognosticate about the ridiculousness of the Left and its last days. Fortunately, Dennis Carlson puts us in completely different territory inviting us to consider the seriousness of the malaise of mainstream life and mainstream education and our need to move beyond conventionalism and the institutional practices of confinement to embrace hope and possibility. Above all, *Leaving Safe Harbors* suggests movement like the movement in Herman Melville's novel *Moby Dick* (1851/2009). It is the suggestion of movement in the context of stasis, where, as George Lipsitz (2004) notes, too many inner-city youth and their schools are "locked on this earth" (p. 1). They are locked in the bureaucratic deployment of schooling that is articulated to a hierarchical organization of society and an unequal access to its social rewards, goods and services. This process is analogous to what Melville lays out on the deck of the *Pequod* in his magnificent novel, *Moby Dick*. Arrayed around Ahab, on the deck of the *Pequod*, is the projection of social classification: first mate, Starbuck; second mate, Stub; third mate, Flask. Then there are the first harpooner, Queequeg, the second harpooner, Tashtego and the third harpooner, Dagoo of third world, Native American and African backgrounds. We are familiar with this penchant for hierarchy and top-down leadership in the university and the school. We have, then, embodied in Carlson's book, echoing Herman Melville, the announcement of a Shakespearean story of tragic proportions on schools that is about to unfold. This is the story of movement and stasis—the vigorous turn in education toward neoliberalism and its false clarity and false promises of greater individual freedom and choice (movement) while consolidating and exacerbating the problems of access and inequality for the minority and working class disadvantaged (stasis). But the matter goes further as we shall see in what follows.

Movement and Stasis. We must try to understand the context of this movement in stasis, this dizziness, this uncertainty that W.B. Yeats defines in "The Second Coming". . . . "the best lacked all conviction" (1994, p. 154). BUT now the worst are in power. The neoconservatives have gained a pervasive hold on society and leaving no child behind in their perverse project of neo-liberalism—the unseemly handing over of schools to private enterprise. If I may be permitted, I will step back for a moment from Carlson's specific reading of education and try to speak to the context in which we operate in schools and the university, the ordeal of intellectual labor and the labor process of teaching and learning in general. I want to talk about the context, the network of new relations that define our times. This is the context of neoliberalism and the specific interpretation of globalization and multiplicity in the modern world undertaken by neoliberal policy-makers. It is a context that has generated a set of dynamics that has transformed modern subject relations to the state and society in the twenty-first century. It is a world marked by movement and stasis but not entirely in the sense that is often invoked in the literature on globalization as a kind of technological determinism and associated binarism. By "binarism" I refer to the oppositional logic that is captured in, say, Zygmunt Bauman's couplet "tourist" versus "vagabond" or Anthony Giddens' "radicals" versus "skeptics" (Bauman, 1998; Giddens, 2003). These binary oppositions, among other things, suggest that those with access to technology are on the move, free of containment and those who are pre-or under-technologized are marching in place, marking time, while the world passes them by. Of course there is some truth to this. But what I want to identify most urgently here is the severe and deepening loss of theodicy and meaning in the educational enterprise generally—a process that is reflected in the broad tendency of neoliberalism to compromise educational institutions and practices.

But these neoliberal logics are even broader in reach and implications. Indeed, it might be argued that instead of the end to the game of totalization announced in the declarations of the *New York Times* article I quoted earlier, that we, late-modern citizens, more than ever, are being seduced, inducted, incorporated into ever-larger discursive systems and materialisms, led forward as much by the state as by multinational capital. We are being seduced by large-scale programs of re-narration of affiliation and exclusion holding out the possibility of identity makeovers, place swapping, and material exchange and immaterial rewards. Our daily lives are being colonized by massive systems of textual production that transgress the boundary lines between private and public life and that seem to have at the same time the ambition to conquer all of global and planetary space. Here, I am talking about the US continuing war on terrorism (even after Osama), new inter-operable information technologies, such as digital face and eye-retina scanning and recognition technology, aimed at gaining fuller access to human characteristics for the purpose of sorting human bodies in a vast domestic and international project of surveillance and human capital extraction, the rise of state-driven post-Fordist authoritarianism in the name of national security, the human genome project and the dream of human perfectability, the aspirations of corporate American sports like basketball and football to conquer the globe, one brand name after another, and one world series at a time (Gates, 2011; King, 2008; Roman, 2005).

How might we understand these developments? How might we theorize their conjunctural relationship to educational institutions? What general organizing principles or terms might we deploy to both sum up these developments and to identify their dominant vectors? It is not enough, as Carson suggests, to offer vain formulations at the level of abstraction of the mode of production. We need to pay proper attention to patterns of historical incorporation and the work of culture and identification practices in specific institutional contexts and programmatic applications.

Neo-liberal Re-articulations

One dominant (but under-diagnosed) complex or network of relations affecting schools can be conceptualized and identified as neo-liberal re-articulations and transformations to which I called attention in the early part of this essay. It is this context of neoliberal hegemony and moral and cultural leadership itself and its relationship to what Michel Foucault has called government (that is, the regulation of conduct of populations through systems of administration and self management of everyday life) that we must examine in order to better understand the specific impact of current political, cultural and economic forces on education, understood here as the promise of the public good.

I want to talk briefly about neo-liberalism in greater detail than I have so far, specifically its particular interpretation of globalization and multiplicity and its transforming impact on the organization of knowledge in education. How do we define neoliberalism? I want to talk about two aspects of this dynamic complex of relations. First, I want to talk about neo-liberalism's relationship to globalization. Second, I will discuss neoliberalism's re-orientation of domestic and public space and institutions of confinement such as schooling.

One way of talking about neo-liberalism as it has arisen in the social science and political science literatures of the last two decades has been to define neo-liberalism in terms of the universalization of the enterprise ethic (Comaroff & Comaroff, 2009). This is to see its logics in the context of multinational capital's strategic translation of globalization (globalization is understood here as the rapid intensification of migration, the amplification of electronic mediation, the movement of economic and cultural capital across borders, and the deepening and stretching of interconnectivity all around the world) and the usurpation of the role of the state in a broad range of economic and political affairs. Within this framework, neoliberalism is simply a new form of liberalism that marks the emergence of the New Right and its distinctive fusion of political and economic formulas—a fusion that integrates eighteenth and nineteenth century notions of free market and laissez-faire into potentially all aspects of contemporary life (Ong, 2006). This is marked by policies, since Reagan and Thatcher, of the extensive deregulation of the economy and markets, the overturning of Keynesianism and the disinvestment of the state in projects of welfare for the poor and the common good. Despite the brutal financial crisis, this is still the working policy commonsense of the dominant powers as well as post-development states such as Taiwan, Korea, and India. There is, then, the systematic reordering of state priorities in which the state's accumulation function is predominant in the modern system of rule at a distance, subordinating the processes of legitimation and democratic involvement of citizens. Of course, many corporations like Nike, Starbucks, and Disney have appropriated Keynesianism, rearticulating it as an ironic substance or residue in the form of philanthropy and thereby morphing it into the role of state-like promoters of ecumenical feel good affiliation, self-help forms of involvement in community, and so forth. Disney, in fact has for over a decade now, provided a super model of community ("of the way we are supposed to be") in the form of the fabricated town, Celebration—the new urbanist heaven in Central Florida, that Andrew Ross insightfully calls "privatopia" (Ross, 1999, p. 228). For as the state disinvests in the public sphere, corporations move in to redefine community in neo-liberal terms absorbing philanthropy into cause-related marketing and the building of new synergies and brand share. From this development, if we were, then, to follow the ideological direction of, say, Teach for America and or the Chicago's Commercial Club (for example, their manifesto *Still Left Behind [2009]*) e.g., by this logic, IBM and Xerox and, earlier, Ross Perot can do more for schools than the government or the state or we the intellectuals in the university—"the bright but useless ones."

The second logic of neo-liberalism, I want to argue, operates decisively through culture, at the point of integration of modern subjects into social institutions and the organization and architecture of domestic and institutional space. Here, neoliberalism strategically addresses the new post-Fordist subject, the new cultural citizen of mobile privatization who exists within the self-contained unit of the home or the school, and so forth and who mediates his or her environment through the new smart technologies of the day driven by computer hardware and software—the smart Zenith TV and DVR that we can program, the remote control, the cell phone, video/digital games (hand-held or console based), and the ultimate phenomenon of moving enclosure since 9/11 of the flag car as the symbol of the nation rid-ing on the back of the mobile patriotic citizen—the moving ground so to speak of a popular post-Fordist authoritarianism. These new technologies have helped to elaborate a discursive order and rearticulate time, duration, and the rhythm of production, consumption and leisure in the constitution of our everyday lives—mobile and sedentary. Further, the mobile digital gadgets, such as the cell phone, the GPS in our car navigation system, the lap-top with wireless internet connection, the iPod, iPad and so forth, which are already widespread in the US and throughout the metropolitan world, complicate the existing negotiation process between movement and stasis by allowing continuous streams of electronic navigation, communication, transaction, entertainment and information retrieval for people on the move. In these digital appliances, the representation of others and their environments looks simple, effortless, fast and shape-shifting. Because these devices operate in networks of digital enclosure and provide prompt information about our environments and others, users require less direct contact with their fellow citizens and need to take into account less and less of a meaningful relation to their locales and environments.

In the context of what Raymond Williams called "mobile-privatization" (1974/1992, p. 20), we now have the ability to look out from within, to be vicariously active, to move while staying in place, to intercourse with the world while hiding in the light and in a state of retreat. To these technologies, we can add the surveillance camera, the fax machine, the scanning machine, the PC, the cable network uplinks in the school that allow us the illusion of control over our physical environment while we monitor, often ourselves, from the safety inside. It is through these new social densities associated with electronic mediation, computerization, and the new digitally and genetically driven biometric technologies of surveillance, identification and verification that neoliberalism operates as a supported master code translating the new terminologies of the Age associated with globalization, movement and stasis, place-swapping and identity make-overs.

The Unmaking and Remaking of Schooling

The university and schooling are not inured from these dynamic material practices associated with neoliberalism. Indeed, neoliberalism has a privileged position in the educational field "as a technique of government, regulation and social control" (Silva, 1994, as cited in Gandin, 2007, p. 182). It is not surprising, then, that the market ethic has been introduced into the educational arena, replacing the public good ethic (Gandin, 2007). Education, Alex Molnar (1996) points out, has been colonized by marketization; school reforms are being discussed in commercial terms, and expressions such as "future consumers," "future workers," and "future taxpayers" are being used in reference to children and school youth. In sum, education is seen "as a product to be evaluated for its economic utility and as a commodity to be bought and sold like anything else in the 'free market'" (Apple, 2000, p. 111).

The subordination of education to economic ends is evident when one looks at recent educational reform initiatives—not only in the U.S., but internationally— whose main rationales are arguments favoring a tighter link between "education and the wider project of 'meeting the needs of the economy'" (Apple, 2006, p. 23). To this end, neoliberal efforts in education aim at reorganizing schooling so the needs of the local and global economy are met by producing human capital sufficiently skilled, adaptable and flexible. In addition to conceiving schools as producers of "human capital," neoliberalism has an equally critical cultural agenda: "It involves radically changing how we think of ourselves and what the goals of schooling should be" (Apple, 2006, p. 23). Under neoliberalism, then, educational institutions are expected to form students for market competition by transforming them into entrepreneurs and to convince them that "competition is a natural phenomenon, with winners and losers" (Gandin, 2007, p. 182).

Nancy Cantor and Paul Courant (2003), for instance, identify three features of neo-liberalism or the universalization of the enterprise ethic that are transforming the life world of schools and universities understood as institutions for the optimization of the public good and molding culture, economy, politics, and ideology into a template of a new educational order. These three neoliberal tendencies can be identified as follows. First, there is virtualization or the process of managing the university as an on-line community and a paperless world. Second, there is vocationalization or the insistence on consistently derived and derivable returns on education. The third tendency in the process of educational neoliberalization is the practice of fiscalization or bottom-line budgeting as the ruling measure of viability of all departments and units of educational institutions. Cantor and Courant understand these trends as fiscal and budgetary dilemmas, I see them here as deeply cultural in the sense that they set off particular configurations of interests, needs, desires, beliefs, and system wide behavioral practices in the life world of universities and schools with respect to ethos and milieu and the organization of knowledge, the regulation of individual and group relations in these institutions, and the sorting and sifting of social and cultural capital.

Virtualization

The first trend that I will discuss here is *virtualization*. Virtualization of educational processes involves the rise and intensification of virtual interactions in more and more of our institutional activities. It is driven forward by our on-line proclivity towards information craving, speed, efficiency, optimization and maximization that now as a set of dispositions is rapidly displacing face-to-face interaction and embodied decision making and community feeling in our institutions. Education in its virtualizing tendency is susceptible to the "Internet paradox"—the other side of deregulation as the centrifugal logic of neo-liberalism and laissez-faire—that is, "dependence on a social technology that often breeds social isolation" and insulation of knowledge and disciplines as much as it facilitates interaction (Cantor and Courant, 2003, p. 5). We now know more about each other's group and society by the proxy of images than by experiential encounter. This is not a Luddite argument, it is as Cantor and Courant suggest the proper concern that "the delivery of education solely on the Internet may rob students of the experience of the clash of ideas out of which emerges empathy with others and a desire for compromise" (p. 5). The arrival of the Internet for some heralded yet another clean technological break with the past. But unlike car manufacturers and fashion designers, we in the humanities and in the social sciences need the past for more than nostalgia and the ephemeral. We cannot jettison it ruthlessly bringing on stream the latest gizmo or style. We need the past to study it to better understand the present and the future. This raises questions bearing upon the status and nature of the contemporary public sphere and the fact that we now seem to have a multiplicity of strongly insulated publics in educational institutions in the Nancy Fraser sense—publics where conversations are shorn off by essentialism and tribalism (Fraser, 1997). Virtualization has not lived up to the promise of universalizing or flattening out our particularisms. Indeed, it may have helped to heighten these latter tendencies, breeding new cultural nationalisms that glow in the dark—each man turning his key of endless data, in his own door, to use the imagery of T.S. Eliot ("And each man fixes his eyes before his feet" [Eliot, 1954, p. 53]) . The fact is that virtualization within the university setting, as an example, has been more often than not dominated by the will to power of university administrations, which now use "the" network for information and image control, surveillance, unidirectional communication, edicts and coercive demands on actors lower down. The promise of openness of the virtual network capacity has been replaced too often by the elaboration of defensive shields sealing off administrative personnel from the rest of campus.

Vocationalization

In the neoliberal scenario, vocationalization is now a ruling logic in curricular arrangements and the overall strategic calculation of educational actors (Ong, 2006). And, "education is positioned in terms of its relationship with the economy and broader state policy [where] an instrumental rationality underlies education policy discourse, manifested in the pervasive rhetoric and values of the market in the representation of educational participants and practices" (Mulderrig, 2003, as cited in Hill, 2003, p. 7). This commodification of education is further advanced by policy documents that foreground the relevance of lifelong learning,[1] a key component developing *workforce versatility* which accommodates the needs of flexible production[2] and "ensures that responsibility for employment tenure belongs to individuals themselves, ensures the possibility for companies to offset responsibility for social and fiscal payments, and enhances the freedom of business in a global environment." (Olssen, 2006, p. 222). In this context, information replaces knowledge in the interests of an ever-changing system of production and educational goals are assessed in terms of the quantitative appropriation of skills and information for the labor market. We are living in the era of a new Taylorism in which knowledge production processes are being bent out of shape for the purposes of information delivery, strategic planning, and value extraction from culture (see for example the strategic plan on globalization of the University of Illinois at Chicago [2006]) At all levels, education has become a market commodity. As Masao Miyoshi (1998) warned us a decade or so ago, in his essay "'Globalization' and the University," transnational capital has overridden the line between the university and its outside enveloping its sinews, reorganizing its infrastructures, closing the distance between education and economy in the privatization of the organization of knowledge. As Miyoshi maintains, university students and administration seek to empty the rigorous and complex content out of curricular knowledge in the humanities, re-labeling it and putting it up for sale. The goal is to maximize returns on investment as in the marketplace: "Higher education is now up to the administrators. And, sooner or later, research too, will be up to the administrators. Of course, we know that administrators are merely in the service of the managers of the society and the economy who exercise their supreme authority vested in the transnational corporate world" (Miyoshi, 1998, p. 267).

This investment in the enterprise ethic within the university has meant that on many campuses there has been an eroding of support for humanities and humanistic social sciences. For example, as Cantor and Courant have pointed out, "representation in superior humanities programs at public universities has dramatically declined between 1982 [and the present]" (2003, p. 5). But, it is precisely these courses that provide the best preparation for democratic citizenship and critical thinking. And, it is indeed the case, that humanities disciplines have consistently produced forms of knowledge that operate as a check on the worst aspects of societal modernization and industrialization. In undertaking our deep investment in the enterprise ethic, we have sacrificed this critical investment in knowledge for taking the pig to the market. One is reminded here of the *Ohio State Journal* of 1870, whose editorial cautioned educators and professionals at the time of the founding of Ohio State University: "[. . .].the lawyer who knows nothing but law, the physician who knows nothing but medicine, and the farmer who knows nothing but farming are on par with each other. They are all alike starved and indigent in the requirement of true culture" (Alexis Cope quoted in Cantor & Courant, 2003, p. 6). In regards to schooling, Richard Hatcher (2001) claims that global capitalism needs to ensure that schools produce effective and flexible workers and that they "subordinate to the personality, ideological and economic requirements of Capital" (Hill, 2003, p. 8). To guarantee this, neoliberalism creates institutional practices and rewards for enforcing the market rationale and competition in education.[3] For instance, World Bank loans given to countries have been conditioned on the implementation of school reforms in line with neoliberal formulations.[4] Similarly, the No Child Left Behind Act in the U.S. contributes to the support of a "global" neoliberal agenda pushing towards an increased presence of market dynamics in education by rewarding managerial practices in schools and by setting rigid standards they should meet in order to receive financial support.

Fiscalization

The latter (vocationalization) is closely tied to the process of fiscalization of the university and schooling, the application of "bottom-line" budgeting, and the proliferation of surveillance and control mechanisms—compulsory and nationally monitored tests, publication of schools and districts performances and "policy emphasis on 'shaming and naming', closing, or privatizing 'failing' schools" (Hill, 2001)—that are arising everywhere as illustrated by the "No Child Left Behind Act" and the "Race to The Top" initiatives of the Obama administration. As we live in a context of chronic budgetary crisis within the economy generally and within education, there are increasing demands for accountability and fiscalization. For instance, in view of the strict limits placed by the state on public funding, income generation has become an increasingly powerful imperative among tertiary institutions (Henkel, 2005). Bruce Johnstone (2002) states that governments worldwide have to supplement their revenues, "not only with 'cost sharing,' but also with sale of faculty services, sale or lease of university facilities, vigorous pursuit of grants and contracts, and fund raising" (p. 4). Concomitantly, research agendas are being made the target of rationalization as public funding in universities becomes oriented to "strategic" researches (Rip, 1997), that are "likely to make at least a background contribution to the solution of recognized current or future practical problems" (Henkel, 2005, p. 160). From this perspective, basic or "pure science" may receive funding only if it is responsive to socially and economically strategic needs. Besides, "the pathway to innovation is now seen as often beginning in industry rather than the university and as entailing more variable, complex, uncertain and interactive patterns of communication and collaboration between the university and industry" (Henkel, 2005, p. 160). More importantly, these institutional constraints are "an insidious way of lessening academic independence" (Musselin, 2005, p. 146) as the nature of the relationship between universities and academics changes under the influence of a managerial perspective that dictates criteria and norms to be applied to academic activities, and ensures that these criteria and norms are respected.

Pervasive measuring, accountability and feasibility pressures have forced the humanistic disciplines to be on the defensive. Neo-liberals have proven themselves particularly adept at blurring and bending political, ideological, cultural faiths to achieve means-end rationalities. We live in such a time on campuses across the United States in which the pressure of rationalization has placed humanistic programs in doubt, forcing them to establish new codes and rules of the game. Programs, particularly in the humanities disciplines, that will never be profit-making enterprises are feeling the pressure of the bottom line. We are trapped in the marketplace logic of student credit hours, the tallying of instructional units, and sponsored research objectives. More teaching, less time off, less pay. Our relevant models are now the business school, the law school, the natural sciences, wherever and however money is to be made there lies self-justification and validation. The immediate casualties are interdisciplinary research, collaborative writing projects, and innovative curricula projects. The more long-term casualties are our students who now see us less as models of thoughtfulness and more as purveyors of knowledge fast food. Likewise, disinvestment in public schooling has "destabilized and weakened its very own immunities as a secular institution in protecting and developing the public good" (Paraskeva, 2007, p. 154). Scholars such as Jurjo Torres Santomé (2001), Michael Apple (2003), among many others, concur, pointing to the ill-fated effects of disinvesting in public education (i.e., deficient infrastructure, lack of material and intellectual resources, low-quality teacher education programs, etc.). In João Paraskeva's view, state disinvestments in public education acted as the needed sign "for the market forces to hijack public schooling from a public social domain to an economic private sphere" (p. 154). Ultimately, education as a public good is being compromised to privatization. Alongside all of these transformations, neoliberalism in education functions by curtailing any kind of critical thinking. Education is reorganized in a way that intends to produce skilled and flexible workers but in so doing hinders a critical engagement with their reality (Harvey, 2000, 2010).

Conclusion

As I have sought to demonstrate the tremendously important discussion of cognitive capitalism generated in this volume must be directly turned on to the topic of education transformations taking place in the new century. A fundamental nexus of associations configure around the metanarratives of neoliberalism and globalization and their existential extension into the educational life of present-day stakeholders and social agents in the school and university settings. Neoliberalism has reoriented educational institutions and has given a new meaning to learning and the goals of education formulated around strategic calculations. Equally important, "the commodification of education rules out the very critical freedom and academic rigor which education requires to be more than indoctrination" (McMurtry, 1991, p. 215). As Jurjo Torres Santomé (2007) asserts, the school curriculum conveys information "that neither reveals nor problematizes the structural causes underlying the cases it appears to denounce" (p. 12). The lack of sustained critical approaches to addressing social issues in educational institutions prevents students from realizing their human potential for the recreation of their own life world. Neoliberalism in education not only compresses critical spaces, but also hinders the likelihood of building democratic school communities as competition "stymies the potential for system-wide policies designed to equalize opportunities" (Marginson, 2006).

Having said all of this about neoliberalism and education, then, our greatest challenge is to create the conditions "for solidaristic, movement-style relations" (Marginson, 2006, p. 219) and counteracting a neoliberal language that "destroys social responsibility and critique, that invites a mindless, consumer-oriented individualism to flourish, and kills off conscience" (Davies, 2005, p. 6). We need to stop the neoliberal appropriation of education by safeguarding the autonomy of the teaching learning process, the autonomy of intellectual production, and the fostering of the reproduction of critical scholars. We need to work toward conditions for widening access for those severely disadvantaged by the current formulas and who are being shunted around from bad educational options to worse ones. Educational discourses and practices need to be reconnected to a progressive emancipatory project based upon solidarity and social justice. These are the central issues at stake even as we set out with Carlson from the "safe harbors" of educational practice and custom, seeking movement in the context of constraint and refusing the stasis of administrative containment and neoliberal myopia. As we struggle to understand the logics of cognitive capitalism as they work back within the educational enterprise itself, we must be mindful of Walter Benjamin's caveat: "There is no document of culture . . . which is not at the same time a document of barbarism" (Benjamin, 2008, p. 124). We must say "no" to the excessive Taylorism and instrumentalism that now crowd out reflexivity and intellectual autonomy in schooling and the academy. We must strive for the harnessing of technology to the worthy purposes of expanding critical access and critical communication in education, extending the vital work of embattled transformative interpretive communities in schooling and the university.

Notes

1. As Bert Lambeir (2005) argues, "lifelong learning is the magic spell in the discourse of educational and economic policymakers, as well as in that of the practitioners of both domains" (p. 350).
2. In relation to this, some scholars contend that the discourses on lifelong learning represent 'a form of biopower' (Marshall, 1995) or self-regulation aiming at reducing the 'time lag' between individual skills and economic and technological innovation (Tuschling and Engemann, 2006, as cited in Olssen, 2006).
3. A similar argument is found in Wendy Brown's (2003) work, where she posits that neoliberalism involves a normative rather than ontological claim about the pervasiveness of economic rationality and takes as its task the development, dissemination, and institutionalization of such rationality.
4. In relation to this, Phillip Jones' (1992) book provides a thorough description of the World Bank's instrumental role in promoting Western ideas about how education and the economy are—or should be—related. Terms such as "external inducement" (Ikenberry, 1990), "direct coercive transfer" (Dolowitz & Marsh, 1996), "exporting ideas" or "policy pusher" (Nedley, 2007) serve to illustrate the promotion of fiscal discipline and other neoliberal measures in poorer countries through donor agencies that condition their loans to the adoption of such measures. For instance, the World Bank demands curricular and structural change in education when it provides loans alleging that those changes contribute to rationalizing and equalizing the delivery of this social good (Weiner, 2005).

References

Apple, M. (2000). *Official knowledge: Democratic education in a conservative age.* New York: Routledge.

Apple, M. (2003). *The state and the politics of knowledge.* New York: Routledge.

Apple, M. (2006). Understanding and interrupting neoliberalism and neoconservatism in education. *Pedagogies: An International Journal, 1*(1), 21–26.

Ball, S. (1999). Performativity and fragmentation in postmodern schooling, in J. Carter (Ed.) *Postmodernity and the fragmentation of welfare.* London: Routledge.

Bansel, P. (2007). Subjects of choice and lifelong learning. *International Journal of Qualitative Studies in Education, 20*(3), 283–300.

Barry, A., Osborne, T. and Rose, N. (1996). *Foucault and Political Reason: Liberalism, neoliberalism and rationalities of government.* Chicago: University of Chicago Press.

Bauman, Z. (1998). *Globalization: The human consequences.* New York: Columbia University Press.

Bauman, Z. (2000). Liquid modernity. Cambridge, UK: Polity.

Bauman, Z. (2009) Does ethics have a chance in a world of consumers? Cambridge, MA.: Harvard University Press.

Benjamin, W. (2008). Eduard Fuchs, collector and historian. In, M. Jennings et al. (Eds), *The Work of Art in the Age of Technological Reproducibility and Other Writings on Media.* (pp. 116–157). Cambridge, MA.: Harvard University Press.

Bourdieu, P. (1998). *Acts of resistance: Against the tyranny of the market.* New York: The New Press.

Brown, W. (2003) Neo-liberalism and the end of liberal democracy. *Theory and Event, 7*(1), 1–25.

Cambridge, E. (2006). Relationships among globalization, development, primary education spending and brain drain in the developing world. 2007. *The Heinz School Review*, 3 (1) .

Cantor, N. and Courant, P. (2003). Scrounging for resources: Reflections on the whys and wherefores of higher education finance. In, *New Directions for Institutional Research* no. 119, pp. 3–12.

Carlson, D. (2002). *Leaving Safe Harbors: Toward a New Progressivism in American Education and Public Life.* New York: Routledge.

Chicago Commercial Club (2009). *Still left behind. Chicago:* Chicago Commercial Club.

Clarke, J. (2007). Subordinating the social? Neo-liberalism and the remaking of welfare capitalism. *Cultural Studies, 21*(6), 974–987.

Comaroff, J., & Comaroff, J. L. (2009). *Ethnicity Inc.* Chicago: University of Chicago Press.

Davies, B., & Bansel, P. (2007). Neoliberalism and education. *International Journal of Qualitative Studies in Education, 20*(3), 247–259.

Davis, D. A. (2007). Narrating the mute: Racializing and racism in a neoliberal moment. *Souls: A Critical Journal of Black Politics, Culture and Society, 9*(4), 346–360.

Dolowitz, D. and Marsh, D. (1996). Who learns from whom: A review of the policy transfer literature. *Political Studies,* 44(2), 343–57.

Du Gay, P. (1996). Organizing identity: Entrepreneurial governance and public management. In S. Hall & P. du Gay (Eds.), *Questions of cultural identity* (pp. 151–169). London: Sage Publications.

Duggan, L. (2003). *The twilight of equality? Neoliberalism, cultural politics, and the attack on democracy.* Boston: Beacon.

Eakin, E. (2003). The latest theory is that theory doesn't matter. *New York Times.* (Art and Ideas, Section D), April 19, p. 9.

Eliot, T.S. (1954). The wasteland I.: The burial of the dead. In, T.S. Eliot, *Selected Poems* (pp. 51–53). London: Faber and Faber.

Fitzsimons, P. (2002). Neoliberalism and education: The autonomous chooser. *Radical Pedagogy,* retrieved on 6/12/07 from: http://radicalpedagogy.icaap.org/content/issue4_2/04_fitzsimons.html

Foucault, M. (1982). The subject and power. Afterword. In H. L. Dreyfus and P. Rabinow *Michel Foucault: Beyond structuralism and hermeneutics*. Chicago: University of Chicago Press, pp. 208–226.

Fraser, N. (1997). Justice interruptus: Critical reflections on the "postsocialist" condition. New York: Routledge.

Gabbard, D. A. (2003). Education IS enforcement: The centrality of compulsory schooling in market societies, in K. Saltman & D. A. Gabbard (Eds.) *Education as enforcement: The militarization and corporatization of schools*. London: Routledge Falmer, pp. 61–80.

Gandin, L. A. (2007). The construction of the citizen school project as an alternative to neoliberal educational policies. *Policy Futures in Education, 5*(2), 179–193).

Gates, K. (2011). *Our biometric future: Facial recognition technology and the culture of surveillance*. New York: New York University Press.

Giddens, A. (2003). *Runaway world: How globalization is reshaping our lives*. New York: Routledge.

Gordon, C. (1991). Governmental rationality: An introduction, in Graham Burchell, Colin Gordon and Peter Miller (Eds.) *The Foucault Effect: Studies in Governmentality*, Hemel Hempstead: Harvester Wheatsheaf, 1–51.

Griffin, P. (2007). Sexing the economy in a neo-liberal world order: Neo-liberal discourse and the (re)production of heteronormative heterosexuality. *British Journal of Politics & International Relations, 9*(2), 220–238.

Habermas, J. (1992). *The structural transformation of the public sphere*. Cambridge, MA.: M.I.T. Press.

Harvey, D. (2000). *Spaces of hope*. Berkeley: University of California Press.

Harvey, D. (2010). *The enigma of capital and the crises of capitalism*. New York: Oxford.

Hatcher, R. (2001). Getting down to business: Schooling in the globalized economy. *Education and Social Justice, 3*(2), 45–59.

Henkel, M. (2005). Academic identity and autonomy in a changing policy, *Environment, Higher Education* 49: 155–176.

Hill, D. (2007). Critical teacher education, new labour, and the global project of neoliberal capital. *Policy Futures in Education, 5*(2), 204–225.

Hill, D. (2004). Books, banks, and bullets: Controlling our minds—the global project of imperialistic and militaristic neo-liberalism and its effect on education policy. *Policy Futures in Education, 2*(3), 504–522.

Hill, D. (2003). Global neo-liberalism, the deformation of education and resistance. *Journal of Critical Educational Policy Studies, 1*(1), 1–26.

Hill, D. (2001). State theory and the neo-liberal reconstruction of schooling and teacher education: A structuralist neo-Marxist critique of postmodernist, quasi-postmodernist, and culturalist neo-Marxist theory. *British Journal of Sociology of Education, 22*(1), 135–155.

Ikenberry, G. J. (1990). The international spread of privatization policies: Inducements, learning and 'Policy Band wagoning', in E. Suleiman and J. Waterbury (Eds.) *The Political Economy of Public Sector Reform and Privatization*. Boulder, CO: Westview Press.

Johnstone, D. B. (2002). *Chinese higher education in the context of the worldwide university agenda*, adapted paper from an address to the Chinese and Foreign University Presidents Forum held in Beijing, PCR, July 2002.

Jones, P. W. (1992). *World Bank financing of education: Lending, learning and development.* London-New York: Routledge.

King, S. (2011). *Pink Ribbons, Inc.: Breast cancer and the politics of philanthropy.* Minneapolis: University of Minnesota Press.

Klees, S. J. (2002). Privatization and neo-liberalism: Ideology and evidence in rhetorical reforms. *Current Issues in Comparative Education, 1* (2), 19–26.

Klein, N. (2007). *The shock doctrine: The rise and fall of disaster capitalism.* Toronto: Knopf.

Klein, N. (2009). *No logo.* New York: Picador.

Kurtz, M. J. (2004). The dilemmas of democracy in the open economy: Lessons from Latin America. *World Politics, 56,* 262–302.

Lambeir, B. (2005). Education as liberation: The politics and techniques of lifelong learning. *Educational Philosophy and Theory, 37*(3), 349–356.

Lemke, T. (2001). The birth of bio-politics: Michel Foucault's lecture at the College de France on neo-liberal governmentality. *Economy and Society, 30*(2), 190–207.

Lipman, P. & Hursh, D. (2007). Renaissance 2010: The reassertion of ruling-class power through neoliberal policies in Chicago. *Policy Futures in Education, 5*(2), 160–178.

Lipsitz, G. (2004). *Locked here on this earth: Spatial politics and black expressive culture.* University of California at Santa Cruz. Unpublished Paper.

Mahoney, P. & Hextall, I. (2000). *Reconstructing teaching standards, performance and accountability.* London: Routledge Falmer.

Marginson, S. (2006). Engaging democratic education in the neoliberal age. *Educational Theory, 56*(2), 205–219.

McChesney, R. (1999). *Profits over people: Neoliberalism and global order.* New York: Seven Stories Press.

McLaren, P., Martin, G., Farahmandpur, R. & Jaramillo, N. (2005). *Teaching against global capitalism and the new imperialism.* Lanham: Rowman & Littlefield.

McMurtry, J. (1991). Education and the market model. *Journal of the Philosophy of Education, 25*(2), 209–217.

Melville, H. (1851/2009). *Moby Dick.* London: Collector's Library.

Miyoshi, M. (1998). "Globalization," culture and the university. In, F. Jameson and Masao Miyoshi (Eds.), *The cultures of globalization.* Durham, NC: Duke University Press.

Molnar, A. (1996). *Giving kids the business: The commercialization of America's schools.* Boulder, CO: Westview Press.

Mulderrig, J. 2003. Consuming education: A critical discourse analysis of social actors in New Labour's education policy, *Journal for Critical Education Policy Studies,* 1(1). Available at www.jceps.com.

Musselin, C. (2005). European academic labor markets in transition. *Higher Education, 49*(1/2), 135–154.

Nairn, K., & Higgins, J. (2007). New Zealand's neoliberal generation: Tracing discourses of economic (ir)rationality. *International Journal of Qualitative Studies in Education, 20*(3), 261–281.

Nedley, A. (2007). Policy transfer and the developing-country experience gap: Taking a southern perspective. Retrieved on 6/3/07 from http://www.york.ac.uk/depts/poli/news/sem3esrc/nedley.pdf.

Olssen, M. (2006). Understanding the mechanisms of neoliberal control: Lifelong learning, flexibility and knowledge capitalism. *International Journal of Lifelong Education* 25(3), pp. 213–230.

Ong, A. (2006). *Neoliberalism as exception: Mutations in citizenship and sovereignty*. Durham, NC: Duke University Press.

Ortner, S. (1994). Theory in anthropology since the sixties. In, N.B. Dirks, G. Eley, and S. Ortner (Eds.), *Culture/Power/History: A Reader in Contemporary Social Theory*. Princeton, NJ: Princeton University.

Paraskeva, J. M. (2007). Kidnapping public schooling: Perversion and normalization of the discursive bases within the epicenter of New Right educational policies. *Policy Futures in Education, 5*(2), p. 137–159.

Quiroz, P. A. (2007). *Adoption in a color-blind society*. Lanham, MD: Rowman & Littlefield.

Rip, A. (1997). A cognitive approach to relevance of science. *Social Science Information, 36(4), 615–640*.

Robertson, S., & Dale, R. (2002). Local states of emergency: The contradictions of neo-liberal governance in education in New Zealand. *British Journal of Sociology of Education, 23*(3), 463–482.

Roman, L. (2005). States of insecurity: Cold war memory, "global citizenship" and its discontents. In C. McCarthy, W. Crichlow, G. Dimitriadis, & N. Dolby (Eds). *Race, Identity and Representation in Education*. New York: Routledge

Ross, A. (1999). *The celebration chronicles: Life, liberty and the pursuit of property values in Disney's new town*. New York: Ballantine Books.

Schiller, D. (2003). Digital capitalism: A status report on the corporate commonwealth of information. In A. Valdivia (Ed.), A companion to media studies (pp. 137–156). Oxford, U.K.: Blackwell.

Schiller, D. (2010). How to think about information. Urbana: University of Illinois Press.

Sennett, R. (1998). The corrosion of character. New York: Norton.

Sennett, R. (2006). The culture of new capitalism. New Haven, CT: Yale University Press.

Sennett, R. (2008). The craftsman. New Haven, CT: Yale University Press.

Silva, T. T. (1994). 'A nova direita e as transformações na pedagogia da política e na política da pedagogia', in T. T. Silva and A A. Gentili (Eds.), *Neoliberalismo, qualidade total e educação: visões críticas*. Petrópolis: Vozes.

Stiglitz, J. (2002). *Globalization and its discontents*. London: Penguin.

Thomas, C. (2001). Global governance, development and human security: Exploring the links. *Third World Quarterly, 22*(2), 159–175.

Torres Santomé, J. (2001). *Educación en tiempos de neoliberalismo*. Madrid: Morata.

Tuschling, A., & Engemann, C. (2006). From education to lifelong learning: The emerging regime of learning in the European Union. *Educational Philosophy and Theory 38* (4):451–469.

U.S. Department of Education, Office of Elementary and Secondary Education (2002). *No Child Left Behind: a desk reference*. Washington, D.C.: U.S. Department of Education.

University of Illinois-Chicago (2006, June 30). Access to excellence. Retrieved from http://www.uillinois.edu/strategicplan/plans/UIC_Strategic_Plan_v1.3_6.30.06.pdf.

Weiner, L. (2005). Neoliberalism, teacher unionism, and the future of public education. *New Politics, 38*, X, no. 2. Retrieved on 6/3/07 from http://www.wpunj.edu/newpol/issue38/wein-cr38.htm.

Whitty, G., Power, S. and Halpin, D. (1998). *Devolution and choice in education: The school, the state and the market.* Buckingham: Open University Press.

Williams, R. (1974/1992). *Television: Technology as cultural form.* New York: Schocken Books.

Yeats, W.B. (1994). *Michael Robartes and the Dancer: Manuscript Materials.* Ithaca, NY: Cornell University.

Contributors

Antonio Negri is an Italian Marxist philosopher. He is known for his activist struggles and books he has written with Michael Hardt. Some of his very widely acclaimed books include *Empire, Multitude: War and Democracy in the Age of Empire,* and *Commonwealth Marx beyond Marx: Lessons on Grundrisse* among many others.

Timothy Brennan works on the relationship between comparative literature, world literature, and global English. He is a member of both the departments of Cultural Studies & Comparative Literature and English, and is affiliated with the Institute for Global Studies and the Institute for Advanced Studies. His essays and course offerings deal with issues of intellectual history, cultural theory, the Marxist and phenomenological traditions, the avant-gardes, theories of colonialism and imperialism, problems of translation, and popular music. He is the author most recently of *Secular Devotion: Afro-Latin Music and Imperial Jazz* (Verso, 2008), and he edited, introduced, and co-translated the first English edition of Alejo Carpentier's classic study, *Music in Cuba* (U of Minnesota P, 2001). His other recent books include *Wars of Position: The Cultural Politics of Left and Right* (Columbia UP, 2006), *Empire in Different Colors* (Revolver, 2007) and *At Home in the World: Cosmopolitanism Now* (Harvard UP, 1997). In 1989, he received an award from the Council of Editors of Learned Journals for his special issue of Modern Fiction Studies titled "Narratives of Colonial Resistance" (1989). Professor Brennan is a recipient of fellowships from the Fulbright Foundation, the National

Endowment for the Humanities, the American Council of Learned Societies, and the McKnight foundation and has taught at Cornell University, the University of Michigan, and the Humboldt University (Berlin). His essays have been translated into Spanish, Italian, Swedish, Polish, Turkish, French, Slovenian, Hungarian, and Japanese, and his writing has appeared in a variety of publications including The Nation, The Times Literary Supplement, *The Cambridge Companion to Postcolonial Studies, Critical Inquiry, The South Atlantic Quarterly, Public Culture, The Chronicle of Higher Education* and the *London Review of Books*.

Jonathan Beller is Professor of Humanities and Media Studies and Critical and Visual Studies and Director of the Graduate Program in Media Studies at The Pratt Institute. His work focuses on the relationship between the rise of industrial and digital forms of imaging and the transformation of political economy, discourse function and the value-form. His books include *The Cinematic Mode of Production: Attention Economy and the Society of the Spectacle* (Dartmouth/UPNE 2006) and *Acquiring Eyes: Philippine Visuality, Nationalist Struggle and the World-Media System* (Ateneo de Manila University Press, 2006). Current projects include *Present Senses: Aesthetics/Affect/Asia in the Global* (with Neferti Tadiar) and *The Tortured Signifier: Signs of the State of Exception*. He is also editing a special issue of *The Scholar and Feminist Online* called *Feminist Media Theory and Iterations of Social Difference*.

George Caffentzis is a Professor of Philosophy and Honors at the University of Southern Maine (Portland). He was a founding member of the Midnight Notes Collective and a founding member and coordinator of the Committee for Academic Freedom in Africa. He has taught and lectured in universities in Africa, Europe and North America. He is the author of many essays on social and political themes. His books include *Clipped Coins, Abused Words and Civil Government: John Locke's Philosophy of Money, A Thousand Flowers: Social Struggles against Structural Adjustment in African Universities* (co-editor) and *No Blood for Oil!*

Tahir Wood is Director of the Academic Planning Unit at the University of the Western Cape, a historically black South African university. He obtained his PhD from the University of Cape Town in 1994. He is the author of various articles and book chapters in the fields of Education, Linguistics and Literature. He has presented conference papers in the United States, New Zealand, Cuba, Germany, Spain, Italy, Hungary, Portugal, Poland and South Africa. Except for very brief periods, he has always lived in Cape Town.

Toby Miller is the author and editor of over 30 books, and has published essays in more than 100 journals and edited collections. His teaching and research cover the media, sports, labor, gender, race, citizenship, politics, and cultural policy, as well as the success of Hollywood overseas and the adverse effects of electronic waste. Miller's work has been translated into Chinese, Japanese, Swedish, German, Spanish and Portuguese. He has been Media Scholar in Residence at Sarai, the Centre for the Study of Developing Societies in India, Becker Lecturer at the University of Iowa, a Queensland Smart Returns Fellow in Australia, Honorary Professor at the Center for Critical and Cultural Studies, University of Queensland, CanWest Visiting Fellow at the Alberta Global Forum in Canada, and an International Research collaborator at the Centre for Cultural Research in Australia. Among his books, *SportSex* was a Choice Outstanding Title for 2002 and A Companion to Film Theory a Choice Outstanding Title for 2004. He is chair of a new Department of Media & Cultural Studies at the University of California, Riverside, and lives near the ocean in Los Angeles.

Mark Coté is a Lecturer in Media and Communication Studies at Victoria University, Melbourne, Australia. He has published extensively on Social Media, Media theory, Autonomist Marxism, and Foucault. He is currently researching the relationship between the human and technology, particularly the dimensions of im/materiality via what he calls the (non)local body. He can be reached at mark.cote@vu.edu.au.

Jennifer Pybus is a Doctoral Candidate in English and Cultural Studies at McMaster University. Her research focuses on the relationship between social networks and youth, with a specific interest in the civic possibilities these virtual spaces can provide to young users who all too often experience the market as an initial site of subjectivization and agency. She can be reached at pybusjr@mcmaster.ca.

Christian Fuchs is chair professor in Media and Communication Studies at Uppsala University's Department of Informatics and Media. He is author of many publications in the fields of Critical Theory, Critical Theory of the Internet, Critical Political Economy of the Media, Critical Political Economy of Digital Media and Critical Information Society Studies. Among his publications are the books *Internet and Society: Social Theory in the Information Age* (Routledge 2008, Paperback 2011) and *Foundations of Critical Media and Information Studies* (Routledge 2011). He is co-editor of the collected volume *Internet and Surveillance: The Challenges of Web 2.0 and Social Media* (Routledge 2011). Fuchs is a board member of the Unified Theory of Information (UTI) Research Group, editor of the journal *tripleC* (cognition, communication, co-operation): *Journal for a Global Sustainable Information Society* and co-ordinator of the research project "Social Networking Sites in the Surveillance Society" (funded by the Austrian Science Fund FWF). Website: http://fuchs.uti.at

Michael A Peters is Professor of Education at the University of Illinois at Urbana-Champaign and Adjunct Professor in the School of Art, Royal Melbourne Institute of Technology (RMIT). He is the executive editor of three journals: *Educational Philosophy and Theory, Policy Futures in Education* and *E-Learning and Digital Media*. His interests span the fields of education, philosophy and policy, and he has written over fifty books, including most recently the trilogy (co-authored with Simon Marginson and Peter Murphy) *Creativity and the Global Knowledge Economy* (2009) *Global Creation: Space, Connection and Universities in the Age of the Knowledge Economy* (2010), *Imagination: Three Models of Imagination in the Age of the Knowledge Economy* (2010) (AESA Critics Book Award 2010); *Subjectivity and Truth: Foucault, Education and the Culture of the Self* (2008) (AESA Critics Book Award 2009), and *Building Knowledge Cultures: Educational and Development in the Age of Knowledge Capitalism* (2006), both with Tina (A.C.) Besley.

Alex Means is a doctoral candidate in the Department of Sociology and Equity Studies in Education at the Ontario Institute for Studies in Education, University of Toronto. His research is based in the intersections of critical theory and the sociology and politics of secondary and higher education particularly as they relate to processes of urbanization and global change. His work has appeared among other places in *Educational Philosophy and Theory, Foucault Studies, Policy Futures in Education*, and the *Review of Education, Pedagogy, and Cultural Studies*. alexmeans1@gmail.com

Silvia Federici is Emerita Professor in Political Philosophy and International Studies at Hofstra University and a long time feminist activist and writer. She is the author of many essays on feminist theory, women and globalization, and feminist struggles. Her published work includes *Caliban and the Witch: Women, the Body, and Primitive Accumulation; A Thousand Flowers: Social Struggles Against Structural Adjustment in African Universities* (co-editor); *Enduring Western Civilization: The Construction of the Concept of the West and its 'Others,'* (editor).

Alberto Toscano teaches in the Department of Sociology at Goldsmiths, University of London. He is the author of *Fanaticism: On the Uses of an Idea* (2010) and *The Theatre of Production: Philosophy and Individuation Between Kant and Deleuze* (2006). He is an editor of the journal *Historical Materialism*.

Ergin Bulut is a doctoral student at the University of Illinois at Urbana-Champaign in the Institute of Communications Research. He received his Bachelor's degree from the Department of Translation and Interpreting and gained his Master's from The Ataturk Institute for Modern Turkish History, both at Bogazici University, Turkey. His research interests broadly include critical theory, political economy, issues of technology, labor and education. He has published on labor in digital capitalism, cultural studies and child labor in Turkey. His dissertation work is on the labor process in the video game industry. He has introduced the work of Michael Apple and Aijaz Ahmad to the Turkish audience.

Nick Dyer-Witheford is a professor at University of Western Ontario in Canada. He has written widely on issues of technology in informational capitalism. His widely acclaimed books include *Cyber-Marx: Cycles and Circuits of Struggle in High Technology Capitalism*, and *Games of Empire* (with Greig de Peuter). He is currently writing a book on the attempts to transform libraries from what he calls 'books to bytes'.

Emma Dowling is a lecturer in Ethics, Governance and Accountability and a member of the Centre for Ethics and Politics at Queen Mary, University of London. She holds a BA in International Studies and Politics and an MSc in Global Ethics from the University of Birmingham, as well as an MRes in Social and Political Theory and a PhD in Politics from Birkbeck, University of London. She is currently interested in the relationship between social and political conflict and global governance processes and institutions and how ethics is increasingly connected to new forms of valorisation and measure. Her work on affect looks at forms of affective labour and deals with immaterial and reproductive labour in its intersections with gender, and also with the role of affect in politics and in knowledge production. She is a co-editor of the 2007 special issue of *Ephemera*, "Immaterial and Affective Labour: Explored" (with Ben Trott and Rodrigo Nunes), and the author of Producing the Dining Experience–Measure, Subjectivity and the Affective Worker, *Ephemera* 7(1): 117–132 (2007).

Cameron McCarthy teaches mass communications theory and cultural studies at the University of Illinois at Urbana-Champaign. He is University Scholar and Communications Scholar in the Department of Educational Policy Studies. Cameron also holds appointments in the Institute of Communications Research and in the Unit for Criticism and Interpretive Theory at the University of Illinois. He has been a visiting scholar and lecturer at Jesus College, the University of Cambridge, York University, the University of Western Ontario, the University of Newcastle, Monash University, the University of Salamanca, Spain, and the University of Queensland. He has published widely on topics related to postcolonialism, problems with neoMarxist writings on race and education, institutional support for teaching, and school ritual and adolescent identities in journals such as *Harvard Educational Review*, *Oxford Review of Education*, *The British Journal of the Sociology of Education*, and the *European Journal of Cultural Studies in Education* among many others. Cameron has authored or co-authored many books such as:

Race and Curriculum (Falmer Press, 1990), *Multicultural Curriculum: New Directions for Social Theory, Practice and Policy* (Routledge, 2000), and *Reading and Teaching the Postcolonial: From Baldwin to Basquiat and Beyond* (Teachers College Press, Columbia University, 2001). With his graduate students, Cameron has published a number of books such as *New Times: Making Sense of Critical/Cultural Theory in a Digital Age* (Peter Lang, 2011) *Foucault, Cultural Studies and Governmentality* (SUNY Press, 2003) and *Race, Identity and Representation in Education* (Routledge, 2005). He co-edited the collection, *Globalizing Cultural Studies*, which was published by Peter Lang (2007). His most recent book (co-edited with Cathryn Teasley of the University of A Coruña, Galicia) is *Transnational Perspectives on Culture, Policy, and Education: Redirecting Cultural Studies in Neoliberal Times* (Peter Lang, 2009). With Angharad Valdivia, Cameron is co-editor of the "Intersections in Communication and Culture" book series at Peter Lang and the Institute of Communications Research at the University of Illinois. He is also one of the Senior Editors of Lang's Global Studies in Education book series. Last academic year, Cameron was a distinguished visiting professor in the Department of English and Communications Studies at the Saint Louis University of Madrid, Madrid, Spain.

Index